Intelligent Systems for Automated Learning and Adaptation:
Emerging Trends and Applications

Raymond Chiong
Swinburne University of Technology (Sarawak Campus), Malaysia

INFORMATION SCIENCE REFERENCE

Hershey · New York

Director of Editorial Content:	Kristin Klinger
Senior Managing Editor:	Jamie Snavely
Assistant Managing Editor:	Michael Brehm
Publishing Assistant:	Sean Woznicki
Typesetter:	Sean Woznicki
Cover Design:	Lisa Tosheff
Printed at:	Yurchak Printing Inc.

Published in the United States of America by
  Information Science Reference (an imprint of IGI Global)
  701 E. Chocolate Avenue
  Hershey PA 17033
  Tel: 717-533-8845
  Fax: 717-533-8661
  E-mail: cust@igi-global.com
  Web site: http://www.igi-global.com/reference

Library of Congress Cataloging-in-Publication Data

Intelligent systems for automated learning and adaptation : emerging trends and applications / Raymond Chiong, editor.
    p. cm.
  Includes bibliographical references and index.
  Summary: "This volume offers intriguing applications, reviews and additions to the methodology of intelligent computing, presenting the emerging trends of state-of-the-art intelligent systems and their practical applications"-- Provided by publisher.

  ISBN 978-1-60566-798-0 (hardcover) -- ISBN 978-1-60566-799-7 (ebook) 1. Computational intelligence. 2. Computational learning theory. I. Chiong, Raymond, 1979-
  Q342.I5643 2010
  006.3'1--dc22
                          2009021568

British Cataloguing in Publication Data
A Cataloguing in Publication record for this book is available from the British Library.

Table of Contents

Section 1
Adaptive Learning Systems

Section 2
Adaptive Evolutionary Systems

Section 3
Adaptive Collective Systems

Detailed Table of Contents

Section 1
Adaptive Learning Systems

The first section deals with adaptive learning systems. In general, an adaptive system is composed of a set of interacting or interdependent entities that is able to adapt its behaviour according to environmental changes or changes in its interacting parts. By focusing on the aspect of adaptation with intelligent learning, this section presents four chapters that use artificial neural networks and other learning technologies in various practical problems.

This chapter presents a set of methodologies and architectures for designing bio-inspired hardware by exploiting the reconfigurability features available in the commercial field programmable gate arrays (FP-GAs). The proposed methods allow a system-on-chip to self-reconfigure in order to adapt the hardware supporting it in a completely autonomous way. An in-depth discussion of a number of architectures, such as neural networks, spiking neuron models, fuzzy systems, cellular automata and random boolean networks, is provided. Various optimisation methodologies including evolution, synaptic weight learning, and so on are also discussed.

This chapter presents a new face recognition system comprising of feature extraction techniques and two Lyapunov theory-based neural networks. The design details of the proposed system are discussed, followed with some experiments on two benchmark databases, ORL and Yale. The experimental results show that the use of Lyapunov theory-based neural networks is quite promising, as both the classifiers achieve higher training speeds as well as higher recognition rates compared to the corresponding conventional classifiers found in the literature.

Chapter 3

This chapter presents a new novelty detection technique called the self-organising novelty detection neural network architecture (SONDE). SONDE is able to learn patterns incrementally in order to represent unknown dynamics and fluctuations of established behaviour in time-series. The accumulated knowledge can subsequently be used to estimate Markov chains for modelling causal relationships. It is then applied to detect and measure temporal and non-temporal novelties. The proposed method is evaluated using various simulations and experiments and the results confirm it to be quite promising.

Chapter 4

This chapter presents a computationally intelligent tool for extending the linear range of an arbitrary sensor. Typical sensors are either highly non-linear or not linear enough to be useful over a wide range of interest, and the proposed technique aims at compensating this problem by using a very efficiently trained neuro-fuzzy hybrid network. The training algorithm is based on the Levenberg-Marquardt algorithm (LMA) and the chapter also describes a simple technique to compute the Jacobian matrix, which is generally considered to be the most difficult step in implementing the LMA. A negative temperature coefficient thermistor sensor with an exponentially decaying characteristic function is linearised to demonstrate the efficacy of the proposed procedure. The experimental results show that the new training algorithm is able to bring the performance index of the network down to the desired error goal much faster.

Section 2

Adaptive Evolutionary Systems

The second section contains five chapters, and each of them is dealing with a unique domain of its own using evolutionary approaches. Evolutionary computing has become a very active research field nowadays, with many examples of successful applications ranging from data analysis and machine learning to telecommunication network design, logistics, scheduling, and technical engineering, among others. Across all these areas, evolutionary approaches have convinced practitioners by the results obtained on hard problems that they are very powerful algorithms.

Salvador García, University of Granada, Spain
José Ramón Cano, University of Jaén, Spain
Francisco Herrera, University of Granada, Spain

This chapter presents a review and analysis of evolutionary prototype selection in data mining and its application over different sizes of data sets, with a special focus on the scaling-up problem. The representative evolutionary prototype selection algorithms are reviewed and described in detail. The performances of these algorithms are analysed in terms of their efficiency and effectiveness via experimental study. The numerical results are then used to determine the benefits and drawbacks of the algorithms.

Thomas Weise, University of Kassel, Germany
Raymond Chiong, Swinburne University of Technology (Sarawak Campus), Malaysia

This chapter presents a systematic review of evolutionary algorithms employed to solve various problems in distributed systems. The review is aimed at providing an insight of evolutionary approaches, in particular genetic algorithms and genetic programming, in solving problems in five different areas of network optimisation: network topology, routing, protocol synthesis, network security, and parameter settings and configuration. Some interesting applications from these areas are discussed in detail with many illustrative examples.

Gary G. Yen, Oklahoma State University, USA

This chapter presents a novel approach based on evolutionary adaptation of the user interface in complex supervisory tasks using a combination of genetic algorithm for constrained optimisation and probabilistic modelling of the user. The proposed algorithm has been tested with an automated user and a group of real users in an air traffic control environment and the results show that it is flexible and easy to use in various problem domains. The results also demonstrate that the method is able to improve human-computer interaction.

Esteban Tlelo-Cuautle, Instituto Nacional de Astrofísica Óptica y Electrónica, México
Ivick Guerra-Gómez, Instituto Nacional de Astrofísica Óptica y Electrónica, México
Carlos Alberto Reyes-García, Instituto Nacional de Astrofísica Óptica y Electrónica, México
Miguel Aurelio Duarte-Villaseñor, Instituto Nacional de Astrofísica Óptica y Electrónica, México

This chapter presents an application that uses particle swarm optimisation (PSO) to size analog circuits which are synthesized by a genetic algorithm from nullor-based descriptions. The analog circuits are first synthesized by applying a genetic algorithm at the transistor level of abstraction, following which the multi-objective PSO evaluates the performances until optimal transistor-sizes are found by using a standard CMOS technology of 0.35μm of integrated circuits. As an example, two synthesized current conveyors (CCII+ and CCII-) are optimised by applying the proposed multi-objective PSO algorithm. The experimental results show that this algorithm is able to improve the performance of the current conveyors in comparison to the algorithms mentioned in the literature.

Chapter 9

    Flávio Teixeira, University of Victoria, Canada
    Alexandre Ricardo Soares Romariz, University of Brasilia, Brazil

This chapter presents the application of a comprehensive statistical analysis for both algorithmic performance comparison and optimal parameter estimation on a multi-objective digital signal processing problem. Several algorithms such as genetic algorithms, particle swarm optimisation, simulated annealing, non-dominated sorting genetic algorithm (NSGA II), and multi-objective simulated annealing (MOSA) are applied to design non-linear digital finite impulse response (FIR) filters. Also, optimal parameter values are obtained using statistical exploratory analysis instead of the common trial and error process. A comprehensive statistical comparison of these algorithms indicates a strong performance from NSGA II and the pure genetic algorithm with weighting scalarization. In particular, it is observed that the latter is able to obtain the best average performances.

Section 3
Adaptive Collective Systems

The last section of the book presents three chapters from diverse fields: social networks, automatic programming, and manufacturing. They, however, do share a common theme – they all exhibit collective intelligence. Collective systems differ from other intelligent systems in a way that the components in these systems do not directly influence the behaviour of one another. The outcomes are often being formed via the collective behaviour of some decentralised, self-organised entities within it.

Chapter 10

    Akira Namatame, National Defense Academy, Japan

This chapter presents an overview of the research examining how the structure of social networks impacts the diffusion process. There is also discussion on how the structure of social networks determines the dynamics of various types of emergent properties that occur within those networks. By focusing on the stylised facts of macroscopic emergent phenomena that are the results of bi-directional interactions, the chapter outlines various circumstances conducive for desirable emergent properties to appear.

Chapter 11

Mariusz Boryczka, University of Silesia, Poland

This chapter presents several improvements to the ant colony programming (ACP) method, including the elimination of introns, the use of a specimen list, and the tuning of the ACP's parameters. While most of these improvements are discussed as a review of the information already present in the literature, the latter is a novel idea. The described method with these improvements seems to be able to solve not only the problem of approximation, but also other problems, such as finding the perfect hash functions or different problems from the game theory.

Chapter 12

Paolo Renna, University of Basilicata, Italy

This chapter presents an innovative coordination mechanism in manufacturing systems by pheromone approach in a multi-agent architecture environment. Comparative studies are conducted between the pre-existing methods in the literature and two proposed methods based on the pheromone approach. Numerical results show that the first proposed method based on the parts' memory is inefficient while the second one based on the queue of a manufacturing cell is able to outperform the efficiency-based approach in case of medium dynamism in the manufacturing environment. Several important conclusions regarding the performance of these new methods are drawn.

Foreword

An amazing collection of state-of-the-art papers on the topic of intelligent, adaptive systems has been assembled by the editor, Raymond Chiong of Swinburne University of Technology (Sarawak Campus), Malaysia in this exciting special volume. He has selected the works of a truly global group of talented researchers. In addition, he has focused on taking a large swath of presentations in order to maximize the benefit of this volume to the widest possible audience. Raymond has merged cutting–edge science, novel and practical applications, methodology analysis, and social commentary into a cohesive unit that is destined to anchor the research of young investigators for many years to come.

A recurring theme throughout this compilation of twelve chapters is the incorporation of adaptation with intelligent learning, evolutionary, and collective systems. The first four chapters deal in various ways with artificial neural networks that learn and adapt based on experience and data tendencies. The next five chapters focus on evolutionary approaches applied in general to problems of optimization of performance and system efficiency. The remaining three chapters are concerned with collective behaviors, where diffusion and emergence in social networks, automatic programming based on ant colony system, and efficient management of manufacturing systems using a pheromone approach are discussed.

This interesting collection of timely contributions is an exceptional blend of current theoretical research and valuable applications to the solution of real world problems. For a discipline to remain relevant, it must nourish innovative research yet provide tools for improving the quality of life and sustainability of our civilization. This new book contains an excellent balance of these two objectives. The common theme of adaptability throughout diverse topics will likely provide considerable interest among practitioners in intelligent systems.

Professor Don Potter
Professor Ron McClendon
Institute for Artificial Intelligence
University of Georgia, USA

Walter D. Potter *is the Director of the Artificial Intelligence Institute, and a Professor of Computer Science. He received his undergraduate degree in Management Science from the University of Tennessee and followed that with many years as a systems analyst in the software development field. He then received advanced degrees in Computer Science from the University of South Carolina where he worked closely with Prof. Larry Kerschberg, the father of expert database systems. His research interests include robotics, knowledge-based systems, genetic algorithms, expert database systems, and advanced information system design. He has worked, as a research fellow, with the Oak Ridge National Laboratory, the US Army Research Institute, and the Westinghouse Savannah River Company. More recently, he has been involved with the USDA Forest Service doing research on ecosystem decision support systems. In 2008, he was awarded the prestigious General Sandy Beaver Special Teaching Award for excellence in teaching by the Franklin College of Arts and Sciences at the University of Georgia.*

Ronald W. McClendon is a Faculty Fellow of the Institute for Artificial Intelligence at the University of Georgia, and a Professor in Biological and Agricultural Engineering of the Faculty of Engineering. He holds the B.S and M.S. in Aerospace Engineering and a Ph.D. in General Engineering from Mississippi State University. He has also served as a faculty member at the University of Pittsburgh and Mississippi State University. He and Prof. Potter routinely team-teach a graduate course in computational intelligence which covers genetic algorithms, particle swarm optimization, neural networks, and fuzzy logic. His area of research is developing decision support systems which incorporate computational intelligence methodologies.

Preface

"Intelligent System" is a broad term, so giving it a precise definition can be difficult. This book deals specifically with systems that have the ability to learn and adapt during their existence in order to achieve certain goals and objectives. It concentrates on methods and approaches that might be generally referred to as "automated learning from experience."

Indeed, most living beings learn from experience rather than from an explicit detailed model of the world around them. They develop a model automatically from observation, refining it as more experience becomes available. It is this "intelligent" model that allows us to predict what would happen to a system under particular conditions, to sort the system inputs into categories, and to optimise the performance of the system in some way. These kind of intelligent and adaptive systems have attracted increasing attention in recent years. They are considerably more robust and flexible than systems based on traditional approaches that have been developed mainly for mathematically well-defined problems. They provide more autonomy and more powerful decision-making ability in uncertain and complex environments. They also adapt better to an unknown environment without needing to explicitly model it.

This special volume has assembled some of the most intriguing applications, reviews and additions to the methodology of intelligent computing. Its main objective is to present the emerging trends of state-of-the-art intelligent systems and their practical applications. It contains open-solicited and invited chapters written by leading researchers, academics and practitioners in the field. All contributions were peer reviewed by two to three reviewers.

TARGET AUDIENCE

This book covers the state-of-the-art plus latest research discoveries and applications of intelligent adaptive systems, thus making it a valuable reference for a large community of audiences. It is an important reference to researchers and academics working in computational intelligence and its related fields, such as multi-agent systems, machine learning, pattern recognition, optimisation, knowledge-based systems, natural computing, and so forth. It will also be appealing to developers, engineers, practitioners, final year undergraduates as well as postgraduate students who may find the ideas and solutions presented fascinating.

ORGANISATION OF THE BOOK

This book comprises 12 chapters, which can be categorised into the following 3 sections:

- Section 1: Adaptive Learning Systems
- Section 2: Adaptive Evolutionary Systems
- Section 3: Adaptive Collective Systems

Section 1: Adaptive Learning Systems

The first section deals with adaptive learning systems. In general, an adaptive system is composed of a set of interacting or interdependent entities that is able to adapt its behaviour according to environmental changes or changes in its interacting parts. By focusing on the aspect of adaptation with intelligent learning, this section presents four chapters that use artificial neural networks and other learning technologies in various practical problems.

Chapter 1, by *Andres Upegui*, presents a set of methodologies and architectures for designing bio-inspired hardware by exploiting the reconfigurability features available in the commercial field programmable gate arrays (FPGAs). The proposed systems, which consist of two main components – the computation engine and an adaptation mechanism, allow a system-on-chip to self-reconfigure in order to adapt the hardware supporting it in a completely autonomous way. The chapter provides an in-depth discussion of the numerous architectures such as neural networks, spiking neuron models, fuzzy systems, and so forth, which could constitute the computation engine. Similarly, various optimisation methodologies including evolution, synaptic weight learning, and so on which could allow the computation engine to adapt for performing a given computation are also discussed.

In chapter 2 *Ang et al.* present a new face recognition system comprising of feature extractions and two custom-designed neural classifiers based on the Lyapunov stability theory: Lyapunov theory-based radial basis function neural network and Lyapunov theory-based multi-layered neural network. The authors first used principal component analysis (PCA) to extract the most expressive facial features to reduce the dimensionality of the original images, and further applied Fischer's linear discriminant (FLD) to obtain the most discriminant features. These features were then passed to the two proposed classifiers for face classification. The simulation results have shown that the proposed system is quite promising as both the classifiers achieve higher training speeds as well as higher recognition rates compared to the corresponding conventional classifiers found in the literature.

In the next chapter (i.e., chapter 3), *Albertini and Mello* propose a new novelty detection technique called self-organising novelty detection neural network architecture (SONDE) which incrementally learns patterns in order to represent unknown dynamics and fluctuations of established behaviour in time-series. The authors use the thus accumulated knowledge to estimate Markov chains to model causal relationships. The subsequent model is then applied to detect and measure temporal and non-temporal novelties. The significance of this chapter lies in the fact that current studies do not fully detect and quantify these temporal novelties nor do they completely consider causal relationships. The proposed method was evaluated using various simulations and experiments and the results confirm the method to be quite promising.

Following which, chapter 4, by *Palit and Anheier*, proposes a computationally intelligent tool for extending the linear range of an arbitrary sensor. Typical sensors are either highly non-linear or not linear enough to be useful over a wide range of interest, and the proposed technique aims at compensating this problem by using a very efficiently trained neuro-fuzzy hybrid network. The training algorithm is based on the Levenberg-Marquardt algorithm (LMA) and the chapter also describes a simple technique to compute the Jacobian matrix, which is generally considered to be the most difficult step in implementing the LMA. A negative temperature coefficient thermistor sensor with an exponentially decaying characteristic function is linearised to demonstrate the efficacy of the proposed procedure. The experimental results show that the new training algorithm is able to bring the performance index of the network down to the desired error goal much faster than any first order training algorithm. What makes the work significant is that the intelligent models developed here could be programmed into low-cost embedded processors or micro-controllers to overcome the losses or performance drifts of components which arise as a result of the additional electronics required for conventional linearisation.

Section 2: Adaptive Evolutionary Systems

The second section contains five chapters, and each of them is dealing with a unique domain of its own using evolutionary approaches. Evolutionary computing has become a very active research field nowadays, with many examples of successful applications ranging from data analysis and machine learning to telecommunication network design, logistics, scheduling, and technical engineering, among others. Across all these areas, evolutionary approaches have convinced practitioners by the results obtained on hard problems that they are very powerful algorithms.

The first chapter of this section, chapter 5 by *García et al.*, presents a review and analysis of evolutionary prototype selection in data mining and its application over different sizes of data sets, with a special focus on the scaling-up problem. The authors review the representative evolutionary prototype selection algorithms of the two common strategies on the use of evolutionary algorithms: general evolutionary models, and models specific to prototype selection. These algorithms are described in detail and their performances analysed in terms of their efficiency and effectiveness. These results are then used to determine the benefits and drawbacks of each model.

Subsequently, chapter 6, by *Weise and Chiong*, gives a systematic overview of the wide array of applications of evolutionary optimisation to distributed systems. The focus, here, is on genetic algorithms and genetic programming and their application in solving problems from five different domains of network optimisation: network topology, routing, protocol synthesis, network security, and parameter settings and configuration. The authors also provide some applications from these areas to serve as illustrative examples. The chapter should be able to encourage readers to incorporate not only evolutionary algorithms but also other bio-inspired methods to solve various dynamic, large scale or *NP*-hard problems faced in network optimisation.

In chapter 7 *Gary Yen* proposes a novel idea based on evolutionary algorithm for adaptation of the user interface in complex supervisory tasks using a combination of genetic algorithm for constrained optimisation and probabilistic modelling of the user. The algorithm has been tested with an automated user and a group of real users in an air traffic control environment and the results have shown that the proposed method is flexible and easy to use in various problem domains. The results also demonstrate that the method is able to improve human-computer interaction and the author argues that the approach is pragmatically a valid design for interface adaptation in complex environments. A significant contribution of this chapter is a general framework for adaptation under ill-defined situations using statistical, non-parametric methods.

In chapter 8 *Tlelo-Cuautle et al.* demonstrate the application of a particle swarm optimisation (PSO) to size analog circuits which are synthesised by a genetic algorithm from nullor-based descriptions. The analog circuits are first synthesised by applying a genetic algorithm at the transistor level of abstraction, following which the multi-objective PSO evaluates the performances until optimal transistor-sizes are found by using a standard CMOS technology of 0.35 μm of integrated circuits. As an example, two synthesised current conveyors (CCII+ and CCII-) were optimised by applying the proposed multi-objective PSO algorithm. The experimental results show that this algorithm is able to improve the performance of the above-mentioned current conveyors in comparison to the algorithms mentioned in the literature.

This section wraps up with its last chapter (i.e., chapter 9), by *Teixeira and Romariz*, that presents the application of a comprehensive statistical analysis for both algorithmic performance comparison and optimal parameter estimation on a multi-objective digital signal processing problem. Several algorithms such as genetic algorithms, particle swarm optimisation, simulated annealing, non-dominated sorting genetic algorithm (NSGA II), and multi-objective simulated annealing (MOSA) are applied to design non-linear digital finite impulse response (FIR) filters. Also, optimal parameter values were obtained using statistical exploratory analysis instead of the common trial and error process. This has allowed the authors to conduct a fair and effective performance comparison among the different approaches. A comprehensive statistical comparison of the above-mentioned algorithms indicates a strong performance from NSGA II and the pure genetic algorithm with weighting scalarization. In particular, it was observed that the latter was able to obtain the best average performances.

Section 3: Adaptive Collective Systems

The last section of the book presents three chapters from diverse fields: social networks, automatic programming, and manufacturing. They, however, do share a common theme – they all exhibit collective intelligence. Collective systems differ from other intelligent systems in a way that the components in these systems do not directly influence the behaviour of one another. The outcomes are often being formed via the collective behaviour of some decentralised, self-organised entities within it.

There is often a lag time between an innovation's first appearance and its adoption by a substantial section of the society. This diffusion process is quite essential in enhancing future innovations by providing feedback about the innovation's utility. Moving away from the engineering and computing systems of the first two sections, chapter 5, by *Akira Namatame*, provides an overview of the research examining how the structure of social networks impacts this diffusion process. There is further discussion on how the structure of social networks determines the dynamics of various types of emergent properties that occur within those networks. By focusing on the stylised facts of macroscopic emergent phenomena that are the results of bi-directional interactions, the chapter outlines various circumstances conducive for desirable emergent properties to appear.

The penultimate chapter of this book, chapter 11 by *Mariusz Boryczka*, presents several improvements to the ant colony programming (ACP) method. Some of these improvements include the elimination of introns - which helps improve the readability of solutions as well as reduce their evaluation time, the use of a specimen list to reduce the solution's construction time, establishing a set of instructions, and tuning of the ACP's parameters. While most of the improvements are discussed as a review of the information already present in the literature, the latter is a novel idea. The described method with these improvements seems to be able to solve not only the problem of approximation, but also other problems, such as finding the perfect hash functions or different problems from the game theory. As an example of the nature-inspired algorithm, this method may be interesting for researchers and academics and may also be developed towards automatic programming.

In the final chapter (i.e., chapter 12), *Paolo Renna* proposes an innovative coordination mechanism in manufacturing systems by pheromone approach in a multi-agent architecture environment. As an illustrative example, the chapter focuses on the job shop scheduling problem in cellular manufacturing systems. Comparative studies are conducted between the pre-existing methods in the literature and two new methods based on the above-mentioned approach. One of these methods is based on the parts' memory whereas the next is based on the queue of a manufacturing cell. Experiments have been conducted in a dynamic environment which is characterised by the following parameters: inter-arrival, machine breakdowns, and processing time efficiency. The experimental results show that the first method based on the parts' memory is inefficient while the second method is able to outperform the efficiency-based approach in case of medium dynamism in the manufacturing environment. The author draws several important conclusions regarding the performance of these new methods which might be helpful while developing new approaches.

Raymond Chiong
Editor

Acknowledgment

In closing, I would like to thank all the authors for their excellent contributions to this book. I also wish to acknowledge the support of the editorial advisory board and the help of all who were involved in the collection and review process of this book. Without them, this book would not have been possible. Special thanks go to all those who provided constructive and comprehensive review comments, as well as those who willingly helped in some last-minute urgent reviews. I would also like to offer my gratitude to Don Potter and Ron McClendon for writing the foreword.

A further special note of thanks goes to the staff members at IGI Global. Their editorial assistance and professional support, from the inception of the initial idea to final publication, have been invaluable. In particular, I would like to thank Tyler Heath who continuously prodded me with e-mail to keep the project on schedule.

Finally, I hope that the readers would enjoy reading this book as much as I have enjoyed putting it together.

Raymond Chiong
April, 2009

Section 1
Adaptive Learning Systems

Chapter 1
Dynamically Reconfigurable Hardware for Evolving Bio-Inspired Architectures

Andres Upegui
Haute Ecole d'Ingénierie et de Gestion du Canton de Vaud, Switzerland

ABSTRACT

During the last few years, reconfigurable computing devices have experienced an impressive development in their resource availability, speed, and configurability. Currently, commercial FPGAs offer the possibility of self-reconfiguring by partially modifying their configuration bit-string, providing high architectural flexibility, while guaranteeing high performance. On the other hand, we have bio-inspired hardware, a large research field taking inspiration from living beings in order to design hardware systems, which includes diverse approaches like evolvable hardware, neural hardware, and fuzzy hardware. Living beings are well known for their high adaptability to environmental changes, featuring very flexible adaptations at several levels. Bio-inspired hardware systems require such flexibility to be provided by the hardware platform on which the system is implemented. Even though some commercial FPGAs provide enhanced reconfigurability features such as partial and dynamic reconfiguration, their utilization is still in the early stages and they are not well supported by FPGA vendors, thus making their inclusion difficult in existing bio-inspired systems. This chapter presents a set of methodologies and architectures for exploiting the reconfigurability advantages of current commercial FPGAs in the design of bio-inspired hardware systems. Among the presented architectures are neural networks, spiking neuron models, fuzzy systems, cellular automata and Random Boolean Networks.

INTRODUCTION

Living beings have managed to survive on earth for the last four billion years. The main reason for such a success is certainly their striking capacity to adapt to changing and adverse environments. They pos-

DOI: 10.4018/978-1-60566-798-0.ch001

sess astonishing faculties to learn from unknown situations, to adapt their behavior and their shape to environmental changes, to self-reproduce while keeping the species' most useful features, and to self-repair without external intervention.

Bio-inspired systems aim to extract some interesting features from these living beings, such as adaptability and fault-tolerance, for including them in human-designed devices. In engineering and science one can find several examples of bio-inspiration: airplane's wings have been inspired from birds, sonar and radar technologies take direct inspiration from bats' navigation system, and vaccines use the knowledge acquired from observing natural immune systems. These are just some of the numerous lessons that scientists and engineers have learned from mother nature. Electronic circuit design has also been inspired by biology at several levels. Biological systems exhibit several desirable features for electronic circuits: robustness, adaptability, development, scalability, and autonomy, among others. Neural hardware and evolvable hardware are two examples where human-designed circuits take inspiration from nature.

Several issues arise when defining the hardware substrate supporting a bio-inspired architecture. Designers must typically design their own integrated circuit, implying a very expensive and time-consuming design process, or they must implement a virtual reconfigurable substrate by using commercial reconfigurable devices, which is very inefficient in terms of resource utilization.

This chapter summarizes three methodologies for conceiving bio-inspired self-reconfigurable systems able to benefit from current commercial FPGAs' dynamic partial reconfigurability. Current design tools and techniques support the implementation of partial self-reconfigurable systems, however, conventional tools and techniques lack the required flexibility for supporting systems featuring on-line architectural adaptation. The proposed systems, along with the proposed bio-inspired techniques, allow a piece of hardware to self-adapt by reconfiguring the hardware supporting it, in an autonomous way, without external human intervention. The main advantage, with respect to existing self-reconfigurable platforms, lies in the fact that every possible architecture to be implemented is not required to be explicitly specified at design time, but it is the platform itself which determines it.

This chapter is organized in seven sections. The background section introduces the required background on dynamically reconfigurable computing devices and bio-inspired hardware systems. The third section, on evolvable hardware devices, introduces the existing hardware platform approaches for supporting evolvable platforms, and proposes a classification of three techniques that may be used to tackle this issue on commercial devices. Then, the section bio-inspired hardware components, describes bio-inspired hardware system as an adaptation mechanism that modifies a computation engine, for developing later in sections five, parametric adaptation, and six, structural adaptation, two types of adaptation – parametric and structural – by giving some illustrative examples. Finally, section seven concludes.

BACKGROUND

Hardware engineers have drawn inspiration from biology for designing and building bio-inspired architectures. A very important issue is the hardware platform supporting them. It is highly desirable for the platform to provide flexibility, scalability, and autonomy. Bringing flexibility to hardware devices is not trivial. An electronic circuit can be seen as a set of basic components (transistors, capacitors, resistances, etc) interconnected in a certain way. Modifying such a circuit implies replacing some components or modifying some of its connections. Performing these modifications would be unfeasible without the concept of *reconfigurability*.

Figure 1. Field programmable gate array - FPGA

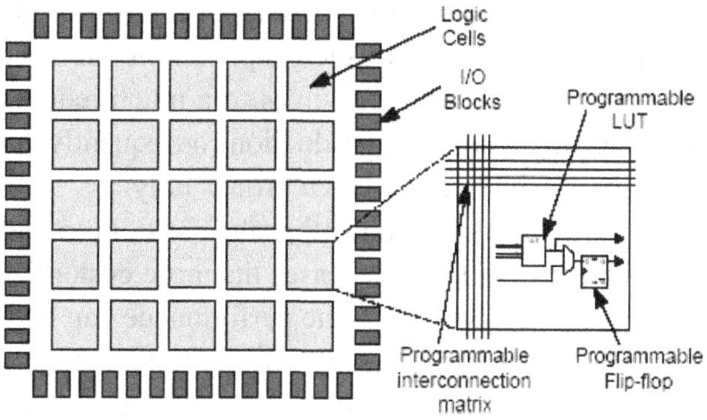

Reconfigurable Computing

An electronic device is said to be configurable when its functionality is not pre-defined at fabrication-time, but can be further specified by a configuration bit-string. Reconfigurable devices permit configuration several times, supporting system upgrades and refinements in a relatively small time scale. Given this architectural flexibility and upgradeability, they constitute the best candidates for supporting bio-inspired architectures: they offer a set of features that permit the implementation of flexible architectures, while still guaranteeing high performance execution.

The main representatives of reconfigurable computing devices are FPGAs (Field Programmable Gate Arrays) (Trimberger, 1994). FPGAs are programmable logic devices that permit the implementation of digital systems. FPGAs are typically composed of an array of uniform logic cells, interconnected through programmable interconnection matrices, that can be configured to perform a given function by means of a configuration bit-string (see figure 1). Additionally, current FPGAs provide specialized functional blocks like microcontrollers, RAM, and embedded arithmetic operators, depending on the targeted application field.

Figure 1 depicts a typical logic cell architecture. Each logic cell is composed of combinatorial and sequential programmable components, whose inputs and outputs are connected to a programmable interconnection matrix. The most used combinatorial components are look-up-tables (LUT), which can be programmed to implement any desired n-input boolean function.

FPGAs' programming is performed by means of a configuration bit-string, which is stored in a configuration memory. This string contains the configuration information for every FPGA's internal elements. Some FPGAs support a *partial reconfiguration*, where a reduced configuration bit-string can reconfigure only a given subset of internal components. *Dynamic partial reconfiguration* (DPR) (Donthi and Haggard, 2003; Hubner et al., 2005) is done while the device is active: certain areas of the device can be reconfigured while other areas remain operational and unaffected by the reprogramming. Unlike a *static partial reconfiguration*, in DPR, the system execution is not interrupted during the reconfiguration. However, the section being reconfigured might become unusable during reconfiguration.

Self-reconfigurable systems (Baumgarte et al., 2003) result in a direct offspring of DPR systems. *Self-reconfigurable systems* can modify their own hardware substrate in order to provide high performance, flexibility, and autonomy. They exhibit high performance due to their hardware's nature. Their high flexibility is achieved thanks to the possibility of modifying their own hardware at run-time by using DPR.

The autonomy is assured by the capability of the platform to modify itself without any external intervention. Several custom platforms have been proposed for supporting reconfigurable systems. Typically, these platforms target an application or a family of such applications. However, custom reconfigurable platforms are application-oriented, restraining themselves to a much reduced market participation or exclusively for academic purpose. This small scale production consequently makes them very expensive, being exclusively available to some privileged research groups only.

Commercial FPGAs typically offer more flexibility than their custom counterparts. Given the tradeoff between performance and flexibility, in most of the cases the more customized architectures can offer a better performance. However, during recent years the performance gap between commercial FPGAs and custom devices has been reduced in an impressive way. Xilinx is the largest FPGA manufacturer, whose devices are among the few supporting dynamic partial reconfiguration. Their Virtex-II family, for instance, fully supports dynamic and self partial reconfigurability. A critical issue when designing a dynamically reconfigurable system is the design flow used for conceiving it. Typical design flows target static designs, where a circuit is synthesized for performing a predefined task. When tackling a problem requiring dynamic reconfigurability, a number of new issues and paradigms arise given the changing nature of the underlying platform implementing the system. Xilinx proposes two design flows for generating partial reconfiguration bit-strings: *module-based* and *difference-based* (Xilinx Corp., 2004b).

The *module-based* flow allows the designer to split the whole system into modules. For each module, the designer generates a partial configuration bit-string starting from an HDL description and goes through the synthesis, mapping, placement, and routing procedures, independently of other modules. With the *difference-based* flow the designer must manually perform low-level changes. Using the *FPGA Editor* (a low level design tool) the designer can manually modify the configuration of several components such as: look-up-table equations, internal RAM contents, multiplexers' selections, etc. After editing the changes, the designer can generate a partial configuration bit-string, containing only the differences between the ''before'' and the ''after'' designs.

A third approach, called *bit-string manipulation* (Upegui and Sanchez, 2005), consists of directly modifying the configuration bit-string by knowing in advance which bits in the string must be modified for obtaining a desired circuit. In this way, one can generate and modify the FPGA configuration bit-string without depending on Xilinx design tools, in an on-chip and on-line manner. The main drawback of this approach is that one must know the bit-string format in advance, and the Virtex-II bit-string format is not documented by the manufacturer. This problem was overcome by reverse engineering some sections of the configuration bit-string for implementing self-reconfigurable adaptive systems (Upegui and Sanchez, 2006a; Upegui and Sanchez, 2006b).

The design methodologies that allow benefiting from such hardware flexibility are still in their early stages. We have identified, in bio-inspiration, a potential approach for tackling the challenging issues found when designing dynamic and self-adapting systems.

Bio-Inspired Hardware

Nature has always stimulated the imagination of humans, but it is only very recently that technology has started supporting the physical implementation of bio-inspired computing systems. They are man-made systems whose architectures and emergent behaviors resemble the structure and behavior of biological organisms (Langton, 1995). Artificial neural networks (ANNs), evolutionary algorithms (EAs), and fuzzy logic are some representatives of a new, different approach to artificial intelligence. These techniques exhibit the following features: (1) they model natural processes such as evolution, learning, development, or reasoning; (2) they are intended to be tolerant of imprecision, uncertainty, partial truth, and approximation; (3) they process numerical information with little or no explicit knowledge representation.

If one considers life on Earth since its very beginning, then the following three levels of organization can be distinguished (Sanchez et al., 1997): (1) Phylogeny, concerning the temporal evolution of a certain genetic material in individuals and species, (2) Epigenesis, concerning the learning process during an individual's lifetime, and (3) Ontogeny, concerning the developmental process of multicellular organisms. Analogous to nature, the space of bio-inspired hardware systems can also be partitioned along these three axes: the phylogenetic axis involves *evolvable hardware*, the ontogenetic axis involves *multicellular developmental hardware*, and the epigenetic axis mainly involves *neural hardware*.

In the case of living beings, adaptation due to evolution is performed through modifications in the DNA (Deoxyribonucleic acid), which constitutes the encoding of every living being on earth. DNA is a double-stranded molecule composed of two chains linked together by the base pairs Adenine, Cytocine, Guanine, and Thymine, constituting a string of symbols from a quaternary alphabet (A, C, G, T). On the other hand, reconfigurable logic devices are configured by a string of symbols from a binary alphabet (0, 1). This string determines the function implemented by each of the programmable components and the connections between each of the switch matrices. Under this description, a rough analogy naturally arises between the DNA and a configuration bit-string, and between a living being and a circuit. In both cases there is a mapping from a string representation to an entity that will perform one or more actions: growing, moving, reproducing, etc. for living beings, or computing a function for circuits.

This analogy between living beings and digital circuits suggests the possibility of applying the principles of artificial evolution to the field of circuit design. Designing analog and digital electrical circuits is, by tradition, a hard engineering task, vulnerable to human errors, and no one can guarantee the optimality of a solution for large circuits. Design automation has become a challenge for tool designers, and given the increasing complexity of circuits, higher abstraction levels of description are needed. Evolvable hardware arises as a promising solution to tackle this problem: from a given behavior specification of a circuit, an EA will search for a configuration bit-string describing a circuit able to satisfy the specification.

EVOLVABLE HARDWARE DEVICES

The hardware substrate supporting the circuit evolution is one of the most important initial decisions to make when evolving hardware. The hardware architecture is closely related to the type of solution being evolved. Reconfigurable hardware platforms have, in most cases, a cellular structure composed of uniform or non-uniform components. In some cases, one can evolve the components' functionality; in others the connectivity; or, in the most powerful platforms, both. FPGAs fit well into this third category: they are composed of configurable logic elements interconnected by configurable switch matrices.

The most basic hardware requirement when evolving hardware is to have a set of high-level or low-level evolvable components: the basic elements from which the evolved circuits will be built (transistors, logic gates, arithmetic functions, functional cells, etc); and an evolvable substrate supporting them: a flexible hardware platform allowing arbitrary configurations mapped from a genome. FPGAs constitute the perfect hardware substrate, given their connectivity and functional flexibility. This evolvable substrate can be implemented using three main techniques: (1) by designing a custom reconfigurable circuit with the desired configurability features; (2) by building a virtual reconfigurable substrate on top of the FPGA logic; and (3) by using the flexibility provided by the FPGAs' configuration logic in performing real partial reconfiguration.

The *first* approach constitutes a very efficient, high-performance, and flexible solution. A good example is the POEtic tissue (Thoma and Sanchez, 2004; Thoma et al., 2004), a computational substrate optimized for the implementation of digital systems inspired by the ontogenetic and epigenetic axes. By designing a custom reconfigurable circuit one can define the desired configurability features which may be useful for the circuit to be evolved. Thus, one can define a certain configuration bit-string structure that may constrain the search space to be explored by the EA to more suitable solutions. The main problem with this approach is the high cost and large development time for designing a custom reconfigurable circuit.

The *second* approach consists of building a virtual reconfigurable circuit on top of a commercial one (Sekanina, 2004a). This way, the designer can also define his own configuration bit-string and can determine which features of the circuit to evolve. This approach has been widely used by several groups (Goeke et al., 1997; Haddow and Tufte, 2000; Sekanina, 2004a; Sekanina, 2004b; Slorach and Sharman, 2000; Upegui et al., 2005; Vinger and Torresen, 2003), exhibiting enhanced flexibility and ease of implementation and incurring the cost of an inefficient use of logic resources.

The *third* approach consists of partially modifying the configuration bit-string of commercial FPGAs. In this way, one can make a better use of FPGA resources: logic functions are directly mapped in the FPGAs' LUTs, and connections are directly mapped to routing switch matrices and multiplexers, incurring the cost of dealing with very low level circuit descriptions (Thompson, 1997; Thompson et al., 1996; Upegui and Sanchez, 2005).

We define three methodologies for evolving hardware by partially reconfiguring Virtex and Virtex-II families in a dynamic way using this *third* approach. Each methodology considers a different level of abstraction and granularity of the basic components used in the evolved circuit. The *modular evolution* methodology is a coarse-grained high level solution, well suited for architecture exploration. The *node evolution* and the *bit-string evolution* methodologies, which are closely related, constitute a fine-grained low level solution, well suited for fine tuning.

Modular Evolution

The modular evolution methodology considers a coarse-grained reconfigurable substrate, where the basic blocks are defined as modules and are described at a high functional level. The methodology uses the module-based partial reconfiguration design flow described in the subsection "Reconfigurable Computing." The main consequence of the features of the module-based DPR is a modular structure, where each module communicates solely with its neighbor modules through a bus macro. This structure matches well with modular architectures, such as layered neural networks, fuzzy systems, multi-stage filtering, etc. These systems require a high degree of adaptability, and can benefit greatly from architecture exploration. However, some design constraints must be respected: inputs and outputs of the full network must be previously fixed, as well as the number of layers and their interconnectivity (number and direction of connections). While each layer can have any kind of internal connectivity, connections among modules are fixed through bus macros and restricted to neighbor layers. The subsection "Topology evolution of ANNs: a course-grained approach" presents the evolution of ANN topologies by using this method.

Node Evolution

The node evolution methodology considers a finer-grained partial reconfiguration than the modular evolution. The basic building blocks are defined at a low functional level and are defined as nodes which are, typically, much smaller than modules. This methodology uses the difference-based partial reconfiguration design flow described in the previous section. Using this technique to modify circuits requires a previous knowledge of the physical placement of the nodes implementing the target function (i.e. the logical function to be evolved) in the FPGA. By using hard-macros one can define placement constraints; one can place each hard-macro and, knowing LUT positions, one can modify them by using the difference-based design flow. Hard-macros must be designed by low level specification of a system (using the FPGA_editor one can define a system in terms of the FPGA's basic components). Every CLB, LUT, multiplexer, and flip-flop must be manually placed, and a semi-automatic routing must be performed. Hard-macros allow physically specifying the exact position of a part of the designed system and its building components in the reconfigurable device.

For using this methodology, the first step is to define an initial HDL description of the system. This description must include as black boxes the nodes to be evolved in the form of hard-macros and placement constraints must be specified for these macros. The system is now ready to be evolved: an EA written in your favorite programming language will map LUT configuration contents from a chromosome and will run a script for modifying the LUT contents in the FPGA_editor. The result is a partial configuration bit-string, containing just the LUT modifications, which will be generated and downloaded to the FPGA.

This methodology provides the possibility of fine tuning systems, incurring the cost of not allowing topological or connection modifications. It is well suited for evolving systems with cellular structures, such as neural networks, fuzzy system rules, or cellular automata, among others, with the main drawback being a dependence on Xilinx tools for modifying LUT contents and generating the configuration bit-string. The subsection "Coevolutionary setup for adapting fuzzy systems" presents the cooperative coevolution of fuzzy systems using this methodology.

Even though the complete placement and routing process is not executed for every individual, it is still not suited for on-system evolution.

Configuration Bit-String Evolution

The previously described evolving methodologies are dependent on Xilinx tools for generating every new partial bit-string, making them unsuitable for on-chip evolution. The configuration bit-string evolution methodology constitutes the finest grained reconfigurable approach, where modifications are performed at the configuration bit-string level. The methodology uses the direct bit-string manipulation design flow described in the previous section in order to directly evolve a subset of the bits describing the circuit.

Directly evolving the configuration bit-string has been done with the XC6200 FPGA family and on other custom platforms (Thompson, 1997). The same principle can be applied for Virtex families, including Virtex-II, Virtex-II-Pro, Virtex-4, and Virtex-5: LUTs' and multiplexers' configurations can be evolved, while keeping a fixed routing. By using hard-macros, as described for the node evolution, one can describe a computing cell. This computing cell can implement a neuron, a fuzzy rule, a simple LUT, or any function, including one or several LUTs; it can also include flip-flops for making the design synchronous, or it can just implement combinatorial circuits. LUTs' and multiplexers' configurations can be modified in an arbitrary way; however, routing must remain fixed. Connectivity among components of a computing cell is manually set when designing the hard-macro; connectivity among computing cells is defined by an HDL description of the full system. Although routing must remain fixed during evolution, LUTs can be evolved as multiplexers, where the selection is done by the configuration bit-string.

For the Virtex family, the XAPP151 (Xilinx Corp., 2004a) describes, in a detailed way, the configuration bit-string, specifying the position of LUT contents in the string. However, for the Virtex-II family this documentation is not available, and just a limited bit-string description can be found in Xilinx Corp. (2005). For tackling this problem, we have reverse-engineered some sections of the configuration bit-string format (Upegui and Sanchez, 2005; Upegui and Sanchez, 2006a). We have used this approach for evolving Cellular Automata rules presented in the subsection "Cellular Automata," and Random Boolean Networks as presented in the subsection "Topology generation for Random Boolean Networks: a fine-grained approach."

BIO-INSPIRED HARDWARE COMPONENTS

In nature, one can identify two levels on which adaptation can be performed in living beings: at the species level, and at the individual level. Adaptation at the species level, also known as evolution, refers to the capability of a given species to adapt to an environment by means of natural selection and reproduction. Adaptation at the individual level, also known as development and learning, refers to the cellular development and the behavioral changes in an individual, which occur during its lifetime while interacting with an environment.

In both artificial and biological systems, adaptation implies modifications. These modifications are presented in several forms depending on the substrate being modified and the mechanism driving the modification. One can roughly consider that epigenesis mainly involves parametric modifications which concern exclusively an individual's adaptation (such as synaptic efficacies in neural systems), while morphological modifications concern both entities (individuals and species), and are mainly driven by phylogeny and ontogeny.

Although artificial adaptation has been widely studied, it has been very elusive to human technology. An example of artificial adaptability is that of ANNs, where adaptability refers to the topological (Reed, 1993; Yao, 1999) or synaptic weight (Hebb, 1949; Hecht-Nielsen, 1989) modifications performed in order to allow it to execute a given task. Several types of adaptability methods can be identified according to the modification done.

On the other hand, topology modification explores different computation and generalizations capabilities of the network. Growing (Perez-Uribe, 1999), pruning (Reed, 1993), and EAs (Yao, 1999) are adaptive methods widely used to modify an ANN topology that will, in association with weight modification, eventually converge to better solutions than the ones found only with synaptic adaptation. We consider, thus, a hybrid adaptation framework, where structural adaptation is performed by modifying the system's topology, allowing a wider exploration of the system's computational capabilities. The evaluation of these capabilities is further done by parametric adaptation (synaptic weight learning in the case of ANNs), finding a solution for the problem at hand.

We consider these adaptation aspects for being specifically implemented in partially reconfigurable devices. By doing it, we consider a model composed of two main components: a *computation engine* and an *adaptation mechanism*. The computation engine is the physical machine able to implement the target function, while the adaptation mechanism is the technique that modifies this computation engine in order to find the target system.

Computation Engine

Universal computation refers to the ability of a machine to simulate any arbitrary computation on a conventional computation model. The complexity of the required machine can vary according to the complexity of the desired computational task. The computational task is highly dependent upon the number of inputs and outputs, and upon the non-linearities of the desired solution.

Among the most famous universal computers, one can find boolean functions and Turing machines. However, in the literature there is a very large number of machines claiming universal computability and, among them, one can find a number of bio-inspired machines. Some of these are ANNs (Hornik et al., 1989; Maass and Markram, 2004; Siegelmann and Sontag, 1991), fuzzy systems (Kosko, 1994; Ying and Chen, 1997), and Cellular Automata (Lindgren and Nordahl, 1990; Sipper, 1996).

We consider the *computation engine* as the hardware implementation of a given function; it can be implemented in the form of one of the aforementioned universal computers, as well as in the form of non-universal ones. Computation engines have a physical existence in hardware, and even though universal computability is not mandatory, it is a much appreciated feature when searching a solution since it guarantees that a solution actually exists. In this chapter, these computation engines are presented in the form of neural networks, fuzzy systems, Cellular Automata, and Random Boolean Networks.

Adaptation Mechanism

An important issue for all of the previously presented computation engines is how to find a solution for a specific problem. The proof of their universal computability guarantees that a solution exists, but how to find it is an open issue. How to find the correct configuration of NAND gates (accepted as universal approximators) for implementing a specific boolean function? How to determine the synaptic weights of a recurrent spiking neural network for discriminating between two pattern classes? How to connect a random boolean network and which rules to use for achieving the desired dynamics? These issues must be addressed by an adaptation mechanism.

The adaptation mechanism provides the possibility of modifying the function described by the computation engine. Two types of adaptation are allowed: *parametric* and *structural*. The first type modifies the values of some registers for parameter tuning and enabling (or disabling) of some module functions without involving major structural changes. The second type takes advantage of the reconfigurable characteristic of FPGAs and intends to modify the architecture of the computation engine by means of partially reconfiguring the FPGA.

PARAMETRIC ADAPTATION

Learning in living beings involves several physiological processes that result in a set of synaptic efficacy modifications, constituting one of the key components of neurobiological research. This synaptic efficacy adaptation exhibited in the brain is an example of parametric adaptation in living beings. In a similar manner, parametric adaptation in bio-inspired hardware is related to minor system modifications.

It consists of parameter tuning of the computation engine by modifying, for instance, a register value or the truth table of a combinatorial function, while keeping the system topology unchanged. The most typical example is that of ANNs, where the computation engine in the form of a neural network implements a function solving the problem at hand; however, it is the adaptation mechanism in the form of a learning algorithm which modifies the synaptic weights.

When bringing these two components to reconfigurable hardware, one must provide the system implementation with a certain plasticity, in order to allow the system to adapt. This plasticity can be provided in the form of a memory or a set of registers storing the synaptic weights to be adapted, which constitutes a classical approach for providing flexibility or programmability in such hardware systems. Another way of providing this plasticity is by allowing the system to be partially reconfigured only in the sections involving the utilization of these parameters.

This section introduces two computation engines with their respective parametric adaptations, including both types of plasticity described in the previous paragraph. In "Coevolutionary setup for adapting fuzzy systems," the computation engine consists of a coevolutionary fuzzy classifier. Then, "Cellular Automata" presents reconfigurable cellular automata, where automata rules are dynamically and partially reconfigured driven by a cellular programming algorithm.

Coevolutionary Setup for Adapting Fuzzy Systems

There are numerous examples where bio-inspired systems yield quite good performance, but often even their creators do not know why and how such systems work since they perform opaque heuristics. Fuzzy systems are an exception among these approaches since they might provide both good results and interpretability. Nevertheless, the construction of fuzzy systems is a hard task involving a lot of correlated parameters, which are often subject to several constraints to satisfy linguistic criteria. For tackling this problem, *Fuzzy CoCo* – an evolutionary technique based on cooperative coevolution – has been conceived to produce accurate and interpretable fuzzy systems (Peña Reyes, 2002).

In Mermoud et al. (2005), they propose a hardware platform for coevolving fuzzy systems by using Fuzzy CoCo in order to speed up both evolution and execution while offering equivalent performance. Fuzzy CoCo is a Cooperative Coevolutionary approach to fuzzy modeling, wherein two coevolving species are defined: data base (membership functions – MFs hereafter) and rule base. It is based on a family of EAs called coevolutionary algorithms, which take inspiration from the way several species cooperate or compete against each other for survival, sharing the same environment.

For modeling the hardware implementation of the system, it is decomposed in a computation engine and an adaptation mechanism. In this case, the computation engine is a fuzzy system and the adaptation mechanism is a coevolutionary algorithm. The architecture is kept modular in order to allow the structural adaptation that will be described in the section "Topology evolution of ANNs: a course-grained approach." However, the main focus here is on parameter tuning.

The fuzzy architecture consists of three layers: (1) *Fuzzification* that transforms crisp input values into membership values. (2) The *rule-based inference*, which computes the firing of each fuzzy rule, providing an activation level for one of the four output MFs. As several rules can propose the same action, the output fuzzy values are aggregated by using an aggregation operator, e.g., *maximum*. Finally, (3) *Defuzzification* produces a crisp output from the resulting aggregated fuzzy set. Inference and defuzzification are merged into a single physical module since the latter is static. Figure 2 shows a top level view of the platform.

Figure 2. Schematic of the evolvable fuzzy platform

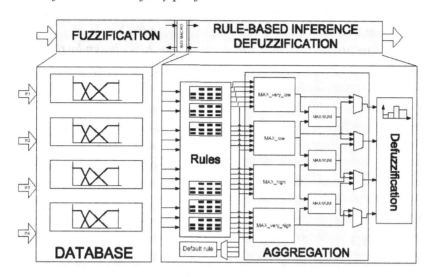

In this architecture, parameter tuning implies modifying lookup table (LUT) functions. The difference-based reconfiguration flow is used, because only small modifications are performed. This method implies two advantages: (1) minimization of the reconfiguration bit-string size and hence the reconfiguration time, and (2) it allows the possibility of automatically generating the bit-string. To achieve that, three hard-macros using LUTs were created for each evolvable part of the platform: the input MF parameters, the inference rules, the aggregation configuration and the output MF parameters. By using the hard-macro's location constraints, one can locate each LUT and hence modify it by using difference-based reconfiguration as described in the subsection "Reconfigurable Computing."

The implemented system has 4 input variables with 3 triangular MFs each. The inference layer contains 20 rules that take up to 4 fuzzy input values from different input variables, though, the system is easily scalable for increasing the number of inputs or rules. For the sake of interpretability, a *default rule* was added, whose effect is important when the other rules are not very active. In this implementation, the default rule has a fixed activation level encoded by the genome. One of the most commonly used defuzzification methods is the *center of areas*, which is very expensive since it includes division.

For maximum flexibility, rules able to include fuzzy *AND* and *OR* operators (i.e., respectively *minimum* and *maximum*) are required. A LUT-based hard-macro allows computing any combination of *AND* and *OR* operators on 4 fuzzy values chosen from among 16 input values. Figure 3 shows an implementation of a fuzzy *AND* between two 4-bit values *a* and *b*.

This implementation has been validated with a classification problem with the Fisher's Iris database. The achieved solution coevolved in the hardware platform exhibited a similar classification accuracy to the one exhibited by the software implementation of the same algorithm.

Cellular Automata

Cellular automata (CA) are discrete time dynamic systems, consisting of an array of identical computing cells (Toffoli and Margolus, 1987; Wolfram, 2002). A cell is defined by a set of discrete states, and a rule for determining the transitions between states. In the array, states are synchronously updated according

Figure 3. Implementation of a 4-bit minimum operator. Each block represents a LUT taking 4 bits as input. The macro is made up of three layers (D, S and V) and four stages (one per bit). The layer D indicates to the next stage whether a decision can be made or not. Once a decision is made, further D units transmit this fact. The layer S indicates which value, a or b, is chosen by the multiplexer V

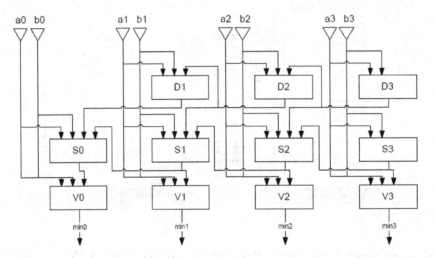

to the rule, which is a function of the current state of the cell itself and the states of the surrounding neighbors. Non-uniform CA differ from their uniform counterparts in their state transition rule diversity. The fact that uniform CA constitute a sub-set of non-uniform CA makes the latter a more general and powerful platform featuring universal computation capabilities (Lindgren and Nordahl, 1990; Sipper, 1996). Several features make them interesting for hardware implementation: they are massively parallel cellular systems, they are easily scalable, and their basic computing unit is closely related to the basic components of digital hardware: logic gates.

For FPGAs, non-uniform CA have an even more direct analogy. A typical FPGA architecture uses LUTs for implementing combinatorial functions, a LUT being the ideal substrate for implementing a modifiable boolean function. Additionally, the ICAP present in Xilinx FPGAs along with the configuration bit-string format description reported in Upegui and Sanchez (2005) allows one to perform an on-line and on-chip modification of CA rules by dynamically reconfiguring the LUTs' configuration.

The system architecture of a self-reconfigurable platform for evolving CA is depicted in figure 4. A MicroBlaze soft-processor running an EA evolves a CA implemented in the reconfigurable device. The CA can be accessed for reading and writing the states through general purpose I/O interfaces. Rule modifications are exclusively performed by the HWICAP peripheral. The HWICAP module allows the MicroBlaze to read and write the FPGA configuration memory through the Internal Configuration Access Port (ICAP) at run time, enabling an evolutive algorithm to modify the circuit structure and functionality during the circuit's operation, specifically in this case, CA state transitions.

The work presented in Upegui and Sanchez (2006b) focuses on 1-d grids, with two states per cell, denoted by *0* and *1*. In such CA, each cell is connected to one local neighbor (cell) on either side, as well as to itself. They present a 1-d CA composed of 50 automata that can be configured for running on free-run mode or on controlled iterative mode. An initial CA state can be configured through the writing interface, for being further read through the reading interface.

Figure 4. System schematic for self-reconfiguring cellular automata

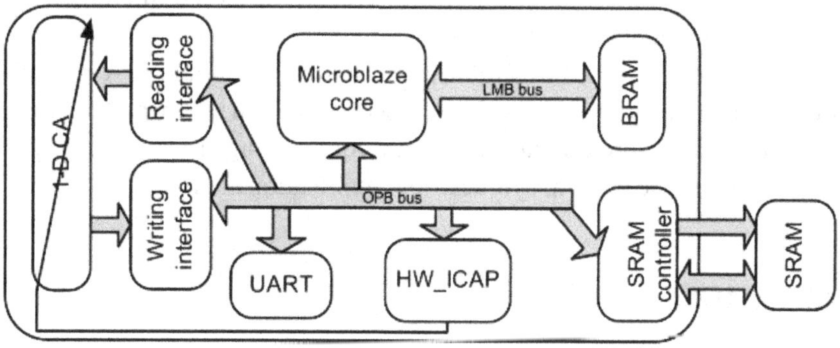

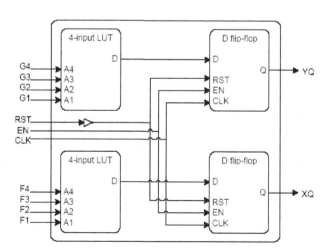

A special interest has been focused on 1-d CA, with two states and two neighbors, given their analogy with FPGA's basic elements (LUTs and flip-flops). Such an automaton implemented in hardware requires a flip-flop, for storing the current state, and a 3-input LUT. The basic logic cell of Virtex-II FPGAs is a slice, which contains 2 flip-flops and 2 4-input LUT, a good fit for implementing two of the above described automaton. Larger automata can be implemented by representing rules with several LUTs.

As explained before, hard-macros allow specifying the exact placement of a desired component in a design. In the previous section, hard-macros are used for instantiating fuzzy rules, which are then evolved from a PC. In this case, the hard-macro depicted in figure 5 has been designed, consisting of a slice containing 2 automata. Then, a 1-d automata array with size 50 was instantiated (i.e. by using 25 hard-macros), where the input A4 of LUTs is set to a constant value of '0', and A3, A2, and A1 receive the signals from the self, lower, and upper states respectively.

As described in Upegui and Sanchez (2005), one can access the LUT configuration of a whole column of slices in a single configuration frame. That is the reason why one must place the set of 25 hard-macros in a single column: for minimizing the number of frames to access. Then, just by reading and writing a single frame, one can evolve the configuration bit-string containing the LUTs' functions. By using this

Figure 5. 2-automata hard-macro

implementation in a Virtex-II 1000 FPGA, one can update CA rules for an array of up to 160 automata by modifying a single frame. It must be noted that for reconfiguring the full Virtex-II 1000, one may configure a full bit-string containing 1104 frames.

The implementation of this self-reconfigurable platform for non-uniform CA was validated with two problems: the firefly synchronization problem, and a pseudo-random number generator. This configuration approach can be used, in a more general framework, for evolving circuits at configuration bit-string level; for instance, for automatic on-chip synthesis of combinational circuits.

STRUCTURAL ADAPTATION

Evolution, development, and learning in living beings imply several types of morphological modifications where the organism structure is involved. Learning and development, closely related, are characterized by a high brain plasticity with a very high rate of neural and synaptic birth and death. Moreover, the whole development process from a single cell to a complete organism implies a highly dynamic structural construction. Evolution, acting in a larger time-scale, also exhibits morphological changes in species from one generation to the next. One can thus identify several types of structural adaptation in living beings, which can happen at different time-scales at both individual and species level.

In bio-inspired reconfigurable hardware systems, structural adaptation is related to major system modifications. It basically refers to topology modifications of the computation engine by modifying; for instance, the number or the type of membership functions in a fuzzy system, the size or the neighborhood of cellular automata, or the connectivity in a neural network. Structural adaptation is mainly associated with the phylogenetic and ontogenetic axes. The phylogenetic axis of bio-inspired hardware, better known as evolvable hardware (EHW), mainly targets the building of logical circuits, implying an architectural construction of the circuit. The ontogenetic axis requires a circuit to be constructed from a genetic description, given a developmental rule. Some examples are the works presented by Haddow et al. (2001) and Roggen et al. (2007). A hardware platform must consequently provide the required flexibility for supporting individuals with the diversity exhibited by genetic descriptions and developmental rules.

Bringing structural flexibility to hardware is very expensive in terms of logic resources, since one must provide a certain configurability that provides such flexibility. In the EHW field, this configurability has been provided by building custom evolvable chips or by using virtual reconfigurable architectures, as introduced in the section "Evolvable hardware devices," with the high costs and inefficiency that those solutions can imply.

In this section, we introduce two approaches for modifying the structure of the computation engine by means of partial reconfiguration: a coarse-grained and a fine-grained approach. The main advantage over previous work is the cost efficiency achieved by the partial reconfigurability of commercial FPGAs. "Topology evolution of ANNs: a course grained approach" presents a technique for evolving a layered spiking neural network by means of *modular evolution*. Subsection "Topology generation for Random Boolean Networks: a fine-grained approach" presents a fine-grained approach, where modifications are not performed at a layer level, but at the level of individual connections by means of *bit-string evolution*.

Topology Evolution of ANNs: A Coarse-Grained Approach

The coarse-grained approach presented in this section considers modules as the lowest-level reconfigurable part of a system. A module can contain a neural network layer, a fuzzy logic inference rule, or a stage in a multistage filter. It is based on the methodology of *modular evolution*, where the module size determines the level of granularity of the reconfiguration. As an example, this section presents the case of evolution of layered spiking neural networks. Different partial configuration bit-strings implementing layer topologies are available for each one of the modules. Then, from a repository of layers, an EA determines the set of layers most adequate for solving the problem. In this way, each layer performs a part of the whole computation.

This type of network fits well into the concept of *modular artificial neural networks* (Ronco and Gawthrop, 1995). Modular ANNs insert a level of hierarchy by considering a network as a set of interconnected modules. At the same time, these modules contain the neurons which are the basic computing nodes for both modular and traditional ANNs. From a bio-inspired perspective, modular ANN are more biologically plausible than their plain counterparts. The brain is not just a bunch of interconnected neurons, but there are specific areas in the brain in-charge of specific tasks.

Another possible approach is the evolution of ANN ensembles (Liu and Yao, 1997). In this case, each module could contain an independent ANN, and an EA would manage a population of them. At the end of the evolution, the provided solution would not be a single ANN, but a set composed of the best individuals. The mapping genotype-phenotype can involve the parametric adaptations already described, as well as the fine-grained topological adaptations that will be described in the next subsection.

The module-based DPR approach fits well for evolving modular topologies. The main consequence of the features of DPR is a modular structure, where each module communicates solely with his neighbor modules. This structure matches well with a layered neural-network topology presented in Upegui et al. (2005), where each reconfigurable module contains a sub-network. Inputs and outputs of the full network are fixed at design time, while each sub-network can have any kind of internal connectivity, connections among sub-networks are fixed and restricted to neighboring sub-networks.

For each module, there exists a pool of different possible configurations. Each configuration contains a sub-network topology (i.e. a certain number of neurons with a given connectivity). As illustrated in figure 6, each module can be configured with different layer topologies, provided that they offer the same external view (i.e. the same inputs and outputs). Several generic layer configurations are generated to obtain a library of layers, which may be used for different applications.

Figure 6. Layout of the reconfigurable network topology

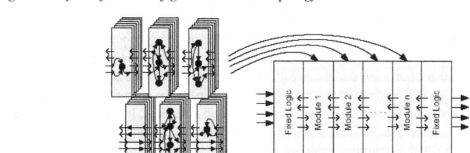

A simple genetic algorithm (GA) is responsible for determining which configuration bit-string is downloaded to the FPGA. The GA considers a full network as an individual. For each application the GA may find the combination of layers that best solves the problem. Input and output fixed modules contain the required logic to code and decode external signals and to evaluate the fitness of the individual depending on the application (the fitness can also be evaluated off-chip). As in any GA the phenotype is mapped from the genome, in this case the combination of layers for a network. Each module has a set of possible configurations and an index is assigned to each configuration. The genome is composed of a vector of these indices.

In a more general framework, one can consider this reconfigurable network as an example of the modular ANN described at the beginning of this subsection. Related work about evolution of modular ANN has been reported in Happel and Murre (1994), where they use modules which are able to categorize and learn in an autonomous way, with an architecture which is evolved at the same time. They thus present, a system involving architectural modular evolution along with individual learning. Such a system fits well in the proposed coarse-grained structural adaptation, where each ANN module corresponds to a reconfigurable module. Learning is performed as a parametric adaptation inside each one of the modules by updating some registers' values.

Topology Generation for Random Boolean Networks: A Fine-Grained Approach

Regular topologies have been shown to perform well for several problems. Layered ANNs are widely used for classification and control tasks, while Cellular Automata dynamics have been widely studied, as they exhibit interesting emergent behaviors. However, biological systems don't use such regular connectivity, it being a critical point when building systems targeting self-adaptation and emergence. An example of a different approach for connecting systems is that of Random Boolean Networks (RBN), a set of randomly interconnected nodes computing different boolean functions (Gershenson, 2002).

Several approaches using arbitrary connectionism have been shown to perform well for several applications. Jaeger and Haas (2004) have shown the suitability of echo state networks (randomly connected recurrent ANNs) to predict chaotic time series, improving accuracy by a factor of 2400 over previous techniques. Maass et al. (2002) present their liquid state machines (randomly connected integrate and fire neurons), which are able to classify noise-corrupted spoken words.

As presented in the background, Xilinx FPGAs can be partially reconfigured by using several design flows. This subsection presents a system exhibiting the maximum autonomy and the maximum flexibility. An FPGA system can self-reconfigure for evolving a part of the circuit in a way similar to the system presented in the subsection "Cellular Automata" for evolving CA. However, unlike CA, this section presents a system with flexible topology. Topological modifications are based on the configuration bit-string description of Upegui and Sanchez (2006a) for dynamically modifying multiplexers' configuration.

A hardware architecture of a cellular system allowing a completely arbitrary connectionism constitutes a very hard routing problem. The main problem faced is scalability. Increasing the array size implies not only increasing the number of cells but also the size of the multiplexers selecting the nodes' inputs. This fact increases the resource requirements exponentially when increasing the amount of nodes. This subsection presents an RBN cell array that allows full implementation scalability. It allows connecting any node with any other; however, some constraints must be respected when creating new connections.

Figure 7 illustrates the RBN cell array: it consists of an array of identical elements, each one containing a rule implemented in a look-up-table (LUT), a flip-flop storing the cells' state, and flexible routing resources implemented in the form of multiplexers.

Figure 7. RBN cell: rule and connectionism implementation

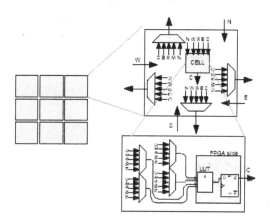

In the 2-d case, each cell has 4 inputs and 4 outputs corresponding to its four cardinal points: north, west, south, and east, which fits well with the current 2-d fabrication technology of integrated circuits. Additional dimensions would require two more inputs per dimension.

An output from the cell can be driven by the cell's state or by any other input, allowing the outputs to act as a bypass from distant cell's states. In a typical 2-d CA, outputs would always be driven by the cell's state. A cell's state is updated by a rule (a boolean function). As cell outputs, rule inputs can be driven by any input or by the cell's state. If two multiplexers select the same driver, the 4-inputs rule becomes a 3-inputs rule, with the possibility of becoming a 1-input rule if all multiplexers select the same input.

In Upegui and Sanchez (2006a), there are presented 3 approaches of generating a random connectionism in this array, with discussion about how to implement them and what problems can arise in each of them. The *first approach* consists of randomly generating the sources for each node by randomly assigning a cell for driving each cell's input. The *second approach* consists of randomly assigning values to multiplexers' selections. The *third approach*, and the one implemented in this work, consists of randomly generating values of multiplexers' selections, while forcing random drivers for floating nets.

They use the same system setup previously described in the subsection "Cellular Automata" for evolving the non-uniform CA (see figure 4). The only difference is that instead of the 1-d CA they used an array of the RBN cells of figure 7. The HWICAP module allows the MicroBlaze to read and write the FPGA configuration memory through the Internal Configuration Access Port (ICAP) at run time, enabling the adaptation algorithm to modify the RBN connections and boolean rules during the circuit's operation.

The RBN cell is implemented as a hard-macro. It is implemented by using the four slices in a CLB. The RBN cell has 4 inputs and outputs from and to its neighbors. Four additional signals are included for system control: CLK, EN, RST, and an output signal for observing the cell's state. A common alternative to using the FPGA's low level resources would be to define the RBN cell as a virtual reconfigurable circuit. In this case, the reconfigurable circuit is described by a high level language and further synthesized, placed, and routed by automatic tools. Implementing the RBN cell in this way, would require 18 Virtex-II slices (5 CLBs), while implementing it by defining a hard-macro for further reconfiguring the logic supporting it requires only 4 slices (1 CLB). In this way, using a virtual reconfigurable substrate would imply an overhead of *x4.5* respective to the implementation in the actual FPGA LUTs and multiplexers.

This system has been validated with the implementation of a *5x6* RBN cell array. After defining an initial random network, an evolutionary algorithm evolved the boolean functions for solving the firefly synchronization problem. In a more general case, this non-regular network can be used for modeling evolving and/or developmental neural systems, gene regulatory networks, or any type of network model featuring a dynamic topology.

CONCLUSION

This chapter presented a set of methodologies and architectures for the conception of bio-inspired self-reconfigurable systems by exploiting the current commercial FPGA's dynamic partial reconfigurability. The methodologies for evolving bio-inspired architectures proposed in this chapter allow three different layers of abstraction. The modular evolution allows a high abstraction level, where the basic components used by the evolution are large functional modules such as ANN layers or fuzzy systems stages. The node evolution involves an intermediate level of abstraction, where the basic components used by the evolution are small functional modules, such as logic gates, neurons, or fuzzy rules. The third methodology, bit-string evolution, involves the lowest abstraction level, where the evolution directly determines the configuration bit-string reconfiguring the FPGA, and provides the possibility of executing the evolution on-chip and on-line.

These methodologies have been applied to several bio-inspired architectures. The implementation of the architectures, along with the methodologies, is based on a model composed of two main components: a computation engine and an adaptation mechanism. The computation engine constitutes the bio-inspired architecture computing the solution. In this chapter these computation engines are presented in the form of spiking neural networks, fuzzy systems, cellular automata, and Random Boolean Networks. The adaptation mechanism, on the other hand, allows the computation engine to adapt for performing a given computation; two basic types of adaptation are proposed: parametric and structural. Parametric adaptation mainly deals with the adjustment of functional parameters, while structural adaptation deals with topological modifications. This adaptation can be present in the form of evolution, synaptic weight learning, or any other global or local optimization algorithm.

The proposed systems, along with the proposed bio-inspired architectures and algorithms, allow a system-on-chip to self-reconfigure in order to adapt the hardware supporting it, in a completely autonomous way. The main advantage of the proposed approach is that, unlike existing self-reconfigurable platforms, it is not required to specify every possible architecture to be implemented at design time, but it is the platform itself which determines it on-line in a completely autonomous way.

In the framework of a more general scope, dynamic self-reconfigurable adaptive systems can be seen as the next step towards bio-inspired hardware systems exhibiting real adaptability. Current systems still require a high degree of human intervention and a very restricted level of adaptability to changing conditions. Future work must tackle these issues by inspiration from the adaptability features observed in living beings. Among these features we can identify a full autonomy, a development driven by environmental and physical constraints instead of human imposed constraints, and a support for structural and parametric adaptation. These approaches will not be used for tackling high performance or critical applications because adaptation is typically not a necessity for them. They may mainly be used in pervasive systems which interact with changing environments and are difficult to upgrade manually. Some examples are human-interaction devices, space devices, or environmental monitoring networks.

Moving towards this direction imposes a set of challenges that may be tackled by advanced engineering and methodologies. Current commercial reconfigurable devices exhibit important limitations: they are expensive, highly power-consuming, and they offer limited reconfiguration capabilities. Future trends towards nanotechnologies may help to tackle these issues. Another current limitation is scalability at several levels. EAs have shown to be limited in the size of genome they can deal with, which is critical when solving discrete problems as digital systems. This problem has been tackled through ontogenetic hardware approaches (Haddow et al., 2001; Roggen et al., 2007) where, starting from a genetic description, the individual develops its architecture driven by construction rules or by interactions with its environment. These devices may also interact among them, making scalability at network level another important issue. These limitations, in general, may not constitute a real obstacle for future works but a set of constraints that will become softer with time.

REFERENCES

Baumgarte, V., Ehlers, G., May, F., Nückel, A., Vorbach, M., & Weinhardt, M. (2003). PACT XPP - a self-reconfigurable data processing architecture. *The Journal of Supercomputing, 26*(2), 167–184. doi:10.1023/A:1024499601571

Donthi, S., & Haggard, R. (2003). A survey of dynamically reconfigurable FPGA devices. In *Proceedings of the 35th Southeastern Symposium on System Theory* (pp. 422-426).

Gershenson, C. (2002). Classification of random Boolean networks. In *Artificial Life VIII: Proceedings of the 8th International Conference on Artificial Life* (pp. 1-8).

Goeke, M., Sipper, M., Mange, D., Stauffer, A., Sanchez, E., & Tomassini, M. (1997). Online autonomous evolware. In *Evolvable Systems: From Biology to Hardware* (LNCS 1259, pp. 96-106). Berlin, Germany: Springer-Verlag.

Haddow, P., & Tufte, G. (2000). An evolvable hardware FPGA for adaptive hardware. In *Proceedings of the IEEE Congress on Evolutionary Computation* (pp. 553-560).

Haddow, P., Tufte, G., & Remortel, P. V. (2001). Shrinking the genotype:L-systems for EHW? In *Proceedings of the 4th International Conference on Evolvable Systems: From Biology to Hardware* (pp. 128-139).

Happel, B., & Murre, J. (1994). Design and evolution of modular neural network architectures. *Neural Networks, 7*(6/7), 985–1004. doi:10.1016/S0893-6080(05)80155-8

Hebb, D. O. (1949). *The organization of behavior*. New York: John Wiley.

Hecht-Nielsen, R. (1989). Theory of the backpropagation neural network. In . *Proceedings of the International Joint Conference on Neural Networks, 1*, 593–606. doi:10.1109/IJCNN.1989.118638

Hornik, K., Stinchcombe, M., & White, H. (1989). Multilayer feedforward networks are universal approximations. *Neural Networks, 2*, 359–366. doi:10.1016/0893-6080(89)90020-8

Hubner, M., Paulsson, K., Stitz, M., & Becker, J. (2005). Novel seamless design-flow for partial and dynamic reconfigurable systems with customized communication structures based on Xilinx Virtex-II FPGAs. In *System Aspects in Organic and Pervasive Computing, Workshop Proceedings* (pp. 39-44).

Jaeger, H., & Haas, H. (2004). Harnessing nonlinearity: Predicting chaotic systems and saving energy in wireless communication. *Science, 304*(5667), 78–80. doi:10.1126/science.1091277

Kosko, B. (1994). Fuzzy systems as universal approximators. *IEEE Transactions on Computers, 43*(11), 1329–1333. doi:10.1109/12.324566

Langton, C. G. (1995). *Artificial life: An overview. Complex adaptive systems.* Cambridge, MA: MIT Press.

Lindgren, C., & Nordahl, M. (1990). Universal computation in simple one dimensional cellular automata. *Complex Systems, 4,* 299–318.

Liu, Y., & Yao, X. (1997). Evolving modular neural networks which generalize well. In *Proceedings of the IEEE Conference on Evolutionary Computation* (pp. 605-610).

Maass, W., & Markram, H. (2004). On the computational power of recurrent circuits of spiking neurons. *Journal of Computer and System Sciences, 69*(4), 593–616. doi:10.1016/j.jcss.2004.04.001

Maass, W., Natschlager, T., & Markram, H. (2002). Real-time computing without stable states: A new framework for neural computation based on perturbations. *Neural Computation, 14*(11), 2531–2560. doi:10.1162/089976602760407955

Mermoud, G., Upegui, A., Pena, C. A., & Sanchez, E. (2005). A dynamically-reconfigurable FPGA platform for evolving fuzzy systems. In *Computational Intelligence and Bioinspired Systems* (LNCS 3512, pp. 572-581). Berlin, Germany: Springer-Verlag.

Peña Reyes, C. A. (2002). *Coevolutionary fuzzy modeling.* Unpublished doctoral dissertation, EPFL.

Perez-Uribe, A. (1999). *Structure-adaptable digital neural networks.* Unpublished doctoral dissertation, EPFL.

Reed, R. (1993). Pruning algorithms - a survey. *IEEE Transactions on Neural Networks, 4*(5), 740–747. doi:10.1109/72.248452

Roggen, D., Federici, D., & Floreano, D. (2007, March). Evolutionary morphogenesis for multi-cellular systems. *Genetic Programming and Evolvable Machines, 8,* 61–96. doi:10.1007/s10710-006-9019-1

Ronco, E., & Gawthrop, P. (May 1995). *Modular neural networks: A state of the art* (Tech. Rep. CSC-9502). Center for System and Control, University of Glasgow.

Sanchez, E., Mange, D., Sipper, M., Tomassini, M., Perez-Uribe, A., & Stauffer, A. (1997). Phylogeny, ontogeny, and epigenesis: Three sources of biological inspiration for softening hardware. In *Evolvable Systems: From Biology to Hardware* (LNCS 1259, pp. 35-54). Berlin, Germany: Springer-Verlag.

Sekanina, L. (2004a). *Evolvable components from theory to hardware implementations.* Berlin, Germany: Springer.

Sekanina, L. (2004b). Virtual reconfigurable devices. In *Evolvable Components from Theory to Hardware Implementations* (pp. 153-168). Berlin, Germany: Springer,-Verlag.

Siegelmann, H., & Sontag, E. (1991). Turing computability with neural nets. *Applied Mathematics Letters, 4*(6), 77–80. doi:10.1016/0893-9659(91)90080-F

Sipper, M. (1996). Co-evolving non-uniform cellular automata to perform computations. *Physica D. Nonlinear Phenomena, 92*(3-4), 193–208. doi:10.1016/0167-2789(95)00286-3

Slorach, C., & Sharman, K. (2000). The design and implementation of custom architectures for evolvable hardware using off-the-shelf programmable devices. In *Evolvable Systems: From Biology to Hardware* (LNCS 1801, pp. 197-207). Berlin, Germany: Springer-Verlag.

Thoma, Y., & Sanchez, E. (2004). A reconfigurable chip for evolvable hardware. In *Proceedings of the Genetic and Evolutionary Computation Conference* (pp. 816-827).

Thoma, Y., Tempesti, G., Sanchez, E., & Arostegui, J. M. M. (2004). POEtic: An electronic tissue for bio-inspired cellular applications. *Bio Systems, 76*(1-3), 191–200. doi:10.1016/j.biosystems.2004.05.023

Thompson, A. (1997). An evolved circuit, intrinsic in silicon, entwined with physics. In *Evolvable Systems: From Biology to Hardware* (LNCS 1259, pp. 390-405). Berlin, Germany: Springer-Verlag.

Thompson, A., Harvey, I., & Husbands, P. (1996). Unconstrained evolution and hard consequences. *Towards Evolvable Hardware, The Evolutionary Engineering Approach* (. *LNCS, 1062*, 136–165.

Toffoli, T., & Margolus, N. (1987). *Cellular automata machines: A new environment for modeling.* Cambridge, MA: MIT Press.

Trimberger, S. (1994). *Field-programmable gate array technology.* Boston: Kluwer Academic Publishers.

Upegui, A., Peña Reyes, C. A., & Sanchez, E. (2005). An FPGA platform for on-line topology exploration of spiking neural networks. *Microprocessors and Microsystems, 29*(5), 211–223. doi:10.1016/j.micpro.2004.08.012

Upegui, A., & Sanchez, E. (2005). Evolving hardware by dynamically reconfiguring Xilinx FPGAs. In *Evolvable Systems: From Biology to Hardware* (LNCS 3637, pp. 56-65).

Upegui, A., & Sanchez, E. (2006a). Evolving hardware with self-reconfigurable connectivity in Xilinx FPGAs. In *Proceedings of the 1st NASA /ESA Conference on Adaptive Hardware and Systems (AHS-2006)* (pp. 153-160). Los Alamitos, CA: IEEE Computer Society.

Upegui, A., & Sanchez, E. (2006b). On-chip and on-line self-reconfigurable adaptable platform: The non-uniform cellular automata case. In *Proceedings of the 20th IEEE International Parallel and Distributed Processing Symposium (IPDPS06)* (p. 206).

Vinger, K., & Torresen, J. (2003). Implementing evolution of FIR-filters efficiently in an FPGA. In *Proceedings of the NASA/DOD Conference on Evolvable Hardware,* Chicago, Illinois (pp. 26-29).

Wolfram, S. (2002). *A new kind of science.* Champaign, IL:Wolfram Media.

Xilinx Corp. (2004a). *XAPP151: Virtex series configuration architecture user guide*. Retrieved from http://www.xilinx.com

Xilinx Corp. (2004b). *XAPP290: Two flows for partial reconfiguration: Module based or difference based*. Retrieved from http://www.xilinx.com

Xilinx Corp. (2005). *Virtex-II platform FPGA user guide*. Retrieved from http://www.xilinx.com

Yao, X. (1999). Evolving artificial neural networks. *Proceedings of the IEEE, 87*(9), 1423–1447. doi:10.1109/5.784219

Ying, H., & Chen, G. (1997). Necessary conditions for some typical fuzzy systems as universal approximators. *Automatica, 33*(7), 1333–1338. doi:10.1016/S0005-1098(97)00026-5

Chapter 2
A Lyapunov Theory–Based Neural Network Approach for Face Recognition

Li-Minn Ang
University of Nottingham Malaysia Campus, Malaysia

King Hann Lim
University of Nottingham Malaysia Campus, Malaysia

Kah Phooi Seng
University of Nottingham Malaysia Campus, Malaysia

Siew Wen Chin
University of Nottingham Malaysia Campus, Malaysia

ABSTRACT

This chapter presents a new face recognition system comprising of feature extraction and the Lyapunov theory-based neural network. It first gives the definition of face recognition which can be broadly divided into (i) feature-based approaches, and (ii) holistic approaches. A general review of both approaches will be given in the chapter. Face features extraction techniques including Principal Component Analysis (PCA) and Fisher's Linear Discriminant (FLD) are discussed. Multilayered neural network (MLNN) and Radial Basis Function neural network (RBF NN) will be reviewed. Two Lyapunov theory-based neural classifiers: (i) Lyapunov theory-based RBF NN, and (ii) Lyapunov theory-based MLNN classifiers are designed based on the Lyapunov stability theory. The design details will be discussed in the chapter. Experiments are performed on two benchmark databases, ORL and Yale. Comparisons with some of the existing conventional techniques are given. Simulation results have shown good performance for face recognition using the Lyapunov theory-based neural network systems.

DOI: 10.4018/978-1-60566-798-0.ch002

INTRODUCTION

Automatic recognition of human faces in dynamic environments has gained a great deal of interest from the communities of image processing, pattern recognition, neural network, biometric and computer vision in the past couple of decades. The active research in face recognition has stimulated the rapid development of numerous applications, including access control, human computer interfaces, security and surveillance, e-commerce, etc. In this chapter, we first give an overview of face recognition. In general, research on face recognition can be grouped into two categories: (i) feature-based approaches and (ii) holistic approaches. Feature-based approaches extract local features such as eyes, nose, mouth and so on to perform spatial face recognition while holistic approaches match the faces as a whole for recognition (Mian, 2007).

Recently, artificial neural networks (ANNs) have been widely applied in face recognition for the reason that neural network based classifiers can incorporate both statistical and structural information to achieve better performance than the simple minimum distance classifiers (Chellappa *et al.*, 1995). There are two structures of ANNs commonly in use, namely *Multilayered neural network* (MLNN) and *Radial Basis Function neural network* (RBF NN). MLNNs are popular in face recognition due to their good learning generalization for complex problems (Jain *et. al.*, 1999). The conventional training of MLNNs is mainly based on optimization theory. In order to search an optimal solution for MLNNs, a number of weight updating algorithms have been developed. The gradient-based *backpropagation* (BP) training algorithms are widely used (Valentin *et al.*, 1994). It is well-known that gradient-based BP training algorithms may have a slow convergence in practice. The search for the global minimum point of a cost function may be trapped at local minima during gradient descent. Furthermore, the global minimum point may not be found, if the MLNN has large bounded input disturbances. Therefore, fast error convergence and strong robustness of the MLNN with the gradient-based BP algorithms may not be guaranteed.

Alternatively, RBF NNs have been applied to many engineering and scientific applications including face recognition (Er *et al.*, 2002; Yang & Paindavoine, 2003). RBF NNs possess the following significant properties: (i) universal approximators (Park & Wsandberg, 1991), and (ii) simple topological structure (Lee & Kil, 1991) which allows straightforward computation using a linearly weighted combination of single hidden-layer neurons. Due to the linear-weighted combiner, the weights can be determined using *least mean square* (LMS) and *recursive least square* (RLS) algorithms. However, these algorithms suffer from several drawbacks and limitations. LMS is highly dependent on the autocorrelation function associated with the input signals and slow convergence. RLS, on the other hand, provides faster convergence but it depends on the implicit or explicit computation of the inverse of the input signal's autocorrelation matrix. This not only implies a higher computational cost, but it can also lead to instability problems (Mueller, 1981). Other gradient search-based training algorithms also suffer from the so-called local minima problem, i.e., the optimization search may stop at a local minimum of the cost function in the weight space if the initial values are arbitrarily chosen. For example, the cost function has a fixed structure in the weight space after the expression of the cost function is chosen. The parameter update law is only a means to search for the global minimum and is independent of the cost function in the weight space.

To overcome the aforementioned problems, a new approach for face recognition using Lyapunov theory-based neural network is presented as illustrated in Figure 1. To further reduce the input dimensions, feature extraction techniques are applied before Lyapunov theory-based neural classifier. First,

Figure 1. Proposed face recognition system

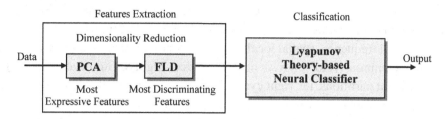

high dimensional data are applied to *Principal Component Analysis* (PCA) to extract the most expressive features, followed by *Fisher's Linear Discriminant* (FLD) to obtain the most discriminating features for dimensionality reduction. Next, these features are passed to Lyapunov theory-based neural classifier for classification. The optimization techniques based on Lyapunov stability theory are adopted from Man *et al.* (1999, 2006) and Seng *et al.* (1999, 2002). Unlike gradient-based training algorithms, Lyapunov adaptive techniques are not used for searching the global minimum point along the cost-function surface in the weight or parameter space. They are aimed at constructing an energy surface with a single global minimum point through the adaptive adjustment of the weights or parameters as time goes to infinity. The classification error can then asymptotically converge to zero. Another important characteristic of the Lyapunov adaptive techniques is that, the effects of the noise disturbances can be eliminated through adaptively updating the weights using the Lyapunov stability theory.

In this chapter, the basic knowledge of face recognition techniques, face features extraction methods and ANNs will be discussed in the background. The detail of designing Lyapunov theory-based neural classifiers based on Lyapunov stability theory will be presented subsequently. For performance evaluation, experiments are conducted on two benchmark face databases: ORL (*Olivetti Research Laboratory*) and Yale. Comparisons with some of the existing conventional techniques are given as well. Meanwhile, the future research trends on Lyapunov theory-based neural networks will be suggested at the end of this chapter.

BACKGROUND

Face recognition is a critical task in human-interaction computerized machine. The key point of face recognition is to automatically distinguish individuals from still images or videos utilising facial appearance such as eyes, nose, mouth, chin and other facial features. It scans a person's face and finds the similarities against a known database. For surveillance and cognitive ability, face recognition systems are nowadays extensively applied to intelligent systems. There are various advanced face recognition techniques being developed for the same ultimate goal: identifying faces efficiently and accurately under any circumstances. Generally, face recognition techniques can be classified into two major categories: (i) feature-based approaches (Bobis *et al.*, 1999; Cagnoni & Poggi, 1999; Ergin & Gülmezoğlu, 2008; Li *et al.*, 2007; Martinez, 1999; Yan *et al.*, 2007), and (ii) holistic approaches (Belhumeur *et al.*, 1997; Hu *et al.*, 2008; Gul, 2003; Kirby & Sirovich, 1990; Sirovich & Kirby, 1987; Zhao *et al.*, 2003).

A feature-based approach, proposed by Bobis *et al.* (1999), was used to perform extraction and measurement of salient features regarding the distance and angle between the local facial features such as eyes, nose and mouth for identifying faces. Meanwhile, Cagnoni & Poggi (1999) segmented the facial features and then transformed them into PCA subspace for better matching results. Martinez (1999) divided face into a few regions followed by PCA transformation. Hidden Markov Models (HMMs) are therefore used to match the facial features for each candidate. In addition, Li *et al.* (2007) characterized facial features by spatial frequency, spatial locality and orientation selection using Gabor wavelet. After that, they performed common vector analysis in kernel space. Ergin & Gülmezoğlu (2008) split a facial region into four different partitions, i.e. right eye, left eye, nose and mouth. These features are extracted and applied to Common Vector Approach for face recognition.

On the other hand, the holistic approach is widely used in face recognition because it extracts extremely represented features from the whole face region with respect to the pixels' intensity values. As an operation, holistic face recognition tries to spot the global facial representations to distinguish faces. It is then followed by cross correlation on the input data compared with database images to seek for the best match (Zhao *et al.*, 2003). There are two widely used eigenspace representations of the face region, namely PCA (Sirovich & Kirby, 1987; Kirby & Sirovich, 1990) and FLD (Belhumeur *et al.*, 1997). PCA is often used to reduce multidimensional data sets to lower dimensions in a subspace for analysis. Likewise, FLD transforms input data to the eigenspace to obtain the discriminant feature points. Other feature extraction techniques such as Discrete Wavelet transform (DWT) (Hu *et al.*, 2008; Jong-Bae & Hang-Joon, 2002) and Discrete Cosine Transform (DCT) (Er *et al.*, 2005; Hafed & Levine, 2001) are applied to reduce image dimension in frequency space.

ANNs have been successfully applied to face recognition because neural network based classifiers can incorporate both statistical and structural information to achieve better performance than the simple minimum distance classifier (Chellappa *et al.*, 1995). The main advantages of applying ANNs to face recognition can be listed as follows: (i) prior knowledge of statistical data is unnecessary, (ii) inherent parallelism, (iii) fault tolerance, (iv) flexibility, and (v) fast classification (Jain *et al.*, 1999, p.291). Two structures of ANNs that are normally found in face recognition are RBF NN (Er *et al.*, 2002, 2005; Thomaz *et al.*, 1998; Zhou *et al.*, 2007) and MLNN (Lin *et al*, 1997; Midorikawa, 1988; Nazeer, 2007; Perry & Carney, 1990; Solheim *et al.*, 1992). Generally, high dimensional data are fed into neural networks for classification. However, high dimensional images are highly redundant, and at the same time increase the complexity of neural systems as well as the network training time. To reduce high dimension input data, face feature extraction techniques are required to reduce the dimension of input image before classification. The following two sections discuss the details of (i) face features extraction, and (ii) classification using ANNs.

Face Features Extraction

Extracting proper features is essential for satisfactory design of any face classifier. Traditionally, PCA has been the standard approach to reduce the high-dimensional original pattern vector space into low-dimensional feature vector space. Numerous studies (Belhumeur *et al.*, 1997; Swets & Weng, 1996; Wang & Tang, 2004; Nazeer, 2007) have been performed between FLD and PCA on face recognition. Wang & Tang (2004) attempted to unify all these subspace methods under the same framework. In this section, PCA is used to reduce the high dimensional input data and generate the most expressive features. FLD is then implemented to generate a set of the most discriminating features.

Principal Component Analysis (PCA)

PCA is used to extract mostly significant features of the multidimensional image in order to reduce raw data dimension. Since Sirovich & Kirby (1987) has proposed the eigenfaces approach based on PCA mathematical tools, the growth of the face recognition technology has dramatically increased. With the *Karhunen-Loève* (KL) transform, the dimensionality of the face pattern is greatly reduced and represented by salient feature vectors. The features in PCA subspace provide more salient and richer information for recognition than the original image (Stan & Anil, 2004).

Let the original image Z_i be a two-dimensional $m \times m$ array. The image is first converted to a vector of dimension m^2. Training images are denoted as $Z = (Z_1, Z_2, ..., Z_n) \subset \Re^{m^2 x n}$ where n is the number of classes. An assumption is made that each image belongs to one of the classes. The covariance matrix (Fukunaga, 1990; Turk & Pentland, 1991) is then defined as:

$$\Gamma = \frac{1}{n}\sum_{i=1}^{n}(Z_i - \bar{Z})(Z_i - \bar{Z})^T = \Phi\Phi^T \tag{1}$$

where $\Phi = (\Phi_1, \Phi_2, ..., \Phi_n) \subset \Re^{m^2 x n}$ and $\bar{Z} = \frac{1}{n}\sum_{i=1}^{n}Z_i$

Subsequently, eigenvalues and eigenvectors of the covariance Γ are calculated. Let $U = (U_1, U_2, ..., U_n) \subset \Re^{m^2 x n} (r < n)$ be the r eigenvectors corresponding to the r largest eigenvalues. The corresponding eigenface-based feature $X \subset \Re^{r x n}$ of the original images $Z \subset \Re^{m^2 x n}$ can be obtained by projecting Z into the eigenface space as:

$$X = U^T Z \tag{2}$$

Fisher's Linear Discriminant (FLD)

Belhumeur *et al.* (1997) proposed FLD to further discriminate the PCA data which are largely affected by the illumination and expression changes. FLD is applied to obtain the most invariant feature of facial images. It selects the linear subspace E, which maximizes the ratio:

$$\frac{\left|E^T S_b E\right|}{\left|E^T S_w E\right|} \tag{3}$$

Let the set of training samples in the eigenface space be $X = (X_1, X_2, ..., X_n) \subset \Re^{r x n}$. To find an optimal low-dimensional subspace, the between-class scatter and the within-class scatter are defined in (4) and (5) respectively.

$$S_B = \sum_{i-1}^{c}n^i(\bar{X}^i - \bar{X})(\bar{X}^i - \bar{X})^T \tag{4}$$

Figure 2. Radial basis function neural network

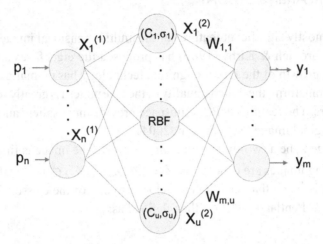

$$S_W = \sum_{i=1}^{c} \sum_{X_i \in n^i} (X_k - \bar{X}^i)(X - \bar{X}^i)^T \qquad (5)$$

where c represents the number of classes and n^i is the number of *i-th* class data. The maximum dimension of linear subspace, E is *c-1*. The discriminating feature vectors P projected from the PCA to the optimal subspace can be calculated as follows:

$$P = E_{optimal}^T X \qquad (6)$$

where $E_{optimal}$ is the FLD optimal projection matrix (Fukunaga,1990; Swets & Weng,1996).

Other Methods

Other feature extraction methods, such as *Discrete Cosine Transform* (DCT) based feature transform and *Discrete Wavelet Transform* (DWT) based feature transform are used to reduce the image dimensionality. DCT (Er *et al.*, 2005; Hafed & Levine, 2001) is a discrete-time version of the Fourier-Cosine series technique. It provides a better approximation of a signal with fewer coefficients in real value. Therefore, DCT is applied on facial images for image size reduction and illumination removal. DWT (Hu *et al.*, 2008; Jong-Bae & Hang-Joon, 2002) is, in general perspective, used to analyze data in frequency domain. Images are decomposed into four sub-bands representation with two-dimensional DWT. The four blocks of decomposition are the approximation coefficients and three detailed coefficients. The details include the horizontal, vertical, and diagonal coefficients. The lower frequency of sub-band is significantly preserved to represent the original data while the higher frequency data suffers from some data loss.

Classification Using Artificial Neural Networks (ANNs)

ANNs are widely used for pattern classification or recognition. Face images are first transformed into a column vector and fed into the ANN as input. The input of the ANN is set to be the image size while the output represents the number of tasks to be classified. Two types of ANNs that are normally used for classification – RBF NN and MLNN are discussed in the following sections.

Radial Basis Function Neural Network (RBF NN)

The traditional three-layer RBF NN, shown in Figure 2, is employed for face recognition. Such a network implements an input-output mapping: $\Re^n \rightarrow \Re^m$. Let the first layer of input vector, $\mathbf{X}^{(1)}$ to be $\mathbf{P} \in \Re^n$ where $\mathbf{P} = \left[p_1, p_2, \cdots, p_n \right]^T$. The RBF centers are denoted as $C_j \in \Re^n (1 \leq j \leq u)$. Each RBF unit is defined as:

$$X_j^{(2)}(P) = \exp(-\frac{\| X^{(1)} - C_j \|^2}{\sigma_j^2}), \quad j = 1, \ldots, u \tag{7}$$

where $\|\cdot\|$ indicates the Euclidean norm on the input space while σ_j is the Gaussian width of the j-th RBF unit. The vector form generated after the RBF neurons is given in (8).

$$\begin{bmatrix} \psi(\|\mathbf{X}^{(1)} - C_1\|^2) \\ \psi(\|\mathbf{X}^{(1)} - C_2\|^2) \\ \vdots \\ \psi(\|\mathbf{X}^{(1)} - C_u\|^2) \end{bmatrix} = \begin{bmatrix} X_1^{(2)} \\ X_2^{(2)} \\ \vdots \\ X_u^{(2)} \end{bmatrix} = \begin{bmatrix} \psi(\|\mathbf{X}^{(1)} - C_1\|^2) \\ \psi(\|\mathbf{X}^{(1)} - C_2\|^2) \\ \vdots \\ \psi(\|\mathbf{X}^{(1)} - C_u\|^2) \end{bmatrix} \begin{bmatrix} X_1^{(2)} \\ X_2^{(2)} \\ \vdots \\ X_u^{(2)} \end{bmatrix} \mathbf{X}^{(2)} = \begin{bmatrix} X_1^{(2)} \\ X_2^{(2)} \\ \vdots \\ X_u^{(2)} \end{bmatrix} = \mathbf{X}^{(2)} \tag{8}$$

where the function $\psi(\cdot)$ is the radial basis function. Consider that the hidden nodes are linearly mapped to the output with the weights in the matrix form as shown in (9).

$$\begin{bmatrix} w_{1,1} & w_{1,2} & \cdots & w_{1,u} \\ w_{2,1} & w_{2,2} & \cdots & w_{2,u} \\ \vdots & \ddots & & \vdots \\ w_{m,1} & \cdots & \cdots & w_{m,u} \end{bmatrix} = \begin{bmatrix} \mathbf{w}_1^T \\ \mathbf{w}_2^T \\ \vdots \\ \mathbf{w}_m^T \end{bmatrix} = \begin{bmatrix} w_{1,1} & w_{1,2} & \cdots & w_{1,u} \\ w_{2,1} & w_{2,2} & \cdots & w_{2,u} \\ \vdots & \ddots & & \vdots \\ w_{m,1} & \cdots & \cdots & w_{m,u} \end{bmatrix} \begin{bmatrix} \mathbf{w}_1^T \\ \mathbf{w}_2^T \\ \vdots \\ \mathbf{w}_m^T \end{bmatrix} \mathbf{W} = \begin{bmatrix} \mathbf{w}_1^T \\ \mathbf{w}_2^T \\ \vdots \\ \mathbf{w}_m^T \end{bmatrix} = \mathbf{W} \tag{9}$$

RBF network establishes a linear function mapping in the output layer. By multiplying equations (8) and (9), the weighted hidden values are summed to be the output vector, $\mathbf{Y}$ as follows:

$$\mathbf{Y} = \mathbf{W}\mathbf{X}^{(2)} \tag{10}$$

Figure 3. Feedforward multilayered neural network

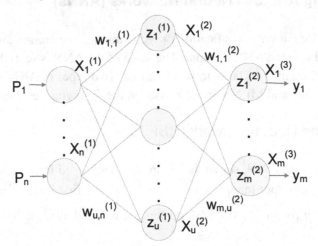

where $\mathbf{Y} = \left[y_1, y_2 \cdots, y_m\right]^T$ and each output node has the relationship in (11).

$$y_r(P) = \sum_{j=1}^{u} X_j^{(2)} w_{r,j}, \quad r = 1, \cdots m \tag{11}$$

Two important parameters are associated with each RBF unit. They are center C_j and gaussian width σ_j. Every center should well represent the corresponding subclass because the classification in RBF NN is mainly measured based on the distances between the input samples and the centers of each subclass. There are different strategies to select RBF centers (Haykin, 1994). These strategies can be classified into supervised (Er *et al.*, 2002, 2005) and unsupervised algorithms (Leonard & Kramer, 1991; Moody & Darken, 1989; Musavi, *et al.*, 1991; Yang & Paindavoine, 2003). Once centers are well selected, the network starts learning the training data with the weight updating scheme.

Learning algorithm plays an important role in updating the weight between hidden and output layer of RBF NN. Conventional RBF with LMS algorithm (Nehrotra *et al.*, 1996; Virginia, 2000) is trained using the gradient descent method which finds the negative gradient on the error curve. It suffers from slow convergence and is trapped in the local minima instead of global error. On the other hand, conventional RBF using RLS method (Birgmeier, 1995; Simon, 2002) computes the inverse of autocorrelation matrix associated with the input data to update the system weights. However, the inversion of RLS algorithm gives instability of system convergence and increases computational cost.

Multilayered Neural Network (MLNN)

A simple feedforward MLNN with one hidden layer is shown in Figure 3. Unlike RBF NN, the activation function of MLNN neurons can be hard-limiter, linear, sigmoid and others. The performance of MLNN system is greatly dependent on the weight updating. Hence, an effective weight updating law with fast weight convergence and error minimization is important. MLNN updates weights recursively in order to do the pattern classification. Weights are connected from every node of *s-th* layer to the nodes in *(s+1)-th* layer where s is the layer's number of the system. Consider that the three layered MLNN has the weight arrangement in (12) & (13):

$$\mathbf{W}^{(1)} = \begin{bmatrix} w_{1,1}^{(1)} & w_{1,2}^{(1)} & \cdots & w_{1,n}^{(1)} \\ \vdots & \ddots & & \vdots \\ w_{u,1}^{(1)} & \cdots & \cdots & w_{u,n}^{(1)} \end{bmatrix} = \begin{bmatrix} \mathbf{w}_1^{(1)T} \\ \vdots \\ \mathbf{w}_u^{(1)T} \end{bmatrix}$$

(12)

$$\mathbf{W}^{(2)} = \begin{bmatrix} w_{1,1}^{(2)} & w_{1,2}^{(2)} & \cdots & w_{1,u}^{(2)} \\ \vdots & \ddots & & \vdots \\ w_{m,1}^{(2)} & \cdots & \cdots & w_{m,u}^{(2)} \end{bmatrix} = \begin{bmatrix} \mathbf{w}_1^{(2)T} \\ \vdots \\ \mathbf{w}_m^{(2)T} \end{bmatrix}$$

(13)

where $\mathbf{W}^{(1)}$ is the weight link between *n-th* input and *u-th* hidden nodes while $\mathbf{W}^{(2)}$ is the weight connection between *u-th* hidden nodes and *m-th* outputs.

Let $\mathbf{X}^{(1)} = \mathbf{P} \in \Re^n$ where $\mathbf{P} = \begin{bmatrix} p_1, p_2, \cdots, p_n \end{bmatrix}^T$ be the input vector. The hidden layer has u nonlinear nodes. The output of the hidden nodes gives the response as in (14) & (15).

$$z_j = \left(\sum_{i=1}^{n} X_i^{(1)} w_{j,i}^{(1)} \right)$$

(14)

$$X_j^{(2)} = F\left(z_j\right)$$

(15)

where $F\left(\cdot\right)$ is the nonlinear function on hidden nodes.

Subsequently, the weighted sum value of the hidden layer is fed into the *m*-th output node, y_r which is defined as:

$$z_r = \left(\sum_{j=1}^{u} X_j^{(2)} w_{r,j}^{(2)} \right)$$

(16)

$$y_r = G\left(z_r\right)$$

(17)

where $G\left(\cdot\right)$ is the nonlinear function on output nodes and $r = 1, 2, ..., m$. Both nonlinear vector functions $F(\cdot)$ and $G(\cdot)$ are assigned to be the sigmoid function where

$$G\left(\cdot\right) = F\left(\cdot\right) = \frac{1}{1 + e^{-\beta(\cdot)}}$$

(18)

and β is a positive constant.

The conventional MLNN (Nehrotra, 1996) is trained using BP method in order to update the weights as well as to minimize the error of the network. The BP method uses the gradient descent algorithm to search for the global minimum in the error surface. It is known that the standard BP training algorithm suffers from slow convergence in practice, and the search for the global minimum point of a cost function may be trapped at local minima. In addition, the global minimum point may not be found if the MLNN has large bounded input disturbances. To solve the abovementioned problems, the Lyapunov theory-based neural networks are designed and discussed in the next section.

CLASSIFICATION USING LYAPUNOV THEORY-BASED RBF NN

Lyapunov stability theory was proposed by a Russian mathematician, A.M. Lyapunov (1892). The basic definition of Lyapunov stability theorem is stated in Vidyasagar (1993, p.157). Consider a function $V(x(t)) : \Re_+ \times \Re^n \rightarrow \Re$ and time-dependent input $x(t) \in \Re^n$ such that: (i) $V(x(t)) \geq 0$ *with the equilibrium zero if and only if x = 0;* (ii) $\dot{V}(x(t)) < 0$.

Then *V(x(t))* is called a Lyapunov function candidate and the system is asymptotically stable in the sense of Lyapunov.

The idea of the Lyapunov theory-based RBF filter was first developed in Seng *et al.* (1999) for adaptive filtering. Other related research works can be found in Man *et al.* (1999, 2006) and Seng *et al.* (1999, 2002). The basic idea of those research works is that: *The candidate of a Lyapunov function V (an energy function) of the tracking error is first chosen. The weights or filter parameters are then adaptively updated, from the output layer to the input layer, to make ΔV < 0.* According to Lyapunov stability theory, the candidate of Lyapunov function is a true Lyapunov function of the error dynamics if the above conditions are satisfied. The training error can then asymptotically converge to zero as time goes to infinity. Unlike the gradient-based training algorithms, Lyapunov adaptive techniques are not used for searching the global minimum point along the cost-function surface in the weight or parameter space, but they are aimed at constructing an energy surface with a single global minimum point through the adaptive adjustment of the weights or parameters as time goes to infinity. The training error can then asymptotically converge to zero.

To design the Lyapunov theory-based neural classifier, Lyapunov function of errors between target outputs and RBF outputs are first defined. The weights are then adjusted based on Lyapunov theory so that errors can asymptotically converge to zero. The selected Lyapunov function has a unique global minimum in the state space. By properly choosing the weight update law in Lyapunov sense, RBF outputs can asymptotically converge to the target outputs. Lyapunov theory provides an optimization method in the state space. In this section, the design in Seng *et al.* (2002) is adopted and modified. The input vector **P** is fed into the RBF node and then passed to the output by the weighted sum with the formulas given in (7)-(11). Initially, for the given desired response $d_r(k)$ of each output node at discrete time k, the Lyapunov function is chosen as:

$$V(k) = e_r^2(k) \tag{19}$$

$$V(k) = (d_r(k) - \mathbf{w}_r^T(k)\mathbf{X}^{(2)}(k))^2 \tag{20}$$

The $V(k)$ is well selected based on the Lyapunov stability theory. As stated in (Seng *et al.*, 2002), the adaptive gain function is selected to be of the form in (21).

$$\mathbf{g}_r(k) = \frac{\mathbf{X}(k)}{\left\|\mathbf{X}(k)\right\|^2}\left[1 - \kappa\left|\frac{e_r(k-1)}{\alpha_r(k)}\right|\right] \tag{21}$$

where $0 \le \kappa < 1$.

Therefore, weights are updated based on the multiplication of gain and the a priori error denoted in (22).

$$\mathbf{w}_r(k) = \mathbf{w}_r(k-1) + \mathbf{g}_r(k)\alpha_r(k) \tag{22}$$

where the estimation of a priori error $\alpha_k(k)$ is defined as follows:

$$\alpha_r(k) = d_r(k) - \mathbf{w}_r^T(k-1)\mathbf{X}(k) \tag{23}$$

In order to prevent the singularities of the gain $g_r(k)$, the equation (21) is modified as:

$$\mathbf{g}_r(k) = \frac{\mathbf{X}(k)}{\lambda_1 + \left\|\mathbf{X}(k)\right\|^2}\left[1 - \kappa\frac{\left|e_r(k-1)\right|}{\lambda_2 + \left|\alpha_r(k)\right|}\right] \tag{24}$$

where λ_1 and λ_2 are small positive integers.

For face recognition, the Lyapunov theory-based RBF network has to be extended to multi-outputs or r-output neurons because there are, in general, numbers of faces to be recognized. Hence, the Lyapunov theory has to be modified as well for multi-outputs.

Remark 1: The theoretical design of Lyapunov theory-based RBF neural system is shown in *Appendix A*. Lyapunov function $V(k)$ is important in constructing a new cost-function of the system. Compared to conventional gradient searching algorithm, Lyapunov-based system constructs the error in the state space with a single minimum point. Regarding the Lyapunov stability theory, $V(k)$ should be selected such that $\Delta V(k) = V(k) - V(k-1) < 0$. For r-output RBF network, $V(k)$ is chosen as in (20). With the parameters pre-defined in expressions (21)-(23), it is proved that $\Delta V(k)$ is a negative value.

Remark 2: Proof of error convergence is shown in *Appendix B*. By applying the Lyapunov function, the error converges to zero exponentially as time increases to infinity. For r-output RBF NN, the classification error $e_r(k)$ is proved to be asymptotically approaching zero as training time increases. It is noted that the error convergence rate is dependent on the positive constant, κ. For faster error convergence, κ should remain a small value, $0 \le \kappa < 1$.

Remark 3: With the modified adaptive gain (24), the error can converge to a ball centered. The proof of error convergence and analysis for r-output RBF NN can be easily obtained by modifying the proof in this reference (Seng *et al.*, 2002).

CLASSIFICATION USING LYAPUNOV THEORY-BASED MLNN

Weights update laws in linear RBF neural network cannot be directly applied to adjust the weights of MLNN. Therefore, the modified Lyapunov theory-based neural classifier is needed for MLNN.

For $\{p_r\} \in \Re^n$ and $\{y_r\} \in \Re^m$, a linear function $h : \Re^n \to \Re^m$ which maps $\{p_r\}$ to $\{\tilde{y}_r\}$ has to be created. By finding the linear mapping $h(\cdot)$, the MLNN system weights in (12)-(13) have to be rearranged in a linear form in the representation of θ_r as follows:

$$\boldsymbol{\theta}_r = \begin{bmatrix} \mathbf{w}_r^{(2)} \\ \mathbf{w}_1^{(1)} \\ \vdots \\ \mathbf{w}_u^{(1)} \end{bmatrix}, \ for \ r = 1, 2, \cdots, m \tag{25}$$

The modified weight, θ_r has M-dimensional structure in $r\text{-}th$ output node where $M = u(n+1) + (u+1)$. Thus, the functional mapping from p_r to y_r is defined as the relationship:

$$y_r = h(\theta_r, \mathbf{p}_r) \tag{26}$$

Assume that the MLNN output has desired output, $\{d_r\} \in \Re^m$. The system is modeled as:

$$d_r = h(\theta_r, \mathbf{p}_r) + u_r \tag{27}$$

where u_r is an observing noise.

By applying Taylor series on eq. (26) with the estimation of θ_t, it is written as follows:

$$h(\theta_r, \mathbf{p}_r) = h(\theta_t, \mathbf{p}_r) + \mathbf{H}_r^T(\theta_r - \theta_t) + H.O.T \tag{28}$$

where H.O.T is high order differentiation term and

$$\mathbf{H}_r = \frac{\partial h(\theta_t, \mathbf{p}_r)}{\partial \theta_t} \tag{29}$$

Substituting the expression (28) into (27) and rearranging the equation, we get

$$d_r - h(\theta_t, \mathbf{p}_r) + \mathbf{H}_r^T \theta_t = \mathbf{H}_r^T \theta_r + u_r$$
$$\tilde{d}_r = \tilde{y}_r + u_r \tag{30}$$

Since the system has been linearly transformed, the input vector of MLNN system is given as the derivative matrix, $\mathbf{H}_r$. The derivative matrix $\mathbf{H}_r$ is defined as follows:

$$\mathbf{H}_r = \begin{bmatrix} \dfrac{\partial y_r}{\partial w_r^{(2)}} \\[8pt] \dfrac{\partial y_r}{\partial w_1^{(1)}} \\ \vdots \\ \dfrac{\partial y_r}{\partial w_u^{(1)}} \end{bmatrix} = \begin{bmatrix} G'(z_r^{(2)})X^{(2)} \\[8pt] G'(z_r^{(2)})w_{r,1}^{(2)}F'(z_1^{(1)})X^{(1)} \\ \vdots \\ \vdots \\ G'(z_r^{(2)})w_{r,u}^{(2)}F'(z_u^{(1)})X^{(1)} \end{bmatrix} \tag{31}$$

where

$$G'(z_r^{(2)}) = z_r^{(2)}(1 - z_r^{(2)}), \; for \; r = 1, \cdots, m$$

$$F'(z_j^{(1)}) = z_j^{(1)}(1 - z_j^{(1)}), \; for \; j = 1, \cdots, u$$

The desired output after linear transformation $\left\{ \tilde{d}_r \right\} \in \Re^m$ is set to be equal to $\left\{ d_r \right\} \in \Re^m$. Therefore, Lyapunov function $V(k)$ for the linear MLNN system is defined as:

$$V(k) = \sum \left(d_r(k) - \tilde{y}_r(k) \right)^2$$
$$= \sum \left(d_r(k) - \mathbf{H}_r^T(k), _r(k) \right)^2 \tag{32}$$

The adaptive gain (21) is modified such that $\Delta V < 0$:

$$\mathbf{g}_r(k) = \frac{\mathbf{H}_r(k)}{\left\| \mathbf{H}_r(k) \right\|^2} \left(1 - \kappa \left| \frac{e_r(k-1)}{\alpha_r(k)} \right| \right) \tag{33}$$

The weight updating algorithm is designed as follows:

$$\boldsymbol{\theta}_r(k) = \boldsymbol{\theta}_r(k-1) + \mathbf{g}_r(k)\alpha_r(k) \tag{34}$$

To prevent the singularities, expression (33) can be modified to:

$$\mathbf{g}_r(t) = \frac{\mathbf{H}_r(k)}{\lambda_1 + \left\| \mathbf{H}_r(k) \right\|^2} \left(1 - \kappa \frac{\left| e_r(k-1) \right|}{\lambda_2 + \left| \alpha_r(k) \right|} \right) \tag{35}$$

where λ_1 and λ_2 are small positive integers.

Remark 4: The theoretical design of Lyapunov theory-based MLNN neural system is shown in *Appendix C*. In MLNN systems, the difference of Lyapunov function defined in (32) is guaranteed in the sense that $\Delta V(k) < 0$ with the equations (33) and (34).

Remark 5: Proof of error convergence is given in *Appendix D*. Similar to the RBF classifier, the error of the modified MLNN for each of the output nodes is approaching zero when time goes to infinity with the expression (33).

EXPERIMENTAL RESULTS

In order to evaluate the Lyapunov theory-based face recognition system, experiments are carried out on the two benchmark databases: ORL and Yale. The ORL database is made up of 400 images with 40 distinct subjects in an upright frontal position. There are variation in lighting levels, facial expression, pose and facial details as depicted in Figure 4(a). In these experiments, a total of 200 images were selected randomly as the training data and another 200 images as the testing set, in which each person has five images. On the other hand, another experiment was done on the Yale database (Belhumeur et al, 1997), where the facial regions are cropped and normalized as illustrated in Figure 4(b). The database contains 165 frontal face images covering 15 individuals taken under 11 different conditions. Each individual has different facial expressions, illumination conditions and small occlusion. 10 images of each individual are selected: five images for the training set and others for the testing data set. Every experimental result is generated based on six simulation runs. An average classification rate is defined as (Er *et al.*, 2002, 2005; Sing *et al.*, 2005):

$$R_{ave} = \frac{\sum_{i=1}^{q} n_c^i}{q n_{tot}} \tag{36}$$

where q is the number of simulation runs, n_c^i is the number of correct classifications for *i-th* run, and n_{tot} is the total number of the testing data for each run.

In the experiments, three sets of different input data size are prepared: (i) original image with 64x64 dimension, (ii) salient features extracted from PCA, and (iii) salient features extracted from PCA and

Figure 4. A subset of face samples in (a) ORL database (Adapted from [The ORL database]), and (b) Yale database © 1997, The Yale University, used with permission

(a) (b)

further discriminated using FLD. These data sets are then passed to the neural network to complete the face recognition analysis. The number of neural inputs is set to be equal to the dimensions of the input space (i.e. number of features from FLD). On the other hand, the number of outputs is equal to the number of classes to be recognized. Centers of RBF hidden neurons are selected based on the mean of the images for each class.

ORL Database Experiments

The RBF classifiers were evaluated using the ORL face database. Three types of RBF classifiers with different learning schemes were used, i.e. conventional RBF1 with LMS learning approach, conventional RBF2 with RLS technique, and the Lyapunov theory-based RBF classifier. The performance and face recognition rates were compared on these RBF systems.

Weight convergence was crucial in the network's learning characteristic. The weights for all RBF classifiers were converged at equilibrium with a random set of initial weights. Figure 5(a) shows one of the weights, where the x-axis denotes the epochs while the y-axis denotes the weight values connected from the hidden layer to the output layer of the RBF network. An epoch represents the efficient time used to train the entire set of input data. Hence, each epoch updated the weights once for the whole training set until the occurrence of weight convergence and this is referred to the batch learning scheme. In addition, the weight of the proposed RBF classifier is converged within 5 epochs, which is faster than other conventional RBF classifiers.

On the other hand, incremental learning scheme updated weights for every training data and the time used to train an input data was represented as an iteration. The training process iteratively updated the weights for every data until the weights reached an equilibrium point. Therefore, an incremental training weight convergence was considered in this context to obtain better observation on weight convergence. Figure 5(b) shows that the Lyapunov theory-based RBF classifier obtained a faster convergence rate than other conventional RBF NNs.

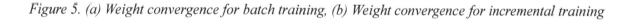

Figure 5. (a) Weight convergence for batch training, (b) Weight convergence for incremental training

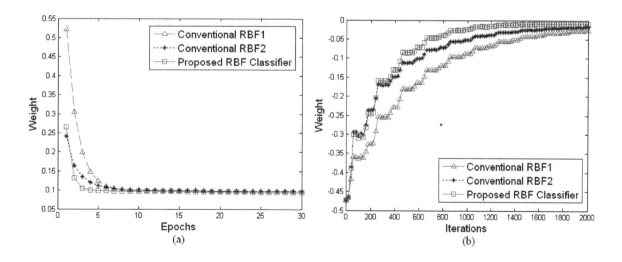

To investigate the performance of the RBF classifiers, testing data were fed into the system and the average recognition rate was calculated using equation (36). Without any features extraction method, the original images were tested with the RBF classifiers. Conventional RBF1 has a recognition rate of 83.75% while the conventional RBF2 has a rate of 85.17%. However, the recognition rate of the proposed classifier is slightly higher at 85.33% compared to the conventional methods. The testing result is shown in Figure 6(a).

According to Er *et al.* (2002), high dimensional input data causes low recognition rate of the network. This is because high dimensional input data and network complexity may need a large training sample size. Therefore, a feature extraction technique such as PCA is used to reduce the image's dimension. From Figure 6(b), the recognition rate is increased along with the increased number of PCA feature points. These classifiers have the optimum performance where the number of PCA feature points is 170. Subsequently, the FLD method was used to obtain the most discriminating features in order to separate the class data further. As shown in Figure 6(c), the performance of PCA combined with FLD

Figure 6. RBF NN results of (a) Recognition rate vs epochs, (b) Recognition rate vs PCA features, and (c) Recognition rate vs PCA+FLD features on ORL database

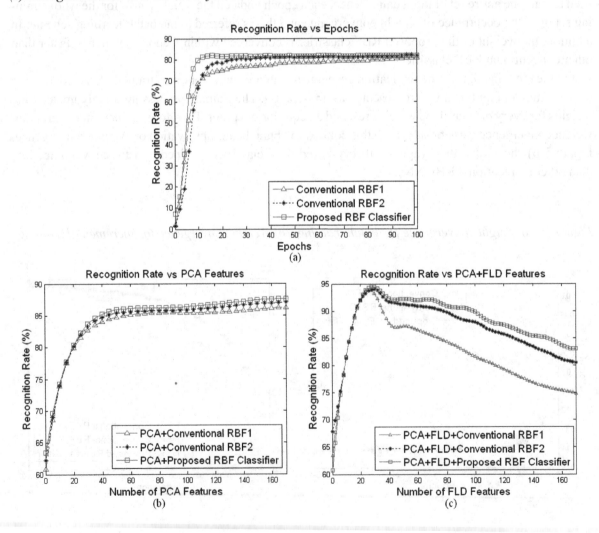

did not improve along with the increase in feature dimension due to the information loss. The optimum performance is obtained with the number of 30 FLD feature points. The Lyapunov theory-based RBF classifier with PCA and FLD testing data achieved a recognition rate of 94.42%.

For MLNN classifiers, it has been reported in Jain *et al.* (1999) and Lawrence *et al.* (1996, 1997) that recognition rates of the MLNN classifiers with PCA features and the *Self-Organizing Map* (SOM) are 58.80% and 60.40% respectively on the ORL database. Both of these MLNNs were trained using conventional BP algorithms. In these experiments, ORL training sets after PCA and FLD features extraction were tested with the conventional MLNN and the Lyapunov theory-based MLNN classifier. The MLNN with BP method had a recognition rate of 59.08% while the MLNN with Lyapunov designed weight update law achieved a recognition rate of 75.40%. The recognition rates of ORL data with different networks are summarized in Table 1.

Yale Database Experiments

The original images were tested in the RBF networks. The conventional RBF1 obtained a recognition rate of 64.89% and the conventional RBF2 had a 65.56% recognition rate. On the other hand, the proposed classifier using Lyapunov function achieved a recognition rate of 66.00%. In Figure 7(a), the RBF system was tested with the testing pattern after the training data had been learned. It showed that the proposed RBF classifier can achieve the highest recognition rate within a few epochs as compared to the other networks.

The classification of higher dimension input needs a complex neural system, and at the same time, the computational time also increases. Therefore, PCA is performed on the input data to extract some significant feature points. As shown in Figure 7(b), the recognition rate increases as the PCA features number is increased. The optimum PCA features for Yale database is 60 where the proposed classifier achieved a 71.70% recognition rate.

The simulations were further tested with PCA and FLD data. As shown in Figure 7(c), the RBF classifiers obtain better results over the result generated in PCA features only. The optimum performance is obtained with 20 FLD features. In the experiment, the proposed RBF classifier had a 92.76% recognition rate. Similar to RBF NN, testing data were fed into a multilayered network. In an MLNN network, the conventional network with BP algorithm obtained a 69.78% recognition rate. On the other hand, the Lyapunov theory-based MLNN achieved 81.78%, which is higher than the conventional one. The overall recognition rates on the Yale database with RBF NNs and MLNNs are summarized in Table 2.

Table 1. Recognition rates on ORL database with RBF NNs and MLNNs

Networks	Recognition Rate
Conventional RBF1	83.75%
Conventional RBF2	85.17%
Proposed RBF Classifier	**94.42%**
Conventional MLNN+PCA	58.80%
Conventional MLNN+SOM	60.40%
Conventional MLNN+PCA+FLD	59.08%
Proposed MLNN Classifier	**75.40%**

Figure 7. RBF NN results of (a) Recognition rate vs epochs, (b) Recognition rate vs PCA features, (c) Recognition rate vs PCA+FLD features on Yale database

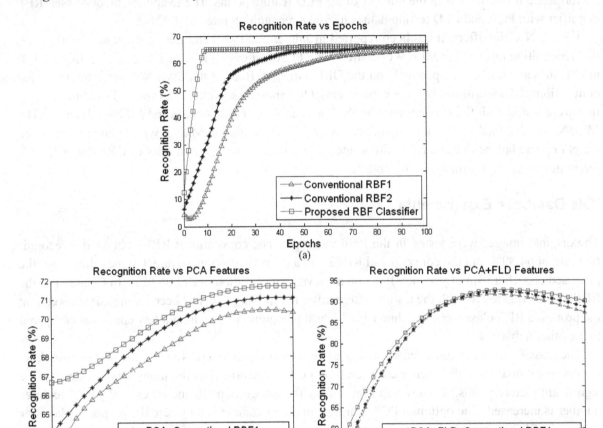

CONCLUSION

This chapter presented a new approach for face recognition using feature extractions and Lyapunov theory-based neural networks. The most expressive facial features are first extracted by PCA which reduces dimensionality of the original face image. The FLD is further applied to obtain the most discriminating features. Those features are then passed to the Lyapunov theory-based neural classifiers for face classification. Two neural network structures, RBF NN and MLNN have been developed based on the Lyapunov stability theory, i.e. (i) Lyapunov theory-based RBF neural classifier, and (ii) Lyapunov theory-based MLNN classifier. Experiments were performed on two benchmark databases, ORL and Yale. The conventional techniques were evaluated and compared with the Lyapunov theory-based neural networks. Simulation results have shown that the Lyapunov-based face recognition system achieves higher training speeds, as well as higher recognition rates. The research on the optimization using Lyapunov stability theory is just in its early stages, and many further works in this area are still under investigation.

Table 2. Recognition rates on Yale database with RBF NNs and MLNNs

Networks	Recognition Rate
Conventional RBF1	64.89%
Conventional RBF2	65.56%
Proposed RBF Classifier	**92.76%**
Conventional MLNN+PCA+FLD	69.78%
Proposed MLNN Classifier	**81.78%**

The trend of using Lyapunov stability theory in ANNs has just started. There is still a lot of room for additional work and development in Lyapunov theory-based neural networks. Differently designed Lyapunov functions and adaptive laws need to be further investigated to improve the parameter convergence and robustness properties of the Lyapunov theory-based neural network. As mentioned in the chapter, Lyapunov stability property possesses the advantage of global error convergence. Hence, it can be applied to other neural network architectures to enhance the system's performance instead of using MLNN and RBF NN. In addition, Lyapunov stability theory can be extended to non-linearity of weight update law in neural network architectures. Moreover, different types of neuron activation functions in the network's hidden layer can be further investigated and tested with Lyapunov stability theory. Also, the optimal neural network architectures may be examined in the future. The applications of Lyapunov theory-based neural networks can be expanded to various aspects of pattern classification.

REFERENCES

Belhumeur, P. N., Hespanha, J. P., & Kriegman, D. J. (1997). Eigenfaces vs. fisherfaces: Recognition using class specific linear projection. *IEEE Transactions on Pattern Analysis and Machine Intelligence, 19*(7), 711–720. doi:10.1109/34.598228

Birgmeier, M. (1995). A fully Kalman-trained radial basis function network for nonlinear speech modeling. In *Proceedings of the IEEE International Conference on Neural Networks,* Perth, Australia (pp. 259-264).

Bobis, C. F., Gonezalez, R. C., Cancelas, J. A., Alvarez, I., & Enguita, J. M. (1999). Face recognition using binary thresholding for features extraction. In *Proceedings of the IEEE International Conference on Image Analysis and Processing,* Venice, Italy (pp. 1077-1080).

Cagnoni, S., Poggi, A., & Porcari, G. L. (1999). A modified modular eigenspace approach to face recognition. In *Proceedings of the 10th International Conference on Image Analysis and Processing,* Venice, Italy (pp 490-495).

Chellappa, R., Wilson, C. L., & Sirohey, S. (1995). Human and machine recognition of faces: A survey. *Proceedings of the IEEE, 83*(5), 705–740. doi:10.1109/5.381842

Database, Y. (n.d.). *Department of computer science, Yale University.* Retrieved from http://cvc.yale.edu/projects/yalefaces/yalefaces.html

Er, M. J., Chen, W. L., & Wu, S. Q. (2005). High-speed face recognition based on discrete cosine transform and RBF neural network. *IEEE Transactions on Neural Networks, 16*(3), 679–691. doi:10.1109/TNN.2005.844909

Er, M. J., Wu, S., Lu, J., & Toh, H. L. (2002). Face recognition with radial basis function (RBF) neural networks. *IEEE Transactions on Neural Networks, 13*(3), 697–710. doi:10.1109/TNN.2002.1000134

Ergin, S., & Gülmezoğlu, M. B. (2008). Face recognition based on face partitions using common vector approach. In *Proceedings of the 3rd International Symposium on Communications, Control and Signal Processing,* St. Julians, Malta (pp. 624-628).

Fukunaga, K. (1990). *Introduction to statistical pattern recognition* (2nd ed.). San Diego, CA: Academic Press Professional.

Gul, A. B. (2003). *Holistic face recognition by dimension reduction*. Unpublished master's thesis, the Middle East Technical University.

Hafed, Z. M., & Levine, M. D. (2001). Face recognition using the discrete cosine transform. *International Journal of Computer Vision, 43*(3), 167–188. doi:10.1023/A:1011183429707

Haykin, S. (1994). *Neural networks: A comprehensive foundation*. Upper Saddle River, NJ: Prentice Hall.

Hu, W., Farooq, O., & Datta, S. (2008). Wavelet based sub-space features for face recognition. In *Proceedings of the International Congress on Image and Signal Processing,* Sanya, Hainan, China (pp. 426-430).

Jain, L. C., Halici, U., Hayashi, I., Lee, S. B., & Tsutsui, S. (1999). *Intelligent biometric techniques in fingerprint and face recognition*. Boca Raton, FL: CRC Press.

Kim, J. B., & Kim, H. J. (2002). Efficient image segmentation based on wavelet and watersheds for video objects extraction. In *Developments in applied artificial intelligence* (LNCS 2358, pp. 67-76). Berlin, Germany: Springer.

Kirby, M., & Sirovich, L. (1990). Application of the Karhunen-Loeve procedure for the characterization of human faces. *IEEE Transactions on Pattern Analysis and Machine Intelligence, 12*, 103–108. doi:10.1109/34.41390

Lawrence, S., Giles, C. L., & Tsoi, A. C. (1996). *What size neural network gives optimal generalization? Convergence properties of backpropagation* (Tech. Rep. UMIACS-TR-96-22 & CS-TR-3617). Institute for Advanced Computer Studies, University of Maryland. Lawrence, S., Giles, C. L., Tsoi, A. C., & Back, A. D. (1997). Face recognition: A convolutional neural-network approach. *IEEE Transactions on Neural Networks, 8*, 98–113. doi:10.1109/72.554195

Lee, S., & Kil, R. M. (1991). A Gaussian potential function network with hierarchically self-organizing learning. *Neural Networks, 4*(2), 207–224. doi:10.1016/0893-6080(91)90005-P

Leonard, J. A., & Kramer, M. A. (1991, April). Radial basis function networks for classifying process faults. *IEEE Control Systems Magazine, 11*, 31–38. doi:10.1109/37.75576

Li, J. B., Chu, S. C., & Pan, J. S. (2007). Facial texture feature based face recognition with common vector analysis in the kernel space. In *Proceedings of the 2nd IEEE International Conference on Industrial Electronics and Applications,* Harbin, China (pp. 714-718).

Lin, S. H., Kung, S. Y., & Lin, L. J. (1997). Face recognition/detection by probabilistic decision- based neural network. *IEEE Transactions on Neural Networks, 8,* 114–132. doi:10.1109/72.554196

Lyapunov, A. M. (1892). *The general problem of the stability of motion.* Kharkov, Ukraine: Kharkov Mathematical Society.

Man, Z. H., Seng, K. P., & Wu, H. R. (1999). Lyapunov stability based adaptive backpropagation for discrete time system. In *Proceedings of the 5th International Symposium on Signal Processing and Its Applications,* Brisbane, Australia (pp. 661-664).

Man, Z. H., Wu, H. R., Sophie, L., & Xinghuo, Y. (2006). A new adaptive backpropagation algorithm based on Lyapunov stability theory for neural networks. *IEEE Transactions on Neural Networks, 17*(6), 1580–1591. doi:10.1109/TNN.2006.880360

Martinez, A. (1999). Face image retrieval using HMMs. In *Proceedings of the IEEE Workshop on Content-based Access of Image and Video Libraries,* Fort Collins, CO (pp. 35-39).

Mian, A. S., Bennamoun, M., & Owens, R. (2007). An efficient multimodal 2D-3D hybrid approach to automatic face recognition. *IEEE Transactions on Pattern Analysis and Machine Intelligence, 29*(11), 1927–1943. doi:10.1109/TPAMI.2007.1105

Midorikawa, H. (1988). The face pattern identification by backpropagation learning procedure. In *Abstracts of the First Annual INNS meeting,* Boston, MA (p. 515).

Moody, T. J., & Darken, C. J. (1989). Fast learning in networks of locally tuned processing units. *Neural Computation, 1*(2), 281–294. doi:10.1162/neco.1989.1.2.281

Mueller, M. (1981). Least-squares algorithms for adaptive equalizers. *The Bell System Technical Journal, 60,* 1905–1925.

Musavi, M. T., Faris, K. B., Chan, K. H., & Ahmed, W. (1991). On the implementation of RBF technique in neural network. In *Proceedings of the Conference on Analysis of Neural Network Applications,* Fairfax, VA (pp. 110-115).

Nazeer, S. A., Omar, N., & Khalid, M. (2007). Face recognition system using artificial neural network approach. In *Proceedings of the International Conference on Signal Processing, Communication and Networking,* Chennai, India (pp. 420-425).

Nehrotra, K., Mohan, C. K., & Ranka, S. (1996). *Element of artificial neural networks.* Cambridge, MA: The MIT Press.

Park, J., & Wsandberg, J. (1991). Universal approximation using radial basis functions network. *Neural Computation, 3,* 246–257. doi:10.1162/neco.1991.3.2.246

Perry, J. L., & Carney, J. M. (1990). Human face recognition using a multilayer perceptron. In *Proceedings of the International Conference on Neural Networks,* Washington, DC (pp. 4-13).

Samaria, F., & Harter, A. (1994). Parameterization of a stochastic model for human face identification. In *Proceedings of 2ⁿᵈ IEEE Workshop on Applications of Computer Vision,* Austin, TX (pp. 138-142).

Seng, K. P., Man, Z. H., & Wu, H. R. (1999). Nonlinear adaptive RBF neural filter with Lyapunov adaptation algorithm and its application to nonlinear channel equalization. In *Proceedings of the 5ᵗʰ International Symposium on Signal Processing and Its Applications,* Brisbane, Australia (pp. 151-154).

Seng, K. P., Man, Z. H., & Wu, H. R. (2002). Lyapunov theory-based radial basis function networks for adaptive filtering. *IEEE Transactions on Circuits and Systems. I, Fundamental Theory and Applications, 49*(8), 1215–1220. doi:10.1109/TCSI.2002.801255

Simon, D. (2002). Training radial basis neural networks with the extended kalman filter. *Neurocomputing, 48,* 455–475. doi:10.1016/S0925-2312(01)00611-7

Sing, J. K., Basu, D. K., Nasipuri, M., & Kundu, M. (2005). Face recognition using point symmetry distance-based RBF network. *Applied Soft Computing, 7,* 58–70. doi:10.1016/j.asoc.2005.02.004

Sirovich, L., & Kirby, M. (1987). Low-dimensional procedure for the characterization of human face. *Journal of the Optical Society of America, 4,* 519–524. doi:10.1364/JOSAA.4.000519

Solheim, I., Paync, T., & Castain, R. (1992). The potential in using backpropagation neural networks for facial verification systems. *Simulations, 58*(5), 306–310.

Stan, Z. L., & Anil, K. J. (2004). *Handbook of face recognition.* New York: Springer-Verlag.

Swets, D. L., & Weng, J. (1996, August). Using discriminant eigenfeatures for image retrieval. *IEEE Transactions on Pattern Analysis and Machine Intelligence, 18*(8), 831–836. doi:10.1109/34.531802

The ORL database. (n.d.). *Cambridge University computer laboratory.* Retrieved from http//www.cam-orl.co.uk/facedatabase.html

Thomaz, C. E., Feitosa, R. Q., & Veiga, A. (1998). Design of radial basis function network as classifier in face recognition using eigenfaces. In *Proceedings of the Vᵗʰ Brazilian Symposium on Neural Networks,* Belo Horizonte, Brazil (pp. 118-123).

Turk, M. A., & Pentland, A. P. (1991). Eigenfaces for recognition. *Journal of Cognitive Neuroscience, 3,* 71–86. doi:10.1162/jocn.1991.3.1.71

Valentin, D., Abdi, H., O'Toole, A. J., & Cottrell, G. W. (1994). Connectionist models of face processing: A survey. *Pattern Recognition, 27,* 1209–1230. doi:10.1016/0031-3203(94)90006-X

Vidyasagar, M. (1993). *Nonlinear systems analysis* (2ⁿᵈ ed.). Englewood Cliffs, NJ: Prentice Hall.

Virginia, E. D. (2000). Biometric identification system using a radial basis network. In *Proceedings of the 34ᵗʰ Annual IEEE International Carnahan Conference on Security Technology,* Ottawa, Ontario, Canada (pp. 47-51).

Wang, X., & Tang, X. (2004). A unified framework for subspace face recognition. *IEEE Transactions on Pattern Analysis and Machine Intelligence, 26*(9), 1222–1228. doi:10.1109/TPAMI.2004.57

Yan, S. C., Wang, H., Tang, X. O., & Huang, T. (2007). Exploring features descriptors for face recognition. In *Proceedings of the 32nd IEEE International Conference on Acoustics, Speech, and Signal Processing*, Honolulu, HI (pp. 629-632).

Yang, F., & Paindavoine, M. (2003). Implementation of an RBF neural network on embedded systems: Real-time face tracking and identity verification. *IEEE Transactions on Neural Networks, 14*(5), 1162–1175. doi:10.1109/TNN.2003.816035

Zhao, W., Chellappa, R., Phillips, P. J., & Rosenfeld, A. (2003). Face recognition: A literature survey. *ACM Computing Surveys, 35*(4), 399–459. doi:10.1145/954339.954342

Zhou, J., Liu, Y., & Chen, Y. H. (2007). Face recognition using kernel PCA and hierarchical RBF network. In *Proceedings of the 6th IEEE International Conference on Computer Information Systems and Industrial Management Applications,* Minneapolis, MN (pp. 239-244).

APPENDIX A

$\forall r \in \left\{ 1, 2, \cdots, m \right\}$,

$$\Delta V(k) = e_r^2(k) - e_r^2(k-1)$$

$$
\begin{aligned}
e_r^2(k) &= \left(d_r(k) - y_r(k) \right)^2 \\
&= \left(d_r(k) - \mathbf{w}_r^T(k)\mathbf{X}(k) \right)^2 \\
&= \left[d_r(k) - (\mathbf{w}_r^T(k-1) + \mathbf{g}_r^T(k)\alpha_r(k))\mathbf{X}(k) \right]^2 \\
&= \left[d_r(k) - \mathbf{w}_r^T(k-1)\mathbf{X}(k) - \mathbf{g}_r^T(k)\alpha_r(k)\mathbf{X}(k) \right]^2 \\
&= \left[\alpha_r(k) - \mathbf{g}_r^T(k)\alpha_r(k)\mathbf{X}(k) \right]^2 \\
&= \alpha_r^2(k)\left[1 - (\frac{\mathbf{X}^T(k)}{\left\| \mathbf{X}(k) \right\|^2}\left[1 - \kappa\left| \frac{e_r(k-1)}{\alpha_r(k)} \right| \right])\mathbf{X}(k) \right]^2 \\
&= \kappa^2 e_r^2(k-1)
\end{aligned}
$$

$$
\begin{aligned}
\Delta V(k) - \kappa^2 e_r^2(k-1) \quad & c_r^2(k-1) \\
&= -(1 - \kappa^2)e_r^2(k-1) \\
&< 0
\end{aligned}
$$

APPENDIX B

$\forall r \in \left\{ 1, 2, \cdots, m \right\}$

$$
\begin{aligned}
e_r(k) &= d_r(k) - y_r(k) \\
&= d_r(k) - w_r^T(k)X(k) \\
&= d_r(k) - (\mathbf{w}_r^T(k-1) + \mathbf{g}_r^T(k)\alpha_r(k))\mathbf{X}(k) \\
&= d_r(k) - \mathbf{w}_r^T(k-1)\mathbf{X}(k) - \mathbf{g}_r^T(k)\alpha_r(k)\mathbf{X}(k) \\
&= \alpha_r(k) - \mathbf{g}_r^T(k)\alpha_r(k)\mathbf{X}(k) \\
&= \left[\alpha_r(k) - \alpha_r(k)(\frac{\mathbf{X}^T(k)}{\left\| \mathbf{X}(k) \right\|^2}\left[1 - \kappa\left| \frac{e_r(k-1)}{\alpha_r(k)} \right| \right])\mathbf{X}(k) \right] \\
&= \kappa\left| e_r(k-1) \right| \mathrm{sgn}(\alpha_k(k))
\end{aligned}
$$

$$\therefore \therefore \left|e_r(k)\right| = \kappa \left|e_r(k-1)\right| \quad \left|e_r(k)\right| = \kappa \left|e_r(k-1)\right|$$

$$\left|e_r(1)\right| = \kappa \left|e_r(0)\right|$$
$$\left|e_r(2)\right| = \kappa \left|e_r(1)\right| = \kappa^2 \left|e_r(0)\right|$$
$$\vdots$$
$$\left|e_r(k)\right| = \lim_{k \to \infty} \kappa^k \left|e_r(0)\right| \approx 0$$

APPENDIX C

$$\forall r \in \left\{1, 2, \cdots, m\right\},$$

$$\Delta V(k) = e^2(k) - e^2(k-1)$$

$$\begin{aligned}
\Delta V(k) &= e_r^2(k) - e_r^2(k-1) \\
&= \left(d_r(k) - y_r(k)\right)^2 - e_r^2(k-1) \\
&= \left(d_r(k) - \mathbf{H}_r^T(k), {}_r(t)\right)^2 - e_r^2(k-1) \\
&= \left[d_r(k) - \mathbf{H}_r^T(k)({}_r(k-1) + \mathbf{g}_r(k)\alpha_r(k))\right]^2 - e_r^2(k-1) \\
&= \left[\alpha_r(k) - \mathbf{H}_r^T(k)\mathbf{g}_r(k)\alpha_r(k)\right]^2 - e_r^2(k-1) \\
&= \alpha_r^2(k)\left[1 - \mathbf{H}_r^T(k)(\frac{\mathbf{H}_r(k)}{\left\|\mathbf{H}_r(k)\right\|^2}\left[1 - \kappa\left|\frac{e_r(k-1)}{u_r(k)}\right|\right])\right]^2 - e_r^2(k-1) \\
&= \kappa^2 e_r^2(k-1) - e_r^2(k-1) \\
&= -(1 - \kappa^2)e_r^2(k-1) < 0
\end{aligned}$$

APPENDIX D

$$\forall r \in \left\{1, 2, \cdots, m\right\}$$

$$
\begin{aligned}
e_r(k) &= d_r(k) - \tilde{y}_r(k) \\
&= d_r(k) - \mathbf{H}_r^T(k),\,_r(t) \\
&= d_r(k) - \mathbf{H}_r^T(k)(,\,_r(k-1) + \mathbf{g}_r(k)\alpha_r(k)) \\
&= d_r(k) - \mathbf{H}_k^T(k),\,_k(k-1) - \mathbf{H}_r^T(k)\mathbf{g}_r(k)\alpha_r(k) \\
&= \alpha_r(k) - \mathbf{H}_r^T(k)\mathbf{g}_r(k)\alpha_r(k) \\
&= \left[\alpha_r(k) - \mathbf{H}_r^T(k)\left(\frac{\mathbf{H}_r(k)}{\left\|\mathbf{H}_r(k)\right\|^2}\left[1 - \kappa\left|\frac{e_r(k-1)}{\alpha_r(k)}\right|\right]\right)\alpha_r(k) \right] \\
&= \kappa\left|e_r(k-1)\right|\operatorname{sgn}(\alpha_r(k))
\end{aligned}
$$

$$
\therefore\ \left|e_r(k)\right| = \kappa\left|e_r(k-1)\right|\ \left|e_r(k)\right| = \kappa\left|e_r(k-1)\right|
$$

$$
\begin{aligned}
\left|e_r(1)\right| &= \kappa\left|e_r(0)\right| \\
\left|e_r(2)\right| &= \kappa\left|e_r(1)\right| = \kappa^2\left|e_r(0)\right| \\
&\vdots \\
\left|e_r(k)\right| &= \lim_{t\to\infty}\kappa^k\left|e_r(0)\right| \approx 0
\end{aligned}
$$

Chapter 3
A Self–Organizing Neural Network to Approach Novelty Detection

Marcelo Keese Albertini
University of São Paulo, Brazil

Rodrigo Fernandes de Mello
University of São Paulo, Brazil

ABSTRACT

Machine learning is a field of artificial intelligence which aims at developing techniques to automatically transfer human knowledge into analytical models. Recently, those techniques have been applied to time series with unknown dynamics and fluctuations in the established behavior patterns, such as human-computer interaction, inspection robotics and climate change. In order to detect novelties in those time series, techniques are required to learn and update knowledge structures, adapting themselves to data tendencies. The learning and updating process should integrate and accommodate novelty events into the normal behavior model, possibly incurring the revaluation of long-term memories. This sort of application has been addressed by the proposal of incremental techniques based on unsupervised neural networks and regression techniques. Such proposals have introduced two new concepts in time-series novelty detection. The first defines the temporal novelty, which indicates the occurrence of unexpected series of events. The second measures how novel a single event is, based on the historical knowledge. However, current studies do not fully consider both concepts of detecting and quantifying temporal novelties. This motivated the proposal of the self-organizing novelty detection neural network architecture (SONDE) which incrementally learns patterns in order to represent unknown dynamics and fluctuation of established behavior. The knowledge accumulated by SONDE is employed to estimate Markov chains which model causal relationships. This architecture is applied to detect and measure temporal and non-temporal novelties. The evaluation of the proposed technique is carried out through simulations and experiments, which have presented promising results.

DOI: 10.4018/978-1-60566-798-0.ch003

INTRODUCTION

Machine learning is a field of artificial intelligence which aims at developing techniques for automatically transferring human knowledge into analytical models (Kecman, 2001). Such techniques support activities in several areas, such as natural language processing (Jelinek, 1997), pattern recognition (Bishop, 2006), search engines (Zhang and Dong, 2000), medical diagnosis (Cox et al., 1982) and fraud detection (Chan and Stolfo, 1998).

With the development of new approaches and learning techniques, researchers identified the need of modeling datasets presenting noise (Barnett and Lewis, 1994), inconsistencies derived from anomalies (Singh, 2002), scarce patterns (Rosen et al., 1996) and information tendency modifications (Spinosa et al., 2007).

The modeling of those datasets has motivated additional studies which originated the novelty detection researches. At the beginning, such studies aimed at identifying rare and unknown information. Such information is observed in, for instance, samples from defective equipments (Tarassenko, 1995; Ypma and Duin, 1997) and exams of patients with rare diseases (Cox et al., 1982). In such cases, data are temporally independent of each other. One example of this situation is the study of breast cancer diagnosis using x-ray image analysis conducted by Tarassenko (1995). That work considers a dataset containing one x-ray exam and one diagnosis per patient which indicates suspected areas. In this kind of application, there is no causal relationship between different patient exams, consequently, previous exams cannot indicate the disease for a new one. Thus, the sequence in which the exams are analyzed is irrelevant.

Another kind of application, named temporal, considers the causal relationship among data sequences (Box and Jenkins, 1976). An example of such application is the analysis of customer's behavior in using credit cards. In such a situation, the debits compose a time series where data are causal dependent. If the customer's debit behavior varies in an unexpected manner (depicting novelty), the credit company could, for example, block the card to prevent frauds.

There are different types of temporal applications, some of which present well-behaved series, where previously obtained data can be used to model the required knowledge and, consequently, describe expected behavior. Using such a model, the novelty detection process comprises labeling patterns which are not consistent with the expectations. An example of such an approach is proposed by Ko et al. (1992) which models the current knowledge by storing input pattern characteristics. New patterns are evaluated by assessing their distances to any other in the model. The pattern is labeled as novelty when the distance is above an *ad hoc* similarity threshold. Other works that present similar approaches include Ypma and Duin (1997) who propose clustering indices based on the unsupervised artificial neural network Self-Organizing Map, and Hayton et al. (2000) who apply a binary classifier based on Support Vector Machines.

Other temporal applications are characterized by series with unknown dynamics and fluctuation in the established behavior of patterns (such as the human interaction with computers (Lane, 1999), inspection robotics (Marsland, 2002) and climate change (Lau and Weng, 1995)). In order to detect novelties in those series, techniques are required to learn and update knowledge structures, and adapting them to data tendencies. The learning and updating process should integrate and accommodate novelty events into the normal behavior model, possibly incurring the revaluation of long-term memories. This sort of application has been addressed by the proposal of incremental techniques such as the ones by Marsland (2002), Ma and Perkins (2003) and Itti and Baldi (2005).

The previously mentioned studies have concurrently introduced two new concepts on time-series novelty detection. The first defines the temporal novelty (Marsland, 2002), which indicates the occurrence of unexpected series of events. For instance, consider the previously presented situation of the credit card fraud where the customer may be used to withdraw some money from the credit account and, afterwards, go shopping. If the customer withdraws money without immediately going shopping or more than one consecutive occasion, a novelty would be detected. Temporal novelties depend on the sequence in which the events occur, and not in the event itself.

The second new concept measures how novel an event is based on historical knowledge (such as presented by Itti and Baldi (2005)). Considering the example of the credit card fraud, any event can be quantified by how unusual it is. Such a metric would extend the previous approach which only characterizes novelties in a binary way (unusual/fraud or not).

However, current studies do not fully employ both concepts of detecting and quantifying temporal novelties. Ma and Perkins (2003) addressed the continuous modeling of time series and attributed confidence levels to novelties, but they did not consider quantifying them. Marsland (2002) who proposed the technique Grow When Required (GWR) considers how familiar a neuron is to a specific pattern (called habituation effect) which gives a simplified notion of novelty degree. By contrast, while such a metric can measure novelties for patterns, it does not consider them for different event sequences. Remarkably, the study by Itti and Baldi (2005), specialized in video streams, considers both concepts but only for short-term temporal novelties.

The previously presented works and the need to detect and quantify temporal novelties motivated the proposal of the Self-Organizing Novelty Detection Neural Network Architecture (SONDE) (Albertini and Mello, 2007), which considers incremental learning to represent unknown dynamics and fluctuation of established behavior patterns. The knowledge accumulated by SONDE is employed to detect and quantify the level of temporal and non-temporal novelties.

This chapter presents the state of the art in novelty detection, including recent studies on detecting temporal novelties. Afterwards, our proposal, the SONDE neural network architecture is detailed, as well as the methodology of applying the architecture when learning time series and detecting novelties. Then, simulations and experiments evaluate SONDE and confirm its applicability. Final remarks present the future directions of this work.

BACKGROUND

In biology, the idea of novelty is related to animal survival mechanisms (Middleton, 1996). In economics, the concept of novelty is related to the price of goods and the creation of specialized sub-markets (Bertarelli and Censolo, 2000). In psychology, the novelty magnitude is defined when characterizing creative behaviors (Kaufmann, 2004). The diversity of novelty definitions has resulted in the need to deal with behavior modifications in different areas.

In computer science and statistics, such need is observed in the development of machine learning techniques which aim at automatically adapting the knowledge in response to changes. In this context, *novelties* refer to the identification of unexpected, rare or unknown information according to a reference knowledge model (Ma and Perkins, 2003).

In the machine learning context, novelty detection techniques are applied in a broad range of applications such as disease diagnosis (Middleton, 1996), climate change identification (Lau and Weng, 1995;

Hasselmann, 1997; Luterbacher et al., 2004) and fault detection in hard disks (Hughes et al., 2002). These applications present peculiarities which must be addressed by the novelty detection techniques. Among the peculiarities are the continuous learning capacity, multi-dimensional non-Euclidean space and forgetfulness. The different applications of novelty detection brought up several synonyms for the term *novelty*, e.g. anomaly, fault, outlier, abrupt change and exception (Hodge and Austin, 2004).

The different terms and definitions have motivated researchers to survey works aimed at mapping and comparing techniques in order to identify development trends. By considering such surveys, apparently distinct areas can be related, contributing to the relationship of concepts and techniques.

Among such surveys is the work by Willsky (1976) which focuses on the area of fault detection in linear dynamic systems. Willsky concludes that fault detection is composed of three tasks: alarm, isolation and estimation. The alarm consists of observing whether any fault has occurred. The isolation problem is about determining the type and the origin of the fault. The estimation involves identifying the extent of the problem (if the fault source is not operating or it is damaged). In such work, the alarm task operates as a novelty detector. Such task is carried through the verification of parameter consistency estimations in system models.

While Willsky focused on the concepts of linear dynamic system detection, other recent surveys involve a broader range of applications and techniques. An example of these surveys is the one by Markou and Singh (2003), extended in Singh and Markou (2005), where techniques are classified according to their paradigms: based on artificial neural networks and statistics. According to the authors, among the neural networks are Multi-Layer Perceptron (MLP), Support Vector Machine, Adaptive Resonance Theory (ART), Radial Basis Function Network (RBF), Hopfield neural network, Self-Organizing Map (SOM), self-associators (for example MLP, Principal Components Analysis and SOM), neural networks based on habituation (e.g. Grow When Required (GWR)), neural trees and oscillatory networks. The statistics techniques include probabilistic methods, hypothesis tests, Hidden Markov Models, K-nearest neighbors, Parzen windows, clustering and string matching approaches (such as the ones applied in artificial immune systems).

In another survey, Hodge and Austin (2004) under the classification of outlier detection identified three approaches with different learning paradigms applied on the knowledge model construction. The first is based on unsupervised learning and labels normal and novelty patterns without previous analysis. The second is a supervised approach based on the classification of previously labeled patterns. The third is a variation of the latter, where only normal patterns are observed during training.

The classifications carried out by Markou and Singh (2003), Singh and Markou (2005) and Hodge and Austin (2004) allow to identify the type of techniques and the learning paradigm, respectively. However, they do not consider peculiarities of the temporal knowledge model construction which are a key factor in this work. This has motivated detailed studies to identify and classify techniques according to the causal relationship (Al-Subaie and Zulkernine, 2006).

From these studies, we propose a classification tree, presented in Figure 1, which allows to identify the techniques applied to detect temporal novelties (similar to the previously presented credit card example), in which unusual sequences of common events should be detected[1] . These techniques address the same problem as SONDE, proposed in this work, although they consider different approaches.

According to our classification tree, there are two branches of novelty detection techniques as shown in Figure 1. The first contains non-temporal approaches and the second, the opposite, where the causal relationships are explicitly explored in order to detect novelties. The branches are detailed as follows.

Figure 1. Classification tree identifying techniques employed to detect temporal novelties

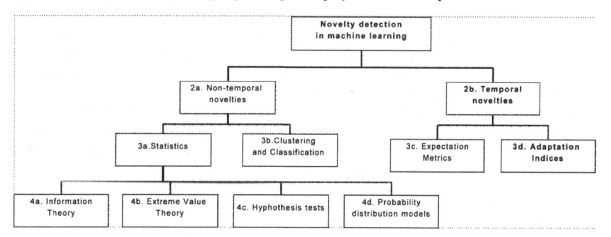

Non-Temporal Novelty Detection

Some techniques do not address the causal relationships of time series events. In our classification, these techniques are divided in two sub-groups according to the considered concepts (node **2a** in Figure 1): *Statistics* (node **3a**), and methods of *Clustering and classification* (node **3b**).

Among the approaches of the sub-group *Statistics* are: *Information Theory* (node **4a**), *Extreme value theory* (node **4b**), *Hypothesis tests* (node **4c**) of Statistics Inference and modeling using *probabilities distribution* (node **4d**).

The approaches based on *Information Theory* consider concepts and theorems targeting the analysis and transmission of information. The basic concept in this branch is the *entropy*, defined by Shannon (1948) as the mean amount of information from a data source and the *self-information* which measures the information for each possible event generated by a source. The concept of *self-information* was considered by Tribus (1961) to quantify surprises. An application of entropy is proposed by Itti and Baldi (2005) who evaluated and compared it with human reaction considering consecutive video frames aimed at establishing a relationship between surprise and the entropy. Itti and Baldi (2005) concluded humans are attracted to higher entropy areas.

The tree element **4b** in Figure 1, representing *Extreme Value Theory* (Roberts, 1999), groups approaches for modeling distributions of the maximum or minimum points of arbitrary populations. Events are characterized as novelty according to the probability given by such distributions. Fisher and Tippett (1928) proved that functions respecting relatively generic conditions are characterized by one of the three asymptotic distributions: Gumbel, Fréchet or Weibull's.

Roberts (1999) considers this theorem when working with extreme region applications. The author applies the Gumbel distribution and an approximation method using Gaussian mixture on two datasets: the first containing information on epilepsy and, the second, noise (defined as novelty) in images. Another work, proposed by Bensalah (2000), considers the Extreme Value Theory to obtain information in financial applications.

Approaches using *Hypothesis Tests from Statistics Inference* evaluate the consistency of model parameter estimation. Examples are presented in the survey by Willsky (1976), which employs the Chi-squared hypothesis test to check the consistency of parameters estimated in electronic systems.

Another example of this element is found in Hughes et al. (2002), which applies the Wilcoxon Rank-Sum hypothesis test (Wilcoxon, 1945; Mann and Whitney, 1947) on a dataset generated by the SMART tool which monitors, analyzes and reports hard disk failures. This work aims at decreasing the false diagnosis alarm rate and the failure prediction. The employed test evaluates whether two data samples are obtained from the same probability distribution function. Additional methods based on hypothesis tests can be found in Barnett and Lewis (1994).

The element *Probability Distributions* refers to techniques for the estimation of models using probability distribution functions. An approach, proposed by Bishop (1995), detects novelties by estimating the density of input data and by labeling information identified in low probability areas. Two similar approaches are proposed: the first by Tarassenko (1995) which aims at detecting masses in mammograms and the second by Lauer (2001) which attempts to determine carriers of a genetic disorder.

The second sub-group (Figure 1) includes methods based on *Clustering and Classification* which are applied in two different ways: considering the *Identification Class* or *Evaluation Metrics*.

The methods considering the *Identification Class* use a supervised approach to differentiate normal and novelty events. An example is the work by Rosen et al. (1996) that adopts a *Multi-layer Perceptron* to identify abnormal tendencies in electronic fetal heart rate tracings (cardiotocograms). Similarly, Spinosa and Carvalho (2005) used the binary classification technique *Support Vector Machine* (SVM), based on the statistical learning theory by Vapnik (1995), to detect novelties in the datasets ALL-AML Leukemia (Golub et al., 1999) and Diffuse Large B-cell Lymphoma (DLBCL) (Alizadeh et al., 2000).

The same concepts were considered by Flexer et al. (2005) who applied novelty detection to retrieve music information based on the spectrum similarity and genre label information. Two central minutes of each music title were considered. Two algorithms were used: the first, called ratio-reject, uses a data density distribution obtained from the classification training phase. The second algorithm, called Knn-reject, creates a neighborhood during the training, which is used for labeling known and novelty data.

The methods under the element *Evaluation Metrics* consider the instability of classification algorithms to novelty detection. An example of this approach is the work by Ypma and Duin (1997) who studied the Self-Organizing Map neural network of Kohonen (1997) using different learning parameters. Each output was mapped through quality representation metrics such as the distance of the two higher activation neurons. According to the experiments, datasets with anomaly generate higher classification errors than normal datasets.

In a similar approach, Tax and Duin (1998) propose the application of a random sampling method, with reposition, where *n* datasets with the same number of elements as the original, are created. Each dataset is classified and the differences are used to define abnormalities. According to the authors, a novelty event causes instability in results.

Temporal Novelty Detection

Techniques capable of detecting temporal novelties explicitly model the data behavior in order to detect modifications in causal relations. Examples of techniques under this class are classified in *Expectation Metrics* (node **3c** in Figure 1) and *Adaptation Indices* (node **4d**).

Techniques of the type *Expectation Metrics* define novelties according to the distance of the actual value and the expected one. Techniques of the class *Adaptation indices* quantify the knowledge model modification after receiving a new pattern.

An example of the element *Expectation Metrics* was proposed by Marsland (2002) who designed an artificial neural network, called Grow When Required (GWR). The GWR neurons are capable of evaluating the pattern frequency using a metric inspired by the biological phenomenon of habituation. In this metric, the higher the neuron habituation, the lesser is the novelty of the pattern related to it. In another example, Ma and Perkins (2003) proposed a technique to define novelties in data sequences which present a minimum of h surprises. The modeling is carried out using a regression function with support vectors, which allows incremental updating. The function provides confidence levels to novelties, considering the consecutive number of surprises.

Techniques for temporal novelty detection under the class *Adaptation Indices* have been recently developed. Among such works is the one by Priebe et al. (2005) which analyzes an email exchange dataset from the North-American energy company Enron. The information was collected from 1998 to 2002, a period in which irregular accounting procedures occurred. The analysis aimed at finding anomalies in the internal communication using graph statistical variation. The authors detected sub-graphs with excessive communication, which characterize anomalies. For detecting novelties in videos, Itti and Baldi (2005) applied relative entropy and divergence of Kullback-Leibler (Kullback, 1959) to measure differences between image probabilistic models over time. Similarly, Gamon (2006) addresses the novelty detection in news documents. Text sentences are modeled using graphs. The addition of new sentences modifies the knowledge model (*e.g.* number of vertices and edges, average connectivity degree and the sum of edge weights).

SELF-ORGANIZING NOVELTY DETECTION NEURAL NETWORK ARCHITECTURE

Time series may present unknown dynamics and behavior fluctuation which require continuous updating of knowledge structures to improve novelty detection. The updating process should integrate and accommodate novelty events into a normal behavior model, possibly incurring the revaluation of long-term memories. This has been addressed by the proposal of incremental techniques which are able to continuously restructure the behavior model without human supervision, such as self-organizing neural networks (Marsland, 2002; Itti and Baldi, 2005) and regression techniques (Ma and Perkins, 2003). However, such techniques present limitations when detecting novelties in unstable series because they do not update normality/novelty thresholds and do not keep track of old knowledge (Itti and Baldi, 2005).

These limitations motivated the proposal of an incremental learning neural network architecture, named Self-Organizing Novelty Detection (SONDE) (Albertini and Mello, 2007), which represents unknown dynamics and fluctuation of established behavior patterns by updating knowledge structures and normality/novelty thresholds. The knowledge accumulated by SONDE is employed to detect temporal and non-temporal novelties as well as to quantify the level of novelties.

The basic knowledge representation unit of SONDE is the neuron which accumulates historical input patterns. The neuron continuously adapts itself according to pattern variations. The SONDE architecture is composed of three layers (Figures 2 and 3): a first input and pre-processing layer – in which patterns are optionally normalized to define a unitary space for multidimensional patterns. This simplifies the SONDE parameterization because all patterns have the same magnitude of norm and they maintain the vector direction; a second layer with neurons – which represents the input pattern knowledge; and the last, named competitive layer – where the selection of the most representative neuron occurs (*Best-*

Figure 2. Self-Organizing Novelty Detection Neural Network Architecture

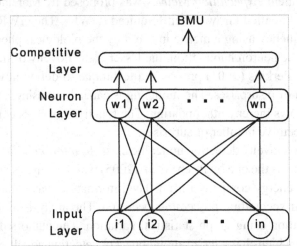

Matching Unit – BMU) for a certain input pattern.

Let a multidimensional input pattern be defined as $\vec{I}_t \in \Re^n$, where t is the time instant. The first SONDE layer may optionally normalize each input pattern $\vec{I}_t$, when $n > 1$, as follows $\vec{I}_t = \dfrac{\vec{I}_t}{\|\vec{I}_t\|}$.

The second layer computes the distance of the pattern $\vec{I}_t$ to each neuron c and informs the last layer about it. Such computation considers three neuron components which are responsible for the individual knowledge representation:

1. the prototype $\vec{w}_c$ represents the tendency of the input patterns classified in the neuron c;
2. the average radius rad_c quantifies the dispersion of input patterns around the prototype $\vec{w}_c$; and
3. the minimum similarity degree $\pm_c$ represents a minimum activation threshold to accept new input patterns.

These components are adapted when the neuron is elected by the competitive layer as the Best-Matching

Figure 3. SONDE architecture: illustration of the neuron c and its components

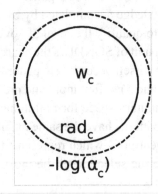

Unit (*BMU*). This adaptation improves the representation of the most recently acquired knowledge according to equations 1 and 2, which are responsible for updating the prototype $\vec{w}_{BMU}$ and the average radius rad_{BMU}, respectively. The adaptation equations follow exponentially weighted moving averages (EWMA) (Smith and Boning, 1997), which allows the incremental update according to inputs. These equations consider the learning parameters $\gamma \in [0,1]$ and $\Omega \in [0,1]$. The higher the parameter values are, the more the network forgets about previous patterns. The neuron adaptation causes an exponential forgetfulness (as illustrated in the next section), allowing the architecture to follow behavior and tendency drifts.

$$\vec{w}_{BMU,t} = (1 - {}^{\scriptscriptstyle 3})\vec{w}_{BMU,t} + {}^{\scriptscriptstyle 3}\,\vec{I}_t \tag{1}$$

$$rad_{BMU,t} = (1 - \copyright)rad_{BMU,t-1} + \copyright \,\|\,\vec{w}_{BMU,t} - \vec{I}_t\,\| \tag{2}$$

The last neuron component, the minimum similarity degree $\pm_{BMU}$, is adapted according to equation 4, where p is the relative modification rate of the average radius rad_{BMU} (equation 3).

$$p = \frac{\|\,rad_{BMU,t} - rad_{BMU,t-1}\,\|}{\|\,max(rad_{BMU,t}, rad_{BMU,t-1})\,\|} \tag{3}$$

$$\pm_{BMU,t} = min\left((1+p)\pm_{BMU,t-1}, \exp^{-(1+p)rad_{BMU,t}}\right) \tag{4}$$

This adaptation mechanism for $\pm_{BMU}$ ensures two learning tendencies, which consider the distance between the average radius (this defines an inner boundary of neuron specialization) and the minimum acceptance threshold for the neuron representation (defined as $-\ln(\pm_{BMU})$), according to equation 5. These tendencies are considered when computing the distance D (equation 5) which is applied by the adaptation mechanism as follows: 1) the greater the distance is, the faster is the specialization to represent input patterns; 2) when patterns are uniformly classified within the neuron's average radius, the similarity threshold $-\ln(\pm_{BMU})$ tends to approach the average radius, which characterizes the neuron's adaptation to the input patterns that it represents.

$$D = |\,rad_{BMU} - \ln(\pm_{BMU})\,| \tag{5}$$

In the third architecture layer, neurons compete to represent each input pattern $\vec{I}_t$. The neuron with the highest activation, a_c, for the current input (equation 6) and that respects the minimum similarity degree, $\pm_c$, is selected as the Best-Matching Unit. Afterwards, the neuron components are updated to represent the new information of $\vec{I}_t$.

$$a_c = \exp(-\|\,\vec{I}_t - \vec{w}_c\,\|) \tag{6}$$

Figure 4. Number of patterns (n) necessary (axis y) to apply a forgetting rate of at least $P \in \{0.0025, 0.0 05, 0.01, 0.02, 0.04, 0.08, 0.16\}$ in a past pattern x_{t-n}, according to the parameter ψ (axis x)

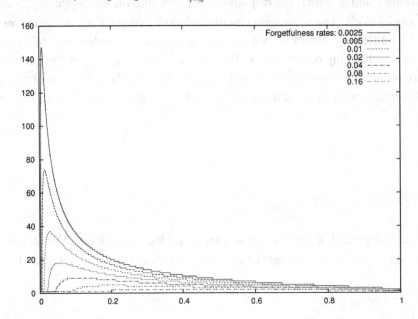

If no neuron is capable of representing the vector $\vec{I}_t$, a new one is created, indicating novelty. The new neuron prototype $\vec{w}_{new}$ is initially set up with the value of the input pattern responsible for the creation. The minimum similarity degree $\pm_{new}$ is defined according to the constant $\pm_0$ and the initial average radius, rad_{new}, equals to $-\ln\left(\pm_0\right)$.

LEARNING BEHAVIOR OF SONDE

Simulations were conducted to evaluate the learning behavior of the SONDE and describe the influence of its learning parameters. Such parameters influence the exponentially weighted moving average (EWMA) equations of the architecture. This motivated the first simulation to compute the forgetfulness effect of EWMA and a second one to evaluate how a neuron adapts and learns considering an uniform distribution $U(0,1)$ of the input patterns.

In the first simulation, an evaluation of neuron adaptation parameters (EWMA weights defined in equations 1 and 2) was conducted aimed at illustrating the learning and forgetting behavior of SONDE. For such evaluation, an equivalent formulation, shown in equation 7 (with weighting parameter $\psi \in [0,1]$), is adopted, because it characterizes the behavior of an hypothetical EWMA.

$$average_t = (1 - \dot{E})average_{t-1} + \dot{E}\,input_t \qquad (7)$$

Using this formulation, we analyze the forgetfulness of the EWMA equation when considering different forgetting rates (P) according to equation 8. This equation represents the forgetfulness caused by n new

Figure 5. Moving average convergence to the mean of an uniform distribution U(0,1)

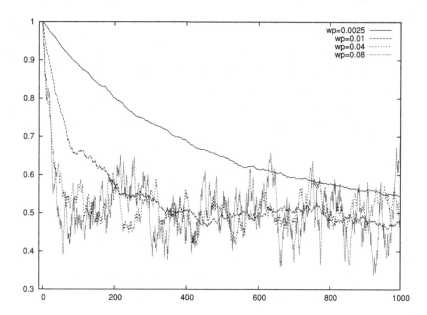

input patterns applied to equation 7. Figure 4 shows the forgetfulness when applying a number of input patterns as previously mentioned. This figure considers different forgetting rates P. Each curve shows the number of patterns necessary to forget the historical behavior (vertical axis) versus the weighting parameter ψ (horizontal axis) defined for different forgetting rates.

$$P \leq \dot{E}(1-\dot{E})^{n-1}, n \in \aleph, n \geq 1 \tag{8}$$

Considering Figure 4, we may estimate a value for the weighting parameter which defines the SONDE neuron's forgetfulness. There are some ways to set such a parameter, one of them is by adopting a ψ regarding the period with the highest values of the auto-correlation function for the input pattern series (such as the curve of forgetting rate $P=0.1$). This helps the neuron's memory to preserve the knowledge of the most important time slice (this is, within the auto-correlation period).

The next simulation involves the learning evaluation of the EWMA (equation 7) when classifying input patterns that follows an uniform distribution $U(0,1)$. The objective is to illustrate the neuron's adaptation capacity. In the first step, we consider a dataset using samples of the $U(0,1)$. Each sample represents the distance of an input pattern to the prototype. In that sense, a value 0 represents an input pattern equal to the prototype and value 1, the farthest input pattern that a neuron could accept. The results of this simulation are presented in Figure 5 where the weighting parameter varies according to $\psi \in \{0.0025, 0.01, 0.04, 0.08\}$. Considering such results, the lower the learning parameter ψ is, the lower is the learning speed and the sensitivity to the pattern noise.

FIRST EXPERIMENTAL RESULTS

This section presents experiments, described in Albertini and Mello (2007), with real-world datasets employed in non-temporal novelty detection. The goal of using these datasets was to validate the SONDE neural network architecture and to perform an initial comparison with other techniques. The datasets were organized in two parts. The first, the training part, with the same class distribution as the original dataset, was submitted to SONDE to learn about data. The second, composed of randomly organized sets, was submitted to evaluate the neural network's capacity to detect novelties. This technique considers the network in a production environment, habituated to certain patterns.

Patterns were normalized in the input layer. Neurons previously created by SONDE, when working on the training dataset, store known information. Any neuron created when working on the randomly distributed patterns points out novelty. The precision, recall and f-measure metrics were adopted to evaluate experiments (Baeza-Yates and Ribeiro-Neto, 1999). The measurements were captured varying in 0.1 units the control parameters γ, Ω and $\pm_0$. Precision is the proportion of true detected novelties over the total number of detected novelties (some events, detected as novelties, may not really be novelties). Recall is the proportion of true detected novelties over the total number of occurred novelties. F-measure is a harmonic average which summarizes the precision and recall results, simplifying the comparison with other techniques.

Biomed

The Biomed dataset[2], created by Larry Cox et. al (Cox et al., 1982), contains patient information and blood measurements obtained from carriers or non-carriers of a genetic disorder. Patterns with NA (not available) elements were removed and the columns of age and 4 blood measurements were used in the experiments. Other available data are: blood measurement date; number of samples per patient and the hospital identifier. The first 127 patterns of non-carriers were submitted to SONDE, after which 194 randomly distributed patterns (127 from non-carriers and 67 from carriers) were submitted. We observe that the best results were obtained with the learning parameters $\gamma=0.3$, $\Omega=0.1$ and $\pm_0 = 0.5$ which are $P=0.85$, $R=0.70$ and *f-measure*=0.77. In this case, 5 neurons were created to generalize the 127 initial patterns of non-carriers. Evaluating all results, we obtained a mean f-measure of 0.59 with standard deviation equal to 0.04 (with mean precision of 0.46 and standard deviation of 0.06; with mean recall of 0.84 and standard deviation of 0.1).

DLBCL

The DLBCL dataset (Diffuse large B-cell lymphoma) (Alizadeh et al., 2000) consists of 47 patterns with 4,026 measurements obtained from patients with tumors. This dataset was prepared using DNA microarrays to characterize the genetic expression in B cells. The obtained measurements show the variation of the proliferation rate, host response and the state of tumor differentiation. These data are classified into two patterns following the stage of B-cell differentiation: germinal and activated. Patients presenting the first type, react better to the treatment.

The 47 patterns were divided into 24 of type germinal and 23 activated. Firstly, the germinal patterns were submitted to SONDE. After that, a set containing all randomly distributed patterns was submitted. We observe that the neural network, in many situations, presented results such as $P=1$, $R=1$ e *f-measure*=1, creating approximatelly 21 neurons to generalize 24 patterns. Apparently, the results are good, although they are too much specalized (almost a neuron per pattern) which results in overfitting.

A better result is obtained with the learning parameters $\gamma=0.2$, $\Omega=0.1$ and $\pm_0 = 0.3$ where $P=0.76$, $R=1.0$ and *f-measure*=0.86. In this case, 3 neurons were generated to generalize 24 patterns, which increases the neural network's capability to detect novelties. Evaluating all results we obtained a mean f-measure of 0.83 with standard deviation of 0.24 (with mean precision of 0.85 and standard deviation of 0.22; with mean recall of 0.83 and standard deviation of 0.26).

ALL-AML Leukemia

The ALL-AML Leukemia dataset (Golub et al., 1999) consists of 72 patterns with 7,129 measurements obtained from acute leukemia carriers classified in the types ALL (acute lymphoblastic leukemia) with 38 patterns, and AML (acute myeloid leukemia) with 34 patterns. Firstly, 38 ALL-type patterns were submitted to SONDE to recognize these characteristics. After that, 72 randomly organized patterns (38 of ALL and 34 of AML) were submitted. In this case an unexpected event is defined by the occurrence of an AML-type pattern. As the DLBCL dataset, this one presented results of $P=1$, $R=1$ e *f-measure*=1 with low generalization, generating approximately a neuron per pattern. A good result was obtained with the learning parameters $\gamma=0.1$, $\Omega=0.4$ and $\pm_0 = 0.6$ where $P=0.65$, $R=1.0$ and *f-measure*=0.76. In this case, 7 neurons were created to generalize 38 initial patterns. Evaluating all results, we obtained a mean f-measure of 0.62 with standard deviation of 0.24 (with mean precision of 0.56 and standard deviation of 0.26; with mean recall of 0.72 and standard deviation of 0.23).

Result Analysis

The experimental results using the dataset Biomed can be compared to the best results obtained by GWR which correctly classified 56 of the 67 carriers and wrongly detected 2 people as carriers, being $P=0.9655$, $R=0.8358$ and *f-measure*=0.8959. Applying a training phase to SONDE, without centroid and radii adaptation in validation phase, with the learning parameters $\gamma=0.075$, $\Omega=0.05$ and $\pm_0 = 0.025$ our approach detected 59 out of the 67 carriers and wrongly classified 8 people as carriers. Thus, a precision $P=0.8805$, recall $R=0.9516$ and *f-measure*=0.9147 were obtained. From the harmonic mean, f-measure, we observe that SONDE presents a better result.

Such results obtained for non-temporal datasets motivated further work in order to represent causal relationships using SONDE and consequently detect novelties in time series, which is described in the following sections.

TIME SERIES MODELING AND NOVELTY LEVEL MEASUREMENT USING SONDE

In the context of this work, time series are sequences of events obtained from causal relationship applications. These applications, common in different areas varying from climate change to neurophysiology, present different characteristics and properties. For certain *well-behaved* time series, it is possible to employ historical data when estimating expected behavior models of the causal relationships. Conversely, some time series present inconsistent relationships which demand the forgetting of old tendencies and incremental behavior model updating. The application of novelty detection techniques on such time series needs to consider the analysis of relationships that supports the detection of temporal novelties. In order to detect such novelties, recent studies (Itti and Baldi, 2005; Al-Subaie and Zulkernine, 2006; Gamon, 2006) developed techniques based on measuring novelty levels, *i.e.*, quantifying the behavioral model changes after inserting a new pattern.

In one of these studies, Gamon (2006) analyzed news topics looking for novel information by modeling the relationships between sentences using a graph-based model. The author also defined novelties according to graph-changing metrics (vertices, edges and weights) and the TextRank method (Mihalcea, 2004). Using a supervised corpora, he modeled the text paragraphs and trained a Support Vector Machine to define the differences among novelty and non-novelty sentences. Itti and Baldi (2005) proposed an approach to novelty detection in videos, employing neural layers to estimate probabilistic models. The estimation process is conducted by counting the activation frequency in short scenes which are matched to Poisson distributions. The novelty measure between scenes is calculated by applying the theoretical information of Kullback-Liebler divergence.

These studies developed specific techniques considering different applications. The first study classified the text contextual characteristics using a non-temporal supervised classifier while the second defined a short-term memory to estimate Poisson distributions of neuron activations.

In order to detect and measure modifications in continuous and non-supervised data streams, we propose the application of the SONDE architecture to estimate Markov chain stochastic processes. Markov chains represent causal relationships through transition probabilities between behavioral states. The Markov property assumes that relationships are composed of a finite number of past terms.

A Markov chain can be formally modeled as a digraph $C=<V,T>$, where V represents the set of behavioral states and T is the set of causal relationships (edges). Each edge in T has an associated weight informing the transition probability between states. Such chain can be represented by a probability transition matrix M (equation 9), with the weights of edges in T from any i to another j corresponding to the element $M(i,j)$.

$$M = \begin{pmatrix} p_{0,0} & \cdots & p_{0,j} \\ \vdots & & \vdots \\ p_{i,0} & \cdots & p_{i,j} \end{pmatrix} \tag{9}$$

The estimation of Markov chains is carried out through the architecture of SONDE, which counts the number of transitions between consecutive *BMU* neurons after each input pattern classification. For each neuron, a corresponding chain state in V is created. The transition matrix estimation M summarizes the number of activations affected by the neuron i followed by the activation of j, this is defined by the element $L(i,j)$ of matrix L in equation 10.

$$L = \begin{pmatrix} L_{0,0} & \cdots & L_{0,j} \\ \vdots & & \vdots \\ L_{i,0} & \cdots & L_{i,j} \end{pmatrix} \tag{10}$$

Each element of the probability matrix $M(i,j)$ is estimated by the division of $L(i,j)$ by the sum $s(i)$ of all transitions which start at the state i (equation 11). As SONDE applies an incremental learning updating technique, the probability matrix M is estimated for each input pattern of the time series at the instant t, which is denoted as M_t .

$$s(i) = \sum_{j=0}^{n-1} L\left(i, j\right)$$

(11)

Using the sequence of Markov chains M_t , which were estimated during the learning of a series, we apply metrics of knowledge variation such as the Shannon entropy (Pincus, 1991) and the Kullback-Liebler divergence (Itti and Baldi, 2005). Such metrics helps to quantify the novelty introduced by the learning of the t-th input pattern into the knowledge model M_{t-1} .

In this work, we propose quantifying novelties using an entropy-based metric as defined by equation 13, where $E(t)$ is the mean state entropy, defined in equation 12, according to the transition probability matrix M_t and the number of states n_t . We observed that such metric has the ability of reflecting non-temporal novelties (i.e. neuron creation).

$$E\left(t\right) = \frac{-\sum_{i}^{n_t} \sum_{j}^{n_t} M_i\left(i, j\right) \log\left(M_t\left(i, j\right)\right)}{n_t}$$

(12)

$$N(t) = |E(t)-E(t-1)|$$

(13)

SIMULATION WITH SHANNON ENTROPY AS NOVELTY METRIC

Three simulations were conducted to illustrate the relation between entropy variation and novelties. The first simulation consists of the detection of noise in a linear signal, the second considers a periodic system to compare temporal and non-temporal novelties, and the third comprises of novelty detection on noisy first-order autoregressive time series. Each simulation is composed of the following steps: SONDE processes input pattern series, estimates Markov chains for each input pattern and computes the entropy-based novelty metric.

The first simulation presents a simple example of noise detection by employing the entropy-based novelty metric defined in equation 13. In this simulation, the task is to identify noise on a constant signal $y=1$. Such noise has the probability p of happening, with intensity following a Gaussian distribution . The results obtained with $p=0.01$, $\mu=0$ and $\sigma^2 = 1$ are shown in Figure 6. In these results, the horizontal axis represents the number of input patterns submitted to SONDE (configured with the following parameters: $\gamma=0.1$, $\Omega=0.1$ and $\pm_0 = 0.4$). For the curve *Inputs*, the vertical axis represents the values of the patterns and, for the curve *Novelty metric*, it represents the novelty intensity. In the same figure, we can observe high variations in the presence of noise, although eventually time lags and false alarms may occur.

The second simulation aims at comparing the entropy-based metric to the non-temporal detection, using the SONDE neuron creation. In this simulation, illustrated in Figure 7, the SONDE receives a

Figure 6. Simulation of noise detection in a constant signal

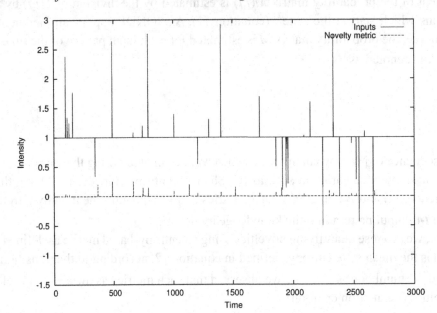

three-valued sequence in the form 123123...123 simulating the behavior of a system. The input pattern sequence is represented by the curve *Inputs* smoothed with a natural cubic spline, which allows better visualization. The curve *Novelty metric* represents the values obtained from the metric proposed in equation 13, using a factor of 10. The curve *States*, also smoothed, represents the current state of the Markov chain. The SONDE learning parameter configuration is: γ=0.1, Ω=0.1 and $\pm_0 = 0.4$.

In this simulation, three tests were conducted to illustrate the detection and level measurement of novelties. The first consisted of the insertion of element 1, a previously known event, in an unexpected order (after another 1). In Figure 7, we observe that such insertion does not cause a neuron creation, but a variation of the novelty metric.

The second situation considered the insertion of a sequence of values 3, which also does not result in neuron creation, but induces an entropy variation. After a sequence of 3s, the *Entropy variation curve* decreases because the input and the sequence were learnt. This variation corresponds to the novelty level after continuous learning. Such temporal novelty level cannot be measured without the modeling of the causal relationship of events.

In the last situation of this simulation, unknown values 4 were introduced causing both novelty metric variation and neuron creation. After the first 4, a negative variation of the novelty metric curve is observed resulting from the insertion a new neuron.

This simulation confirms that novelty detection based only on neuron creation, i.e. a non-temporal novelty metric, does not satisfy the requirements of time-series applications as it does not represent temporal novelties (occurred at the moment of unexpected events 1 and 3). In a similar manner, novelty level attenuation (demonstrated during the learning of the sequence of several 3s) cannot be obtained from similarity-based techniques.

The last simulation was performed to illustrate the entropy-based novelty metric applied to a more complex and real-life-based application which considers noise on time series. In this simulation, a data

Figure 7. Simulation comparing non-temporal and temporal novelty detection in a periodic sequence of three values

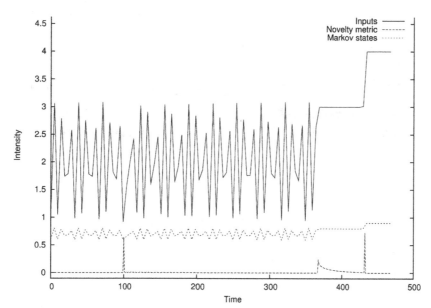

sequence is generated by a first-order autoregressive stochastic process in the form $x_t = \varphi x_{t-1} + a_t$, where a_t is a Gaussian random variable with mean 0 and variance 0.1. The data sequence is comprised of 3,000 points, where the first 1,000 points were obtained from a stationary parameter $\varphi = 0.1$, the following 1,000 from a non-stationary parameter $\varphi = 1$ and the last 1,000 with the same behavior as the first one ($\varphi = 0.1$). These points were learnt by SONDE using the learning parameters γ=0.1, Ω=0.01 and $\pm_0 = 0.4$.

Figure 8 presents the data input in the curve *Inputs*, the novelty metric output (with a shifting factor of 2 and scaling factor of 5 – to improve visualization) in curve *Entropy variation* and the Markov chain states (with a reducing scale factor of 10 – to improve visualization) in the curve *States*. We observe a novelty metric variation during the transitions between stationary and non-stationary processes and when data is abruptly modified from the previously known values.

AN EXPERIMENT BASED ON MEASURED DATA

To our knowledge, the only method that measures novelty levels on temporal data was proposed by (Itti and Baldi, 2005). However, this method is not suitable for time series because it is specialized for video and relies on neuron maps to analyze and estimate probability distribution functions. In order to compare the proposed approach to another incremental method for detection of temporal novelties, we performed experiments using the dataset Laser offered by the Santa Fe Institute (Ma and Perkins, 2003). The Laser dataset presents experimental data with chaotic attractors which approximatelly follows the Lorenz model (Huebner et al., 1989). In the experiments conducted by (Ma and Perkins, 2003), they employed an incremental Support Vector Regression technique to select the time-frames (sequence of data) presenting novel events, without evaluating their novelty intensity.

Figure 8. Novelty detection on noisy first-order autoregressive time series

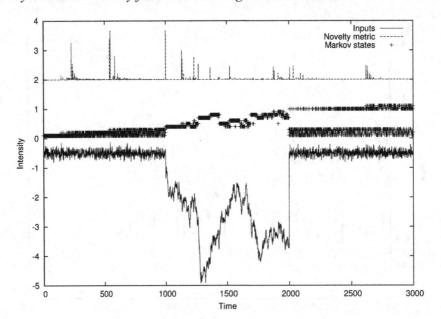

Figures 9 and 10 present results of applying the proposed approach on the Laser dataset with the learning parameters $\gamma=0.1$, $\Omega=0.1$ and $\pm_0 = 0.001$. These results are different from those obtained by Ma and Perkins (2003), where data from 0 to 200 were used only for training. After the training phase, novelties were only identified in the time-frames of about time instants 450 and 600, during approximatelly 10 instants.

In our results (Figure 10), the SONDE identified high novelty levels on the first 200 observations; this is during the learning phase which was not presented by Ma and Perkins (2003). From 200 on, we observe novelty levels attributed to two kinds of variations: extreme values, such as at points 602 and 934; and structural variations, such as at points 312, 320 and 650. While the extreme values can be easily perceived in Figure 9, the structural variations are better observed in Figure 10 which shows only the data points. It is important to observe that the novelties recognized on structural variations occur when data trajectories are increasing their chaoticity, pointing out temporal novelties.

CONCLUSION

This chapter presented the state-of-the-art in novelty detection, including recent studies on temporal novelty detection. In order to detect and measure temporal novelties, causal characteristics must be incrementally learnt. Current studies do not fully detect and quantify these temporal novelties nor do they completely consider causal relationships. This motivated the design of Self-Organizing Novelty Detection (SONDE), a self-organizing neural network which incrementally learns input patterns in order to represent unknown dynamics and fluctuation of the established behavior. The knowledge accumulated by SONDE is employed to estimate Markov chains which model causal relationships. Such model is applied to detect and measure temporal and non-temporal novelties. The evaluation of the proposed

Figure 9. Novelty detection considering the Laser dataset

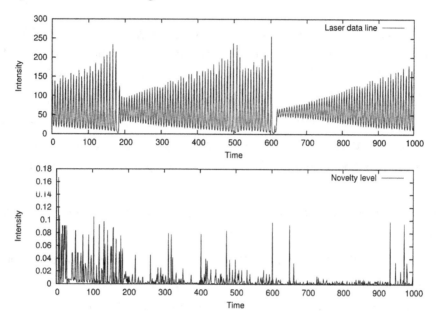

Figure 10. Novelty detection considering the Laser dataset: showing data points

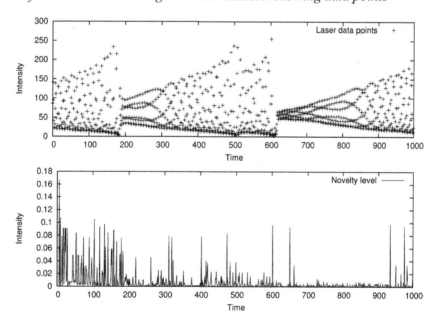

technique was conducted through simulations and experiments, which have presented promising results. Currently, we are investigating other metrics to characterize series behavior such as the Kullback-Leibler divergence, Lyapunov numbers and Hurst exponent. Further directions of this work include the analysis of the long-term influence of causal relationships, the development of a control to adapt the learning parameters which will improve the SONDE incremental learning, the evaluation of the novelty level quality and comparison to other approaches.

REFERENCES

Al-Subaie, M., & Zulkernine, M. (2006). Efficacy of hidden Markov models over neural networks in anomaly intrusion detection. In *Proceedings of the 30th Annual International Computer Software and Applications Conference (COMPSAC '06)* (pp. 325-332). Washington, DC: IEEE Computer Society.

Albertini, M. K., & Mello, R. F. (2007). A self-organizing neural network for detecting novelties. In *Proceedings of the ACM symposium on Applied Computing (SAC '07)* (pp. 462-466). New York: ACM.

Alizadeh, A. A., Eisen, M. B., Davis, E. E., Ma, C., Lossos, I. S., & Rosenwald, A. (2000). Distinct types of diffuse large B-cell lymphoma identified by gene expression profiling. *Nature, 403*(6769), 503–511. doi:10.1038/35000501

Baeza-Yates, R. A., & Ribeiro-Neto, B. A. (1999). *Modern information retrieval.* New York: ACM Press / Addison-Wesley.

Barnett, V., & Lewis, T. (1994). *Outliers in statistical data.* New York: John Wiley & Sons.

Bensalah, Y. (2000). *Steps in applying extreme value theory to finance: A review* (Working Notes 00-20). Bank of Canada. Retrieved from http://ideas.repec.org/p/bca/bocawp/00-20.html

Bertarelli, S., & Censolo, R. (2000). Preference for novelty and price behaviour (Working Papers 383). Dipartimento Scienze Economiche, Università di Bologna.

Bishop, C. M. (1995). *Neural networks for pattern recognition.* Oxford, UK: Oxford University Press.

Bishop, C. M. (2006). *Pattern recognition and machine learning (Information science and statistics).* Berlin, Germany: Springer-Verlag.

Box, G. E. P., & Jenkins, G. M. (1976). *Time series analysis, forecasting, and control.* San Francisco: Holden-Day.

Chan, P., & Stolfo, S. (1998). Toward scalable learning with non-uniform class and cost distributions: A case study in credit card fraud detection. In *Proceedings of the 4th International Conference on Knowledge Discovery and Data Mining* (pp. 164-168).

Cox, L., Johnson, M., & Kafadar, K. (1982). Exposition of statistical graphics technology. In *ASA Proceedings Statistical Computation Section* (pp. 55-56).

Fisher, R. A., & Tippett, L. (1928). Limiting forms for the frequency distribution of the largest or smallest member of a sample. *Proceedings of the Cambridge Philosophical Society, 24,* 180–190. doi:10.1017/S0305004100015681

Flexer, A., Pampalk, E., & Widmer, G. (2005). Novelty detection based on spectral similarity of songs. In *Proceedings of 6th International Conference on Music Information Retrieval* (pp. 260-263).

Gamon, M. (2006). Graph-based text representation for novelty detection. In *Proceedings of TextGraphs: the Second Workshop on Graph Based Methods for Natural Language Processing* (pp. 17-24). New York: Association for Computational Linguistics.

Golub, T. R., Slonim, D. K., Tamayo, P., Huard, C., Gaasenbeek, M., & Mesirov, J. P. (1999). Molecular classification of cancer: Class discovery and class prediction by gene expression monitoring. *Science, 286*(5439), 531–537. doi:10.1126/science.286.5439.531

Hasselmann, K. (1997). Multi-pattern fingerprint method for detection and attribution of climate change. *Climate Dynamics, 13*(9), 601–611. doi:10.1007/s003820050185

Hayton, P., Scholkopf, B., Tarassenko, L., & Anuzis, P. (2000). Support vector novelty detection applied to jet engine vibration spectra. In *Advances in Neural Information Processing Systems* (pp. 946-952).

Hodge, V., & Austin, J. (2004). A survey of outlier detection methodologies. *Artificial Intelligence Review, 22*(2), 85–126.

Huebner, U., Klische, W., Abraham, N. B., & Weiss, C. O. (1989). Comparison of Lorenz-like laser behavior with the Lorenz model. In *Coherence and Quantum Optics VI* (p. 517). New York: Plenum Press.

Hughes, G., Murray, J., Kreutz-Delgado, K., & Elkan, C. (2002). Improved disk-drive failure warnings. *IEEE Transactions on Reliability, 51*(3), 350–357. doi:10.1109/TR.2002.802886

Itti, L., & Baldi, P. (2005). A principled approach to detecting surprising events in video. In *Proceedings of the IEEE Computer Society Conference on Computer Vision and Pattern Recognition (CVPR'05) - Volume 1* (pp. 631-637). Washington, DC: IEEE Computer Society.

Jelinek, F. (1997). *Statistical methods for speech recognition*. Cambridge, MA: MIT Press.

Kaufmann, G. (2004). Two kinds of creativity - but which ones? *Creativity and Innovation Management, 13*(3), 154–165. doi:10.1111/j.0963-1690.2004.00305.x

Kecman, V. (2001). *Learning and soft computing*. Cambridge, MA: MIT Press.

Ko, H., Baran, R., & Arozullah, M. (1992). Neural network based novelty filtering for signal detection enhancement. In *Proceedings of the 35th Midwest Symposium on Circuits and Systems* (Vol 1, pp. 252-255).

Kohonen, T. (1997). *Self-organizing maps*. Berlin, Germany: Springer-Verlag.

Kullback, S. (1959). *Information theory and statistics*. New York: John Wiley and Sons.

Lane, T. (1999). Hidden Markov models for human/computer interface modeling. In *IJCAI-99 Workshop on Learning About Users* (pp. 35-44).

Lau, K.-M., & Weng, H. (1995). Climate signal detection using wavelet transform: How to make a time series sing. *Bulletin of the American Meteorological Society, 76*(12), 2391–2402. doi:10.1175/1520-0477(1995)076<2391:CSDUWT>2.0.CO;2

Lauer, M. (2001). A mixture approach to novelty detection using training data with outliers. In *Proceedings of the 12th European Conference on Machine Learning (ECML '01)*, London, UK (pp. 300-311). Berlin, Germany: Springer-Verlag.

Luterbacher, J., Dietrich, D., Xoplaki, E., Grosjean, M., & Wanner, H. (2004). European seasonal and annual temperature variability, trends, and extremes since 1500. *Science, 303*(5663), 1499–1503. doi:10.1126/science.1093877

Ma, J., & Perkins, S. (2003). Online novelty detection on temporal sequences. In *Proceedings of the 9th ACM SIGKDD International Conference on Knowledge Discovery and Data Mining (KDD '03)* (pp. 613-618). New York: ACM.

Mann, H. B., & Whitney, D. R. (1947). On a test of whether one of two random variables is stochastically larger than the other. *Annals of Mathematical Statistics, 18*(1), 50–60. doi:10.1214/aoms/1177730491

Markou, M., & Singh, S. (2003). Novelty detection: A review - part 1: Statistical approaches, part2: Neural network based approaches. *Signal Processing, 83*(12), 2481–2497, 2499–2521. doi:10.1016/j.sigpro.2003.07.018

Marsland, S. (2002). *On-line novelty detection through self-organisation, with application to inspection robotics*. Unpublished doctoral dissertation, University of Manchester, UK.

Middleton, E. (1996). Adaptation level and 'animal spirits'. *Journal of Economic Psychology, 17*(4), 479–498. doi:10.1016/0167-4870(96)00020-7

Mihalcea, R. (2004). Graph-based ranking algorithms for sentence extraction, applied to text summarization. In *Proceedings of the 42nd Annual Meeting of the Association for Computational Linguistics.*

Pincus, S. (1991). Approximate entropy as a measure of system complexity. *Proceedings of the National Academy of Sciences of the United States of America, 88*, 2297–2301. doi:10.1073/pnas.88.6.2297

Priebe, C., Conroy, J., Marchette, D., & Park, Y. (2005). Scan statistics on Enron graphs. *Computational & Mathematical Organization Theory, 11*(3), 229–247. doi:10.1007/s10588-005-5378-z

Roberts, S. J. (1999). Novelty detection using extreme value statistics. *Vision, Image and Signal Processing . IEEE Proceedings, 146*(3), 124–129.

Rosen, B. E., Soriano, D., Bylander, T., & Ortiz-Zuazaga, H. (1996). Training a neural network to recognize artifacts and decelerations in cardiotocograms. In *Proceedings of the AAAI Spring Symposium on Artificial Intelligence in Medicine: Applicat. Current Technol. Working Notes.*

Shannon, C. (1948). A mathematical theory of communication. *The Bell System Technical Journal, 27*, 379–423, 623–656.

Singh, S. (2002). Anomaly detection using negative selection based on the r-contiguous matching rule. In J. Timmis & P. J. Bentley (Eds.), *Proceedings of the 1st International Conference on Artificial Immune Systems (ICARIS)*, University of Kent at Canterbury (pp. 99-106).

Singh, S., & Markou, M. (2005). A black hole novelty detector for video analysis. *Pattern Analysis & Applications, 8*(1), 102–114. doi:10.1007/s10044-005-0248-3

Smith, T., & Boning, D. (1997). A self-tuning EWMA controller utilizing artificial neural network function approximation techniques. *IEEE Transactions on Components, Packaging, and Manufacturing Technology Part C, 20*(2), 121–132. doi:10.1109/3476.622882

Spinosa, E. J., & de Carvalho, A. C. (2005). Combining one-class classifiers for robust novelty detection in gene expression data. In *Advances in bioinformatics and computational biology* (LNCS 3594, pp. 54-64). Berlin, Germany: Springer.

Spinosa, E. J., de Leon, F., de Carvalho, A. P., & Jo, G. (2007). Olindda: A cluster-based approach for detecting novelty and concept drift in data streams. In *Proceedings of the ACM Symposium on Applied computing (SAC '07)* (pp. 448-452). New York: ACM.

Tarassenko, L. (1995). Novelty detection for the identification of masses in mammograms. In *Proceedings of the 4th IEEE International Conference on Artificial Neural Networks*, Cambridge, UK (Vol. 4, pp. 442-447).

Tax, D., & Duin, R. (1998). Outlier detection using classifier instability. In A. Amin, D. Dori, P. Pudil, & H. Freeman (Eds.), *Advances in pattern recognition* (LNCS 1451, pp. 593-601.) Berlin, Germany: Springer-Verlag.

Tribus, M. (1961). *Thermostatistics and thermodynamics*. D. van Nostrand Company, Inc.

Vapnik, V. N. (1995). *The nature of statistical learning theory*. Berlin, Germany: Springer-Verlag.

Wilcoxon, F. (1945). Individual comparisons by ranking methods. *Biometrics Bulletin, 1*(6), 80–83. doi:10.2307/3001968

Willsky, A. (1976). A survey of design methods for failure detection in dynamic systems. *Automatica, 12*, 601–611. doi:10.1016/0005-1098(76)90041-8

Ypma, A., & Duin, R. P. W. (1997). Novelty detection using self-organizing maps. In *Progress in connectionist-based information systems* (Vol. 2, pp. 1322-1325). Berlin, Germany: Springer-Verlag.

Zhang, D., & Dong, Y. (2000). An efficient algorithm to rank Web resources. In *Proceedings of the 9th International World Wide Web Conference on Computer Networks: the International Journal of Computer and Telecommunications Networking* (pp. 449-455). Amsterdam: North-Holland Publishing Co.

ENDNOTES

[1] The temporal classification of techniques is important in the context of this work. Other studies may classify using different criteria such as the data dimensionality, the model space to represent the knowledge, etc.

[2] Available at: http://lib.stat.cmu.edu/datasets/

Chapter 4
Efficient Training Algorithm for Neuro–Fuzzy Network and its Application to Nonlinear Sensor Characteristic Linearization

Ajoy K. Palit
University of Bremen, Germany

Walter Anheier
University of Bremen, Germany

ABSTRACT

An ideal linear sensor is one for which input and output values are always proportional. Typical sensors are, in general, highly nonlinear or seldom sufficiently linear enough to be useful over a wide range or span of interest. Due to the requirement of tedious effort in designing sensor circuits with sufficient linearity for some applications, the word nonlinearity has acquired a pejorative connotation. Hence, a computationally intelligent tool for extending the linear range of an arbitrary sensor is proposed. The linearization technique is carried out by a very efficiently trained neuro-fuzzy hybrid network which compensates for the sensor's nonlinear characteristic. The training algorithm is very efficient in the sense that it can bring the performance index of the network, such as the sum squared error (SSE), down to the desired error goal much faster than any first order training algorithm. Linearization of a negative temperature coefficient thermistor sensor with an exponentially decaying characteristic function is used as an application example, which demonstrates the efficacy of the procedure. The proposed linearization technique is also applicable for any nonlinear sensor (such as J-type thermocouple or pH sensor), whose output is a monotonically increasing/decreasing function.

INTRODUCTION

Within the artificial intelligence society, the term *computational intelligence* is largely understood as a collection of intelligent computational methodologies such as fuzzy-logic-based computing, neuro-

DOI: 10.4018/978-1-60566-798-0.ch004

computing, and evolutionary computation that help in solving complex computational problems in science and technology which are not solvable or at least not easily solvable by using the conventional mathematical methods (Palit and Popovic, 2005). In the 1990s a growing number of publications on the successful combination of intelligent computational technologies - neural, fuzzy and evolutionary computation - have been reported. Since then hybrid systems, such as neuro-fuzzy networks, have been studied intensively due to their several advantages over the individual constituents. For instance, neural networks have been combined with fuzzy logic resulting in neuro-fuzzy or fuzzy-neural systems in which:

- Neural networks tune the parameters of the fuzzy logic systems, which are used in developing the adaptive fuzzy controllers as implemented in the Adaptive Network-Based Fuzzy Inference System (ANFIS) proposed by Jang (1993).
- Fuzzy logic systems monitor the performance of the neural network and adapt its parameters optimally, for instance, in order to achieve the nonlinear mapping and/or the function approximation to any desired accuracy (Wang and Mendel, 1992a).
- Fuzzy logic is used to control the learning rate of neural networks to avoid the creeping phenomenon in the network while approaching the solution minimum (Arabshahi et al., 1992).

In addition to many applications and improvements, several theoretical results such as universal function approximation capability of neuro-fuzzy networks have also been obtained (Wang, 1994; Wang and Mendel, 1992b). In this chapter, the same feature (universal approximation capability) of the hybrid networks has been exploited for the linearization of highly nonlinear sensor characteristics.

Usually, some particular types of well defined sensor nonlinearities (exponentially rising or exponentially decaying) are compensated by hardware techniques (i.e. by using logarithmic converter) as reported by Patranabis et al. (1988). However, the hardware based linearization procedure lacks the portability i.e. the same procedure cannot be applied so easily to other categories of sensor nonlinearities. In contrast, the linearization technique based on computationally intelligent technology (software based linearization) can very easily be applied to almost all types of sensor nonlinearities. A similar approach but with artificial neural networks has already been reported by Medrano-Marques and Martin-Del-Brio (2001).

However, it is to be noted that the success of software based linearization process based on neural networks and/or neuro-fuzzy networks highly depends on the optimal tuning of (fuzzy) system parameters. Therefore, in this chapter, a training algorithm based on Levenberg-Marquardt approach has been presented that can be applied to fine-tune the free parameters of the hybrid neuro-fuzzy network very efficiently. The training algorithm is very efficient in the sense that it can bring the performance index (sum squared error value) of the network down to the desired error goal much faster than any first order training algorithm (backpropagation algorithm). Thereafter, as an application example, linearization of a negative temperature co-efficient (NTC) type of thermistor sensor has been considered.

The rest of the chapter is organized as follows. The next section presents the structure of the selected neuro-fuzzy network and its training algorithm. Thereafter, the sensor characteristic linearization has been presented as an application example. In the same section, the linearization technique of an arbitrarily chosen nonlinear sensor and the experimental simulations are presented. Finally, the chapter concludes with a brief discussion.

NEURO-FUZZY NETWORK

We propose, here, a hybrid neuro-fuzzy network for the purpose of linearization of nonlinear sensor's characteristics. The main advantage of such a hybrid neuro-fuzzy approach is that it exploits the merits of both neural networks and fuzzy logic based modeling techniques. For instance, the fuzzy models are based on fuzzy "If-Then" rules and are, to some extent, transparent to interpretation and analysis by human experts. In contrast, the neural networks based model has the unique learning ability. In this chapter, hybrid neuro-fuzzy network is constructed by the multi-layer feed-forward network representation of fuzzy logic system as described in (1) - (4). The fuzzy logic system considered here is based on Takagi-Sugeno (TS) type of fuzzy model and with Gaussian membership functions (GMF), product inference rule, and a weighted average defuzzifier.

$$f\left(\mathbf{x}\right) = \sum_{l=1}^{M}\left(\beta^l \cdot y_{TS}^l\right)\Big/\beta^l \tag{1}$$

$$y_{TS}^l = \left(\theta_0^l + \theta_1^l x_1 + \cdots + \theta_n^l x_n\right). \tag{2}$$

$$\beta^l = \prod_{i=1}^{n}\mu_{G_i^l}\left(x_i\right), \text{ with } \mu_{G_i^l}\left(x_i\right) = \exp\left\{-\left(x_i - c_i^l\right)^2\Big/\left(\sigma_i^l\right)^2\right\}. \tag{3}$$

Here, we assume that the mean parameter i.e. $c_i^l \in U_i$, and the variance parameter of Gaussian membership functions i.e. $\sigma_i^l > 0$, and the lth rule (Takagi-Sugeno) consequent i.e. $y_{TS}^l \in V$, where U_i and V are universes of discourse for the ith input, and single output of the fuzzy logic system respectively and the input vector $x = \left(x_1, x_2, \cdots, x_n\right)$, $x_i \in U_i$. The corresponding lth rule (Takagi-Sugeno) from the above fuzzy logic system can be written as follows:

R^l: If x_1 is G_1^l and x_2 is G_2^l and ... and x_n is G_n^l
Then $\quad y_{TS}^l = \left(\theta_0^l + \theta_1^l x_1 + \cdots + \theta_n^l x_n\right).$ \tag{4}

In the above fuzzy logic model and also in the fuzzy rule, x_i with i = 1, 2, 3, ..., n; are the n inputs to the fuzzy logic system and f is the output from the fuzzy logic system. Similarly, G_i^l, with i = 1, 2, 3, ..., n; and with l = 1, 2, 3, ..., M; are the $\left(M \times n\right)$ Gaussian membership functions (GMFs) with corresponding mean and variance parameters as $\left(c_i^l, \sigma_i^l\right)$ respectively. y_{TS}^l is the output consequent of lth fuzzy rule.

Note that Gaussian membership functions shown in the rule antecedents (i.e. in "If" parts) actually represent the linguistic terms such as low, medium and high, etc. or slow, moderate and fast, etc. It is clear that because of the crisp output function, the rule stated in (4) is a Takagi-Sugeno (TS) type of fuzzy rule. In the above fuzzy logic system, the Gaussian membership function has been deliberately selected as it is continuous and differentiable at all points, which are essential criteria for first or second order derivative based training algorithms. As mentioned earlier, the above fuzzy logic system is a universal

Figure 1. Multi-input single-output neuro-fuzzy network

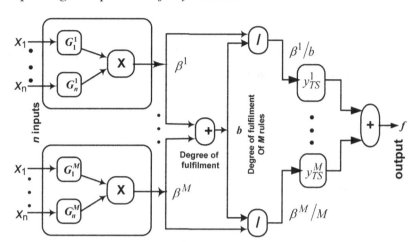

function approximator and hence, the similar feature will later be exploited to approximate the inverted characteristic function of the sensor (see Figure 6).

Note that by carefully observing the functional forms of (1) - (4), it can be seen that the above fuzzy logic system can be represented as a three-layer multi-input and single-output feed-forward network as shown in Figure 1. Because of neuro-implementation of a TS type of fuzzy logic system, Figure 1 actually represents a TS type multi-input single-output (MISO) neuro-fuzzy network. Here, instead of connecting weights and biases as in neural networks, we have the mean $\left(c_i^l\right)$ and the variance $\left(\sigma_i^l\right)$ parameters of the Gaussian membership functions, along with $\left(\theta_0^l, \theta_i^l\right)$ i.e. y_{TS}^l from the TS rules consequent as the equivalent free parameters. The neuro-fuzzy network implemented above with a sufficiently large number of optimally tuned free parameters (i.e. with a large number of tuned rules) can approximate any nonlinear function to any degree of accuracy based on the given input-output data pairs.

EFFICIENT TRAINING ALGORITHM FOR NEURO-FUZZY NETWORKS

The TS type of fuzzy logic system, once represented as the equivalent multi-input single-output feed-forward network (Figure 1), can generally be trained using any classical training algorithm of neural networks. However, because of much faster convergence speed, the Levenberg-Marquardt training is generally preferred to the standard backpropagation algorithm (Hagan and Menhaj, 1994).

Levenberg-Marquardt Algorithm (LMA)

If a function $V\left(w\right)$ is to be minimized with respect to the parameter vector w using Newton's method, the updated parameter vector w is defined as:

$$\Delta w = -\left[\nabla^2 V\left(w\right)\right]^{-1}. \nabla V\left(w\right)$$

(5a)

$$w(k+1) = w(k) + \Delta w \tag{5b}$$

In equation (5a), $\nabla^2 V(w)$ is the Hessian matrix and $\nabla V(w)$ is the gradient of $V(w)$. If the function $V(w)$ is taken to be a sum squared error (SSE) function as follows:

$$V(w) = 0.5 \cdot \sum_{r=1}^{N} e_r^2(w) \tag{6}$$

then the gradient of $V(w)$ and the Hessian matrix $\nabla^2 V(w)$ are generally defined as:

$$\nabla V(w) = J^T(w) \cdot e(w) \tag{7a}$$

$$\nabla^2 V(w) = J^T(w) \cdot J(w) + \sum_{r=1}^{N} e_r(w) \nabla^2 e_r(w) \tag{7b}$$

where, the Jacobian matrix $J(w)$ is as follows:

$$J(w) = \begin{bmatrix} \dfrac{\partial e_1(w)}{\partial w_1} & \dfrac{\partial e_1(w)}{\partial w_2} & \cdots & \dfrac{\partial e_1(w)}{\partial w_N} \\ \dfrac{\partial e_2(w)}{\partial w_1} & \dfrac{\partial e_2(w)}{\partial w_2} & \cdots & \dfrac{\partial e_2(w)}{\partial w_N} \\ \vdots & \vdots & & \vdots \\ \dfrac{\partial e_N(w)}{\partial w_1} & \dfrac{\partial e_N(w)}{\partial w_2} & \cdots & \dfrac{\partial e_N(w)}{\partial w_N} \end{bmatrix} \tag{7c}$$

From (7c), it can be seen that the dimension of the Jacobian matrix is $(N \times N_p)$, where N is the number of training samples and N_p is the number of adjustable (free) parameters in the entire network. For the Gauss-Newton method, the second term in (7b) is assumed to be zero. Therefore, the updated equation according to (5a) will be:

$$\Delta w = -\left[J^T(w) \cdot J(w) \right]^{-1} \cdot J^T(w) \cdot e(w) \tag{8a}$$

Now the Levenberg-Marquardt's modification of the Gauss-Newton method is:

$$\Delta w = -\left[J^T(w) \cdot J(w) + \mu \cdot I \right]^{-1} \cdot J^T(w) \cdot e(w) \tag{8b}$$

where I is the $\left(N_p \times N_p\right)$ identity matrix, and the parameter μ is multiplied or divided by some factor whenever the iteration step increases or decreases the value of $V\left(w\right)$.

Here, the updated equation according to (5b) is:

$$w\left(k+1\right) = w\left(k\right) - \left[J^T\left(w\right)\cdot J\left(w\right) + \mu\cdot I\right]^{-1}\cdot J^T\left(w\right)\cdot e\left(w\right) \tag{8c}$$

It is important to note that for a large μ the algorithm becomes the steepest descent algorithm with step size $1/\mu$, and for small μ, i.e. $\mu \approx 0$, it becomes the Gauss-Newton method.

Furthermore, as shown in equation (9a), the modified error index (MEI) term $V_{MEI}(w)$ can also be added to the original SSE function V(w) in order to further improve the training convergence (Xiaosong et. al., 1995). The corresponding gradient with MEI can now be defined by using a Jacobian matrix as (see Palit et. al. (2009) for detailed derivation):

$$V_{new}\left(w\right) = \left(V\left(w\right) + V_{MEI}\left(w\right)\right), \quad and$$
$$V_{new}\left(w\right) = 0.5\cdot\left[\sum_{r=1}^{N} e_r^2\left(w\right) + \gamma\sum_{r=1}^{N}\left(e_r\left(w\right) - e_{avg}\right)^2\right] \tag{9a}$$

Therefore, $\nabla V_{new}\left(w\right) = J^T\left(w\right)\cdot\left[e\left(w\right) + \gamma\cdot\left(e\left(w\right) - e_{avg}\right)\right]$ (9b)

In the above equations $e\left(w\right) = \left[e_1\left(w\right), e_2\left(w\right), \cdots, e_N\left(w\right)\right]^T$ is the column vector of errors, $e_{avg} = \left(e_1\left(w\right) + e_2\left(w\right) + \cdots + e_N\left(w\right)\right)/N$ is the average training error in each epoch, while γ is a constant factor such that $\gamma << 1$, which needs to be chosen appropriately.

Computation of the Jacobian Matrix

The computations of the Jacobian matrices are considered to be the most difficult step in implementing the LMA. Therefore, in this section, we describe a simple technique to compute, layer by layer, the Jacobian matrix from the backpropagation results reported in Palit and Popovic (2005). Layer-wise or parameter-wise computation of Jacobian matrix is possible because, as stated in equations (10a) - (10b), the final contents of the Hessian matrix remain unaltered even if the whole Jacobian is divided into smaller parts. Furthermore, this partition of the Jacobian matrix helps to avoid computer memory shortage problem, which usually occurred earlier with old computers for extremely large neural and/or neuro-fuzzy networks.

$$\nabla^2 V\left(w\right) \approx \left[J^T\left(w\right)\right]\cdot\left[J\left(w\right)\right] = \left[J_1^T\left(w\right)\cdot J_1\left(w\right), \; J_2^T\left(w\right)\cdot J_2\left(w\right)\right] \tag{10a}$$

$$\left[J\left(w\right)\right] = \begin{bmatrix} J_1\left(w\right) \\ J_2\left(w\right) \end{bmatrix} \quad and \quad \left[J^T\left(w\right)\right] = \left[J_1^T\left(w\right), J_2^T\left(w\right)\right] \tag{10b}$$

For the computation of the Jacobian matrix, the results obtained from the backpropagation algorithm will be extensively used, where the derivatives of the **sum squared error** S with respect to the network's adjustable parameters namely $\left(\theta_0^l, \theta_i^l\right)$ and $\left(c_i^l, \sigma_i^l\right)$ for the fuzzy logic system (1) - (4) have already been computed (see Palit et. al., 2009).

Therefore, the gradient $\nabla V\left(\theta_0^l\right)$ derived in the backpropagation algorithm can be written as:

$$\nabla V\left(\theta_0^l\right) \equiv \left(\partial S / \partial \theta_0^l\right) = \left\{\beta^l / b\right\}\left(f - d\right) \tag{11}$$

where, f and d are the vectors of actual output and desired output respectively for all training samples of the Takagi-Sugeno type MISO neuro-fuzzy network; and $b = \left(\beta^1 + \beta^2 + \cdots + \beta^M\right)$ is the summation of degrees of fulfillment of M fuzzy rules (see Palit and Popovic (2005) for details). Now, by comparing (11) and (12), where the gradient $\nabla V\left(w\right)$ is expressed as the transpose of the Jacobian matrix multiplied by the network's error vector, i.e.

$$\nabla V\left(w\right) = J^T\left(w\right) \cdot e\left(w\right) \tag{12}$$

the corresponding Jacobian matrix and the transpose of Jacobian matrix for the parameter $\left(\theta_0^l\right)$ of the neuro-fuzzy network can be written as:

$$J^T\left(\theta_0^l\right) = \left[\beta^l / b\right] \tag{13a}$$

$$J\left(\theta_0^l\right) = \left[\beta^l / b\right]^T \tag{13b}$$

where the prediction error of neuro-fuzzy network is written as:

$$e\left(\theta_0^l\right) = \left(f - d\right) \tag{14}$$

If the normalized prediction error of the neuro-fuzzy network is considered, then, instead of equations (13a) and (13b), the corresponding Jacobian and transpose of Jacobian matrix will be as follows:

$$J^T\left(\theta_0^l\right) = \left[\beta^l\right] \quad \text{and} \quad J\left(\theta_0^l\right) = \left[\beta^l\right]^T \tag{15}$$

This is because the normalized prediction error for any free parameter vector (w) of the MISO neuro-fuzzy network is

$$e_{normalized}\left(w\right) = \left(f - d\right)/b \tag{16}$$

Similarly, the transpose of the Jacobian matrix and the Jacobian matrix itself for the parameter $\left(\theta_i^l\right)$ of the neuro-fuzzy network can be written as:

$$J^T\left(\theta_i^l\right) = \left[\left(\beta^l/b\right)\cdot x_i\right] \tag{17a}$$

$$J\left(\theta_i^l\right) = \left[\left(\beta^l/b\right)\cdot x_i\right]^T \tag{17b}$$

Also, by considering normalized prediction error from (16), equations (17a)-(17b) then become:

$$J^T\left(\theta_i^l\right) = \left[\beta^l \cdot x_i\right] \quad \text{and} \quad J\left(\theta_i^l\right) = \left[\beta^l \cdot x_i\right]^T \tag{18}$$

Now, the Jacobian matrix computations of the remaining parameters $\left(c_i^l, \sigma_i^l\right)$ are performed similarly taking into consideration the normalized prediction error of equation (16).

$$J^T\left(c_i^l\right) = \left[2\cdot\beta^l\cdot\left(y_{TS}^l - f\right)\cdot\left(x_i - c_i^l\right)\Big/\left(\sigma_i^l\right)^2\right] \tag{19a}$$

$$J\left(c_i^l\right) = \left[2\cdot\beta^l\cdot\left(y_{TS}^l - f\right)\cdot\left(x_i - c_i^l\right)\Big/\left(\sigma_i^l\right)^2\right]^T \tag{19b}$$

Finally,

$$J^T\left(\sigma_i^l\right) = \left[2\cdot\beta^l\cdot\left(y_{TS}^l - f\right)\cdot\left(x_i - c_i^l\right)^2\Big/\left(\sigma_i^l\right)^3\right] \tag{20a}$$

$$J\left(\sigma_i^l\right) = \left[2\cdot\beta^l\cdot\left(y_{TS}^l - f\right)\cdot\left(x_i - c_i^l\right)^2\Big/\left(\sigma_i^l\right)^3\right]^T \tag{20b}$$

The above procedure actually describes the layer by layer computation of Jacobian matrices for various parameters of neuro-fuzzy network from the backpropagation results (see Palit and Popovic (2005) for details). It is to be noted that while computing the Jacobian matrices care has to be taken so that the dimensions of the Jacobian matrices match correctly with $\left(N \times N_p\right)$, where N = number of training samples (input-output training data sets) and N_p = number of adjustable parameters in the network layer considered.

Oscillation Control During Network Training

The proposed Levenberg-Marquardt algorithm with a modified error index extension of the original SSE function as the new performance function, in general, is very efficient and much faster than both the pure backpropagation algorithm and the pure LMA in training the neuro-fuzzy network considered in this chapter. However, the performance function (SSE) of the network is not always guaranteed to reduce towards the desired error goal in every epoch of training. This means that training may sometimes proceed in the opposite direction resulting in a continuous increase in SSE (instead of reduction after every epoch) or even oscillation, thus giving rise to a longer training time or even an undesirable training performance. In order to guarantee a satisfactory training performance, two sets of adjustable parameters are recommended to be stored. If the updated or new set of adjustable parameters reduces the network's SSE function in the following epoch then the same set of parameters is used for further training and the value of the μ parameter is reduced. Otherwise, if the SSE tends to increase beyond some factor, say WF (wildness factor of oscillation and WF can be 1.01, for example) times the current SSE with new set of parameters, then the new set is discarded and training proceeds with the old set of parameters. Thereafter, a new direction of training is sought with the old set of parameters and with a higher value of the μ parameter. In this way, in every epoch SSE is either decreased steadily or at least maintained within the region of current performance value.

APPLICATION EXAMPLE: SENSOR CHARACTERISTIC LINEARIZATION

The proposed neuro-fuzzy approach will be applied for the nonlinear sensor characteristic's linearization. The linearization technique described in the next few sections is so general that it can be applied to any arbitrary sensor, whose output is a monotonically increasing/decreasing function. Again, the proposed linearization technique can be applied to both highly nonlinear and partially nonlinear sensors where the (small) linear operating regions of the sensors need to be further increased to some extent. However, for the purpose of testing the efficacy of the proposed neuro-fuzzy approach, we have selected an NTC type of thermistor sensor which provides an exponentially decaying nonlinearity. As per Patranabis et. al. (1988) the linearization of this type of nonlinearity is, in fact, not so simple.

Problem Description: Need for Sensor Linearization

Sensors are widely used in various industries, business premises, automated systems, home and domestic appliances and so on, for quick and precise measurements of various physical process variables such as temperature, pressure, level, flow, vibration, force, motion, moisture content, humidity, pH, chemical measurements, etc. An ideal linear sensor is one for which the cause and effect are in proportion for all input and output values. However, typical sensors are, in general, highly nonlinear or seldom sufficiently linear enough to be useful over a wide range or span of interest. The nonlinearity associated with these sensors often creates several difficulties in direct digital read-out or in control applications. Sensor nonlinearity is not only associated with its type or nature but also with other factors like manufacturing tolerances, environmental effects and performance drifts due to aging; these factors contribute to the sensor's nonlinearity and bring up a need for frequent calibration of the sensor. Additionally, the signal conditioning circuits used for linearization may also sometimes contribute to the nonlinearity. For instance, the popularly used instrumentation bridge also introduces a form of nonlinearity, which modifies the inherent characteristics of the sensor. All these influencing factors bring up the need to linearize the response of the sensors in order to maintain it in a usable form for the final measurement and/or control applications.

Conventional Linearization Methods

In order to convert the nonlinear sensor's response into a linear output, several analog and digital techniques are commonly used. For instance, for the sensors with exponentially rising characteristic function, Patranabis et. al. (1988) proposed the logarithmic converter (analog hardware technique) for linearizing the response characteristic. On the other hand, for the sensors with exponentially decaying characteristic function, an additional inverting function was required and therefore, Patranabis et. al. (1988) used the log-converter and a FET. The latter analog method is then compared with the simple "single-stroke" digital technique. Ghosh and Patranabis (1992) also proposed a simple algorithm-oriented digital technique that utilized a truncated power series to linearize the thermistor type sensor characteristics. In their linearization method, early truncation of the power series also reduced the computation time considerably.

Another linearization technique, which is conceptually the simplest, is a read-only-memory (ROM) based look-up table. In this method, the entire dynamic range of the sensor and the conversion table for the measurand are stored in the ROM. The digital equivalent of the measurand is obtained by addressing the ROM. Another method is a nonlinear coding scheme utilized with the help of a digital to analog converter (DAC), and the measurand is linearly encoded by a nonlinear decoding function. The classical statistical regression modeling is also used to determine the polynomial approximation of the sensor's characteristics (Khan et. al., 2002).

Selected Nonlinear Sensor and Its Characteristic Function

As aforementioned, an NTC type of thermistor (temperature) sensor has been considered for this chapter. A thermistor is usually made up of semiconductor material and its resistance is temperature dependent. The actual characteristic of an NTC thermistor can be described by the exponential relation. This approach, however, is only suitable for describing a restricted range around the rated temperature or resistance with sufficient accuracy. The resistance-temperature relationship of thermistor is usually provided by the manufacturer in tabular form. The resistance-versus-temperature relationship of a thermistor is given by:

$$R_T = R_{T_0} \exp\left[\beta\left(\frac{1}{T} - \frac{1}{T_0}\right)\right] \tag{21}$$

where R_T = thermistor resistance (Ohm) at temperature T degree K (Kelvin), R_{T_0} = thermistor nominal resistance (Ohm) at temperature T_0 degree K and β = thermistor material constant. This standardized curve represented by (21) has been experimentally determined with utmost accuracy.

The β value is determined by the ceramic material and represents the slope of the resistance temperature curve. In (21), the β value is defined by two points (R_T, T) and (R_{T0}, T_0) of the R/T curve. In mathematical form, it can be described as:

$$\beta = T \cdot \frac{T_0}{(T - T_0)} \ln\left(\frac{R_{T_0}}{R_T}\right) \tag{22}$$

The specifications of the thermistor under consideration are as follows for the entire operating range: R_{T_0} = 10000 Ohm, T_0 = 298 degree Kelvin, or 25 degree Celsius, β = 3548 and operating range = -15 degree Celsius to 80 degree Celsius.

The resistance-temperature characteristic of the thermistor under consideration is shown in Figure 2. One can easily see the nonlinearity of resistance associated with temperature from Figure 2. This response characteristic of the thermistor and the above mentioned specifications are taken as reference for building the inverted nonlinear function using neuro-fuzzy network.

Signal Conditioning for Thermistor Sensor

The thermistor resistance changes with the change in excitation temperature to which the thermistor is being exposed. This change in resistance can easily be measured by connecting the thermistor to a balanced bridge. Wheatstone's bridge is most frequently used for such a measurement. Another simplified scheme could be the use of a voltage divider as shown in Figure 3. The advantage of such simple signal conditioning unit is that one can get the nonlinear voltage signal corresponding to the input temperature with less electronic circuits.

The output voltage (V_{out}) in Figure 3 can be computed for the change in thermistor resistance (R_{therm}) with the following equation:

$$V_{out} = V_{in} \cdot \frac{1}{1 + \left(\dfrac{R_{therm}}{R} \right)}$$

(23)

Figure 2. Temperature versus resistance curve of an NTC thermistor

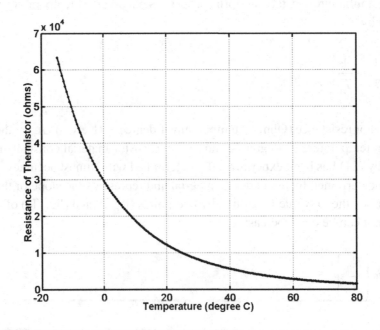

Figure 3. Signal conditioner for measurement of temperature using NTC thermistor

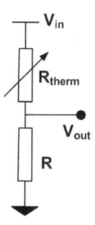

where, R_{therm} = thermistor resistance (Ohm), R = fixed resistance (typically, 1000 Ohms), V_{in} = excitation voltage (typically, 1 Volt) and V_{out} = nonlinear output voltage (Volts).

Three temperature-voltage characteristic curves for the above scheme are shown in Figure 4 for three different conditions. For all three conditions, the output voltage (V_{out}) remains nonlinear as it depends on the thermistor resistance R_{therm}. The output voltage (V_{out}) can be made larger by using a higher input voltage (V_{in}). Changing the input voltage (V_{in}) while the resistance (R) remains fixed will definitely change the temperature versus V_{out} characteristic plot. However, the response in all cases will be nonlinear. We have considered the fixed resistance (R) of value 1000 Ohms and the input excitation voltage (V_{in}) of value 1.0 Volt purposefully (see top-left plot in Figure 4) to simulate the highly nonlinear sensor characteristic, which we will later demonstrate on the linearization capability of the neuro-fuzzy model. The input excitation voltages (V_{in}) for other two plots are set to 5.0 Volts, whereas the respective values of fixed resistances (R) in top-right and bottom plots are set to 1000 Ohms and 10000 Ohms. So, notice that using the above signal conditioning scheme, we have produced three different types of nonlinear characteristics of an NTC thermistor sensor.

Proposed Neuro-Fuzzy Modeling for Sensor Linearization

The main objective here is to use computationally intelligent tool for sensor characteristic linearization. Since V_{out} is presently known from the voltage divider, we can use this nonlinear voltage information (V_{out}) as one of the input data to the neuro-fuzzy network and train the network subsequently using the proposed Levenberg-Marquardt algorithm. The purpose of the network training is to model the $V_{outmirror}$ curve, which is practically the inverse response characteristic of the temperature versus the V_{out} curve with respect to the blue tangent line (see Figure 5).

Figure 6 shows the schematic block diagram for sensor characteristic linearization using a neuro-fuzzy model. It depicts the precise neuro-fuzzy model of the inverse response characteristic of the selected thermistor, i.e. the $V_{outmirror}(t)$ curve when subsequently added to the (V_{out} - $V_{outmirror}$)/2 signal, produces the linear output response (tangent) or $V_{outlinear}(t)$. In order to model the inverse response characteristic curve by neuro-fuzzy network properly, in addition to the application of nonlinear output voltage (V_{out}) from signal conditioner, the thermistor resistance (R_{therm}) values corresponding to the known excitation

Figure 4. Thermistor excitation temperature vs. V_{out} plot

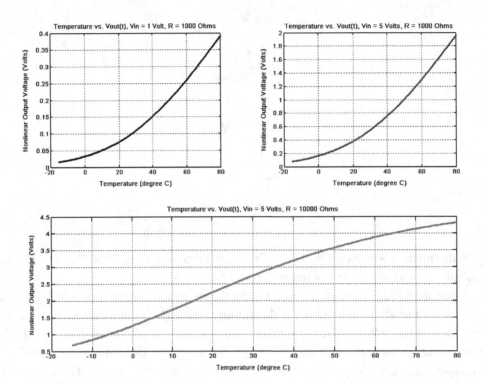

temperatures (t deg. C or T = t + 273 deg. K) were also applied as the second input to the neuro-fuzzy network. The desired output from the neuro-fuzzy network after successful training is the inverse response characteristic of the thermistor or $V_{outmirror}(t)$. Theoretically, the various data points of the $V_{outmirror}(t)$ curve can be computed very easily using the formula given below.

$$V_{outlinear}(t) = (a \cdot t + b), \quad where \quad T = (t + 273)^{\circ} K \tag{24}$$

$$V_{outmirror}(t) = (2 \cdot V_{outlinear}(t) - V_{out}(t)) \tag{25}$$

Note that in the above equations, $V_{outlinear}(t)$ actually represents the tangent drawn at any suitable point on the $V_{out}(t)$ nonlinear output curve and the constants a and b are the slope and intercept from the Voltage axis (Y-axis) respectively.

EXPERIMENTAL SIMULATION AND RESULTS

In this section, we describe the experimental simulation performed with the selected neuro-fuzzy network which has two inputs, one output and 10 fuzzy rules. Therefore, 10 Gaussian membership functions

Figure 5. V_{out} (t) (Temperature vs. nonlinear output voltage, red curve), $V_{outlinear}$ (t)(tangent, blue line) and $V_{outmirror}$ (t)(inverse response characteristic, black curve)

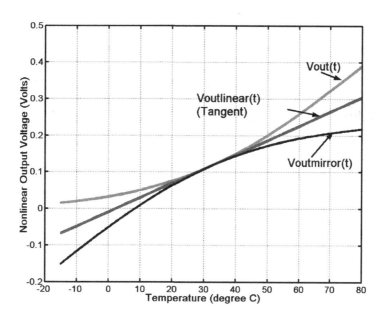

were also selected for each input and the rule antecedents. In order to train the neuro-fuzzy network, an input-output data matrix or XIO matrix was created with three columns, where the first two columns were the two inputs to the network and the third column was the desired output from the network. The generated XIO matrix is shown below:

$$XIO = \begin{bmatrix} V_{out}(t_1) & R_{t_1} & V_{outmirror}(t_1) \\ V_{out}(t_2) & R_{t_2} & V_{outmirror}(t_2) \\ \vdots & \vdots & \vdots \\ V_{out}(t_{192}) & R_{t_{192}} & V_{outmirror}(t_{192}) \end{bmatrix}$$

(26)

All three columns of the XIO matrix were separately normalized applying the equations (27) and (28) given below, so that the normalized input and output data values were always within the desired range of 0 to 1.

Given a row vector $\mathbf{u} = [u_1, u_2, u_3, ..., u_q]$, with q data points, the scaled and normalized row vector $\mathbf{u}_{nsc}$ can be written as

$$\mathbf{u}_{nsc} = K_0[(u_1 - u_{min}), (u_2 - u_{min}), (u_3 - u_{min}), ..., (u_q - u_{min})] + u_{lo}.$$

(27)

$$K_0 = (u_{hi} - u_{lo})/(u_{max} - u_{min})$$

(28)

Figure 6. Neuro-fuzzy model for sensor characteristic linearization

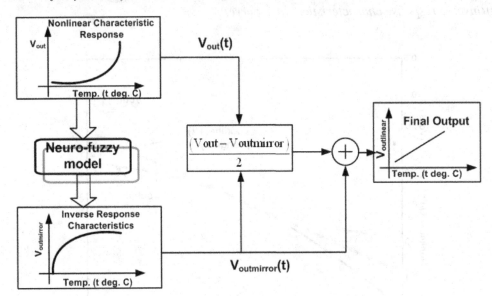

Figure 7. Training performance of neuro-fuzzy network when trained with proposed LMA

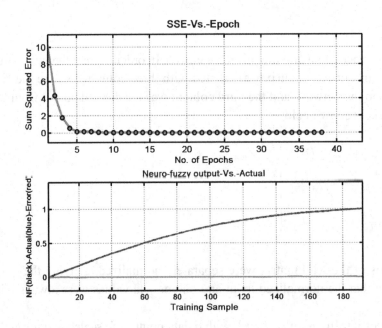

In the above equations u_{max} and u_{min} are the maximum and minimum values respectively of the row vector (**u** vector), and $u_{hi} = 1$, $u_{lo} = 0$ are the desired highest and lowest values respectively of the scaled or normalized row vector (**u_{nsc}** vector).

For the network's training, the entire input-output data set (i.e. 1 to 192 rows of XIO matrix) was used and the network's training was performed with randomly generated initial free parameters values. The training performance of the network is depicted in Figure 7 and Figure 8.

Figure 8. Neuro-fuzzy modeling of inverse sensor characteristic

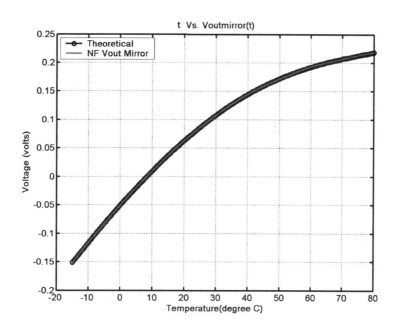

Figure 7 shows the training performance of the selected neuro-fuzzy network when trained with the proposed Levenberg-Marquardt algorithm. The upper-half of Figure 7 demonstrates that the performance function (SSE), in this case, was brought down very quickly from its initial SSE value of 10.547 to the desired error goal (final SSE value) of 9.045e-005 within only 38 epochs. Furthermore, the epoch versus SSE curve demonstrates that training does not exhibit any oscillation. The lower-half of Figure 7 demonstrates that the neuro-fuzzy network has modeled the inverse response characteristic ($V_{outmirror}$ (t)) curve very accurately and thereby giving rise to a practically very smooth error line through 0 values.

Again, Figure 8 shows that the neuro-fuzzy network has modeled the temperature t vs. $V_{outmirror}$(t) curve very accurately as the neuro-fuzzy network's output after the training completely overlaps the desired output. This resulted in a corresponding training accuracy of SSE = 9.045e-005 and MSE (mean square error) = 9.4219e-007.

Furthermore, adopting the linearization technique depicted in the schematic block diagram of Figure 6, the linearization achieved with the neuro-fuzzy network is further demonstrated in Figure 9. Figure 9 clearly shows that the linearization result obtained with the neuro-fuzzy approach overlaps the theoretical tangent line very much, which was computed using equation (24). Again, after getting the linearized thermistor output with the neuro-fuzzy modeling approach, the linearity of the final sensor output is tested for five different randomly selected temperature points. It was observed that the slopes between the different points for all such cases differ very marginally, as the maximum difference in the slope was found to be 0.000682.

Moreover, in order to validate the efficacy of the linearization process built with the help of the neuro-fuzzy model, five different thermistor resistance (i.e. R_{therm}) values and the five nonlinear voltage output (V_{out}) values from the signal conditioning unit were randomly selected corresponding to five known temperature (t) data points. The selected five R_{therm} and V_{out} values were then presented to the

Figure 9. Linearization achieved with neuro-fuzzy modeling approach

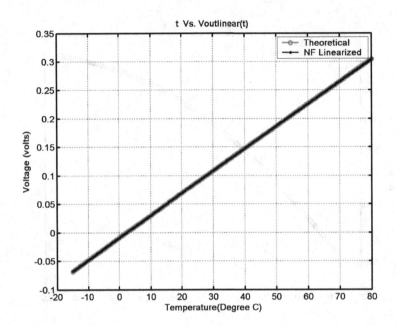

trained neuro-fuzzy network as the five test data sets and the corresponding five predicted neuro-fuzzy output values (i.e. five predicted $V_{outmirror}$ values) were recorded and further processed to generate five corresponding $V_{outlinear}$ values as described in the schematic block diagram of Figure 6. It was observed that the five computed $V_{outlinear}$ values correspond very accurately to their respective known temperature data points which were not exposed to the neuro-fuzzy network at all.

As further application examples, the two remaining sensor characteristic curves from Figure 4 were also considered. It is needless to mention that in both the cases, the neuro-fuzzy network had accurately modeled the inverse response characteristic functions, which finally resulted in high quality linearization performances with this proposed technique.

CONCLUSION

In this chapter, an efficient training algorithm has been presented to train the Takagi-Sugeno type neuro-fuzzy network much speedily. Since the proposed training algorithm is primarily based on the Levenberg-Marquardt algorithm, the chapter also describes a simple technique to compute the Jacobian matrix, which is usually considered to be the most difficult step in implementing the LMA. The trained network is then applied for the linearization of a highly nonlinear sensor. Sensor characteristics linearization has always been a very important task for various applications, which includes the direct digital read out and control applications. It has been observed that neuro-fuzzy networks can very efficiently capture or approximate the inverse response characteristics of a nonlinear sensor, which in turn, helps in generating a highly linearized output from the nonlinear sensor. The intelligent models developed here can easily be programmed into low-cost embedded processors or micro-controller (16 bit or 32 bit), which will enable us to avoid the additional electronics required for linearization using the conventional techniques and thus help to overcome the losses or performance drifts of components due to the additional electronics. The presented results clearly show the excellent performance of the neuro-fuzzy network in linearizing the highly nonlinear sensor characteristics.

The algorithm should also be tested with other nonlinear sensors such as J-type thermocouple and pH sensor, and the accuracy of the results obtained here should be compared with other software/hardware based approaches, which are currently left as the future directions of this work.

ACKNOWLEDGMENT

The authors gratefully thank Mr. Sandeep Mane, an M.Sc student of Information and Automation Engineering department, who performed several simulation experiments written in MATLAB source code for this research work under the guidance of the first author.

REFERENCES

Arabshahi, P., Choi, J. J., Marks, R. J., & Caudell, T. P. (1992). Fuzzy control of backpropagation. In *Proceedings of the IEEE International Conference on Fuzzy Systems,* San Diego, CA (pp. 967-972).

Ghosh, D., & Patranabis, D. (1992). Software based linearisation of thermistor type nonlinearity. *IEE Proceedings-G, Circuits . Devices and Systems, 139*(3), 339–342.

Hagan, M. T., & Menhaj, M. B. (1994). Training feedforward networks with the Marquardt algorithm. *IEEE Transactions on Neural Networks, 5*(6), 989–993. doi:10.1109/72.329697

Jang, J. S. R. (1993). ANFIS: Adaptive network based fuzzy inference system. *IEEE Transactions on Systems, Man, and Cybernetics, 23*(3), 665–685. doi:10.1109/21.256541

Khan, S. A., Shahani, D. T., & Agarwala, A. K. (2002). Sensor calibration and compensation using artificial neural networks. *ISA Transactions, 42*(3), 337–352. doi:10.1016/S0019-0578(07)60138-4

Medrano-Marques, N. J., & Martin-Del-Brio, B. (2001). Sensor linearization with neural networks. *IEEE Transactions on Industrial Electronics, 48*(6), 1288–1290. doi:10.1109/41.969414

Palit, A. K., Anheier, W., & Popovic, D. (2009). Electrical load forecasting using neural-fuzzy approach. In R. Chiong (Ed.), *Natural intelligence for scheduling, planning and packing problems.* Heidelberg, Germany: Springer-Verlag.

Palit, A. K., & Babuška, R. (2001). Efficient training algorithm for neuro-fuzzy network. In *Proceedings of the 10th IEEE International Conference on Fuzzy Systems,* Melbourne, Australia (pp. 1367-1371).

Palit, A. K., & Popovic, D. (2005). *Computational intelligence in time series forecasting: Theory and engineering applications.* London: Springer-Verlag.

Patranabis, D., Ghosh, S., & Bakshi, C. (1988). Linearizing transducer characteristics. *IEEE Transactions on Instrumentation and Measurement, 37*(1), 66–69. doi:10.1109/19.2666

Wang, L. X. (1994). *Adaptive fuzzy systems and control: Design and stability analysis.* Upper Saddle River, NJ: Prentice-Hall.

Wang, L. X., & Mendel, J. M. (1992a). Back-propagation fuzzy system as nonlinear dynamic system identifiers. In *Proceedings of the IEEE International Conference on Fuzzy Systems,* San Diego, CA (pp. 1409-1418).

Wang, L. X., & Mendel, J. M. (1992b). Fuzzy basis functions, universal approximation and orthogonal least squares learning. *IEEE Transactions on Neural Networks, 3,* 807–814. doi:10.1109/72.159070

Xiaosong, D., Popovic, D., & Schulz-Ekloff, G. (1995). Oscillation-resisting in the learning of backpropagation neural networks. In *Proceedings of the 3rd IFAC/IFIP Workshop on Algorithms and Architectures for Real-time Control,* Ostend, Belgium (pp. 21-25).

Section 2
Adaptive Evolutionary Systems

Chapter 5

A Review on Evolutionary Prototype Selection:
An Empirical Study of Performance and Efficiency

Salvador García
University of Granada, Spain

José Ramón Cano
University of Jaén, Spain

Francisco Herrera
University of Granada, Spain

ABSTRACT

Evolutionary algorithms have been successfully used in different data mining problems. Given that the prototype selection problem could be seen as a combinatorial problem, evolutionary algorithms have been used to solve it with promising results. This chapter presents an evolutionary data mining application known as evolutionary prototype selection. Various approaches have been proposed in the literature following two strategies on the use of evolutionary algorithms: general evolutionary models and models specific to prototype selection problem. In this chapter, the authors review the representative evolutionary prototype selection algorithms proposed, give their description and analyze their performance in terms of efficiency and effectiveness. They study their performance considering different sizes of the data sets, and analyze their behavior when the database scales up. The results are statistically contrasted in order to argue the benefits and drawbacks of each model.

INTRODUCTION

In supervised classification problems, we usually have a training set of samples (prototypes, instances) in which each example is labeled according to a given class. In the group of supervised classifiers, we can find the Nearest Neighbor (NN) rule method (Papadopoulos & Manolopoulos, 2004; Shakhnarovich

DOI: 10.4018/978-1-60566-798-0.ch005

et al., 2006) that predicts the class of a new prototype by computing a similarity measure (Pekalska et al., 2006) between this prototype and all prototypes from the training set, called the k-Nearest Neighbors (k-NN) classifier. In the k-NN classifier, k nearest neighbors vote to decide the class of the new instance to classify. A specific case is the 1-NN, where just the nearest neighbor is considered to take the decision.

Recent studies show that k-NN classifiers could be improved by employing numerous procedures. Among them, we could cite proposals on instance reduction (Liu & Motoda, 2002; Wilson & Martinez, 2000) for incorporating weights for improving classification (Paredes & Vidal, 2006), and for accelerating classification task (Gómez-Ballester et al., 2006), etc.

Prototype Selection (PS) is an instance reduction process consisting of maintaining those instances that are more relevant in the classification task of the k-NN algorithm and removing the redundant ones. This attempts to reduce the number of rows in the data set without any loss in classification accuracy and obtain an improvement in the classifier. Various approaches of PS algorithms have been proposed in the literature, see Wilson & Martinez (2000) and Grochowski & Jankowski (2004) for a review. Another process used for reducing the number of instances in the training data is the prototype generation, which consists of building new examples by combining or computing several metrics among the original data and including them into the subset of the training data (Lozano et al., 2006).

Evolutionary Algorithms (EAs) have been successfully used in different data mining problems (see Freitas, 2002; Ghosh & Jain, 2005; García-Pedrajas & Ortiz-Boyer, 2007). Given that PS problem could be regarded as a combinatorial problem, EAs have been used to solve it with promising results (Cano et al., 2003). We termed such approaches as Evolutionary Prototype Selection (EPS).

The increase in the numbers of training samples is a staple problem in PS (which is known as the Scaling Up Problem). This problem produces excessive storage requirement, increases time complexity, and affects generalization accuracy. These drawbacks are present in EPS too, because they result in an increment in chromosome size and execution time and also lead to a decrease in convergence capabilities of the EA. Traditional EPS approaches generally suffer from excessively slow convergence between solutions because of their failure to exploit local information. This often limits the practicality of EAs on many large-scale problems where computational time is a crucial consideration. A first rapprochement on the use of EAs when this problem scales up can be found in Cano et al. (2005).

The aim of this paper is to present a review of the EPS algorithms proposed, provide their description and analyze their performance in terms of efficiency and effectiveness. We will study their performance considering different sizes of the data sets, aimed at studying their behavior when the database scales up. The results will be statistically contrasted in order to argue the benefits and drawbacks of each model.

This chapter is organized in the following manner. Section 2 presents the PS task formally and the scaling problem involved when the size of the data set increases. A review of EPS is given in Section 3. In Section 4 we describe the EPS methods studied. Details of empirical experiments and results obtained are reported in Section 5. Section 6 contains a brief summary of the work and the conclusions reached.

BACKGROUND

PS methods are instance selection methods (Liu & Motoda, 2002) which attempt to find training sets offering the best classification accuracy by using the nearest neighbor rule (1-NN), considering the distance measure as the Euclidean one.

A formal specification of the problem is the following: Let X_p be an example where $X_p = (X_{p1}, X_{p2}, ..., X_{pm}, X_{pc})$, with X_p belonging to a class c given by X_{pc} and an m-dimensional space in which X_{pi} is the value of the i-th feature of the p-th sample. Then, let us assume that there is a training set TR which consists of n instances of X_p and a test set TS composed of t instances of X_p. Let $S \subseteq TR$ be the subset of selected samples that resulted from the execution of a PS algorithm, then we classify a new pattern from TS by the 1-NN rule acting over S. The whole data set is noted as D and it is composed by the union of TR and TS.

Wilson & Martinez (2000) suggest that the determination of the k value in the k-NN classifier may depend on the proposal of the PS algorithm. Setting k greater than 1 decreases the algorithm's sensitivity to noise and tends to smoothen the decision boundaries. In some PS algorithms, a value k > 1 may be convenient, when the interest lies in protecting the classification task of noisy instances. In any case, Wilson states that it may be appropriate to find a value of k to use during the reduction process, and then re-determine the best value of k in the classification task. In EPS we have used the value k = 1, given that EAs need to have the greatest possible sensitivity to noise during the reduction process. In this manner, an EPS algorithm can better detect the noisy instances and the redundant ones in order to find a good subset of instances perfectly adapted to the simplest method of the nearest neighbors. By considering only an instance during the evolutionary process, the reduction-accuracy trade-off is more balanced and the efficiency is improved. The implication of this fact is the use of k = 1 in the classification, as Wilson points out.

Considering the size of the data sets, any algorithm is affected when the size of the problem it is applied to increases. This is the Scaling Up problem leading to:

- Excessive storage requirements.
- Increment of time complexity.
- Decrement of generalization capacity, introducing noise and over-fitting.

A way of avoiding the drawbacks of this problem was proposed in Cano et al. (2005), where a stratified strategy divides the initial data set into disjoint strata with equal class distribution. The number of strata chosen will determine their size, depending on the size of the data set. Using the proper number of strata we can significantly reduce the training set and avoid the drawbacks mentioned above. This proper number is fixed empirically.

Following the stratified strategy, the initial data set D is divided into t disjoint sets D_j, strata of equal size, $D_1, D_2, ..., D_t$ maintaining class distribution within each subset. Then, PS algorithms will be applied to each D_j obtaining a selected subset DS_j. Stratified Prototype Subset Selected (SPSS) is defined as:

$$SPSS = \bigcup_{j \in J} DS_j, \{1, 2, .., t\}$$
$$TS = D / \bigcup D_j$$

(1)

The nearest neighbor classifier is then evaluated using the SPSS set as the training set, and the TS set as test. PS has been used in the past for training set selection. A possible way to improve the behavior of predictive models, their precision and interpretability, is to extract them from suitable reduced or selected training sets. Training set selection can be developed using PS algorithms. In Sebban & Nock (2000), they study the effect of the learning set size in decision trees performances.

STATE-OF-THE-ART OF EVOLUTIONARY PROTOTYPE SELECTION

The necessity of the EPS algorithms is discussed in Cano et al. (2003), where the authors differentiate between the selection based on heuristics (which appears in classic non-evolutionary PS algorithms, like for example CNN, IB3 or DROP described in Wilson & Martinez (2000)) and the selection developed by EPS algorithms. EPS presents a strategy that combines inner and boundary points. It does not tend to select instances depending on their a priori position in the search space (inner class or limit ones). EPS selects the instances that increase the accuracy rates independently of their a priori position.

The EPS algorithms consider a population of chromosomes which evolve to reach the solution. The chromosomes are generally binary in nature. A chromosome consists of n genes (one for each instance in the training set) with two possible states: 0 and 1. If the gene is 1, then its associated instance is included in the subset selected. If it is 0, then this does not occur.

In this section, we will review the some important works that have included or proposed an EPS model. The first appearance of the application of an EA to the PS problem can be found in Kuncheva (1995). Kuncheva applied a Genetic Algorithm (GA) to select a reference set for the k-NN rule. Her GA maps the TR set onto a chromosome structure composed of genes, each with two possible states (binary representation). The computed fitness function measures the error rate by the application of the k-NN rule. This GA was improved in Kuncheva & Bezdek (1998) and Ishibuchi & Nakashima (1999).

At this point, all EPS algorithms considered above adapt a classical GA model to the PS problem. Later, EPS algorithms more conditioned to the problem were developed. The first example of this can be found in Sierra et al. (2001). In this paper, an Estimation of Distribution Algorithm (EDA) is used.

A GA design for obtaining an optimal nearest neighbor classifier based on orthogonal arrays is proposed in Ho et al. (2002). Then, the technical term EPS has been adopted by Cano et al. (2003), in which they analyze the behavior of different EAs, steady-state GAs (SSGAs), GGAs, the CHC model (Eshelman, 1991) and PBIL (Baluja, 1994). The representation of solutions as chromosomes follows the guidelines in Kuncheva (1995), but the fitness function used in these models combines two values: classification rate (*clas rat*) by using 1-NN classifier and percentage reduction of prototypes of S with regards to TR (*perc red*):

$$Fitness(S) = \alpha \cdot clas\ rat + (1 - \alpha) \cdot perc\ red \tag{2}$$

One of the more recent approaches is the Memetic Algorithms (MAs). They are heuristic searches in optimization problems that combine a population-based algorithm with a local search. The MA used by García et al. (2008) incorporates an ad hoc local search specifically designed for optimizing the search in prototype selection problem with the aim of tackling the scaling up problem.

As a multi-objective approach, we can find an EPS algorithm in Chen et al. (2005). The multi-objective optimization of the PS problem is beyond of the scope of this chapter and may be considered as an open problem, together with the design of mechanisms for comparing the Pareto set against a solution obtained by a single-objective GA. This is by taking into consideration the fact that the form of the Pareto front in the test set could not follow the same structure as that in the training set, which is used for the evolution process.

Figure 1. Pseudocode for the GGA Model

1.- Evaluation of individual fitness.
2.- Formation of a gene pool (intermediate population) through selection mechanism.
3.- Recombination through crossover.
4.- Mutation operator.
5.- Check termination criterion and continue in step 1.

EVOLUTIONARY PROTOTYPE SELECTION ALGORITHMS

In this section, the four models developed in Cano et al. (2003) and Eshelman (1991) together with the Intelligent Genetic Algorithm (IGA) by Ho et al. (2002) and the MA-EPS proposal by García et al. (2008) are described.

Generational Genetic Algorithm (GGA)

The basic idea in GGA (Goldberg, 2002) is to maintain a population of chromosomes, which represent plausible solutions to the particular problem that evolves over successive iterations (generations) through a process of competition and controlled variation. Each chromosome in the population has an associated fitness to determine which chromosomes are to be used to form new ones in the competition process. This process is called selection. The new chromosomes are created using genetic operators such as crossover and mutation. The classical model of GAs is the GGA (Figure 1), which consists of three operations:

The selection mechanism produces a new population P(t) with copies of chromosomes from P(t − 1). The number of copies received for each chromosome depends on its fitness; chromosomes with higher fitness usually have a greater chance of contributing copies to P(t). Then, the crossover and mutation operators are applied to P(t).

Crossover takes two individuals called parents and produces two new individuals called the offspring by swapping parts of the parents. In its simplest form, the operator works by exchanging substrings after a randomly selected crossover point. The crossover operator is usually not applied to all pairs of chromosomes in the new population. A random choice is made, where the likelihood of crossover being applied depends on probability defined by the crossover rate.

Mutation serves to prevent premature loss of population diversity by randomly sampling new points in the search space. Mutation rates are kept small, however, otherwise the process degenerates into a random search. In the case of bit strings, mutation is applied by flipping one or more random bits in a string with a probability equal to the mutation rate. Termination may be triggered by reaching a maximum number of generations or by finding an acceptable solution according to some criterion.

We must point out that the GGA described in Cano et al. (2003) is really an improved model of Kuncheva's and Ishibuchi's GGAs.

Steady-State Genetic Algorithm (SSGA)

In SSGA usually one or two offspring are produced in each generation. Parents are selected to produce offspring and then a decision is made as to which individuals in the population are to be deleted in order to make room for the new offspring. The basic algorithm steps of SSGA are shown in Figure 2.

Figure 2. Pseudocode for the SSGA Model

---

1. Select two parents from the population.
2. Create one/two offspring using crossover and mutation.
3. Evaluate the offspring with the fitness function.
4. Select one/two individuals in the population, to be replaced by the offspring.
5. Decide if this/these individuals will be replaced.
6. Check termination criterion and continue in step 1.

In step 4, one can choose the replacement strategy (e.g., replacement of the worst, the oldest, or a randomly chosen individual), and step 5, the replacement condition (e.g., replacement if the new individual is better, or unconditional replacement). A widely used combination is to replace the worst individual only if the new individual is better. We will call this strategy the standard replacement strategy. In Goldberg & Deb (1991), it was suggested that the deletion of the worst individuals induced a high selective pressure, even when the parents were selected randomly.

Population-Based Incremental Learning (PBIL)

PBIL (Baluja, 1994) is a specific EDA designed for binary search spaces. The PBIL algorithm attempts to explicitly maintain statistics about the search space to decide where to sample next.

The objective of the algorithm is to create a real valued probability vector Vp, which, when sampled, reveals high quality solution vectors with high probability. For example, if a good solution can be encoded as a string of alternating 0s and 1s, a possible final Vp would be 0.01, 0.99, 0.01, 0.99, etc. Initially, the values of Vp are set to 0.5. Sampling from this vector yields random solution vectors because the

Figure 3. Pseudocode for the PBIL Model

---

1. A number of solution vectors (N samples) are generated based on the probabilities specified in Vp.
2. Vp is pushed toward the generated solution vector with the highest evaluation Sbest: Vp[i] = Vp[i] · (1 − LR) + Sbest[i] · LR, where LR is the learning rate which specifies how close the steps are to the best solution.
3. Vp is pushed far away from the worst evaluation, Sworse, where Sbest and Sworse differ in the following way:

If Sbest[i] <> Sworse[i] then
$$Vp[i] = Vp[i] \cdot (1 - Negat_{LR}) + Sbest[i] \cdot Negat\_LR$$

Negat_LR is the negative learning rate, which specifies how far away the steps are from the worst solution.
4. After the probability vector is updated, sampling the updated probability vector produces a new set of solution vectors, and the cycle is continued.

Figure 4. Pseudocode of CHC algorithm

---

1. t=0
2. Initialize(Pa ,ConvergenceCount)
3. While not TerminationCriterion(t,Pa) do
    4. Parents = SelectionParents(Pa)
    5. Offspring = HUX(Parents)
    6. Evaluate(Offspring)
    7. Pn = ElitistSelection(Offspring,Pa)
    8. If not modified(Pa ,Pn) then
        9. ConvergenceCount = ConvergenceCount - 1
        10. if ConvergenceCount = 0 then
            11. Pn = Restart(Pa)
            12. Initialize(ConvergenceCount)
        13. end if
    14. end if
    15. t = t + 1
    16. Pa = Pn
17. end while

---

probability of generating a 1 or 0 is equal. As the search progresses, the values of Vp gradually shift to represent high evaluation solution vectors through the following process.

The pseudocode of PBIL is available in Figure 3.

Furthermore, PBIL applies mutations to Vp, with an aim similar to mutation in the case of GAs: to inhibit premature convergence. Mutations affect Vp with low probability Pm in a random direction noted as MutShif.

CHC

During each generation the CHC (Eshelman, 1991) develops the following steps (see Figure 4). Where Pa is the initial population, Pn is the population at iteration n, and ConvergenceCount is the counter used to measure the convergence.

CHC also implements a form of heterogeneous recombination using HUX, a special recombination operator. HUX exchanges half of the bits that differ between parents, where the bit position to be exchanged is randomly determined. CHC also employs a method of incest prevention. Before applying HUX to two parents, the Hamming distance between them is measured. Only those parents who differ from each other by at least some number of bits (mating threshold) are mated. The initial threshold is set to L/4, where L is the length of the chromosomes. If no offspring are inserted into the new population then the threshold is reduced by one.

No mutation is applied during the recombination phase. Instead, when the population converges or the search stops making progress (i.e., the difference of threshold has dropped to zero, and no new offspring are being generated which are better than any members of the parent population), the population is reinitialized to introduce diversity in the search process. The chromosome representing the best

Figure 5. Pseudocode for the IGA Model

---

1. Initialization. Randomly generate an initial population with Npop individuals.
2. Evaluation. Evaluate the fitness function values of all individuals.
3. Selection. Use the rank selection method that replaces the worst Ps Npop individuals to form a new population, where Ps is the selection probability.
4. Crossover. Randomly select Pc Npop individuals to perform IC, where Pc is the crossover probability
5. Mutation. Apply the conventional bit-inverse mutation operator to the population using a mutation probability Pm. The best individual is retained without being subject to the mutation operation.
6. Termination Criterion. If a pre-specified termination condition is met, end the algorithm. Otherwise, go to Step 2.

---

solution found over the course of the search is used as a template to reseed the population. Reseeding of the population is accomplished by randomly changing 35% of the bits in the template chromosome to form each of the other N − 1 new chromosomes in the population. The search is then resumed.

Intelligent Genetic Algorithm (IGA)

Ho et al. (2002) propose IGA based on the Orthogonal experimental design used for PS and Feature Selection. In order to prepare IGA to be applied as a PS method only, we ignore its feature selection functionality. IGA is basically a GGA that incorporates an Intelligent Crossover (IC) operator. IC builds an Orthogonal Array (OA) from the parents and searches within the OA for the two best individuals according to the fitness function. It takes about $2 \log_2 (\gamma+1)$ fitness evaluations to perform an IC operation, where γ is the number of bits that differ between both parents. Note that the application of IC on large-size chromosomes (resulting chromosomes from large size data sets) would require a high number of evaluations. The basic algorithm steps of IGA are shown in Figure 5.

Steady-State Memetic Algorithm (SSMA)

García et al. (2008) make use of a local search (LS) or meme specifically developed for the PS problem. SSMAs integrate global and local searches more tightly than generational memetic algorithms. This interweaving of the global and local search phases allows the two to influence each other, e.g., the SSGA chooses good starting points, and LS provides an accurate representation of that region of the domain. This LS scheme assigns a probability value to each chromosome generated by crossover and mutation, c_{new}:

$$P_{LS} = \begin{cases} 1, & if \ f(C_{new}) \ is \ better \ than \ f(C_{worst}) \\ 0.625 & otherwise \end{cases}$$

(3)

Figure 6. Pseudocode for the SSMA

---

1. Initialize population.
2. While (not termination criterion) do
    3. Use Binary Tournament to select two parents
    4. Apply crossover operator to create offspring (Off1 , Off2)
    5. Apply mutation to Off1 and Of f2
    6. Evaluate Off1 and Off2
    7. For each Offi
        8. Invoke Adaptive-P_{LS} -mechanism to obtain P_{LSi} for Offi
        9. If $u(0, 1) < P_{LSi}$ then
            10. Perform meme optimization for Offi
        11. End if
    12. End for
    13. Employ standard replacement for Off1 and Off2
14. End while
15. Return the best chromosome

---

where f is the fitness function and C_{worst} is the current worst element in the population. As was observed by Hart (1994), applying LS to as little of 5% of each population results in a faster convergence toward good solutions.

Figure 6 shows the SSMA pseudocode.

Note that $u(0,1)$ is a value in the uniform distribution [0,1] and 'standard replacement' means that the worst individual is replaced only if the new individual is better. The Adaptive-P_{LS} –mechanism is an adaptive fitness-based method (García et al., 2008). A brief description of the meme specifically developed for the prototype selection task is shown in Figure 9 in the Appendix section.

EXPERIMENTAL STUDY

This section presents the framework used in the experimental study carried out together with the results obtained. To scale the problem appropriately, we have used three sizes of data sets: small, medium and large. We intend to study the behavior of the algorithms when the size of the data set increases. When considering large data sets, a stratification process (Cano et al., 2005) is used for obtaining strata of medium size. The small-size data sets are summarized in Table 1 and medium and large data sets can be seen in Table 2. The data sets have been taken from the UCI Machine Learning Database Repository (Asuncion & Newman, 2007).

We will distinguish two models of partitions used in this work:

- Ten fold cross-validation classic (Tfcv classic): where TR_i, i = 1, ..., 10 is 90% of D and TS_i is its complementary 10% of D, with D being the initial data set. It is obtained as Equations 4 and 5 indicate.

Table 1. Small Data Sets Characteristics

Name	N. Instances	N. Features.	N. Classes
Bupa	345	7	2
Cleveland	297	13	5
Glass	294	9	7
Iris	150	4	3
Led7Digit	500	7	10
Lymphography	148	18	4
Monks	432	6	2
Pima	768	8	2
Wine	178	13	3
Wisconsin	683	9	2

Table 2. Medium and Large Data Sets Characteristics

Name	N. Instances	N. Features.	N. Classes
Nursery	12960	8	5
Page-Blocks	5476	10	5
Pen-Based	10992	16	10
Ringnorm	7400	20	2
Satimage	6435	36	7
SpamBase	4597	57	2
Splice	3190	60	3
Thyroid	7200	21	3
Adult (large)	45222	14	2

$$TR_i = \bigcup_{j \in J} D_j, J = \{ J \mid \quad 1 \le j \le (i-1) and (i+1) \le j \le 10 \}$$

$$\quad (4)$$

$$TS_i = D \setminus TR_i$$

$$\quad (5)$$

- Ten fold cross validation strat (Tfcv strat (Cano et al., 2005)): where SPSSi is generated using the DS_j instead of D_j. Following the stratified strategy, the initial data set D is divided into t disjoint sets D_j, strata of equal size, D_1, D_2, ..., D_t maintaining class distribution within each subset. Then, the PS algorithms will be applied to each D_j obtaining a selected subset DS_j. Stratified Prototype Subset Selected (SPSS) is defined as:

$$SPSS_i = \bigcup_{j \in J} DS_j, J = \{ j \mid 1 \le j \le b \cdot (i-1) and (i \cdot b) + 1 \le j \le t \}$$

$$\quad (6)$$

Table 3. Parameters used in PS Algorithms

Algorithm	Parameters
CHC	Pop = 50, Eval = 10000, α = 0.5
IGA	Pop = 10, Eval = 10000
GGA	pm = 0.01, α = 0.5
PBIL	Pm = 0.001, Pc = 0.6, Pop = 50
SSGA	Eval = 10000, α = 0.5
SSMA	LR = 0.1, Mutshift = 0.05, pm = 0.02, Pop = 50

The data sets considered are partitioned using the tfcv classic (see Equations 4 and 5) except for the Adult data set, which is partitioned using the tfcv strat procedure with t = 10 and b = 1 (see Equation 6). The algorithms have been run for 3 trials over each partition and we show the average results over these trials.

Whether small, medium or large data sets are evaluated, the parameters used are the same, as specified in Table 3. They are specified by following the indications given by their respective authors. With respect to the standard EAs employed in the study, GGA and SSGA, the selection strategy is the binary tournament. The mutation operator is the same as used in SSMA. In the SSGA experiments, we use the standard replacement strategy given in Goldberg & Deb (1991). The crossover operator used by both the algorithms defines two cut points and interchanges the substrings of bits.

To compare the results, we propose the use of non-parametric tests, according to the recommendations made by Demsar (2006). They are safer than parametric tests since they do not assume normal distribution or homogeneity of variance. As such, these non-parametric tests can be applied to classification accuracies, error ratios or any other measure for evaluation of classifiers, even including model sizes and computation times. Empirical results suggest that they are also stronger than the parametric test. Demsar recommends a set of simple, safe, and robust non-parametric tests for statistical comparisons of classifiers. We will use two tests for different purposes: the first is the Iman and Davenport test (Iman & Davenport, 1980), derived from the Friedman test, which is equivalent to the repeated-measures ANOVA. Under the null-hypothesis, which states that all the algorithms are equivalent, a rejection of this hypothesis implies the existence of differences in performance among the algorithms studied; the second is the Wilcoxon Signed-Ranks test (Sheskin, 2003) - this is analogous to the paired t-test in non-parametrical statistical procedures. Therefore, it is a pairwise test that aims to detect significant differences in the behavior of two algorithms. We will present three types of tables according to the subsequent structure.

The complete results' tables show the average of the results obtained by each algorithm in all the evaluated data sets (small or medium group of data sets). These tables are grouped in columns by the algorithms. For each algorithm, they show the average reduction, accuracy in training and accuracy in test data with their respective standard deviations (see for example Tables 4 and 5). The last two rows compute the average and the standard deviation over the average results obtained on each data set, respectively.

Wilcoxon's test tables for n×n comparisons: Given that the evaluation of only the mean classification accuracy over all the data sets would hide important information and that each data set represents a different classification problem with different degrees of difficulty, we have included a second type of table that shows a statistical comparison of methods over multiple data sets. As we have mentioned, Demsar

(2006) recommends a set of simple, safe, and robust non-parametric tests for statistical comparison of classifiers, one of which is the Wilcoxon Signed-Ranks test (Sheskin, 2003). In our study, we always consider a level of significance of $\alpha < 0.05$. Let d_i be the difference between the performance scores of the two classifiers on i-th out of N data sets. The differences are ranked according to their absolute values; average ranks are assigned in case of ties. Let R+ be the sum of the ranks for the data sets in which the second algorithm outperformed the first, and R− the sum of ranks for the opposite. Ranks of $d_i = 0$ are split evenly among the sums; if there are an odd number of them, one is ignored:

$$R+ = \sum_{d_i>0} rank(d_i) + \frac{1}{2}\sum_{d_i=0} rank(d_i) \tag{7}$$

$$R- = \sum_{d_i<0} rank(d_i) + \frac{1}{2}\sum_{d_i=0} rank(d_i) \tag{8}$$

Let T be the smaller one of the sums, $T = \min(R+, R-)$.

The Wilcoxon signed ranks test is more sensitive than the t-test. It assumes commensurability of differences, but only qualitatively: greater differences are still valued more, which is probably to be desired, but absolute magnitudes are ignored. From the statistical point of view, the test is safer since it does not assume normal distributions. Also outliers (exceptionally good/bad performances on a few data sets) have less effect on Wilcoxon's signed rank test than on the t-test. Wilcoxon's test assumes continuous differences di, which therefore should not be rounded to, say, one or two decimal places since this would decrease the power of the test due to a high number of ties. A Wilcoxon table (see Table 7), in this chapter, is divided into two parts: in the first part, we carry out a Wilcoxon test using the accuracy classification in the test set as the performance measure; while in the second part, a balance of reduction and classification accuracy is used as the performance measure. This balance corresponds to 0.5 · clas rat + 0.5 · perc red. The structure of the tables presents Nalg × (Nalg + 2) cells to compare all the algorithms in them. In each of the Nalg × Nalg cells three symbols can appear: +, - or =. They show that the algorithm situated in that row is better (+), worse (-) or equal (=) in behavior (accuracy or balance accuracy-reduction) to the algorithm that appears in the column. The penultimate column represents the number of algorithms with worse or equal behavior to the one that appears in the row (without considering the algorithm itself) and the last column represents the number of algorithms with worse behavior than the one that appears in the row.

Computation of Iman and Davenport statistic tables: We follow the indications given in Demsar (2006) by carrying out Iman and Davenport test. This test ranks the algorithms for each data set separately, starting by assigning the rank of 1 to the best performing algorithm. Let r_i be the rank of the j-th of k algorithms on the i-th of N data sets. The Iman and Davenport statistic is defined as:

$$F_F = \frac{(N-1)x_F^2}{N(k-1) - x_F^2} \tag{9}$$

$$x_F^2 = \frac{12N}{k(k+1)}\left[\sum_j \left(\frac{1}{N}\sum_i r_i^j\right)^2 - \frac{k(k+1)^2}{4}\right] \tag{10}$$

where X_F is the Friedman statistic and F_F is distributed according to the F-distribution with $k - 1$ and $(k - 1)(N - 1)$ degrees of freedom.

These tables are made up of four columns (see Table 6). In the first and the second columns, information about the conditions of the experiment is indicated: the type of result that is measured and the scale of the data sets, respectively. In the third column, the computed value of F_F is shown and, in the last column, the corresponding critical value of the F-distribution table with $\alpha = 0.05$ is indicated. If the value F_F is higher than its associated critical value, then the null-hypothesis is rejected (this implies a significant difference in results among all methods considered).

We divide the experimental study into three parts: The comparison among EPS algorithms, the analysis of their behavior in a large size training data set case, and a study of the time complexity for EPS.

Part I: Analysis of Evolutionary Prototype Selection Algorithms

In this section, we carry out a comparison that includes all EPS algorithms described in this chapter. Tables 4 and 5 show the average results for EPS algorithms run over the small and medium data sets respectively. The values in bold denote the best results.

The results of the Iman and Davenport test are presented in Table 6. Tables 7 and 8 present the statistical differences according to Wilcoxon's test among EPS algorithms, considering accuracy performance and accuracy-reduction balance performance respectively.

The following conclusions from examination of Tables 4 to 8 can be pointed out:

- In Table 4, SSMA achieves the best test accuracy rate. EPS algorithms are prone to over-fitting and thus, obtain a good accuracy in the training data but not in the test data. The SSMA proposal does not remark this behavior in a noticeable way.
- When the problem scales up, in Table 5, SSMA presents the best reduction and accuracy in the training and test data rates.
- The Iman-Davenport statistic (presented in Table 6) indicates the existence of significant differences in results among all EPS approaches studied.
- Considering only the performance in classification over test data in Table 7, all algorithms are very competitive. Statistically, SSMA always obtains subsets of prototypes with equal performance to the remaining EPS methods, improving GGA with the use of small databases and GGA and CHC when the problem scales up to a medium size.
- When the reduction objective is included in the measure of quality, in Table 8, SSMA obtains the best result. Only CHC presents the same behavior in small data sets. When the problem scales up, SSMA again outperforms CHC.

Part II: A Large Case Study

We have seen the promising results offered by SSMA in small and medium sized databases. However, a size limit of data sets exists which makes the execution of an EPS algorithm over them impossible. This limit depends on the algorithms employed, the properties of data treated and the easiness of reduction of instances in the data set. We could argue that, surely, it may not be possible to handle a data set consisting of more than 20,000 instances with EPS due to the time complexity of the evaluations of

Table 4. Average Results for EPS Algorithms over Small Data Sets

Data set	Measure	CHC Red.	CHC Tra.	CHC Tst.	GGA Red.	GGA Tra.	GGA Tst.	IGA Red.	IGA Tra.	IGA Tst.	PBIL Red.	PBIL Tra.	PBIL Tst.	SSGA Red.	SSGA Tra.	SSGA Tst.	SSMA Red.	SSMA Tra.	SSMA Tst.
Bupa	Mean	97.13	73.24	58.76	92.27	78.58	59.57	81.61	83.09	63.69	91.3	78.39	64.61	90.82	79.19	62.25	95.01	76.55	63.99
	Std.dev.	0.81	1.49	6.75	1.48	1.1	7.39	1.93	1.47	9.27	0.91	1.05	4.64	1.87	1.67	7.18	0.72	1.41	4.11
Cleveland	Mean	98.35	63.48	58.75	95.45	64.76	54.8	86.32	68.72	51.49	94.94	64.98	55.77	94.02	65.16	52.52	97.84	63.51	57.47
	Std.dev.	0.3	0.92	5.91	0.87	1	5.45	2.15	1.03	7.16	0.83	0.8	4.94	1.09	1.45	6.29	0.72	0.92	6.51
Glass	Mean	94.34	74.04	65.39	90.91	76.44	65.87	80.74	82.55	68.89	91.06	76.18	64.58	90.34	75.86	65.83	92.58	76.12	66.07
	Std.dev.	0.86	1.51	9.97	0.99	1.91	13.28	1.82	1.65	0.7	1.66	2.36	9.49	1.69	1.94	12.37	1.32	1.74	10.51
Iris	Mean	96.81	97.41	96.67	95.56	97.63	94	93.33	98.81	94	96.07	98.07	96	95.41	97.41	95.33	96.07	97.93	95.33
	Std.dev.	0.47	0.76	3.33	0.33	0.55	4.67	0.66	0.49	3.59	0.58	0.76	4.42	0.93	0.68	4.27	0.67	1.4	5.21
Lec7Digit	Mean	96.58	68.71	64	95.64	68.64	63.8	95.16	65.89	67.6	93.91	68.67	66	95.71	66.44	64.8	96.71	54.11	75.4
	Std.dev.	0.18	2.88	7.32	0.18	3.27	4.85	0.33	2.21	4.18	0.78	3.09	2.53	0.37	3.18	5.15	0.45	8.78	4.29
Lymphography	Mean	96.55	54.36	39.49	91.96	57.21	35.26	86.27	60.59	40.57	94.75	54.88	41.71	92.33	55.57	43.62	94.67	55.78	42.88
	Std.dev.	0.68	1.42	9.99	1.5	1.52	9.83	2.2	2.35	11.1	1.31	1.92	13.85	2.32	3.11	9.94	1.52	2.51	12.12
Monks	Mean	99.05	96.86	97.27	93.98	94.62	92.3	84.83	98.15	85.75	92.34	94.57	89.17	92.31	94.88	93.39	97.66	97.22	96.58
	Std.dev.	0.23	0.42	2.65	0.73	0.99	3.71	1.61	0.81	6.98	1.13	1.31	7.15	1.08	1.27	3.72	1.27	1.31	3.26
Pima	Mean	98.78	80.14	75.53	95.11	81.57	70.73	86	86.81	70.84	91.9	82.03	72.27	94.23	83.02	73.32	97.38	82.15	73.21
	Std.dev.	0.28	0.87	3.11	0.75	0.7	4.87	0.71	0.78	2.68	0.49	0.57	2.96	0.64	0.97	4.53	0.68	0.67	5.5
Wine	Mean	96.94	98.69	94.93	95.69	98.69	93.82	93.76	99.88	94.97	96.32	98.63	94.41	94.69	98.69	97.19	96.44	98.69	93.82
	Std.dev.	0.51	0.81	4.62	0.71	0.9	4.61	1.01	0.25	6.78	0.59	0.73	5.56	1.29	0.81	3.75	0.68	0.34	6.31
Wisconsin	Mean	99.44	97.57	96.56	99.08	97.71	96	98.22	98.04	95.28	98.54	97.66	96.99	99.06	97.76	96.57	99.38	97.65	96.57
	Std.dev.	0.08	0.28	2.42	0.2	0.18	2.46	0.42	0.23	3.33	0.28	0.23	1.86	0.26	0.25	3.08	0.09	0.19	2.32
GLOBAL	Mean	**97.40**	80.45	74.74	94.57	81.59	72.62	88.62	**84.25**	73.31	94.11	81.41	74.15	93.89	81.4	74.48	96.38	79.97	**76.13**
	Std.dev.	1.53	16.27	20.63	2.37	15.13	20.69	6.03	14.86	18.95	2.47	15.58	19.08	2.58	15.63	19.86	1.92	17.76	18.94

Table 5. *Average Results for EPS Algorithms over Medium Data Sets*

Data set	Measure	CHC			GGA			IGA			PBIL			SSGA			SSMA		
		Red.	Tra.	Tst.	Red.	Tra.	Tst.	Red.	Tra.	Tst.	Red.	Tra.	Tst.	Red.	Tra.	Tst.	Red.	Tra.	Tst.
Nursery	Mean	93.6	74.98	74.07	88.62	82.78	80.55	69.54	87.78	82.88	79.99	86.43	83.46	90.16	84,96	80,56	94,07	88,07	85,28
	Std.dev.	0.82	0.88	1.98	0.24	0.32	0.94	0.19	0.17	1.1	0.23	0.21	0.92	0.17	0,27	0,79	0,89	0,24	0,81
Page-Blocks	Mean	99.66	94.84	94.32	93.15	95.7	94.99	73.34	96.5	95.39	85.75	96.04	95.41	96.77	96,11	95,12	99,18	96,03	95,05
	Std.dev.	0.04	0.24	0.79	0.21	0.17	0.83	0.28	0.13	0.8	0.29	0.14	0.51	0.16	0,19	0,75	0,09	0,12	1,03
Pen-Based	Mean	98.91	95.87	95.87	91.65	98.7	98.27	73.95	99.32	98.94	83.32	99.08	98.74	95.27	98,95	98,37	98,56	98,74	98,04
	Std.dev.	0.12	0.29	0.62	0.2	0.11	0.32	0.55	0.08	0.28	0.15	0.1	0.35	0.07	0,12	0,29	0,28	0,16	0,6
Ring	Mean	99.59	88.08	87.7	90.14	80.11	77.45	67.11	82.66	77.07	81.08	81.64	76.65	93.31	87,71	84,36	98,88	95,53	92,66
	Std.dev.	0.05	1.07	1.51	0.28	0.44	1.66	0.17	0.25	0.82	0.2	0.39	1.17	0.22	0,44	0,94	0,13	0,38	0,89
Satimage	Mean	99.51	87.63	86.59	91.58	90.64	88.7	71.14	92.14	89.25	83.88	91.34	88.97	94.84	91,77	88,95	98,36	91,98	89,39
	Std.dev.	0.1	0.32	0.9	0.24	0.21	1.01	0.52	0.25	1.3	0.32	0.27	1.16	0.21	0,23	1,31	0,23	0,35	0,89
Spambase	Mean	99.53	87.63	86.84	91.71	89.39	87.3	68.7	91.08	87.82	84.76	90.53	87.77	94.79	90,94	87,64	98,12	91,23	88,3
	Std.dev.	0.05	0.9	1.64	0.29	0.52	1.68	0.46	0.36	1.46	0.43	0.44	0.9	0.24	0,42	2,18	0,22	0,55	1,49
Splice	Mean	99.14	75.41	71.57	91.13	78.96	72.51	65.28	80.95	73.73	83.9	80.92	74.11	93.07	83,16	72,92	97,04	83,6	74,7
	Std.dev.	0.16	0.76	1.66	0.53	0.83	2.7	0.62	0.37	1.52	0.5	0.44	1.57	0.49	0,5	1,84	0,48	0,38	2,67
Thyroid	Mean	99.9	92.72	92.53	92.45	93.64	93.32	71.71	93.16	91.94	84.38	93.51	93.1	96.65	93,78	93,58	99,83	94,32	93,82
	Std.dev.	0.03	2.51	2.45	0.18	0.3	0.5	0.27	0.18	0.71	0.29	0.16	0.81	0.16	0,2	0,5	0,07	0,14	0,54
GLOBAL	Mean	**98.73**	87.15	86.19	91.3	83.74	86.64	70.1	90.45	87.13	83.38	89.94	87.28	94.36	90,92	87,69	98,01	**92,44**	**89,66**
	Std.dev.	2.1	8.05	8.97	1.4	7.38	9.07	3.01	6.37	8.74	1.92	6.53	8.75	2.16	5,43	8,33	1,79	4,85	7,28

Table 6. Iman and Davenport Statistic for EPS Algorithms

Performance	Scale	F	Critical Value
Accuracy	Small	2.568	2.422
Accuracy	Medium	5.645	2.485
Accuracy-Reduction	Small	14.936	2.422
Accuracy-Reduction	Medium	179.667	2.485

Table 7. Wilcoxon Table for EPS Algorithms Considering Accuracy Performance

Small Data Sets								
	6	5	4	3	2	1	>=	>
CHC (1)	=	=	=	=	+		5	1
GGA (2)	-	-	=	=		-	2	0
IGA (3)	=	=	=		=	=	5	0
PBIL (4)	=	=		=	=	=	5	0
SSGA (5)	=		=	=	+	=	5	1
SSMA (6)		=	=	=	+	=	5	1
Medium Data Sets								
	6	5	4	3	2	1	>=	>
CHC (1)	-	=	=	=	=		4	0
GGA (2)	-	-	=	=		=	3	0
IGA (3)	=	=	=		=	=	5	0
PBIL (4)	=	=		=	=	=	5	0
SSGA (5)	=		=	=	+	=	5	1
SSMA (6)		=	=	=	+	+	5	2

$O(n^2m)$, n being the number of instances and m the number of features. The SSMA proposal may have this limitation.

In this case, Cano et al. (2005) recommend the use of stratification, which could be combined with a cross-validation procedure as can be seen in Equation 6. By using the Tfcv-Strat, we have run the algorithms considered in this study over the Adult data set with t = 10 and b = 1. We chose these parameters to obtain subsets whose size is not too large as well as to show the effectiveness of the combination of an EPS and the stratification procedure.

Figure 7 shows a representation of the two objectives: reduction and test accuracy. Each algorithm located in the graph gets its position from the average values of each measure evaluated (exact position corresponding to the beginning of the name of the algorithm). Across the graph, there is a line that represents the threshold of test accuracy achieved by the 1-NN algorithm without preprocessing.

As we can see, all EPS methods are above the 1-NN horizontal line. The graph clearly emphasizes three methods as the best with their position at top-right in the graph. In addition to this, we can remark that the SSMA algorithm achieves the highest accuracy rate, and it is only surpassed in the reduction objective by the CHC model.

Table 8. Wilcoxon Table for EPS Algorithms Considering Reduction-Accuracy Balance Performance

Small Data Sets	6	5	4	3	2	1	>=	>
CHC (1)	=	+	+	+	+		5	4
GGA (2)	-	=	=	+		-	3	1
IGA (3)	-	-	-		-	-	0	0
PBIL (4)	-	=		+	=	-	3	1
SSGA (5)	-		=	+	=	-	3	1
SSMA (6)		+	+	+	+	=	5	4
Medium Data Sets	6	5	4	3	2	1	>=	>
CHC (1)	-	=	+	+	+		4	3
GGA (2)	-	-	+	+		-	2	2
IGA (3)	-	-	-		-	-	0	0
PBIL (4)	-	-		+	-	-	1	1
SSGA (5)	-		+	+	+	=	4	3
SSMA (6)		+	+	+	+	+	5	5

Figure 7. Accuracy in test vs. reduction in adult data set for EPS algorithms

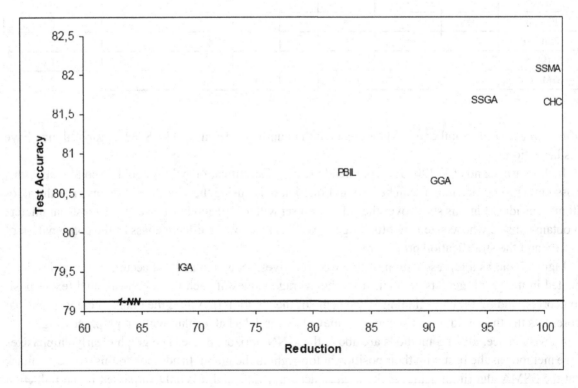

Figure 8. Run-time in seconds for EPS over medium size data sets

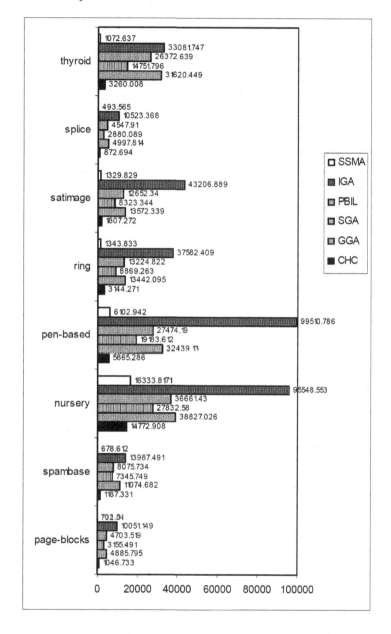

Part III: Time Complexity Analysis for EPS

A way of estimating the efficiency of EPS algorithms is to conduct an empirical study. This implies a study of the execution time of each method by using different sizes of training data. We have shown the results obtained by using a graphical representation in Figure 8 for medium size data sets.

As can be seen in Figure 8, the most efficient EPS algorithms are SSMA and CHC. Time complexity of an algorithm basically depends on two factors:

- Reduction Capacity: When an EPS algorithm can quickly reduce the subset of instances selected in the chromosome, an evaluation will have to compute the nearest neighbors over less data in order to calculate the fitness value. CHC and SSMA are inclined toward the tendency of removing instances and then improving classification accuracy, thus obtaining a good reduction rate. Remaining EPS algorithms try to improve both objectives simultaneously.
- Operational Cost: In this case, any algorithm has an operational cost of time in all its procedures. For example, a GGA algorithm must sort and apply crossover and mutation operators to a part of the population, whereas PBIL must generate new populations from a single probability vector that receives all possible modifications. This explains why GGA takes more time than PBIL even if the former has a higher reduction rate than the latter. SSMA takes advantage of the partial evaluation mechanism, which is an efficient procedure to evaluate chromosomes.

CONCLUSION

This chapter presented a review and analysis of Evolutionary Prototype Selection and their application over different sizes of data sets, paying special attention to the scaling up problem. An experimental study was carried out to establish a comparison among the evolutionary approaches studied in the literature. The main conclusions reached are as follows:

- The SSMA exhibits a good reduction rate and computational time with respect to other EPS schemes.
- When the PS problem scales up, the tendency on the part of classical EPS is to inappropriately converge to two objectives (accuracy and reduction) at the same time.
- Considering all types of data sets, SSMA outperforms or equals all methods when both objectives have the same importance. Furthermore, in terms of test accuracy, it usually outperforms other methods that obtain good rates of reduction.

Finally, we would like to conclude that the SSMA proposal allows EPS to be competitive when the size of the databases increases, tackling the scaling up problem with excellent results.

REFERENCES

Asuncion, A., & Newman, D. J. (2007). *UCI repository of machine learning databases*. Retrieved September 25, 2008, from http://archive.ics.uci.edu/ml/

Baluja, S. (1994). *Population-based incremental learning: A method for integrating genetic search based function optimization and competitive learning* (Tech. Rep. CMU-CS-94-163). Pittsburgh, PA, USA.

Cano, J. R., Herrera, F., & Lozano, M. (2003). Using evolutionary algorithms as instance selection for data reduction in KDD: An experimental study. *IEEE Transactions on Evolutionary Computation, 7*(6), 561–575. doi:10.1109/TEVC.2003.819265

Cano, J. R., Herrera, F., & Lozano, M. (2005). Stratification for scaling up evolutionary prototype selection. *Pattern Recognition Letters, 26*(7), 953–963. doi:10.1016/j.patrec.2004.09.043

Chen, J.-H., Chen, H.-M., & Ho, S.-Y. (2005). Design of nearest neighbor classifiers: Multi-objective approach. *International Journal of Approximate Reasoning, 40*(1-2), 3–22. doi:10.1016/j.ijar.2004.11.009

Demsar, J. (2006). Statistical comparisons of classifiers over multiple data sets. *Journal of Machine Learning Research, 7*, 1–30.

Eshelman, L. J. (1991). The CHC adaptative search algorithm: How to have safe search when engaging in nontraditional genetic recombination. In G. J. E. Rawlins (Ed.), *Foundations of genetic algorithms* (pp. 265-283).

Freitas, A. A. (2002). *Data mining and knowledge discovery with evolutionary algorithms*. Berlin, Germany: Springer-Verlag.

García, S., Cano, J. R., & Herrera, F. (2008). A memetic algorithm for evolutionary prototype selection: A scaling up approach. *Pattern Recognition, 41*(8), 2693–2709. doi:10.1016/j.patcog.2008.02.006

García-Pedrajas, N., & Ortiz-Boyer, D. (2007). A cooperative constructive method for neural networks for pattern recognition. *Pattern Recognition, 40*(1), 80–98. doi:10.1016/j.patcog.2006.06.024

Ghosh, A., & Jain, L. C. (Eds.). (2005). *Evolutionary computation in data mining*. Berlin, Germany: Springer-Verlag.

Goldberg, D. E. (2002). *The design of competent genetic algorithms: Steps toward a computational theory of innovation*. Amsterdam: Kluwer Academic Publishers.

Goldberg, D. E., & Deb, K. (1991). A comparative analysis of selection schemes used in genetic algorithms. In G. J. E. Rawlins (Ed.), *Foundations of genetic algorithms* (pp. 69-93).

Gómez-Ballester, E., Micó, L., & Oncina, J. (2006). Some approaches to improve tree-based nearest neighbour search algorithms. *Pattern Recognition, 39*(2), 171–179. doi:10.1016/j.patcog.2005.06.007

Grochowski, M., & Jankowski, N. (2004). Comparison of instance selection algorithms II. Results and comments. In *Proceedings of the International Conference on Artificial Intelligence and Soft Computing* (LNCS 3070, pp. 580-585). Berlin, Germany: Springer-Verlag.

Hart, W. E. (1994). *Adaptive global optimization with local search*. Unpublished doctoral dissertation, University of California, San Diego.

Ho, S.-Y., Liu, C.-C., & Liu, S. (2002). Design of an optimal nearest neighbor classifier using an intelligent genetic algorithm. *Pattern Recognition Letters, 23*(13), 1495–1503. doi:10.1016/S0167-8655(02)00109-5

Iman, R. L., & Davenport, J. M. (1980). Approximations of the critical region of the friedman statistic. *Communications in Statistics, A9*(6), 571–595. doi:10.1080/03610928008827904

Ishibuchi, H., & Nakashima, T. (1999). Evolution of reference sets in nearest neighbor classification. In *Proceedings of the Second Asia-Pacific Conference on Simulated Evolution and Learning on Simulated Evolution and Learning* (LNCS 1585, pp. 82-89). Berlin, Germany: Springer-Verlag.

Kim, S.-W., & Oommen, B. J. (2007). On using prototype reduction schemes to optimize dissimilarity-based classification. *Pattern Recognition, 40*(11), 2946–2957. doi:10.1016/j.patcog.2007.03.006

Kuncheva, L. I. (1995). Editing for the k-nearest neighbors rule by a genetic algorithm. *Pattern Recognition Letters, 16*, 809–814. doi:10.1016/0167-8655(95)00047-K

Kuncheva, L. I., & Bezdek, J. C. (1998). Nearest prototype classification: Clustering, genetic algorithms, or random search? *IEEE Transactions on Systems, Man, and Cybernetics, 28*(1), 160–164. doi:10.1109/5326.661099

Liu, H., & Motoda, H. (2002). On issues of instance selection. *Data Mining and Knowledge Discovery, 6*(2), 115–130. doi:10.1023/A:1014056429969

Lozano, M., Sotoca, J. M., Sánchez, J. S., Pla, F., Pekalska, E., & Duin, R. P. W. (2006). Experimental study on prototype optimisation algorithms for prototype-based classification in vector spaces. *Pattern Recognition, 39*(10), 1827–1838. doi:10.1016/j.patcog.2006.04.005

Papadopoulos, A. N., & Manolopoulos, Y. (2004). *Nearest neighbor search: A database perspective.* Berlin, Germany: Springer-Verlag Telos.

Paredes, R., & Vidal, E. (2006). Learning prototypes and distances: A prototype reduction technique based on nearest neighbor error minimization. *Pattern Recognition, 39*(2), 180–188. doi:10.1016/j.patcog.2005.06.001

Pekalska, E., Duin, R. P. W., & Paclík, P. (2006). Prototype selection for dissimilarity-based classifiers. *Pattern Recognition, 39*(2), 189–208. doi:10.1016/j.patcog.2005.06.012

Prototype selection and feature subset selection by estimation of distribution algorithms: A case study in the survival of cirrhotic patients treated with tips. In *Proceedings of the 8th Conference on AI in Medicine in Europe* (pp. 20-29). London: Springer-Verlag.

Sebban, M., & Nock, R. (2000). Instance pruning as an information preserving problem. In *Proceedings of the First Conference on Knowledge Discovery and Data Mining* (pp. 174-179).

Shakhnarovich, G., Darrel, T., & Indyk, P. (Eds.). (2006). *Nearest-neighbor methods in learning and vision: Theory and practice.* Cambridge, MA: MIT Press.

Sheskin, D. J. (2003). *Handbook of parametric and nonparametric statistical procedures.* Boca Raton, FL: CRC Press.

APPENDIX

Figure 9. Example of a move in meme procedure and a partial evaluation

Class	Instances
A	$\{1,2,3,4,5,6,7\}$
B	$\{8,9,10,11,12,13\}$

	Current Solution	$\rightarrow$	Neighbour Solution
Representation	0110110100010	$\rightarrow$	0100110100010
U structure	$\{3,5,8,8,3,2,6,2,8,8,3,2,3\}$	$\rightarrow$	$\{\mathbf{12},5,8,8,\mathbf{2},2,6,2,8,8,\mathbf{8},2,\mathbf{8}\}$
Gain	$\{1,1,0,0,1,1,1,0,1,1,0,0,0\}$	$\rightarrow$	$\{-1,\cdot,\cdot,\cdot,0,\cdot,\cdot,\cdot,\cdot,\cdot,+1,\cdot,+1\}$
Correct classified patterns	7	$\rightarrow$	$7-1+1+1$

Partial evaluation account: $\mathrm{PE} = \frac{N_{nu}}{n} = \frac{4}{13}$

Number of correct classified patterns: 8

Chapter 6
Evolutionary Approaches and Their Applications to Distributed Systems

Thomas Weise
University of Kassel, Germany

Raymond Chiong
Swinburne University of Technology (Sarawak Campus), Malaysia

ABSTRACT

The ubiquitous presence of distributed systems has drastically changed the way the world interacts, and impacted not only the economics and governance but also the society at large. It is therefore important for the architecture and infrastructure within the distributed environment to be continuously renewed in order to cope with the rapid changes driven by the innovative technologies. However, many problems in distributed computing are either of dynamic nature, large scale, NP complete, or a combination of any of these. In most cases, exact solutions are hardly found. As a result, a number of intelligent nature-inspired algorithms have been used recently, as these algorithms are capable of achieving good quality solutions in reasonable computational time. Among all the nature-inspired algorithms, evolutionary algorithms are considerably the most extensively applied ones. This chapter presents a systematic review of evolutionary algorithms employed to solve various problems related to distributed systems. The review is aimed at providing an insight of evolutionary approaches, in particular genetic algorithms and genetic programming, in solving problems in five different areas of network optimization: network topology, routing, protocol synthesis, network security, and parameter settings and configuration. Some interesting applications from these areas will be discussed in detail with the use of illustrative examples.

INTRODUCTION

Distributed systems are everywhere, from the World Wide Web, interconnected banking systems, distributed real-time automotive systems, distributed manufacturing systems, e-commerce systems, e-government systems, e-learning systems, to even mobile phone networks. They provide communication

DOI: 10.4018/978-1-60566-798-0.ch006

infrastructures, both world-wide through the Internet as well as locally by connecting different modules of computer devices or as body area networks. Virtually, every computer system today is either already part of a distributed system or may become one in the near future (Tanenbaum & van Steen, 2002).

These days, Internet technologies, protocols, and applications are growing into maturity and most of them have been widely researched. New forms of networks and distributed computing have also emerged in recent years. Amongst them, we can find wireless networks, sensor networks, smart home environments and other ubiquitous computing applications. Many aspects of these distributed systems are configurable or are dependent on parameter settings, e.g. topology, security, and routing. Finding good configurations and settings for distributed systems is therefore one of the key requirements of today's Information Technology (IT) industry. Yet, many problems in distributed computing are either of dynamic nature, large scale, *NP* complete, or a combination of any of these. In most cases, exact solutions are hardly found in practice.

Evolutionary Computation (EC) is a family of the nature-inspired metaheuristic optimization methods. It is well-known for its ability to find satisfactory solutions within a reasonable amount of time, thus very suitable for solving problems of this nature. The study by Sinclair (1999a) reported that more than 120 papers had been published on work which employed EC for optimizing network topologies and dimension, node placement, routing, and wavelength or frequency allocation. The very comprehensive Master's thesis of Kampstra (Kampstra, 2005; Kampstra et al., 2006) builds on this aforementioned study and classifies over 400 papers. In the year 2000 alone, two books (Corne, Oates, & Smith, 2000 and Pedrycz & Vasilakos, 2000b) have been published on the applications of EC to networking. Many summary papers have been published on this subject ever since (Şekercioğlu, Pitsilides, & Vasilakos, 2001; Pedrycz & Vasilakos, 2000a; Théraulaz & Bonabeau, 2000; Vasilakos, Anagnostakis, & Pedrycz, 2001; Alba & Chicano, 2006; Cortés Achedad et al., 2008). Figure 1 gives an overview of the different areas of applications tackled and the techniques applied by the papers listed in the technical report of Weise et al. (2008).

Most of these summaries concentrate on giving an overview in the form of a more prosaic version of paper listings. In this chapter, our focus is to give a clear and detailed in-depth discussion of multiple examples of applications and also introduce the optimization algorithms utilized in them. On one hand, such descriptions make the subject more tangible for audiences rooted in only one of the two subject areas involved. On the other hand, we believe that describing some of the most interesting works in great detail will illustrate the ingenuity with which many researchers have found elegant and simple solutions based on evolutionary optimization to hard problems in distributed systems.

Before we discuss examples of the variety of possible applications of EC in distributed systems, the next section will first outline the basic concepts and background of evolutionary algorithms, and then elaborate on two of them we are focusing on: genetic algorithms and genetic programming. Following which, different methods to synthesize or to improve network topologies are outlined in Section 3. Adaptive and evolved routing protocols will be discussed in Section 4 and different approaches to the generation of protocols with evolutionary algorithms are summarized in Section 5. In Section 6, we illustrate how evolutionary optimization can be used even to improve network security before ending our review on applications with software configuration and parameter adaption approaches in Section 7. Section 8 brings forth the concluding remarks.

Figure 1. The number of papers analyzed in the technical report of Weise et al (2008), broken down to application area and optimization method.

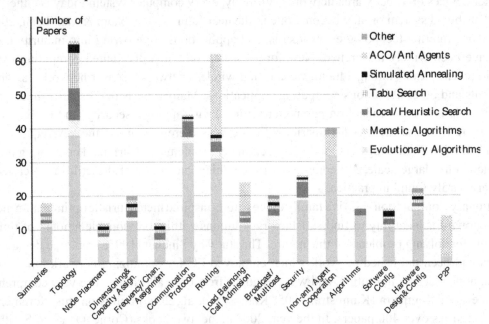

EVOLUTIONARY ALGORITHMS

Evolutionary algorithms are generic, population-based metaheuristic optimization algorithms that use biology-inspired mechanisms like mutation, crossover, natural selection, and survival of the fittest (Bäck, 1996; Bäck, Fogel, & Michalewicz, 1997; Bäck, Hammel, & Schwefel, 1997). The advantage of evolutionary algorithms as compared to other optimization methods is their "black box" character that makes only very few assumptions about the underlying objective functions. Furthermore, the definition of objective functions usually requires lesser insight into the structure of the problem space than the manual construction of an admissible heuristic. Evolutionary algorithms therefore perform consistently well in many different problem categories.

Similar to the evolutionary process in nature, we can distinguish the space of genotypes G (called search space) and the space of phenotypes X (the problem space). The concept of G corresponds to the set of all possible DNA sequences in nature on which the reproductive mechanisms such as sexual recombination and mutation work. In evolutionary algorithms, the definition of G and the operations applied to its elements $g \in G$ is often problem-dependent, but there also exists a set of well-researched and widely used representations.

The living organisms in nature emerge through a process called embryogenesis from the DNA. This process is copied in evolutionary algorithms in a simplified manner: a genotype-phenotype mapping (*gpm*) maps genotypes $g \in G$ to candidate solutions (i.e. phenotypes) $x \in X$.

The phenotypes represent the possible solutions of an optimization problem and are rated by a set of objective functions $f \in F$. Based on its objective values in comparison to the objective values of other individuals in the population, a fitness value can be assigned to each individual. Every living creature has features which influence its fitness positively or negatively. For a fish, such features could be the

Figure 2. The basic cycle of evolutionary algorithms.

Initial Population	Evaluation	Fitness Assignment
create an initial population of random individuals	compute the objective values of the solution candidates	use the objective values to determine fitness values

Reproduction	Selection
create new individuals from the mating pool by crossover and mutation	select the fittest individuals for reproduction

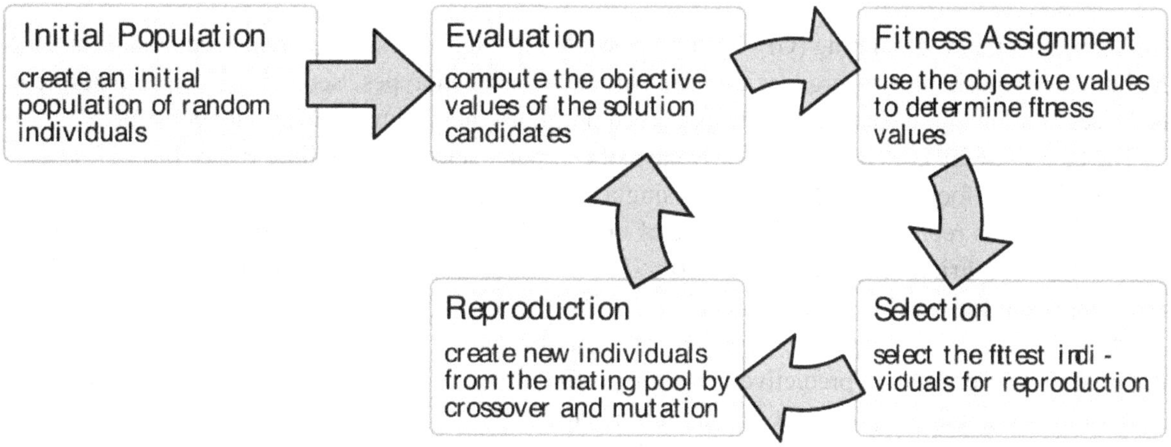

maximum swimming speed, its size and stamina, whether it is cunning or has sophisticated social behavior, its energy and food consumption, and so on. From this point of view, the natural evolution is a multi-objective optimization process, and like in evolutionary algorithms, the objectives may conflict with each other: with the size of the fish, the number of potential predators decreases but its energy consumption also increases. The fitness in nature corresponds to the number of offspring that a creature will produce. The fitness of a fish depends on its "objective values" in relation to other individuals of the population. A fish considered slow in one school could be fastest in another.

Again copying nature, evolutionary algorithms utilize sexual and asexual reproduction, which are implemented in the form of crossover and mutation operators and create new genotypes from existing ones. Since the best candidate solutions are selected with the highest probability, we expect the offspring resulting from the reproduction to also exhibit good characteristics and, hopefully, even better ones. The cycle of reproduction, genotype-phenotype mapping, objective function computation, fitness assignment, and selection as sketched in Figure 2 will be repeated until the termination criterion is met.

Genetic Algorithms

Genetic Algorithms (GA) are a subclass of evolutionary algorithms where the elements of the search space G are binary strings ($G=B^n$) or arrays of other elementary types (Goldberg, 1989; Holland, 1975; Heitkötter & Beasley, 1998; Whitley, 1994). The roots of GA go back to the mid-1950s, where biologists like Barricelli (1954; 1957; 1963) and the computer scientist Fraser (1957) began to apply computer-aided simulations in order to gain more insight into genetic processes and the natural evolution and selection. Bremermann (1962) and Bledsoe (1961a; 1961b; 1962a; 1962b) used evolutionary approaches based on binary string genomes for solving inequalities, for function optimization, and for determining the weights in neural networks (Bledsoe & Browning, 1959) in the early 1960s. At the end of that decade, important research on such search spaces was contributed by Bagley (1967), Cavicchio, Jr. (1970; 1972), and Frantz (1972) – all based on the ideas of Holland at the University of Michigan. As a result of Holland's work (Holland, 1962; 1969; 1975; 1967), GA as a new problem solving approach could be formalized and finally became widely recognized and popular.

Genetic Programming

The term Genetic Programming (GP) has two possible meanings. First, it is often used to subsume all evolutionary algorithms that produce tree data structures as phenotypes. Second, we can also define it as the set of all evolutionary algorithms that breed programs, algorithms, and similar constructs.

The history of GP goes back to the early days of computer science (Angeline, 1998). In 1957, Friedberg left the first footprints in this area by using a learning algorithm to stepwise improve a program. The program was represented as a sequence of instructions for a theoretical computer called Herman (Friedberg, 1958; Friedberg, Dunham, & North, 1959). Friedberg did not use an evolutionary, population-based approach for searching the programs.

The evolutionary programming approach for evolving finite state machines dates back to Fogel et al. (1966). In order to build predictive behaviors, different forms of mutation (but no crossover) were used for creating offspring from successful individuals.

Fourteen years later, the next generation of scientists began to look for ways to evolve programs. New results were reported by Smith (1980) in his PhD thesis. Forsyth (1981) evolved trees denoting fully bracketed Boolean expressions for classification problems (Forsyth, 1981; Forsyth & Rada, 1986; Forsyth, 1989).

GP became fully accepted at the end of this productive decade mainly because of the work of Koza (1988; 1989). He also studied many benchmark applications of GP, such as learning of Boolean functions (Koza, 1990c; 1990d), the Artificial Ant problem (Koza, 1990b; 1990a; 1992), and symbolic regression (Koza, 1990c; 1992), a method for obtaining mathematical expressions that match given data samples.

OPTIMIZING NETWORK TOPOLOGY

The topology of a network is a graph that defines which of the nodes are able to communicate with each other. The structure of any network, be it a distributed system, a social network, or a transportation system, can be described as such a graph. Especially for communication networks, the topology and the features of the nodes and links are very important since they define the maximum throughput, the latency and hops between the nodes, the robustness in terms of link failures, and the installation costs. These are also exactly the objectives which can be optimized when global optimization algorithms, such as evolutionary algorithms, are used to design the networks, the network topologies, and the features of the hardware to be utilized.

The application of EC in this area has a very long tradition, starting with the works of Coombs & Davis (1987), Michalewicz (1991), and Kumar et al. (1993). Before the year 2000, more than 30 papers had been published in this area (Sinclair, 1999b) and the number is still increasing. In this section, we will outline three interesting applications of topology optimization tasks: the Terminal Assignment Problem, the self-organized improvement of singular networks, and an European research initiative for planning a large-scale optical network.

Solving the Terminal Assignment Problem

The goal of the Terminal Assignment Problem is to determine the minimum cost links to connect a given set of nodes (the terminals) to another (disjoint) set of nodes (the concentrators). The required capacity of each terminal is known and may vary from terminal to terminal. The capacities of the concentrators are also known and so are the costs for linking them to the terminals. Each terminal must be linked to exactly one concentrator in a way that the maximum capacity of no concentrator is exceeded. An assignment has to be found under the objective of minimizing the total costs. This problem is *NP*-hard (Kershenbaum, 1993), except for the special case where all terminals have the same capacity requirements and all concentrators have the same capacity.

Abuali et al. (1994) were the first researchers who applied GAs to instances of this problem, where the capacity of all concentrators was equal. Khuri & Chiu (1997) investigated the utility of different heuristic algorithms, including greedy approaches and GAs for the general case where the capacities of the single concentrators differ. In their first genetic approach, Khuri & Chiu (1997) use a terminal-centric representation in the form of a string genome $G=X=N^n$ consisting of natural numbers, where n is the number of terminals. The value of a gene s_i from the genotype/phenotype string $S = (s_1, s_2, .., s_n)$ stands for the concentrator to which the ith terminal is connected. Strings that are infeasible, i.e., violate at least one of the constraints given above, are penalized with an offset separating them from all feasible solutions. Additionally, Khuri & Chiu (1997) also applied their grouping GA (GGA) to this problem. The results of their work indicated that the first GA provides better results than the greedy approach which, in turn, outperformed the grouping GA.

Yao et al. (2005) applied a hybrid evolutionary algorithm (i.e., a Memetic Algorithm) to a multi-objective variant of this problem where, besides the total cost, the number of concentrators used is also variable and subject to minimization. They furthermore abandon the terminal-centric representation in favor of a concentrator-centric genome consisting of m trees of depth 1, where m is the number of concentrators. Each concentrator is represented as the root of a tree and terminals are leaves linked to these roots. If a root has no children, then the corresponding concentrator is not used. The experimental results of Yao et al. (2005) showed that evolutionary algorithms hybridized with Lamarckian or Baldwin local search both perform approximately equally well and are suitable for solving the Terminal Assignment Problem. The concentrator-based representation also proved to be advantageous compared to the terminal-centric genome in these experiments.

Singular, Selfish, and Self-Organized (S³) Networks

Another interesting topology optimization approach is the iterative online method for self-organizing networks of selfish nodes defined by Zweig (2007). Her algorithm is not population-based – at any point in time there is exactly one (singular) network. In each time step, one node may modify the edges to its neighbors by either adding one connection (from itself) to another node or removing one edge attached to it.

If this modification seems to be advantageous from the perspective of the node (therefore the *selfish*), it is committed, otherwise it is rejected. As a measure for the utility of a modification, a node may, for instance, compute the maximum distance from itself to any other node or the sum of the distances to all other nodes. In Lehmann & Kaufmann (2005), it is shown that self-organization algorithms minimiz-

Figure 3. The initial network design of the EON network.

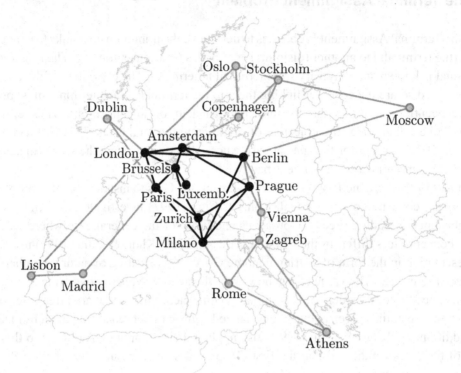

ing such objectives can decrease the diameter of a network down to a certain threshold in polynomial time.

Zweig (2007) refers to this approach as an evolutionary algorithm in the sense of stepwise improvements. Since its population has the size of one and only a unary reproduction operator is used, one may rather consider it as a hill climbing approach with "evolutionary" aspects in the sense of steady improvements.

Optimization of an Optical Network for Europe

The last application of global optimization to topology optimization that we will discuss here is the research project 239 of the European Cooperation in the field of Scientific and Technical Research (COST). The partners in the COST Action 239 (General Secretariat of the Council of the European Union; COST Secretariat, 1994) studied the feasibility of plans for an European Optical Network (EON), a transparent optical overlay network capable of carrying all the international traffic between 20 of the main centers of Europe (Aiyarak, Saket, & Sinclair, 1997). The initial design for this network is illustrated in Figure 4. Sinclair (1995) evolved a network topology for EON using a GA with an objective function that took the estimated traffic on the links between the nodes and weights of the nodes themselves into account. This way, he was able to achieve significant improvements of both costs and reliability compared to the topology initially designed (O'Mahony, Sinclair, & Mikac, 1993). A group of researchers under his leadership later applied a similar GA to optimize the route and wave length assignment as well for such a network. Again, they obtained results superior to initial expectations (Tan & Sinclair, 1995).

Figure 4. The genotype representing the connection matrix of the nine central nodes of EON.

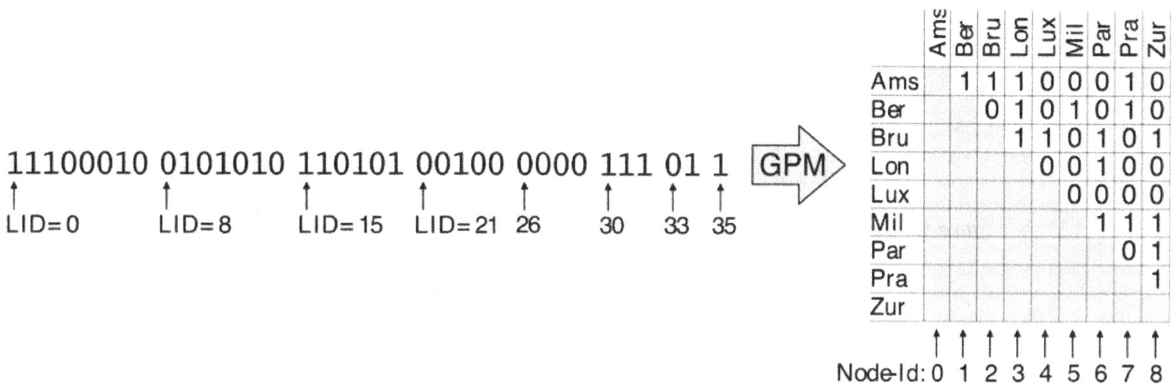
11100010 0101010 110101 00100 0000 111 01 1
LID=0
LID=8
LID=15
LID=21
26
30
33
35
GPM
Ams Ber Bru Lon Lux Mil Par Pra Zur
Ams 1 1 1 0 0 0 1 0
Ber 0 1 0 1 0 1 0
Bru 1 1 0 1 0 1
Lon 0 0 1 0 0
Lux 0 0 0 0
Mil 1 1 1
Par 0 1
Pra 1
Zur
Node-Id: 0 1 2 3 4 5 6 7 8

In Aiyarak et al. (1997) and Sinclair (1999b), they tried out four different GP approaches for the topology optimization problem and compared them with the initial GA. We will outline the representations used in these approaches on the example from Sinclair (1995) concerning only the $N = 9$ central nodes (Amsterdam, Berlin, Brussels, London, Luxembourg, Milan, Paris, Prague, and Zurich). In Figure 3, the black dots stand for these central nodes and the black lines for the (initially planned) connections between them.

The Genetic Algorithm

In his original GA-approach, Sinclair used a genome where each of the $L = 0.5\ N(N - 1) = 0.5 * 9 * 8 = 36$ possible links between these nine metropolises was represented by one bit. When a bit in the genotype is set, the corresponding link is present in the network plan. The central topology from Figure 3 thus translates to the genotype sketched in Figure 4 (which effectively encodes the connection matrix).

Genetic Programming with a Relational Function Set

In the GP approach with a relational function set (RFS), a function is LinkThere (LID) was evolved which evaluates to *1* if the link LID is present and *0* otherwise. Therefore, each of the $L = 36$ possible links is associated with a unique number from the interval $0..L\text{-}1$. The terminal symbols available for GP are the link ID LID (i.e., the parameters of isLinkThere) and constants. As function set, addition (+) and subtraction (-) modulo L are provided together with "greater than" (>) and "less than" (<) which return *1* if their first argument is greater or lesser than their second one. The decision function returns the value of its second argument if the first one equals to *1* and the value of the third one otherwise. Since the function evolved could return values from *0* to $L - 1$, a wrapper function was used which mapped these values to either *0* or *1*. Figure 5.1 sketches how such a symbolic regression-like GP representation of the bit string from Figure 4 may look like, using the LIDs as defined there.

Figure 5. Snippets from the GP representations of the bit string from Figure 4.

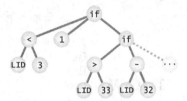

Figure 5.1 The RFS approach.

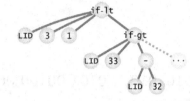

Figure 5.2 The decision tree method (DT).

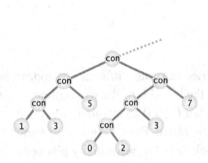

Figure 5.3 The connective approach (CN).

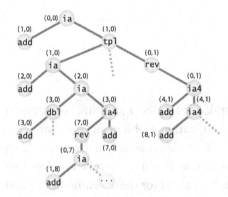

Figure 5.4 The node-pair encoding GP (NP2).

Genetic Programming for Decision Trees

With their DT-GP approach, Aiyarak et al. (1997) extended this method by combing the < and > operators with the if statement, yielding the new if-lt and if-gt expression. With this modification, they wanted to evolve decision trees and hoped to reduce the computational effort for finding solutions. For illustration purposes, we translated the program from Figure 5.1 to this representation and depict the result in Figure 5.2.

Genetic Programming – The Connective Approach

The third GP approach (called connected nodes, or CN for short) differs very much from the other two. As terminal symbols, it only uses node identifiers and it has only one function, con (Sinclair, 1999b). con simply adds a link between the two nodes identified by its parameters and returns its first argument. The tree in Figure 5.3 describes how the network defined in Figure 4 can be derived.

Node-Pair Encoding GP

Inspired by the edge encoding method of Luke & Spector (1996), Sinclair designed another GP method for topology synthesis. His node-pair encoding (NP) involves a tree-to-graph genotype-phenotype mapping which explicitly constructs a network (Sinclair, 1999b; 2000). Table 1 illustrates parts of the function and terminal sets of two NP variants, which only differ in the number of children of the function nodes (noted in the columns NP1 and NP2). NP programs work with tuples *(a, b)* of node IDs with

Table 1. An excerpt of the node-types of the NP-approaches.

Abbreviation	NP1	NP2	Description
rev	1	1	reverse: *(a, b)* → *(b, a)*
ia	1	2	modulo-increment *a*: *(a, b)* → *(a + 1 mod N, a)*
ia2	1	2	modulo-increment *a* by *2*: *(a, b)* → *(a + 2 mod N, a)*
ia4	1	2	modulo-increment *a* by *4*: *(a, b)* → *(a + 4 mod N, a)*
dbl	2	2	plain doubling: pass node pair to both children
add	1	0	if $a \neq b$ create link between a and b
…	…	…	…
nop	0	0	do nothing (terminal)

$a, b \in [0..N-1]$ ($N = 9$ for our example). The program tree is processed from top to bottom and begins with the input *(0, 0)* to the root node. Each node can manipulate the first element of the tuple (with the functions ia, ia2, …), rotate it, create or cut a connection between the two nodes in the tuple (add or cut), or simply do nothing (nop). If it has children, it will pass the (resulting) node tuple to all its children. Figure 5.4 illustrates how a program snippet in NP2 representation is executed and the values of the node tuples at the different levels.

Summary

Aiyarak et al. (1997) tested the first three GP approaches (RFS, DT, and CN) and found that none of them produced solutions with better fitness than the original GA method. RFS-GP performed the worst. The DT method was better than CN on a small test set containing only the nine central nodes and scored even with the GA. On the complete EON network, CN in turn outperformed DT but was still worse than the solution provided by the GA. All GP approaches needed much (at least five times) more individual evaluations to find their solution than the GA. These results were confirmed in Sinclair (1999b), where CN and the two versions of NP were compared with the GA. Again, the GA was the best approach, but NP2 found the best result for one of the five test problems and came close to the GA in all other runs. Still, the experiments with GP needed much longer than those with the GA.

The lesson from these experiments is that the representation issue, i.e., the way in which candidate solutions are encoded, is very important in optimization. Sometimes a simple, fixed-length bit string can outperform more complex approaches. Even if only one class of algorithms (like GP) is applied, modifications in the representation used can still lead to vast differences in performance.

OPTIMIZING ROUTING

Routing is the method by which messages are relayed over multiple nodes in a network in order to convey them to their destination. Naturally, there often exist multiple different routes from a source to a destination. The objective of a routing algorithm is to guide the messages along the shortest[1] possible route. However, a path in the network may get blocked if any of its nodes are congested, i.e., they have to process too many messages at once. Then again, additional paths may become available as new nodes

Figure 6. An evolved routing rule set (left) with target node 0 for the specified network (right).

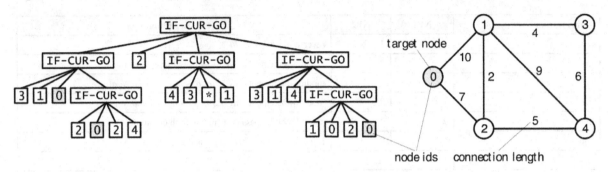

are connected. Hence, routing algorithms have to avoid congestion and should incorporate new links as soon as possible in order to increase the network utility.

In this section, we will discuss six approaches for improving routing with global optimization algorithms, spanning from the evolution of routing rules, adaptive routing with ant agents, to the synthesis of broadcast algorithms and the enhancement of search request distribution in peer-to-peer networks.

Evolving Fault-Tolerant Routing Rules

Routing is tightly coupled with the problem of finding the shortest paths from one vertex in a graph to all others. This problem was solved by Dijkstra (1959). About 40 years later, Kirkwood, Shami, and Sinclair (Kirkwood et al., 1997; Shami, Kirkwood, & Sinclair, 1997) used GP to breed robust routing rules for networks where links may fail.

Their GP system takes the ID of a target node and a graph (containing this node) as input. Each node in the graph has a unique ID and each connection has a certain length. The system then breeds routing rules in the form of LISP S-expressions. In the context of this application, these expressions are trees consisting of nested instances of the domain-specific IF-CUR-GO instruction. The four parameters W, X, Y, and Z of this instruction as well as its return value each represent a node ID. On each node reached by a message, the routing rule is evaluated and the message is sent to the node whose ID is returned. IF-CUR-GO W X Y Z evaluates to X if the current node is W, X and W are directly connected, and X has not yet been visited twice. It returns Y if one of the latter two conditions is violated and Z if the current node is not W.

As per objective function, Kirkwood et al. (1997) use the difference in length between the optimal route (computed with Dijkstra's algorithm) and the routes obtained with the evolved scheme on the target network with and without simulated link failures. The results of the evolution were rules that are very robust against connection loss and, for instance, find correct routes in two thirds of all the cases even if 47% of the connections have broken down. In Figure 6, a routing rule set resulting from one of the experiments (Kirkwood et al., 1997) is displayed on the left. It routes messages through the graph sketched on the right-hand side to node 0.

Genetic Adaptive Routing

Over the Internet, messages are forwarded to their destinations on the basis of routing tables. These tables can be filled using, for example, Dijkstra's algorithm. They contain either the address of the next hop, i.e., the next computer to send a packet to, or the complete routes to each possible destination (source routing). Protocols like RIP (Hedrick, 1988) and OSPF (Moy, 1989) build and distribute such tables, but disregard dynamic aspects like communication latency.

Munetomo, Takai, and Sato (Munetomo et al., 1997; Munetomo, Takai, & Sato, 1998a; 1998b; Munetomo, 1999) contributed GARA, the genetic adaptive routing algorithm, for building and maintaining routing tables for source routing. GARA runs independently on every node in the network. Each node maintains a list of multiple complete routes to the most frequently contacted communication partners. After a specific number of packets have been sent along a route, an additional packet is sent for observing the communication latency. The fitness of the routes and their likeliness for being chosen then corresponds to this delay. In Figure 7, the table with the destinations most frequently addressed by node 0 is sketched in the context of an example network.

From time to time, path genetic operators such as path mutation and path crossover, both illustrated in Figure 8, are applied to routes with the same destination. With these operators, new paths are discovered and made available for message propagation. Path mutation simply exchanges a node within a route with another one (Figure 8.2). Path crossover (Figure 8.1) is applied to two routes that pass through one common point (other than their source and destination). The sub-paths before and after that point are exchanged. Selection is performed when the routing table exceeds a specific size. By utilizing these evolutionary primitives, GARA becomes a self-organizing system able to adapt to changing network situations and to discover new routes, thus challenging established protocols on equal footing.

Ant-Based Routing

The routing of network messages or phone calls through a telecommunication system remotely resembles the transportation of food by ants to their nest (Théraulaz & Bonabeau, 2000).

First Steps by Schoonderwoerd et al.

Schoonderwoerd et al. (Schoonderwoerd et al., 1996; 1997; Schoonderwoerd, 1996) have developed a routing method based on this analogy in the form of an online Ant Colony Optimization approach. In their system, the nodes exchange control messages (the ants) from time to time in order to build and maintain "pheromone tables" used for routing. In principle, a pheromone table of a node with m neighbors is an $n \times m$ matrix where n is the total number of nodes in the network. For any of the n possible destinations, it contains a probability that a message is routed to any of the m neighbors. At each time step during Schoonderwoerd's simulations, any node can launch an ant with a random destination. Whenever an ant created by node i arrives at node j coming from node k, it will update the pheromone table P_j of j according to

$$P_j[i,k] = \frac{P_j[i,k] + \Delta}{1 + \Delta}$$

(1)

Figure 7. The table with the most frequently used routes of node 0.

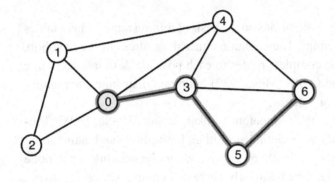

Dest.	Routes	Delay	Weight
1	(0,1)	10	1.0
2	(0,1,2)	100	0.4
	(0,2)	80	0.6
5	(0,3,5)	270	0.7
	(0,4,6,5)	420	0.3
6	(0,1,4,3,6)	210	0.4
	(0,3,6)	250	0.5
	(0,3,5,6)	490	0.1

Figure 8. The Path Genetic Operations in GARA.

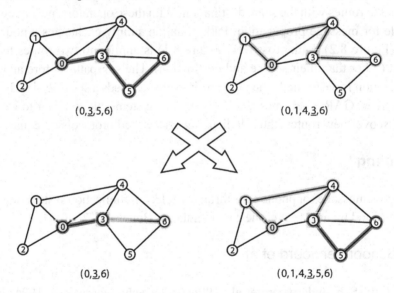

(0,3,5,6)   (0,1,4,3,6)

(0,3,6)   (0,1,4,3,5,6)

Figure 8.1 The Path Crossover Operator.

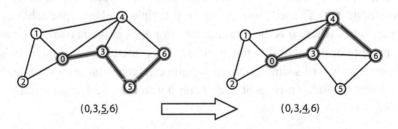

(0,3,5,6)   (0,3,4,6)

Figure 8.2 The Path Mutation Operator.

$$\forall l \in \left[1..n\right], \ l \neq k \, P_j\left[i,l\right] \ = \frac{P_j\left[i,l\right]}{1+\Delta}$$

(2)

In other words, the probability of selecting node k as next hop for future messages with destination i is increased while decreasing the probabilities of the other possible next hops of such a message. The total cumulative probability of all hops together stays 1. This update method modifies the probabilities for messages travelling into the opposite direction of the ants. It indirectly influences the forward probability of the path taken by the ant since subsequent ants moving to node i along it will again have backward influence which then points to the original forward direction.

Schoonderwoerd adds an "age" to the ants which is increased in every hop in order to foster the usage of short pathways. Δ becomes a function which decreases with the age of the ant. Thus, the older an ant, i.e., the longer the path it has travelled, the lower will be its influence on guiding future ants along this path. Congested relay stations can artificially increase the age of the ants passing them and may also delay the ants on their way. This will decrease their traffic.

New routes can be discovered by introducing a factor f: $0 < f < 1$ which denotes a probability that the next hop of an ant is chosen totally randomly whereas the pheromone table is used for the decision with probability $1 - f$. In summary, Schoonderwoerd et al. (1996) presented a decentralized and self-organized online optimization process for communication networks which can be generalized to arbitrary routing problems. The simple behavior of their ants leads to interesting, emergent overall configurations of the network this approach is applied to.

AntNet

Di Caro and Dorigo (Di Caro & Dorigo, 1998a; 1998b; Di Caro, 2004) develop this concept further in their AntNet algorithm. For each node j, it builds a routing table P_j which has basically the same structure as the ones used by Schoonderwoerd et al.[2] What has changed is the way this matrix is updated.

Regularly, every node s sends an agent (forward ant) $F_{s \to d}$ to a node $d \neq s$ in order to discover feasible and efficient paths. The selection of d is randomized but biased to the direction of nodes which exchange high traffic with s. Forward ants share the same queues as data packets, so they will experience the same delays (Di Caro & Dorigo, 1998a). Such an ant agent keeps a history of its route and of the times needed for its sections.

At each node j, the traveling ant $F_{s \to d}$ selects the next node to visit according to:

$$P(j \to i) \ = \frac{P_j\left[d,i\right] + \alpha l\left(i\right)}{1+\alpha(m-1)}$$

(3)

where $P(j \to i)$ is the probability that i is chosen as the next node and $P_j[d,i]$ is the routing table entry which describes the expected utility of i as next hop for messages going to d.[3] m is the number of neighbors of node j and $l(i)$ is a value proportional to the queue length for destination i normalized to the unit interval. The influence of $l(i)$ makes the system more reactive to the current traffic situation. It is weighted by the factor α which usually takes on values between 0.2 and 0.5.

If the forward ant $F_{s \to d}$ detects that it somehow travelled in a loop, it dies. Otherwise, when it arrives at its destination d, it is converted into a backward agent $B_{d \to s}$ which travels back to s along the same route that $F_{s \to d}$ took. When arriving at a node j coming from a node i, the entry for choosing i as next hop for messages going to d in the routing table of j is updated as follows: $P_j[i,d] = P_j[i,d] + r(1 - P_j[i,d])$ (4) where $r \in [0, 1]$ is a reinforcement factor, a measure of goodness of the observed trip time, based on a statistical model for the local traffic M (also updated by the agents) and the time. By multiplying r with $(1 - P_j[i,d])$, small probabilities are increased more proportionally, which allows faster exploration of new, potentially good routes. After this update, the corresponding column of P_j is normalized again.

Global Information?

The simulations of Di Caro & Dorigo (1998a) show that AntNet is an efficient and robust routing algorithm. However, they make the assumption that global information is available. Every node holds a routing table with entries defining how to send messages to any other node. Such global information is normally not available and furthermore would also be subject to constant changes if routers are added to or removed from the network. Liang et al. (2002; 2006) point out this weakness and test a LocalAnt algorithm restricted to routing tables with only two entries for each neighboring node (for the neighbor itself and the probability to route over this node to other destinations). They show that, under these more realistic conditions, the efficiency of the algorithm is much lower than in the case where global information is available (the original approach is called GlobalAnt in this context). Liang et al. (2006) propose a distributed algorithm where each node holds a population of individuals encoding routes. These individuals travel over the network as genetic agents and, subsequently, as backward agents similar to the AntNet approach and are subject to recombination, mutation, and aging. According to their study (Liang et al., 2006), the performance of this method falls in between those of LocalAnt and GlobalAnt.

Genetic Programming of Broadcasting Algorithms

Routing does not necessarily concern the delivery of messages to single destinations only, but may also involve $1: n$ communications, i.e., broadcasts and multicast. Broadcasting in a network (represented as a graph) is the process of spreading information initially known only by a single node to all other nodes. Comellas & Giménez (1998) formulated an optimization problem with the following constraints:

1. Only a node which already knows the information can spread it further.
2. A node can only send one message per time step.
3. A node can only send a message over vertices which are connected to it.

The goal of their work was to find the broadcasting scheme which disseminates the information to all nodes in the shortest possible time. They used GP for growing such broadcasting algorithms for two-dimensional directed grids, toroidal grids, hypercubes, cube-connected cycles, and butterfly graphs. For the butterfly graph, a solution even better than the best known upper bound at that time (Klasing, Monien, Peine, & Stöhr, 1992) was found, whereas in all other cases, (known) optimal algorithms evolved. (Listing 1)

In their experiments, Comellas & Giménez (1998) used Standard GP for evolving Lisp S-expressions. The function set for the directed 2-grid example contained the following expressions:

Listing 1. The optimal broadcasting scheme evolved for 2-dimensional, directed grids.

1	(Prog3 (IfOri (Prog2 (IfTurn0 MoveHor)
2	(IfTurn1 MoveVer)))
3	(IfProcHor (Prog3 (IfTurn0 MoveHor)
4	(IfTurn0 MoveVer)
5	(IfTurn1 MoveHor)))
6	(IfProcVer (IfTurn0 MoveVer)))

1. IfOri executes its parameter action if the node the program runs on was the one which initially knew the information to be disseminated.
2. IfProcHor and IfProcVer execute their parameter if they received the information from a horizontally or vertically adjacent node, respectively.
3. Proc1, Proc2, Proc3, and Proc4 concatenate 1, 2, 3, or 4 instructions to a sequential block.
4. IfTurn0/IfTurn1 execute their actions only in the first/second time step after the node received the information.

As terminal symbols, MoveHor and MoveVer are available, which send the information to the next horizontally or vertically adjacent node, as well as NULL which does nothing. For computing the objective values, the algorithms evolved were applied to an example graph. The number of nodes reached was counted and multiplied by a factor T. From this value, 2 is subtracted for each condition value or NULL action and 4 for each other action in the tree. The number of the ProgN functions had no influence on fitness. Listing 1 illustrates the result delivered by GP for two-dimensional directed grids.

In Figure 9, we applied this algorithm to a 5×5 grid. The gray nodes have no knowledge about the information and turn black once they receive it. It is interesting to know that the IfTurn0 MoveVer in line 4 of Listing 1, although seemingly useless (Comellas & Giménez, 1998), is important. Without it, the last node in the second line in the network illustrated in Figure 9 would not be reached in time step 5 but in step 6, since the MoveHor action cannot be executed by the last node in the first line. With the MoveVert instruction with the same preconditions, an unnecessary pause is avoided. For the other topologies mentioned, Comellas & Giménez (1998) used modified function and terminal sets and obtained optimal results, too.

Optimizing Collective Communication

Recently, Jaroš & Dvořák (2008) developed a scheduling technique for similar collective communication (CC) tasks based on evolutionary algorithms. Their work addresses high-performance multi-processor systems where single CPUs are connected via NoCs (networks on chip). Jaroš and Dvořák experiment with one-to-all broadcast (OAB), all-to-all broadcast (AAB), one-to-all scatter (OAS, a private message to each partner), and all-to-all scatter (AAS).

Each collective communication process is considered as a set of point-to-point communications which can be further partitioned into subsets. The communications in each subset are executed in parallel and the subsets themselves are executed one after the other in a sequence of synchronized steps. The CC scheduling problem is defined as finding a minimal partition without causing conflicts.

Figure 9. The application of Listing 1 to a 5×5 grid.

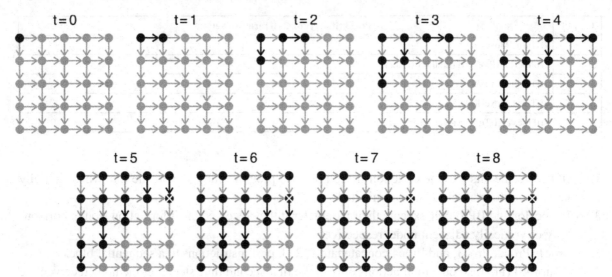

Jaroš & Dvořák (2008) introduced different encodings for broadcast and scatter communication as well as special reproduction and repairing operators. Their objective function corresponds to the number of conflicts that a schedule introduces, i.e., the number of times two point-to-point communications share the same link in the same time step. The experimental results showed that this approach is very efficient and even led to an improvement of the theoretical lower bounds of the number of steps needed for AAS communication.

Improving Gnutella

The Gnutella network (Gnutella, 2000; Ripeanu, Foster, & Iamnitchi, 2002) is one of the oldest and simplest peer-to-peer file sharing systems. In Gnutella, each node only interacts with neighboring nodes which it chooses at startup. Normally, a node picks seven such neighbors and tries to maintain connections to them.

As the last application example in this section, we summarize how Iles & Deugo (2002) use GP for improving routing in such networks. Their idea was to evolve rules for dynamically setting the number of neighbor nodes and for selecting (and possibly exchanging) them. These rules use information the peer-to-peer node can aggregate over time, like the (current) number of neighbors, the bandwidth of the node, the bandwidth of the neighbor nodes, and the duration of the connections to them. The expressions produced by GP led to significant performance improvements in simulations.

The results of the experiments of Iles & Deugo (2002) still use a fixed number of neighbors, but tend to prefer five or six partner nodes instead of Gnutella's default of seven. The way these neighbors are picked, however, becomes a dynamic process depending on multiple aggregated parameters such as the distance in hops and number of search hits to the candidate nodes.

Figure 10. The scenario for protocol synthesis as used in de Araújo et al. (2003a).

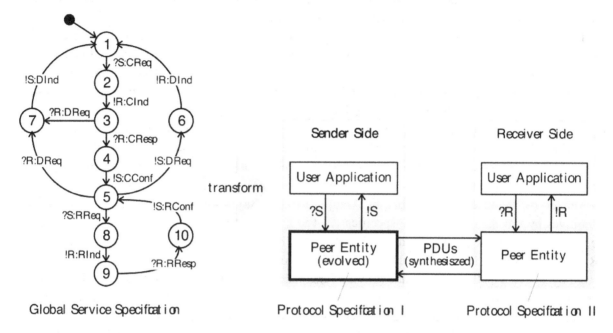

SYNTHESIZING PROTOCOLS

Protocols like IP (Information Sciences Institute, 1981) and TCP (Cerf, Dalal, & Sunshine, 1974) are the rules for message and information exchange in a network. Depending on the application, protocols can become arbitrarily complex and strongly influence the efficiency and robustness of a distributed system.

Transformation of Petri Net-Based Specifications

Yamaguchi et al. (1995) define the problem of transforming a service specification in the form of a Petri Net with registers (PNR) to a protocol specification in the same format. Later, El-Fakihy et al. (1999) showed how to solve this problem efficiently with GAs under the objective of minimizing communication costs.

Transformation of Finite State Machine-Based Specifications

A similar approach for synthesizing protocol specifications from service specifications has been contributed by de Araújo et al. (2003a; 2003b). We will use the communication protocol example given in de Araújo et al. (2003a) to summarize this method in which all specifications are represented as finite state machines.

In Figure 10, we sketch the starting situation from de Araújo et al. (2003a). At the left side, a global service specification is defined in the form of a finite state machine which describes the interactions that take place in a communication protocol between a sender and a receiver. It contains only the interaction primitives between a user (or a user application) and the peer entities, where ?xyz represents an input message to xyz and !xyz stands for the output of xyz to the user. Events on the sender side are marked with S and those occurring at the receiver are annotated with R.

The finite state machine starts in state 1. On the sender side, the user may then issue a connection request CReq causing a transition to state 2. A window indicating an incoming connection CInd may pop up at the receiver side, for instance, which then can either be confirmed ($3 \rightarrow 4$) or declined ($3 \rightarrow 7$). In the latter case, a disconnection indication will ensue on the sender side whereas the former transition leads to a connection confirmation. A connection may be reconnected (states 5, 8, 9, 10) or be closed by either the sender ($5 \rightarrow 6$) or the receiver ($5 \rightarrow 7$) with a disconnect request DReq, causing a disconnect indication DInd (may be in the form of a window) to occur on the other end.

The goal is to evolve a finite state machine that governs the behavior of one of the two protocol partners and to synthesize the messages (Protocol Data Units, PDUs[4]) that have to be exchanged between the sender and the receiver. Therefore, de Araújo et al. (2003a) first create a sequence of interaction primitives by traversing the service specification FSM. In this traversal, all state transitions need to be visited. One such sequence could be (?S:CReq, !R:CInd, ?R:CResp, !S:CConf, ?S:RReq, !R:RInd, ?R:RResp, !S:RConf, !S:DReq, !R:DInd, …). It is obvious that if one event on the sender side is followed by an event on the receiver side (or vice versa) and the second event is not triggered by the user (?xyz), a message (i.e., a PDU) has to be exchanged between the two sides. These PDUs can either be automatically generated or predefined and then inserted into the sequence, resulting in the list (?S:CReq, pduConReq, !R:CInd, ?R:CResp, pduConAcc, !S:CConf, ?S:RReq, pduReiReq, !R:RInd, ?R:RResp, pduReiAcc, !S:RConf, !S:DReq, pduDisInd, !R:DInd, …), for instance.

From this list, the message exchanges which concern the protocol peer to be evolved are extracted. The experiments presented in de Araújo et al. (2003a) were focused on the sender side protocol, which here results in the following tuples: ((?S:CReq, pduConAcc), (pduConAcc, !S:CConf), (?S:RReq, pduReiReq), (pduReiAcc, !S:RConf), (!S:DReq, pduDisInd), (?S:CReq, pduConReq), …).

In order to allow the synthesized protocol to react to all possible messages in all states, random non-expected inputs are added to the list like ((CReq, pduConAcc), (CReq, NULL), (pduConAcc, CConf), …). Such a list is then encoded and used as a test set during individual evaluation. For the evolution of the protocol FSM, de Araújo et al. (2003a) use the GP ernel (GPK) of Hörner (1996) which supports variable-length genomes. The objective function compares the behavior of a candidate solution with the expectations and counts the number of correct outputs.

Figure 11 illustrates the state-based representation (SBR) used by de Araújo et al. (2003a) to encode protocol finite state machines. The genotypes are divided into genes and each gene represents one state. The total number of states is variable. For each possible input, every gene contains one tuple of two numbers. The first number in this tuple represents the next state and the second one stands for the output of the corresponding transition.

The receiver side of the protocol was evolved in the same manner (de Araújo et al., 2003a) and the results were able to pass an automated equivalence check. The good performance reported further indicates the high utility of this approach for protocol synthesis.

Evolving Fraglet-Based Protocols

In his seminal work, Tschudin (2003) introduced Fraglets, a new artificial chemistry suitable for the development and even evolution of network protocols. Fraglets represent an execution model for communication protocols which resembles chemical reactions.

Figure 11. The best individual from the experiment in de Araújo et al. (2003a).

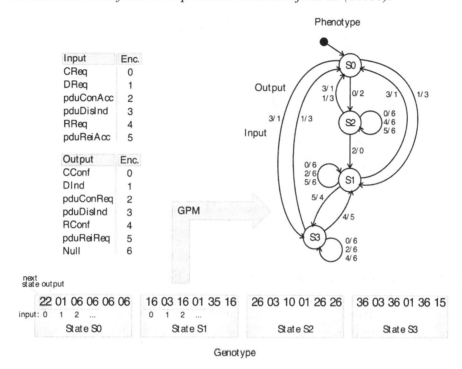

Fraglets are symbolic strings of the form $[s_1:s_2:\ldots:s_n]$. The symbols s_i either represent control information or payload. Each node in the network has a Fraglet store which corresponds to a reaction vessel in chemistry. Such vessels usually contain equal molecules multiple times and the same goes for Fraglet stores which can be implemented as multisets keeping track of the multiplicity of the Fraglets they contain.

Tschudin (2003) defines a simple prefix programming language for Fraglets. It has a fixed instruction set comprising transformation and reaction rules. Transformations like dup and nop modify a single Fraglet whereas the reactions match and matchP combine two Fraglets. For the definition of these rules in Table 2, we will use the syntax $[s_1:s_2:\ldots:tail]$ where s_i is a symbol and tail is a possibly empty sequence of symbols.

This form of protocol representation is predestined for automated synthesis via evolutionary algorithms: Fraglets have almost no syntactical constraints and can represent complicated protocols in a compact manner. Tschudin (2003) focused on the offline evolution of protocols using a GA. A complete communication system was simulated for a given number of time steps during the evaluation of each individual. The objective values denote the correlation of the behavior observed during the simulation and the target behavior. While Tschudin's results substantiate that the evolutionary methods are suitable to optimize existing Fraglet protocols, they also indicated that the evolution of new distributed algorithms is difficult because of a strong tendency to overfitting. Furthermore, it is hard to define objective functions which can reward "partially correct" behavior, since this term is a contradiction in itself. This is known as the all-or-nothing property in GP.

Table 2. Some of the most common Fraglet tags (commands).

Tag	transformation/reaction
dup	[dup:t:a:tail] → [t:a:a:tail] duplicate a single symbol
exch	[exch:t:a:b:tail] → [t:b:a:tail] swap two tags
fork	[fork:a:b:tail] → [a:tail], [b:tail] copy Fraglet tail with different header symbols
pop2	[pop2:h:t:a:tail] → [h:a], [t:tail] pop head element a out of list [a:b:tail]
match	[match:a:tail$_1$], [a:tail$_2$] → [tail$_1$:tail$_2$] two Fraglets react, their tails are concatenated
matchP	[matchP:a:tail$_1$], [a:tail$_2$] → [matchP:a:tail$_1$], [tail1:tail$_2$] catalyst match, i.e., the matchP tag is persistent

Online Protocol Adaptation and Evolution with Fraglets

Autonomic networks are networks where manual management is not desired or hard to realize, such as systems of hundreds of gadgets in an e-home, sensor networks, or arbitrary mesh networks with wireless and wired links. Yamamoto & Tschudin (2005) pointed out that software in such networks should be self-modifying so as to be able to react to unforeseen network situations. They distinguish two forms of such reactions – adaption and evolution.

Adaption is the short-term reconfiguration of existing modules whereas evolution stands for the modification of the old functionality and the discovery of new functionality and happens on a larger timescale. Software with these abilities probably cannot predict whether the effects of a modification are positive or negative in advance and therefore, need to be resilient in order to mitigate faulty code that could evolve. In Tschudin & Yamamoto (2005), they showed that such resilience can be achieved to a certain degree by introducing redundancy into Fraglet protocols.

Complementing Tschudin's work on offline protocol synthesis and optimization (Tschudin, 2003), Yamamoto & Tschudin (2005) describe online protocol evolution as a continuously ongoing, decentralized, and asynchronous process of constant competition and selection of the most feasible modules. GP with mutation and homologous crossover is chosen for accomplishing these features. The fitness measure (subject to maximization) is the performance of the protocols as perceived by the applications running on the network. The score of a candidate solution (i.e., a protocol) is incremented if it behaves correctly and decremented whenever an error is detected. The resource consumption in terms of the memory allocated by the protocols is penalized proportionally. In Yamamoto & Tschudin (2006), populations were created containing a mix of different confirmed delivery and reliable delivery protocols for messages. These populations were then confronted with either reliable or unreliable transmission challenges and were able to adapt to these conditions quickly. When the environment changed, e.g. when a formerly reliable channel became unreliable, the degree of re-adaptation was, however, unsatisfying. The loss of diversity due to the selection of only highly fit protocols during the adaptation phase could not be compensated by mutation in these first experiments. Further information on approaches for evolutionary online optimization of communication protocols can be found in the report Framework for Distributed

On-line Evolution of Protocols and Services from the EU-sponsored project BIONETS (Miorandi et al., 2007).

Learning Communication Patterns for Agents

The term protocol stands not only for the way data is exchanged over a network connection but has a much wider meaning which also subsumes the patterns of communication between humans or animals. Agents are a metaphor for all kinds of autonomous systems in computer science and the last issue which we will look at in this section is the evolution of communication protocols for such systems.

Some early experiments in evolving communication patterns for autonomous agents were conducted by Werner & Dyer (1992) on the example of artificial creatures. In their simulation, blind male animals capable of hearing and moving need to be guided by immobile females which can see and are able to produce sounds. They used a GA with an integer string genome encoding the weights and biases of recurrent neural networks for both the females and the males. The evolution, however, was not performed by a regular GA. Instead, it took place in the simulated environment where the females lead the males to their location. When they meet, two offspring will be produced by applying standard crossover and mutation to their genome.

Based on their co-evolutionary strategy (Iba, 1996), Iba et al. (1997) evolve communication protocols used by agents for cooperative predator-prey pursuit and robot navigation tasks (Iba, 1998). Mackin & Tazaki (1999; 2000; 2002) focus on evolving communication patterns for multi-agent systems modeling a market place. They use a divide-and-conquer approach to evolve the code for sending and receiving the messages exchanged amongst the agents in independent (automatically defined) functions with GP. While starting with a scenario where each trading agent only has a single objective in Mackin & Tazaki (1999), the evolutionary approach is extended to multi-objective GP. By building separate communication trees for each objective, Mackin & Tazaki (2000) allow the agents to weight three objectives in their experiments: to buy the highest volume at lowest price and to collect the best performing services for buying agents, and to sell the highest volume at the highest price while collecting the highest value return for selling agents.

OPTIMIZING NETWORK SECURITY

Network security is one of the most vital aspects when developing distributed systems. The detection of ongoing malicious activities in a network as well as the generation of protocols which are safe against attacks are only two facets of this area. Here we will discuss how global optimization methods can be applied to both of them.

Intrusion Detection

According to Heady et al. (1990), an intrusion is "any set of actions that attempt to compromise the integrity, confidentiality or availability of a resource". These attacks most often come from the outside through network connections to the Internet. intrusion detection systems[5] (IDS) identify such unwanted manipulation of computer systems. Generally, a network connection can be described by a broad set of features concerning its content, time- or traffic-based details, and host-related data. Analysis of these features boils down to data mining. Global optimization methods can be utilized for improving the efficiency of classifiers that decide whether a dataset containing the features of a connection belongs to normal or abnormal (possible intrusive) traffic.

Lu & Traore (2004), for instance, evolve intrusion detection rules with tree-based GP. A similar approach is followed by Folino et al. (2005), who apply the AdaBoost ensemble method of Freund & Schapire (1996) in conjunction with the distributed evolution of decision trees. Heady et al. (1990), on the other hand, use classical Learning Classifier Systems. Linear GP also seems to be very efficient in growing such intrusion detectors, as shown by Mukkamala et al. (2004), for example. D. Song (2003) and D. Song, Heywood, & Zincir-Heywood (2003) use their page-based LGP variant (see Heywood & Zincir-Heywood, 2002) for this purpose. In LaRoche & Zincir-Heywood (2005), they extend this approach for identifying attacks on 802.11 WLAN networks. Hansen et al. (2007) apply a homologous crossover operation to the evolution of linear machine-code structures for intrusion detection to prevent cyber-terrorism.

Security Protocol Generation

Perrig & Song (2000) focus their work on the automatic generation of security protocols such as mutual authentication protocols. In the first step of this process, they use an iterative deepening depth-first search (IDDFS) algorithm to list all protocols that can be composed using a predefined set of primitives. The limit for this search is not the depth in the search space, but a value of a specified cost function which sums up user-specified costs of the single primitives of a protocol. Since the space of all protocols is very large, simplifying assumptions like the absence of redundant message fields and commutativity of the fields are made. Perrig & Song (2000) conduct experiments with the goal of synthesizing mutual authentication protocols. In these experiments, the IDDFS still generates tens of thousands of individuals even with the restrictions defined above. Therefore, a pruning algorithm is added which removes obviously flawed protocols such as those which openly disclose private keys in messages. In this pruning process, vulnerabilities to impersonation attempts or replay attacks are also checked. Only a few hundred candidate protocols survive this pruning routine in the experiments mentioned. These candidates may still be incorrect and are therefore screened with Song's Athena security protocol checker (Song, 1999). As a result, two correct symmetric and one correct asymmetric protocols were synthesized, where the symmetric one was even simpler than the *Symmetric-Key Three-Pass Mutual Authentication Protocol* standardized 1993 by the ISO (ISO, 1993). In 2001, Song et al. (2001) added a code generator that transforms the generated protocol specifications to Java to their system.

OPTIMIZING PARAMETERS AND CONFIGURATIONS

Protocols, distributed algorithms, and topologies can be optimized in order to create robust and efficient distributed applications. The efficiency of such applications strongly depends on their parameter settings and configuration as well. Today's web servers, for instance, have a variety of tuning parameters such as the thread pool size, the maximum number of connections queued, and the number of requests which can be served simultaneously. It is hard to find optimal settings, especially when applications consist of web front ends, application servers hosting the business logic, and database servers in the back end.

The configurations of these subsystems are not independent. Instead, there are epistatic and synergetic effects which are often highly complicated and hard to simulate offline.

Optimal Application Server Configuration

Xi et al. (2004) developed a smart hill climbing algorithm and applied it to application server configuration. This optimization process only needs about ten online performance samples of a running WebSphere brokerage system for fine-tuning its parameters in order to achieve near-optimal results.

Distributed Agent Evolution for Service Management

In the work of Nakano & Suda (2004; 2005; 2007), network services are represented by mobile agents. An agent capable of behaviors like replication, migration, and termination could, for instance, stand for a HTTP server. A behavior i is triggered when a corresponding weighted sum surpasses a certain threshold θ_i (Nakano & Suda, 2005). This sum incorporates environmental information such as the request rate and the resource costs as well as the internal state of the agent like its age and energy level. The weights of the factors in this sum are subject to optimization.

The agents are equipped with energy values. They obtain energy by performing services for the user and spend energy for resource access and replication. If the energy of an agent is depleted, the agent dies, i.e., its service is terminated. Agents may create new agents by replication or reproduction. Replication corresponds to mutation in evolutionary algorithms, leading to a child with slightly changed weight vectors. Reproduction is basically a crossover operation where a partner is selected within n hops in the network based on three measures: the time a user has to wait between requesting and receiving a service, the number of hops a service request travels from the user to the executing agent, and the energy efficiency.

With their experiments, Nakano & Suda (2005) showed that their approach allows the services, i.e., the agents, to adapt to changing conditions such as network failures, varying workload, and changing platform costs (which is reflected in energy consumption).

Protocol Configuration

In his master's thesis, Grace (2000) uses GP to evolve configurations for the JavaGroups (JavaGroups, 1999–2008) reliable group communication framework. The behavior of a JavaGroups instance depends on a protocol stack specification in the form of a string which is passed in when it is created. This specification determines which protocol layers will be present in the stack. Grace (2000) showed that the evolution of communication protocol configurations for predefined scenarios, such as reliable, ordered multicast, is feasible with his approach.

Evolving Protocol Adapters

In distributed systems with components manufactured by different organizations, inter-process communication[6] (IPC) can become problematic. Therefore, protocol adapters are applied, which are components that mediate between different protocols. In the worst case, the number of required adapters rises quadratically with the number of processes in the system. Hence, creating them by hand is infeasible and automated solutions are required. Van Belle et al. (2003) evolve such protocol adapters in the form of classifier systems representing Petri nets with a GA. They show the viability of this method by the example of an adapter for a locking protocol for process synchronization. Similar to our own experience, they found that evolving components of distributed systems always requires special means (Van Belle et al., 2003) of overfitting prevention in order to stop the system from generating useless implementations that just respond with the wanted messages but do not perform the work they are supposed to do. A discussion of the use of Learning Classifier System for the purpose of protocol adapter synthesis can be found in Van Belle's PhD thesis (Van Belle, 2001).

CONCLUDING REMARKS

In this chapter, we presented a systematic review of the wide variety of applications of evolutionary optimization to distributed systems. For the last ten years, this has been one of the most active research areas in EC, with many researchers steadily contributing new and enhanced approaches.

We discussed many interesting works in detail. Yet, we can only offer a small glimpse of the real amount of work available. The Master's thesis of Kampstra (2005) is now four years old and referenced over 400 papers. Apart from these 400 papers, we believe there should exist at least another 200 contributions that were not mentioned in his list or not yet been published when the list was compiled.

Practitioners in the area of networking or telecommunication tend to feel skeptical when it comes to the utilization of ideas like (informed) randomization or bio-inspired approaches for optimizing, managing, or controlling their systems. One argument against the use of metaheuristics is that the worse case results may be unpredictably bad although they may provide good solutions on average.

Nevertheless, certain problems (like the Terminal Assignment Problem, see Section 3.1) are *NP*-hard and therefore can only be solved efficiently with such approaches. This, of course, goes hand in hand with a certain trade-off in terms of optimality, for instance. In static design scenarios, the worst case situations in which an evolutionary algorithm would create inferior solutions can be ruled out by checking its results before the actual deployment or realization.

Furthermore, additional application-specific constraints are often imposed on standard problems in practice. The influence of these constraints on the problem's hardness and the applicability of the well-known solutions is not always easy to comprehend. Thus, incorporating the constraints into an optimization procedure tends to be much easier than customizing a problem-specific heuristic algorithm. Assume that we want to find fast routes in a network which are also robust against a certain fraction of failed links. If we have an evolutionary algorithm with an objective function that measures the time a message travels in a fully functional network, it is intuitively clear that we can extend this approach by simply applying this function to a couple of scenarios with randomly created link failures, too. Creating a corresponding extension of Dijkstra's algorithm, however, is less straightforward.

Evolutionary approaches have not only shown their efficiency in static optimization problems, but are proven to be especially robust in dynamic applications, too. This is particularly interesting in the looming age of networks of larger scale. Wireless networks (Rappaport, 2001; Goldsmith, 2005; Molisch, 2005), sensor networks (Ilyas & Mahgoub, 2004), wireless sensor networks, Smart Home networks (Harper, 2003; Harke, 2003), ubiquitous computing (Greenfield, 2006; Krumm et al., 2007), and more require self-organization, efficient routing, optimal parameter settings, and power management. We are sure that nature and biology-inspired global optimization methods will provide viable answers to many of these questions which will become more and more eminent in the near future.

When condensing the essence of this chapter down to a single sentence, "Evolutionary Computing in Telecommunications – A likely EC success story", the title of Kampstra's thesis, may fit best. However, we believe that the word *likely* is no longer required, since many of the methods developed have already reached engineering-level applicability.

REFERENCES

Abuali, F. N., Schoenefeld, D. A., & Wainwright, R. L. (1994). Terminal assignment in a communications network using genetic algorithms. In *Proceedings of the 22nd Annual ACM Computer Science Conference on Scaling Up: Meeting the Challenge of Complexity in Real-World Computing Applications,* Phoenix, AZ (pp. 74-81).

Aiyarak, P., Saket, A. S., & Sinclair, M. C. (1997). Genetic programming approaches for minimum cost topology optimisation of optical telecommunication networks. In *Proceedings of the 2nd International Conference on Genetic Algorithms in Engineering Systems: Innovations and Applications,* Glasgow, UK (pp. 415-420).

Alba, E., & Chicano, J. F. (2006). Evolutionary algorithms in telecommunications. In *Proceedings of the IEEE Mediterranean Electrotechnical Conference,* Málaga, Spain (pp. 795-798).

Angeline, P. J. (1998). A historical perspective on the evolution of executable structures. *Fundamenta Informaticae, 35*(1-4), 179–195.

Bäck, T. (1996). *Evolutionary algorithms in theory and practice: Evolution strategies, evolutionary programming, genetic algorithms.* Oxford, UK: Oxford University Press.

Bäck, T., Fogel, D. B., & Michalewicz, Z. (Eds.). (1997). *Handbook of evolutionary computation.* London: Taylor & Francis.

Bäck, T., Hammel, U., & Schwefel, H.-P. (1997). Evolutionary computation: Comments on the history and current state. *IEEE Transactions on Evolutionary Computation, 1*(1), 3–17. doi:10.1109/4235.585888

Bagley, J. D. (1967). *The behavior of adaptive systems which employ genetic and correlation algorithms.* Unpublished doctoral dissertation, The University of Michigan, Ann Arbor, MI, USA.

Barricelli, N. A. (1954). Esempi numerici di processi di evoluzione. *Methodos, 6*(21-22), 45–68.

Barricelli, N. A. (1957). Symbiogenetic evolution processes realized by artificial methods. *Methodos, 9*(35-36), 143–182.

Barricelli, N. A. (1963). Numerical testing of evolution theories. Part II. Preliminary tests of performance, symbiogenesis and terrestrial life. *Acta Biotheoretica, 16*(3/4), 99–126. doi:10.1007/BF01556602

Bledsoe, W. W. W. (1961a). *Lethally dependent genes using instant selection* (Tech. Rep. No. PRI 1). Palo Alto, CA, USA: Panoramic Research Inc.

Bledsoe, W. W. W. (1961b). *The use of biological concepts in the analytical study of systems* (Tech. Rep. No. PRI 2). Palo Alto, CA, USA: Panoramic Research, Inc.

Bledsoe, W. W. W. (1962a). *An analysis of genetic populations*. (Tech. Rep.). Palo Alto, CA, USA: Panoramic Research Inc.

Bledsoe, W. W. W. (1962b). *The evolutionary method in hill climbing: Convergence rates*. (Tech. Rep.). Palo Alto, CA, USA: Panoramic Research Inc.

Bledsoe, W. W. W., & Browning, I. (1959). Pattern recognition and reading by machine. In *Proceedings of the Eastern Joint Computer Conference (EJCC) – Papers and Discussions Presented at the Joint IRE - AIEE - ACM Computer Conference,* Boston, MA (pp. 225-232).

Bremermann, H. J. (1962). Optimization through evolution and recombination. In M. C. Yovits, G. T. Jacobi, & G. D. Goldstein (Eds.), *Self-organizing systems* (pp. 93-106). Washington, DC: Spartan Books.

Cavicchio, D. J., Jr. (1970). *Adaptive search using simulated evolution*. Unpublished doctoral disseration, The University of Michigan, Ann Arbor, MI, USA.

Cavicchio, D. J., Jr. (1972). Reproductive adaptive plans. In *Proceedings of the ACM Annual Conference* (pp. 60-70). New York: ACM Press.

Cerf, V., Dalal, Y., & Sunshine, C. (1974). *Specification of Internet transmission control program* (Request for Comments (RFC) No. 675). Network Working Group.

Comellas, F., & Giménez, G. (1998). Genetic programming to design communication algorithms for parallel architectures. *Parallel Processing Letters*, *8*(4), 549–560. doi:10.1142/S0129626498000547

Coombs, S., & Davis, L. (1987). Genetic algorithms and communication link speed design: Constraints and operators. In *Proceedings of the 2nd International Conference on Genetic Algorithms and their Application* (pp. 257-260). Hillsdale, NJ: L. Erlbaum Associates Inc.

Corne, D. W., Oates, M. J., & Smith, G. D. (Eds.). (2000). *Telecommunications optimization: Heuristic and adaptive techniques*. New York: John Wiley & Sons.

Cortés Achedad, P., Onieva Giménez, L., Muñuzuri Sanz, J., & Guadix Martín, J. (2008). A revision of evolutionary computation techniques in telecommunications and an application for the network global planning problem. In A. Yang, Y. Shan, & L. T. Bui (Eds.), *Success in evolutionary computation* (pp. 239-262). Berlin, Germany: Springer-Verlag.

de Araújo, S. G., de Castro Pinto Pedroza, A., & de Mesquita Filho, A. C. (2003a). Evolutionary synthesis of communication protocols. In *Proceedings of the 10th International Conference on Telecommunications,* Tahiti, French Polynesia (pp. 986-993).

de Araújo, S. G., de Castro Pinto Pedroza, A., & de Mesquita Filho, A. C. (2003b). Uma metodologia de projeto de protocolos de comunicação baseada em técnicas evolutivas. In *Proceedings of the XX Simpósio Brasileiro de Telecomunicaçãoes*, Rio de Janeiro, Brazil.

Di Caro, G. (2004). *Ant colony optimization and its application to adaptive routing in telecommunication networks*. Unpublished doctoral dissertation, Université Libre de Bruxelles, Brussels, Belgium.

Di Caro, G., & Dorigo, M. (1998a). Antnet: Distributed stigmergetic control for communications networks. [JAIR]. *Journal of Artificial Intelligence Research, 9*, 317–365.

Di Caro, G., & Dorigo, M. (1998b). Two ant colony algorithms for best-effort routing in datagram networks. In *Proceedings of the 10th IASTED International Conference on Parallel and Distributed Computing and Systems* (pp. 541-546). Calgary, Canada: ACTA Press.

Dijkstra, E. W. (1959). A note on two problems in connexion with graphs. *Numerische Mathematik, 1*, 269–271. doi:10.1007/BF01386390

El-Fakihy, K., Yamaguchi, H., & von Bochmann, G. (1999). A method and a genetic algorithm for deriving protocols for distributed applications with minimum communication cost. In *Proceedings of 11th IASTED International Conference on Parallel and Distributed Computing and Systems* (pp. 863-868). Calgary, Canada: ACTA Press.

Fogel, L. J., Owens, A. J., & Walsh, M. J. (1966). *Artificial intelligence through simulated evolution*. New York: John Wiley & Sons.

Folino, G., Pizzuti, C., & Spezzano, G. (2005). GP ensemble for distributed intrusion detection systems. In *Proceedings of the 3rd International Conference on Advances in Pattern Recognition* (LNCS Vol. 3686, pp. 54-62). Berlin, Germany: Springer-Verlag.

Forsyth, R. (1981). BEAGLE a darwinian approach to pattern recognition. *Kybernetes, 10*, 159–166. doi:10.1108/eb005587

Forsyth, R. (1989). The evolution of intelligence. In R. Forsyth (Ed.), *Machine learning, principles and techniques* (pp. 65-82). Boca Raton, FL: Chapman and Hall.

Forsyth, R., & Rada, R. (1986). *Machine learning applications in expert systems and information retrieval*. Chichester, UK: Ellis Horwood.

Frantz, D. R. (1972). *Nonlinearities in genetic adaptive search*. Unpublished doctoral disseratation, The University of Michigan, Ann Arbor, MI, USA.

Fraser, A. S. (1957). Simulation of genetic systems by automatic digital computers. *Australian Journal of Biological Sciences, 10*, 484–491.

Freund, Y., & Schapire, R. E. (1996). Experiments with a new boosting algorithm. In *Proceedings of the 13th International Conference on Machine Learning,* Bari, Italy (pp. 148-156).

Friedberg, R. M. (1958). A learning machine: Part I. *IBM Journal of Research and Development, 2*, 2–13.

Friedberg, R. M., Dunham, B., & North, J. H. (1959). A learning machine: Part II. *IBM Journal of Research and Development, 3*(3), 282–287.

General Secretariat of the Council of the European Union. COST Secretariat. (1994). *Cost 1991–1992* (Vol. 7). Luxembourg: Office for Official Publications of the European Communities.

Gnutella. (2000). *The Gnutella protocol specification v0.4* [Computer software manual].

Goldberg, D. E. (1989). *Genetic algorithms in search, optimization, and machine learning.* Reading, MA: Addison-Wesley Longman Publishing Co., Inc.

Goldsmith, A. (2005). *Wireless communications.* Cambridge, UK: Cambridge University Press.

Grace, P. (2000). *Genetic programming and protocol configuration.* Unpublished master's thesis, Lancaster University, Lancaster, UK.

Greenfield, A. (2006). *Everyware: The dawning age of ubiquitous computing.* Berkeley, CA: New Riders Publishing.

Hansen, J. V., Lowry, P. B., Meservy, R., & McDonald, D. (2007). Genetic programming for prevention of cyberterrorism through previous dynamic and evolving intrusion detection. *Decision Support Systems, 43*(4), 1362–1374. doi:10.1016/j.dss.2006.04.004

Harke, W. (2003). *Smart home – vernetzung von haustechnik und kommunikationssystemen im wohnungsbau.* Hüthig Verlag/C. F. Müller.

Harper, R. (Ed.). (2003). *Inside the smart home.* Berlin, Germany: Springer-Verlag.

Heady, R., Luger, G., Maccabe, A., & Servilla, M. (1990). *The architecture of a network level intrusion detection system* (Tech. Rep. No. CS90-20, LA-SUB–93-219, W-7405-ENG-36, DE97002400). Department of Computer Science, University of New Mexico, USA.

Hedrick, C. (1988). *Routing information protocol* (Request for Comments (RFC) No. 1058). Internet Engineering Task Force (IETF), Internet Society (ISOC).

Heitkötter, J., & Beasley, D. (Eds.). (1998). *Hitch-hiker's guide to evolutionary computation: A list of frequently asked questions (FAQ).* ENCORE (The EvolutioNary Computation REpository Network).

Heywood, M. I., & Zincir-Heywood, A. N. (2002). Dynamic page-based linear genetic programming. *IEEE Transactions on Systems, Man, and Cybernetics. Part B, Cybernetics, 32*(3), 380–388. doi:10.1109/TSMCB.2002.999814

Holland, J. H. (1962). Outline for a logical theory of adaptive systems. *Journal of the ACM, 9*(3), 297–314. doi:10.1145/321127.321128

Holland, J. H. (1967). *Nonlinear environments permitting efficient adaptation (Vol. II).* New York: Academic Press.

Holland, J. H. (1969). Adaptive plans optimal for payoff-only environments. In *Proceedings of the 2nd Hawaii International Conference on System Sciences, Periodicals,* North Hollywood, CA (pp. 917-920).

Holland, J. H. (1975). *Adaptation in natural and artificial systems: An introductory analysis with applications to biology, control, and artificial intelligence.* Ann Arbor, MI: The University of Michigan Press.

Hörner, H. (1996). *A C++ class library for GP: Vienna University of economics genetic programming kernel (release 1.0, operating instructions)* (Tech. Rep.). Vienna University of Economics.

Iba, H. (1996). Emergent cooperation for multiple agents using genetic programming. In *PPSN IV: Proceedings of the 4th International Conference on Parallel Problem Solving from Nature* (pp. 32-41). Berlin, Germany: Springer-Verlag.

Iba, H. (1998). Evolutionary learning of communicating agents. *Information Sciences – Informatics and Computer Science . International Journal (Toronto, Ont.), 108*(1-4), 181–205.

Iba, H., Nozoe, T., & Ueda, K. (1997). Evolving communicating agents based on genetic programming. In *Proceedings of the IEEE International Conference on Evolutionary Computation* (pp. 297-302). Piscataway, NJ: IEEE Press.

Iles, M., & Deugo, D. L. (2002). A search for routing strategies in a peer-to-peer network using genetic programming. In *Proceedings of the 21st IEEE Symposium on Reliable Distributed Systems* (pp. 341-346). Washington, DC: IEEE Computer Society.

Ilyas, M., & Mahgoub, I. (Eds.). (2004). *Handbook of sensor networks: Compact wireless and wired sensing systems*. Boca Raton, FL: CRC Press.

Information Sciences Institute. University of Southern California, (1981). *Internet protocol, DARPA Internet program protocol specification* (RFC No. 791). Defense Advanced Research Projects Agency, Information Processing Techniques Office, Arlington, USA.

ISO. (1993). Information technology – security techniques – entity authentication – part 3: Mechanisms using digital signature techniques (ISO/IEC No. 9798-3). *International Standards Organization (ISO)*. (JTC 1 Information technology. TC/SC: JTC 1/SC 27. Status: withdrawn)

Jaroš, J., & Dvořák, V. (2008). An evolutionary design technique for collective communications on optimal diameter-degree networks. In *Proceedings of the Genetic and Evolutionary Computation Conference* (pp. 1539-1546). New York: ACM Press.

Javagroups – a reliable multicast communication toolkit for Java [Computer Software Manual]. (1999–2008). Cornell University and SourceForge.

Kampstra, P. (2005). *Evolutionary computing in telecommunications – a likely EC success story*. Unpublished master's thesis, Vrije Universiteit, Amsterdam, the Netherlands.

Kampstra, P., van der Mei, R. D., & Eiben, Á. E. (2006). *Evolutionary computing in telecommunication network design: A survey*. Retrieved from http://www.few.vu.nl/~mei/articles/2006/kampstra/art.pdf

Kershenbaum, A. (1993). *Telecommunications network design algorithms*. New York: McGraw-Hill.

Khuri, S., & Chiu, T. (1997). Heuristic algorithms for the terminal assignment problem. In *Proceedings of the ACM Symposium on Applied Computing* (pp. 247-251). New York: ACM Press.

Kirkwood, I. M. A., Shami, S. H., & Sinclair, M. C. (1997). Discovering simple fault-tolerant routing rules using genetic programming. In *Proceedings of the International Conference on Artificial Neural Networks and Genetic Algorithms,* Norwich, UK (pp. 285-288).

Klasing, R., Monien, B., Peine, R., & Stöhr, E. (1992). Broadcasting in butterfly and de Bruijn networks. In A. Finkel & M. Jantzen (Eds.), *Proceedings of 9th Annual Symposium on Theoretical Aspects of Computer Science* (pp. 351-362). Berlin, Germany: Springer-Verlag.

Koza, J. R. (1988). *Non-linear genetic algorithms for solving problems*. Washington, DC: United States Patent and Trademark Office.

Koza, J. R. (1989). Hierarchical Genetic Algorithms Operating on Populations of Computer Programs. *Proceedings of the 11th International Joint Conference on Artificial Intelligence* (pp. 768–774). Detroit, USA.

Koza, J. R. (1990a). Evolution and co-evolution of computer programs to control independent-acting agents. In *From Animals to Animats: Proceedings of the 1st International Conference on Simulation of Adaptive Behavior,* Paris, France (pp. 366-375).

Koza, J. R. (1990b). Genetic evolution and co-evolution of computer programs. In *Artificial Life II: Proceedings of the Workshop on Artificial Life,* Santa Fe, NM (pp. 603-629).

Koza, J. R. (1990c). *The genetic programming paradigm: Genetically breeding populations of computer programs to solve problems.* (Tech. Rep. No. STAN-CS-90-1314). Computer Science Department, Stanford University, USA.

Koza, J. R. (1990d). A hierarchical approach to learning the Boolean multiplexer function. In *Proceedings of the 1st Workshop on Foundations of Genetic Algorithms,* Indiana, USA (pp. 171-191).

Koza, J. R. (1992). *Genetic programming: On the programming of computers by means of natural selection.* Cambridge, mA: The MIT Press.

Krumm, J., Abowd, G. D., Seneviratne, A., & Strang, T. (Eds.). (2007). *Proceedings of the 9th International Conference on Ubiquitous Computing* (LNCS 4717). Berlin, Germany: Springer-Verlag.

Kumar, A., Pathak, R. M., Gupta, M. C., & Gupta, Y. P. (1993). Genetic algorithm based approach for designing computer network topologies. In *Proceedings of the ACM Conference on Computer Science* (pp. 358-365). New York: ACM Press.

LaRoche, P., & Zincir-Heywood, A. N. (2005). 802.11 network intrusion detection using genetic programming. In *Proceedings of the Workshops on Genetic and Evolutionary Computation* (pp. 170-171). New York: ACM Press.

Lehmann, K. A., & Kaufmann, M. (2005). Evolutionary algorithms for the self-organized evolution of networks. In *Proceedings of the Conference on Genetic and Evolutionary Computation* (pp. 563-570). New York: ACM Press.

Liang, S., Zincir-Heywood, A. N., & Heywood, M. I. (2002). The effect of routing under local information using a social insect metaphor. In *Proceedings of the Congress on Evolutionary Computation* (pp. 1438-1443). Washington, DC: IEEE Computer Society.

Liang, S., Zincir-Heywood, A. N., & Heywood, M. I. (2006). Adding more intelligence to the network routing problem: Antnet and Ga-Agents. *Applied Soft Computing, 6*(3), 244–257. doi:10.1016/j.asoc.2005.01.005

Lu, W., & Traore, I. (2004). Detecting new forms of network intrusions using genetic programming. *Computational Intelligence, 20*(3), 475–494. doi:10.1111/j.0824-7935.2004.00247.x

Luke, S., & Spector, L. (1996). Evolving graphs and networks with edge encoding: A preliminary report. In *Late Breaking Papers at the First Annual Conference Genetic Programming (GP-96)*, Stanford University, CA, USA.

Mackin, K. J., & Tazaki, E. (1999). Emergent agent communication in multi-agent systems using automatically defined function genetic programming (ADFGP). In *Proceedings of the IEEE International Conference on Systems, Man, and Cybernetics*, Tokyo, Japan (pp. 138-142).

Mackin, K. J., & Tazaki, E. (2000). Unsupervised training of multiobjective agent communication using genetic programming. In *Proceedings of the 4ᵗʰ International Conference on Knowledge-Based Intelligent Information Engineering Systems & Allied Technologies*, Brighton, UK (pp. 738-741).

Mackin, K. J., & Tazaki, E. (2002). Multiagent communication combining genetic programming and pheromone communication. *Kybernetes, 31*(6), 827–843. doi:10.1108/03684920210432808

Michalewicz, Z. (1991). A step towards optimal topology of communication networks. In V. Libby (Ed.), *Proceedings of the Data Structures and Target Classification, the SPIE's International Symposium on Optical Engineering and Photonics in Aerospace Sensing* (pp. 112-122). SPIE – The International Society for Optical Engineering.

Miorandi, D., Dini, P., Altman, E., & Kameda, H. (2007). *WP 2.2 – paradigm applications and mapping, D2.2.2 framework for distributed on-line evolution of protocols and services* (2ⁿᵈ ed.). BIOlogically inspired NETwork and Services (BIONETS) and Future and Emerging Technologies (FET) project of the EU.

Molisch, A. F. (2005). *Wireless communications*. New York: John Wiley & Sons/IEEE Press.

Moy, J. (1989). *The OSPF specification* (Request for Comments (RFC) No. 1131). Internet Engineering Task Force (IETF), Internet Society (ISOC).

Mukkamala, S., Sung, A. H., & Abraham, A. (2004). Modeling intrusion detection systems using linear genetic programming approach. In R. Orchard, C. Yang, & M. Ali (Eds.), *Proceedings of the 17ᵗʰ International Conference on Industrial and Engineering Applications of Artificial Intelligence and Expert Systems* (LNCS 3029, pp. 633-642). Berlin, Germany: Springer-Verlag.

Munetomo, M. (1999). Designing genetic algorithms for adaptive routing algorithms in the Internet. In *Proceedings of the GECCO'99 Workshop on Evolutionary Telecommunications: Past, Present and Future*, Orlando, FL (pp. 215-216).

Munetomo, M., Takai, Y., & Sato, Y. (1997). An adaptive network routing algorithm employing path genetic operators. In *Proceedings of the 7ᵗʰ International Conference on Genetic Algorithms*, East Lansing, MI (pp. 643-649).

Munetomo, M., Takai, Y., & Sato, Y. (1998a). An adaptive routing algorithm with load balancing by a genetic algorithm. [IPSJ]. *Transactions of the Information Processing Society of Japan, 39*(2), 219–227.

Munetomo, M., Takai, Y., & Sato, Y. (1998b). A migration scheme for the genetic adaptive routing algorithm. In *Proceedings of the IEEE Conference on Systems, Man, and Cybernetics* (pp. 2774-2779). Piscataway, NJ: IEEE Press.

Nakano, T., & Suda, T. (2004). Adaptive and evolvable network services. In *Proceedings of the Genetic and Evolutionary Computation Conference* (LNCS 3102, pp. 151-162). Berlin, Germany: Springer-Verlag.

Nakano, T., & Suda, T. (2005). Self-organizing network services with evolutionary adaptation. *IEEE Transactions on Neural Networks, 16*(5), 1269–1278. doi:10.1109/TNN.2005.853421

Nakano, T., & Suda, T. (2007). Applying biological principles to designs of network services. *Applied Soft Computing, 7*(3), 870–878. doi:10.1016/j.asoc.2006.04.006

O'Mahony, M., Sinclair, M. C., & Mikac, B. (1993). Ultra-high capacity optical transmission network: European research project COST 239. In M. Kos (Ed.), *Proceedings of the International Conference on Telecommunications,* Zagreb, Croatia (pp. 33-45).

Pedrycz, W., & Vasilakos, A. V. (2000a). Computational intelligence: A development environment for telecommunications networks. In W. Pedrycz & A. V. Vasilakos (Eds.), *Computational intelligence in telecommunications networks* (pp. 1-27). Boca Raton, FL: CRC Press.

Pedrycz, W., & Vasilakos, A. V. (Eds.). (2000b). *Computational intelligence in telecommunications networks*. Boca Raton, FL: CRC Press.

Perrig, A., & Song, D. X. (2000). A first step towards the automatic generation of security protocols. In *Proceedings of the Symposium on Network and Distributed Systems Security,* San Diego, CA (pp. 73-83).

Raghavendra, C. S., Sivalingam, K. M., & Znati, T. (Eds.). (2004). *Wireless sensor networks* (ERCOF-TAC Series). Amsterdam: Springer Netherlands.

Rappaport, T. S. (2001). *Wireless communications: Principles and practice*. Upper Saddle River, NJ: Prentice Hall.

Ripeanu, M., Foster, I., & Iamnitchi, A. (2002). Mapping the Gnutella network: Properties of large-scale peer-to-peer systems and implications for system design. *IEEE Internet Computing Journal, 6*(1), 50–57. doi:10.1109/4236.978369

Schoonderwoerd, R. (1996). *Collective intelligence for network control*. Unpublished master's thesis, Delft University of Technology, Delft, the Netherlands.

Schoonderwoerd, R., Holland, O. E., & Bruten, J. L. (1997). Ant-like agents for load balancing in telecommunications networks. In J. Miller (Ed.), *Proceedings of the 1st International Conference on Autonomous Agents* (pp. 209-216). New York: ACM Press.

Schoonderwoerd, R., Holland, O. E., Bruten, J. L., & Rothkrantz, L. J. M. (1996). Ant-based load balancing in telecommunications networks. *Adaptive Behavior, 5*(2), 169–207. doi:10.1177/105971239700500203

Şckercioğlu, Y. A., Pitsilides, A., & Vasilakos, A. V. (2001). Computational intelligence in management of ATM networks: A survey of current state of research. *Soft Computing, 5*(4), 257–263. doi:10.1007/s005000100099

Shami, S. H., Kirkwood, I. M. A., & Sinclair, M. C. (1997). Evolving simple fault-tolerant routing rules using genetic programming. *Electronics Letters, 33*(17), 1440–1441. doi:10.1049/el:19970996

Sharples, N. P. (1999). Evolutionary approaches to adaptive protocol design. In D. Pearce (Ed.), *CSRP 512: The 12th White House Papers Graduate Research in Cognitive and Computing Sciences at Sussex,* Brighton, UK (pp. 60-62).

Sharples, N. P. (2001). *Evolutionary approaches to adaptive protocol design.* Unpublished doctoral dissertation, University of Sussex, Brighton, UK.

Sharples, N. P., & Wakeman, I. (2000). Protocol construction using genetic search techniques. In S. Cagnoni et al. (Eds.), *Real-world applications of evolutionary computing* (LNCS 1803, pp. 235-246). Berlin, Germany: Springer-Verlag.

Sinclair, M. C. (1995). Minimum cost topology optimisation of the COST 239 European optical network. In *Proceedings of the International Conference on Artificial Neural Networks and Genetic Algorithms* (pp. 26-29). Berlin, Germany: Springer-Verlag.

Sinclair, M. C. (1999a). Evolutionary telecommunications: A summary. In *Proceedings of the GEC-CO'99 Workshop on Evolutionary Telecommunications: Past, Present and Future,* Orlando, FL (pp. 209-212).

Sinclair, M. C. (1999b). Optical mesh network topology design using node-pair encoding genetic programming. In *Proceedings of the Genetic and Evolutionary Computation Conference,* Orlando, FL (pp. 1192–1197).

Sinclair, M. C. (2000). Node-pair encoding genetic programming for optical mesh network topology design. In D. W. Corne et al. (Eds.), *Telecommunications optimization: Heuristic and adaptive techniques* (pp. 99-114). New York: John Wiley & Sons.

Smith, S. F. (1980). *A learning system based on genetic adaptive algorithms.* Unpublished doctoral dissertation, University of Pittsburgh, Pittsburgh, PA, USA.

Song, D. (2003). *A Linear genetic programming approach to intrusion detection.* Unpublished master's thesis, Dalhousie University, Halifax, Nova Scotia, Canada.

Song, D., Heywood, M. I., & Zincir-Heywood, A. N. (2003). A linear genetic programming approach to intrusion detection. In *Proceedings of the Genetic and Evolutionary Computation Conference* (LNCS 2724, pp. 2325-2336). Berlin, Germany: Springer-Verlag.

Song, D. X. (1999). Athena: A new efficient automatic checker for security protocol analysis. In *Proceedings of 12th IEEE Computer Security Foundations Workshop* (pp. 192-202). Piscataway, NJ: IEEE Press.

Song, D. X., Perrig, A., & Phan, D. (2001). AGVI – automatic generation, verification, and implementation of security protocols. In *Proceedings of the 13th International Conference on Computer Aided Verification* (LNCS 2102, pp. 241-245). Berlin, Germany: Springer-Verlag.

Tan, L. G., & Sinclair, M. C. (1995). Wavelength assignment between the central nodes of the COST 239 European optical network. In *Proceedings of the 11th UK Performance Engineering Workshop*, Liverpool, UK (pp. 235-247).

Tanenbaum, A. S., & van Steen, M. (2002). *Distributed systems: Principles and paradigms*. Upper Saddle River, NJ: Prentice Hall.

Théraulaz, G., & Bonabeau, E. (2000). Swarm smarts. *Scientific American, 282*(3), 72–79.

Tschudin, C. F. (2003). Fraglets – a metabolistic execution model for communication protocols. In *Proceedings of 2nd Annual Symposium on Autonomous Intelligent Networks and Systems (AINS 2003)*, Menlo Park, CA.

Tschudin, C. F., & Yamamoto, L. A. R. (2005). A metabolic approach to protocol resilience. In M. Smirnov (Ed.), *Autonomic communication* (LNCS 3457, pp. 191-206). Berlin, Germany: Springer-Verlag.

Van Belle, W. (2001). *Automatic generation of concurrency adaptors by means of learning algorithms*. Unpublished doctoral dissertation, Vrije Universiteit Brussel, Brussel, Belgium.

Van Belle, W., Mens, T., & D'Hondt, T. (2003). Using genetic programming to generate protocol adaptors for interprocess communication. In A. M. Tyrrell, P. C. Haddow, & J. Torresen (Eds.), In *Proceedings of the 5th International Conference on Evolvable Systems: From Biology to Hardware* (LNCS 2606, pp. 67-73). Berlin, Germany: Springer-Verlag.

Vasilakos, A. V., Anagnostakis, K. G., & Pedrycz, W. (2001). Application of computational intelligence techniques in active networks. *Soft Computing – A Fusion of Foundations . Methodologies and Applications, 5*(4), 264–271.

Weise, T., Skubch, H., Zapf, M., & Geihs, K. (2008). *Global optimization algorithms and their application to distributed systems* (Kasseler Informatikschriften (KIS) No. 2008, 3). Distributed Systems Group, University of Kassel, Germany.

Werner, G. M., & Dyer, M. G. (1992). Evolution of communication in artificial organisms. In C. Langton et al. (Eds.), *Artificial life II* (pp. 659-687). Redwood City, CA: Addison-Wesley.

Whitley, L. D. (1994). A genetic algorithm tutorial. *Statistics and Computing, 4*(2), 65–85. doi:10.1007/BF00175354

Xi, B., Liu, Z., Raghavachari, M., Xia, C. H., & Zhang, L. (2004). A smart hill-climbing algorithm for application server configuration. In *Proceedings of the 13th International Conference on World Wide Web* (pp. 287-296). New York: ACM Press.

Yamaguchi, H., Okano, K., Higashino, T., & Taniguchi, K. (1995). Synthesis of protocol entities' specifications from service specifications in a petri net model with registers. In *Proceedings of the 15th International Conference on Distributed Computing Systems* (pp. 510-517). Washington, DC: IEEE Computer Society.

Yamamoto, L. A. R., & Tschudin, C. F. (2005). Genetic evolution of protocol implementations and configurations. In *Proceedings of the IFIP/IEEE International Workshop on Self-Managed Systems and Services (SELFMAN 2005)*, Nice, France.

Yamamoto, L. A. R., & Tschudin, C. F. (2006). Experiments on the automatic evolution of protocols using genetic programming. In I. Stavrakakis & M. Smirnov (Eds.), *Autonomic communication* (LNCS 3854, pp. 13-28). Berlin, Germany: Springer-Verlag.

Yao, X., Wang, F., Padmanabhan, K., & Salcedo-Sanz, S. (2005). Hybrid evolutionary approaches to terminal assignment in communications networks. In W. E. Hart, N. Krasnogor, & J. E. Smith (Eds.), *Recent advances in memetic algorithms* (pp. 129-159). Berlin, Germany: Springer-Verlag.

Zweig, K. A. (2007). *On local behavior and global structures in the evolution of complex networks*. Unpublished doctoral dissertation, University of Tübingen, Tübingen, Germany.

ENDNOTES

[1]   According to some appropriate metric such as latency.

[2]   Except for naming changes and that the rows and columns are switched - we will ignore these minor differences here.

[3]   Again, notice that we have switched the columns and rows in Di Caro and Dorigo's approach in order to relate it to that of Schoonderwoerd et al.

[4]   http://en.wikipedia.org/wiki/Protocol data unit [accessed 2008-06-21]

[5]   http://en.wikipedia.org/wiki/Intrusion detection system [accessed 2008-06-16]

[6]   http://en.wikipedia.org/wiki/Inter-process communication [accessed 2008-06-23]

Chapter 7
Evolutionary Based Adaptive User Interfaces in Complex Supervisory Tasks

Gary G. Yen
Oklahoma State University, USA

ABSTRACT

In this chapter, the author proposes a novel idea based on evolutionary algorithm for adaptation of the user interface in complex supervisory tasks. Under the assumption that the user behavior is stationary and that the user has limited cognitive and motor abilities, the author has shown that a combination of genetic algorithm for constrained optimization and probabilistic modeling of the user may evolve the adaptive interface to the level of personalization. The non-parametric statistics has been employed to evaluate the feasibility of the ranking approach. The method proposed is flexible and easy to use in various problem domains. The author has tested the method with an automated user and a group of real users in an air traffic control environment. The automated user, implemented for initial tests, is built under the same assumptions as a real user. In the second step, the author has exploited the adaptive interface through a group of real users and collected subjective ratings using questionnaires. The author has shown that the proposed method can effectively improve human-computer interaction and his approach is pragmatically a valid design for the interface adaptation in complex environments.

INTRODUCTION

Humans and computers form teams in complex environments such as in aviation, glass cockpit, nuclear power plants, manufacturing lines, and command and control scenarios. The computers generally undertake the automation part while the human is responsible for the supervision of the overall task or interrupts the process at the higher level. Task sharing is generally done at design time, using Fitts list (Fitts, 1951). Automation was thought to be the remedy to the problems resulting from human errors.

DOI: 10.4018/978-1-60566-798-0.ch007

However, Billings has argued that automation in aviation, for example, has not put an end to the accidents (Billings, 1997). It is commonly believed that as the tasks allocated to the computer increase, the cognitive load of the human (supervisor) grows, hence causing inevitable errors.

One of many reasons for the errors under automation is the reduced situation awareness, which is defined as "the perception of the elements in the environment within a duration of time, the comprehension of their meaning, and the projection of their status" by Endsley (1988). Endsley has also developed Situation Awareness Global Assessment Technique (SAGAT), a questionnaire to measure perceived load on the operator. He claims that automation leads to under-utilization of the human's skills and leads to errors. He also added that the automated process under supervision is no longer transparent to the human, hence leads to erroneous decisions under time pressure. Facts mentioned above inspire the idea of the adaptation of the interface. By these means researchers believe that computers can tailor their behavior according to the environment and the personal traits of the user. This adaptation can result in more efficient and effective interaction between human and computer, hence improve the quality of the operations (Wilson *et al.*, 2000). What is proposed in this chapter is to exploit the meta-heuristic searching ability of the genetic algorithm in evolving the user interface based upon certain performance measures. What could be evolved include the position, size, shape, color of each element and even the way how they appear and change in the screen.

In this chapter, we propose a new approach to the adaptive interface design. We develop a generalized and easy-to-implement framework for the adaptation of the interfaces. The section "Literature Review on Concpetual Framework for Adaptation" presents a literature review of the adaptive interface domain. It is not our intent to give a complete taxonomy of the adaptive interfaces under this section; however, this discussion will help the readers to understand our approach easily. The section also justifies the conceptual details of the proposed algorithm. In the section "Proposed Method" we give abstract definitions of the adaptation method. This way readers may adapt the algorithm for their own domain of interest. The fourth section, "Air Traffic Control," presents an application in the Air Traffic Control (ATC) task implementation. With this sample implementation, we aim to give more concrete basis for our approach. The fifth section, "Results," provides some statistical analyses of the results and finally we will conclude with the sixth section.

LITERATURE REVIEW ON CONCEPTUAL FRAMEWORK FOR ADAPTATION

In the introduction, we have mentioned that adaptation of the interface is deemed to be the remedy for human errors in complex environments. The interface adaptation, on the other hand, is not a straightforward task. Difficulty lies in first assessing the user's state of mind (goal-subgoal structure), state of psychology (situation awareness), and level of vigilance. All of these are non-deterministic and hard to model. Secondly, defining an appropriate adaptation behavior for the interface; and thirdly timeliness of the adaptation (Horvitz, 1999) are the other difficulties. Since the work undertaken in this area of research is not well defined, and hard to attack without an appropriate tool, we need to define a framework before we can start the discussion. There are three steps to be considered in adaptation of the interface. Many papers have been written on adaptation and adaptation methods, however Rothrock *et al.* (2002) have defined a simple and comprehensive framework for adaptation. In this study we will follow Rothrock's methodology: identification of variables that call for adaptation, determination of necessary modifications to the interface and selection of decision inference mechanism.

Table 1. Adaptation variables

1. User Performance
2. User Goals
3. Cognitive Workload
4. User Situation Awareness
5. User Knowledge
6. Groups Profiles 7. Situation Variables 8. Task Variables

The above classification is not the only framework for adaptation. Please see (Benyon and Murray, 1993) and (Norcio and Stanley, 1989) for additional references. We will give detailed definitions and possible interpretations of the three-step methodology defined in (Rothrock *et al.*, 2002) in the next three subsections.

Variables that Call for Adaptation

According to Rothrock's methodology, interface adaptation should be triggered by some factors. Because of this, we should consider variables that call for adaptation in order to define the adaptation. Table 1 lists some variables that were considered to be triggers in the literature.

1) User performance is generally defined as an error percentage in performing a task, as well as the time required to perform a task (Rouse *et al.*, 1988). Examples of this kind of metric include reaction time, capturing a simple target, and tracking deviation. Difficulty in measuring the user performance lies in the lack of deterministic mapping between the mental process of the user and task performance. For example, the response latency score does not always reflects the complexity of the mental process or level of mental workload.

2) User goals consist of sub-level or higher level goal structures to accomplish a task. According to (Brusilovsky, 1996), sub-level user goals can change easily, yet high level goals are stable. Because of this reason adaptation should aim to discover higher level goals.

3) Cognitive workload is a highly elaborated topic in the human ergonomics field. It has been shown that both high and low cognitive workloads adversely affect task performance (Bi and Salvendy, 1994). The "multiple resource theory" is the predominant theory in human cognition research (Wickens, 1992). There are three different assessment techniques commonly used to measure cognitive workload, none of which is proven to be correct or reliable. The first technique is called the psychophysical method. An electroencephalogram (EEG) or Event-Related Potentials (ERP) are in this category (Prinzel *et al.*, 2001). New techniques in this group are evaluating the brain potentials and neuro-imaging (Sanderson *et al.*, 2003). The second technique is called subjective measures. This technique relies on the users self assessing their cognitive load. Questionnaires are employed in order to collect the value of the assessment. The best known questionnaires are the NASA Task Load Index (TLX) (Hart and Staveland, 1988) and the Subjective Workload Assessment Technique (SWAT) (Reid and Nygren, 1988). The third technique is called secondary task method. The operator is required to do the secondary task concurrently with the primary task. The secondary

Table 2. Interface modification methods

1. Content adaptation
2. Dialog adaptation
3. Task allocation
4. Decision support

task is used to measure the vigilance or situation awareness. Like in any other method, there is an ongoing debate on assessment of workload level using secondary task (Pew, 1979). On the other hand, Kaber and Riley (1999) showed that secondary task performance can be used for triggering the adaptation. Wilson *et al.* (2000) has shown that using neural networks for assessing user mental workload enhances the task performance.

4) User situation awareness, as defined earlier, can be measured by SAGAT (Endsley, 1988) and Situation Awareness Rating Technique (SART) questionnaires. On the other hand, the Situation Awareness Model for Pilot-in-the-Loop Evaluation (SAMPLE) is designed to measure the awareness in real-time without questioning the operator.

5) User knowledge is generally used in Human Computer Interface (HCI) domain and multimedia systems (Brusilovsky, 1996). For example, each user has a student model in adaptive tutoring systems. This helps the interface to define the way the information should be presented. The same student model may also help to define the best way to explain a topic of interest, such as in mathematics tutoring systems.

6) Group profiles are generally used for web browsing or news article suggestion. It is an important and promising aspect of adaptation because it overcomes the human evaluation barrier by using other user's habits in the group. For example, GroupLens (Suchak and Lacovou, 1994) filters Netnews by suggesting the news that another person has already read and rated. Wu *et al.* (2001) uses a group model to help users in a web browsing task.

7) Situation variables can also trigger adaptation. This happens when a process goes from a normal state to a disturbed state. In these situations the user/operator is stressed very quickly by the number of alarms generated. The interface should help the operator to find the problem and solve it (Viano *et al.*, 2000). Situation variables include system state, environmental conditions, social traits, etc.

8) Task variables are like situation variables but are generally associated with the error or fault in the process or the system.

Interface Modification Methods

Although there is a vast amount of literature from different domains and a vast amount of approaches for specific applications we can classify interface modification methods into four categories. These categories are given in Table 2.

1) Content adaptation is one of the most applied methodologies in multimedia adaptation as mentioned in Brusilovsky (1996). Selection of information with respect to user goals is considered in Francisco-Revilla and Shipman (2000). The abstraction level of the information depending on user vigilance is considered in Sanderson *et al.* (2003). Spatial layout of the information is implemented

Table 3. Adaptation algorithms

1. Naïve Bayesian
2. Nearest neighborhood
3. PEBLS (Parallel Exemplar Based Learning System)
4. Decision tree
5. Rocchio's algorithm
6. Perceptron (multilayered feedforward neural network)
7. Multi-layer neural network

by Masui (1994) by using adaptive methods for graph layouts in user interfaces. Modality of information is proposed for simultaneous tasks. Augmentation of information is proposed in Adelman, *et al.* (2004) for distributed team decision environments.

2) Dialog adaptation is considered as an alternative to interface adaptation. A good example of this is the different ordering of the menu entries according to usage frequency (Mathe and Chen, 1996). Another example of dialog adaptation is to collapse the number of steps for frequent tasks by creating shortcuts such as macros.

3) Task allocation or level of automation is also considered. This field is researched extensively in the aviation systems such as glass cockpit or ATC. A major issue is the level of automation defined in Sheridan and Verbank (1978). It simply classifies levels of automation into ten levels ranging from totally human undertaking to a complete autonomy of the machine.

4) Decision support is considered as a knowledge/rule based system. The system helps to make decisions by employing the coded knowledge of the expert at design time. It is important especially when decisions are required under time pressure.

Inference Mechanism

This subsection briefly overviews the selection of decision inference mechanism. Generally interface can be inferred from the data collected and can change its own mapping. These mechanisms can be regarded as a classifier based on user's habits, levels of knowledge, levels of workload or efficiency and the output is the specific interface chosen. Pazzani and Billsus (1997) have compared the pros and cons of different algorithms. They are listed in Table 3. These algorithms are used in order to infer from the trigger condition. The user and the computer evaluation data were selected according to the criteria explained in the subsection "Variables that Call for Adaptation." For example, Wilson *et al.* (2000) have used neural networks for assessment of the user workload.

Methods defined above were used as classifiers. Previous treatment of the interface adaptation was in the sense of dichotomy. Two interfaces were designed and data related to user interaction was collected. One of the methods was used for offline training. Finally, a trained algorithm was used for real-time adaptation. Our algorithm treats the problem from the optimization point of view and learning is done in real-time. A genetic algorithm (GA) is used to optimize these properties.

Figure 1. Interface adaptation flow chart

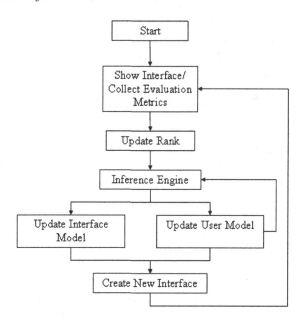

PROPOSED METHOD

We would like to introduce a generalized framework for the adaptation of user interface in complex environments. Our approach is finding the mapping between two spaces of interest as pointed out by Takagi (2001), which are the psychological and the parameter spaces. Here we define psychological space as a level of preference and comfort using the interface for a given user. On the other hand, the parameter space is defined as the possible combinations of parameters related to the interface that could be tuned in order to increase preference value of the interface in the corresponding psychology space. Takagi suggests that there is a desired interface for each user. Psychological distance between this desired interface and the current interface should be minimized in order to increase the efficiency. We will split our framework into three subsections in order to be consistent with the literature reviewed and for ease of explanation. The next three subsections will cover these parts. Meanwhile, the general flow of the algorithm is given in Figure 1.

We will define the psychological and parameter spaces in more concrete manner before we continue to explain the detailed procedures of the proposed method.

Definition 1: If $\mathring{A}$ is a set of operators defined for the interface (interface model) and A is a subset of $\left\{A \middle| A \subset \mathring{A}\right\}$ and X is the operator's psychological space then $f : A \rightarrow X$ is a mapping from interface to psychological space. □

Generally $\dim(\mathring{A}) \geq \dim(X)$ since human perception may not compare to the fineness of parameter space of the interface. Please note $\dim(\cdot)$ is referred to as the dimension of the space under consideration. For example alarm tone of 1 KHz can alert the operator as much as 1.01 KHz can do. Takagi (2001) proposes to use a neural network in order to model f and this can correspond to user model in Benyon and Murray (1993). The actual mapping function that maps the interface to the psychology space is not known analytically and is affected by personal, psychological, and environmental factors.

Assumption 1: f is a stationary stochastic mapping from the parameter space to the psychology space. f is dependent on $\mathring{A}$ which is assumed to span the cognitive space. □

Assumption 1 states that depending on the application domain, $\mathring{A}$ should be selected carefully so that the resultant interface would correspond to a different region in X in order to be evaluated effectively. If we go back to our monotone alarm example, small difference between frequencies would correspond to the same alert level in user psychology space and thus will not be able to span the whole psychological space.

Interaction Evaluation Method

Even if Assumption 1 is satisfied, it is still not easy to evaluate an interface. First reason is the burden of evaluation. The user may not be willing to answer frequent questions; even so, it may lead to degradation of vigilance and concentration loss. In addition to these factors there is no generic and proven way defined for acquiring this information from the user. Some metrics are defined to acquire this information such as psycho-physiological, subjective and performance metrics (Prinzel, 2003). The subjective methods such as NASA-TLX (Task Load Index) are not appropriate for online analysis since it requires the user to respond to a set of questions after interacting with the interface. Psycho-physiological methods (Prinzel *et al.*, 2001; Sanderson *et al.*, 2003) are inconvenient for the user since most of them require connecting the user to the interface via some wires. Finally performance metrics seem to be more appropriate, efficient and inexpensive for assessing user interaction level. Performance data can be collected online through the user's interaction with the interface. This is the first phase of our design as shown in Figure 1. Interaction begins, as soon as an interface is shown to the user. Some values such as goal accomplishment time, number of errors, number of actions, etc. can be used to infer the level of comfort and efficiency of the interface. These values can be fed to the inference engine which will be covered in the next subsection.

Inference Engine

Data collection methods for evaluation of the interface may vary, but data is independent of the collection method. This acquired data is not dependable and often very noisy. "Noise" here is used to emphasize the stochastic behavior of the user. That is, the same interface can receive different scores at different times. We are using a non-parametric approach to handle this problem, because any data collected as a measure of performance, should be regarded as in an ordinal scale, which means data can be ordered as better or worse. Data values of any kind cannot be considered as an interval scale since the relative difference between the values is not meaningful. This is also true for subjective and performance measures. The second reason we employ a non-parametric method is to decrease the variability of the scores. One method proposed in non-parametric statistics is using the rank values, i.e. the preprocessing of the data before it is sent to the inference engine.

If we had a perfect mapping function $f : A \rightarrow X$, we could use it to find the best interface. However it is not available and we are not interested in finding the exact mapping function f, since it is too hard if not impossible. Instead every new interface is ranked with respect to other interfaces which have been shown through interaction. We propose this method in order to create the mapping by sampling different possible interfaces. This approach has been applied before (Claude-Nicolas and Seth, 2000; Masui, 1994) in a sense of dichotomy but adaptation was not continuous. Gervasio *et al.* (1999) have used past information without considering the importance of the context during user evaluation. Claude-Nicolas and Seth's approach is very similar and tries to find a linear classifier to separate two classes which are labeled as good and bad. They have not considered the linear separability of these points. In our approach, however, changing the interface triggers re-ranking of all the interfaces that have been shown to the user up to that point in time. Re-arrangement of the interfaces helps to fine tune the topology of *f*. Ranking can be applied to multiple metrics collected upon interaction and the sum of ranks can be assigned as the final evaluation of interface given proper weighting.

Some amount of forgetting is also applied to the model. Forgetting is a simple pruning of the earliest (temporal) interface from the pool of interfaces that has been shown to the user, thus corresponding to a sliding time window during the evolution. This sort of pruning is chosen to be the forgetting factor in order to accommodate the fast changing characteristics of the user such as fatigue, vigilance, etc. We drop the oldest interface regardless of its fitness value. This pruning approach is beneficial since it can adapt to high frequency changes due to the user forgetting about the past events. On the other hand, this method also leads to pruning of candidate solutions regardless of their potential usefulness and makes it even harder for the algorithm to find the best interface. Ranking is done relying on the problem dependent features of the interface that have been identified during the design time. Although these features are problem dependent, flexibility of the ranking approach will be less of a constraint on choosing the features. Equation (1) shows ranking formula where $R(.)$ is defined as monotonically increasing function from performance of the interface to the rank of the interface within other interfaces.

$$R(A_{ij}) < R(A_{kj}) \quad \Leftrightarrow \quad A_{ij} < A_{kj}, \forall i, j, k \in \Re \tag{1}$$

where $i, k = 1, 2, \cdots, n$ is the interface number and A_{ij} and A_{kj} are the *j*th metric associated to interface *i* and *k*, respectively, $j = 1, 2, \cdots, m$. A new interface will be shown to the user and the desired measurements are collected in a given period of time. Results will be ranked with respect to the earlier interfaces and rank values will be used as fitness value of the interface (1).

An inference engine will generate new interface with the help of the user model which will be covered in the next subsection. Our aim is to consider inference as an optimization problem, search space being the parameter space of the interface while objective space is the psychological space of the user. The relation between these two is the calculated rank. Although different optimization techniques can be applied to this problem, we have used GA as mentioned before. The complexity of the problem arises from the lack of well-defined objective functions and noisy evaluations. We prefer to apply GA in the search for two reasons. The first reason is to take advantage of stochastic search method employed, and the second reason is the flexibility of GA search in difficult problems such as discontinuity in function surface and constraint satisfaction.

User Model

The scores from the interface evaluation are fed into the inference engine after the ranking scheme is employed and GA is used as an inference engine to search for a better interface. Yet the power of GA comes from being a population based algorithm. In the interface design, finding the fitness of any candidate solution is very expensive. We cannot evaluate many interfaces at a given time since we don't

Table 4. Pseudo code for adaptation algorithm

```
InitInterface();
Do {
collectData();
updateUserModel();
If (timerTriggered()) then
reRankAllInterfaces();
\\GA part
selectParentInterfaces();
doCrossOver();
doMutation();
\\End of GA part
if MOD(numIterations) = maxPopLength then
\\Prune the oldest interface
pruneInterfacePop();
reRankAllInterfaces();
end if
end if
} while (numIterations < maxIteration);
```

want to disturb the user extensively. Although we always log the past individuals (interface models) and create a temporary population for GA, we are not able to test more than one individual (interface model) in each generation. We have used probabilistic approach to overcome this problem. The user model is given in Definition 2.

Definition 2: The user model which is used to approximate f in Definition 1 is a multivariate Gaussian with $U = G(\mu, \sigma)$. $\Theta = [\mu, \sigma]$ is the model parameter. Every interface is subject to pre-evaluation and their scores are calculated as $P(A = \text{good} \mid \Theta = \theta)$ where $\{A \mid A \subset \text{Å}\}$. □

The next interface is chosen according to this probability. Before going into more detail we would like to clarify why we need to define a mapping for evaluation of interface components. First, the user is able to interact with only one interface model. Under this assumption we can evaluate only one interface in a given time period. However GA can create more than one offspring (interface models). In order to evaluate the interfaces without showing them to the user, we need an estimator of user preferences which were defined within the user model.

The pseudocode for the algorithm is given in Table 4. The *updateUserModel* subroutine contains the adaptation of a multivariate Gaussian function. After defining our adaptation method we can discuss the process of selecting the interface model from the interface population. An individual is defined by the combination of features dependent on the problem domain that can be selected to adapt the interface to the current user. Due to the inherent flexibility of GA these features can be chosen from discrete or continues variables.

AIR TRAFFIC CONTROL

In this section, domain specific components will be defined and separated from the general framework and better understanding of the algorithm will be pursued through an example. A generalized framework for online adaptation being the ultimate goal, we have implemented our approach using an ATC (Air Traffic Control) test bed. We have used this example because recent studies have shown that the adap-

Table 5. Interface features specific for ATC testbed

1. Information Acquisition
  • Change update time [0-50]
  • Activate sound crash/shoot/both [0-3]
  • Whether to apply Fitt's rule [0-1]
  • Mouse pointer arrow/cross/nodrop [0-2]

2. Information Analysis
  • Show current score [0-1]
  • Activate right click [0-1] when it locates the possible crash
  • Number of planes [1-maxNum]

3. Action Implementation
  • Add list box [0-1] automatically activate linking
  • Clear planes by right click [0-1]

4. Decision Making
  • Rank list box by entry sequence/speed/position/possible accident [0-3]
  • Increase size/change color of possible crash site [0-2]

tation of this type of interface would improve the performance of operators. In one study Kaber *et al.* (2002) have shown moving targets (airplanes) to the user. The user is supposed to clear the targets, by clicking on them before they leave the display. Contrary to what was explained in Kaber *et al.* (2002), we did not employ an impaired vision with a moving window, or use two-step clearance method for each plane. However, we have used number of airplanes presented and number of airplanes cleared as performance measures. We will start with domain specific components of interface model as defined in Definition 1. Taxonomy for domain specific interface modification techniques was defined for ATC in Laois and Giannacourou (1995).

Table 5 shows interface features chosen to be implemented in the experimental testbed. Numbers in squared brackets are possible values that a feature can assume respectively with linguistic explanations. Now that the problem dependent features are selected, our interface model (A in Definition 1) to be used under evaluation will be the possible combinations of this features. For example

$$\left\{ A \middle| A \quad \begin{bmatrix} 30 & 1 & 1 & 0 & 40 & 1 & 0 & 0 & 0 & 0 & 1 \end{bmatrix} \in \mathring{A} \right\} \text{ is interpreted as:}$$

- Update interval will be 30 sample times [30];
- Activate the sound for crash of the plane [1];
- Apply Fitt's rule [1];
- Don't show the current score [0];
- Number of maximum airplanes is 40 [40];
- Locate possible crash site on right click [1];
- Don't add list box [0];
- Rank list box by time sequence of entry [0];
- Mouse pointer shape over the plane is arrow [0];
- Don't do any change at possible crash site [0];
- Right click clear planes from the interface [1];

All kinds of interfaces (genomes) will be subjected to adaptation under genetic operators. Resulting children will be evaluated by user model U as explained in Definition 2. Depending on a candidate interface's conditional probability, it will be selected to be shown to the user for a predetermined interval of time. Multivariate Gaussian approximation of the user (user model U in Definition 2) is also updated through evolution of the interfaces along with the performance as given in Equation (2). Model parameter μ is adapted by using Equation (3) and σ is adapted dynamically by Equation (4).

$$P_n^a = \mathrm{hardlim}(P_n^a - P_n)(\lambda P_{n-1}^a + (1-\lambda)P_n) \tag{2}$$

$$\mu_n = \mathrm{hardlim}(P_n^a - P_n)(\gamma \mu_{n-1} + (1-\gamma)(\mu_{n-1} - A_{n-1})) \tag{3}$$

$$\sigma_n = \mathrm{hardlim}(P_n^a - P_n)(\tau \sigma_{n-1} + \delta) \tag{4}$$

where P_n^a is the weighted average performance throughout the interaction. The corresponding $\lambda < 1$ is the filter coefficient. P_n is the last performance at time n. μ_n is the mean of Gaussian at time n and the corresponding $\gamma < 1$ is generally called the learning constant. $\theta_n = \begin{bmatrix} \mu_n & \sigma_n \end{bmatrix}$ is the model parameter and $\left\{ A_{n-1} \big| A_{n-1} \subset \text{Å} \right\}$ is the current interface model. σ_n is the diagonal elements of the covariance matrix of the multivariate Gaussian. Cross-correlation effects of parameters were not considered for simplicity. $\tau < 1$ is the convergence rate of the variance. δ is a constant and is used in Equation (4) to prevent variance from approaching zero and creating singularity. The steady state value of δ can be determined for every parameter in the interface using Equation (5).

$$\lim_{n \to \infty} \sigma_n^j = \frac{\delta_j}{1 - \tau}, j = 1, 2, \cdots, m \tag{5}$$

is the jth diagonal element of the covariance metric associated to model. *hardlim* is referred to as the hard limit function (i.e., $\mathrm{hardlim}(x) = 1$, if $x > 0$ and $\mathrm{hardlim}(x) = 0$, otherwise). Equation (3) is a modified version of the instar rule for associative learning and is very similar to the non-projectional learning algorithm scheme explained in the learning automata (Thathachar and Sastry 2002). As can be easily seen from Equation (3), our user model is nothing but a localization function for the search used in GA. Initially GA is free to explore the subset of parameter space since the initial variance was set to a big number. As iteration continues, the user model limits the search space since variance converges to a steady state value as given in Equation (5). Because $P(A = \text{good} \big| \Theta = \theta)$ would be very small for the interface models away (Euclidian distance sense) from μ_n they would not be selected as candidates for the next iteration. This will naturally lead to an exploration of the search space in contrast to an exploitation. At this point, we can assign a probability value to each interface using the user model U. One of these interfaces will then be shown at the next iteration according to their probability. New scores will be used for fine-tuning the evaluation function through the re-ranking mechanism.

As mentioned above we can select more then one measure to evaluate the interface due to the flexibility of the ranking method. We can collect the following data set for each interface for a fixed interval of time;

- number of mouse clicks,
- number of unsuccessful mouse clicks,

Table 6. Ranking procedure

Interval Number	# of mouse clicks /Rank	# of unsuccessful mouse clicks/ Rank	# of planes shown /Rank	\# of destroyed plane/ Rank	Total Rank
1	55/2	5/2	60/1*	3/1.5**	6.5
2	43/1	3/1	55/2*	3/1.5**	5.5

* Higher number of planes is better than smaller number of planes
** Equal numbers are assigned middle ranks

- number of air planes presented to the user, and
- number of air planes destroyed before successful clearance.

We have also collected the total mouse shift, but it was not very informative for ranking. For each performance measure, we assign a rank to an interface. Adding up the total rank assigned to one interface is used for ordering. Tables 6 and 7 give an example. Each row is assumed to be an interface model as explained above. The reason for the ranking procedure is to reduce the variability of data. Also, as we have claimed before, data is in an ordinal scale, and values can be interpreted only as bigger or smaller in relation to other data. Assume now a new interface was presented to user, re-ranking will be applied every time a new evaluation is available. For a new interface, this procedure is demonstrated in Table 7.

For now we are using only total ranks as fitness measure but these ranks can also be used in statistical analysis. Subroutines listed in Table 4 also include selectParentInterfaces(), doCrossOver(), and doMutation() for ATC case study and are briefly discussed below. The parent selection algorithm, selectParentInterfaces(), implements roulette wheel selection. In this method, fitter individuals are selected with higher probability. Crossover operation, doCrossOver(), applies uniform crossover. Given two parents, we create one child by selecting one of its parent's genes at each location with equal probability. Finally the mutation operator, doMutation(), is applied to the child with a very low probability. We use real_valued crossover, and random assignment is used at the locations where discrete variations are assumed.

RESULTS

Results are collected under two different categories. The automated user is designed to test the algorithm while real users are employed to show the validity of the approach in real world environment.

Table 7. Re-ranking procedure

Interval Number	# of mouse clicks /Rank	# of unsuccessful mouse clicks/ Rank	# of planes shown /Rank	\# of destroyed plane/Rank	Total Rank
1	55/3*	5/2	60/1	3/2.5*	8.5
2	43/1	3/1	55/2	3/2.5*	6.5
3	45/2	6/3	54/3	2/1	9

* Updated after the addition of the new interface (compare with Table 6)

Automated User Model

The automated user model is a multivariate Gaussian and is very similar to the user model that was defined earlier but with one difference in that μ and σ^2 of the automated user are fixed. The automated user randomly selects a plane and attempts to clear it. The probability of the automated user clearing the plane is calculated by substituting the interface model A into the automated user model.

The first category of the experiments is used to validate the ranking approach for the evaluation of interfaces. Two different kinds of interface models (one is closer in Euclidian distance to the preferred interface of the automated user than the other) without adaptation have been presented to the automated user. We test the hypothesis, "if distribution of the populations from which these samples came from is the same." We can rephrase the hypothesis as follows, "is the ranking procedure a consistent measure for different types of interfaces?" We have used the Kolmogorov-Smirnov (KS-2) test (Terrell, 1999) to compare the distribution of two samples from the same interface model. The resulting test statistic value for m = 20, n = 20 was K = 0.2 and the null hypothesis was accepted with observed significance level (p-value = 0.7710) for preferred interface; and K = 0.2105 and the null hypothesis was accepted with observed significance level (p-value = 0.7415) for non-preferred interface. The second test for the first category of experiments was to test if two different interfaces could be distinguished as better or worse using the ranking procedure. Data was ranked using all of the values (preferred and non-preferred interfaces together). We have used the t-test to see if the difference in means is significant. We have also used the Lilliefors test (Terrell, 1999) for goodness of fit to a normal distribution on both sample data before we use the t-test. Lilliefors test accepts null hypothesis with a p-value = 0.1096 and a p-value = 0.1454 for preferred and non-preferred interfaces, respectively. Finally a two tailed t-test rejects the null hypothesis (the distributions are same) with a p-value = 3.6637e-14. Our results show that we can use the ranking scheme for estimating the relative goodness of the interface.

The second category of experiments was conducted for adaptation of interface under these assumptions. At this point we have developed a test procedure to see if we can adapt the interface for different users. Starting interface parameters were $\begin{bmatrix} 50 & 0 & 1 & 0 & 40 & 0 & 1 & 0 & 0 & 0 & 1 \end{bmatrix}$. The first one thousand and eighty iterations were conducted with the automated user preference vector being $\begin{bmatrix} 10 & 1 & 1 & 0 & 40 & 0 & 1 & 3 & 0 & 2 & 0 \end{bmatrix}$ and at the instance of one thousand and eighty one, the preference vector for the automated user was changed to $\begin{bmatrix} 50 & 3 & 0 & 1 & 40 & 0 & 1 & 1 & 2 & 0 & 1 \end{bmatrix}$ This is preferred if changing the automated user in the simulation would be recognized by the adaptation algorithm.

Figure 2 shows the improvement in the errors (i.e., number of unsuccessful mouse clicks and number of airplanes destroyed before successful clearance). This is the data we have collected for the ranking procedure and GA was running to improve this performance. Results were given for a total of 2,160 iterations. This means we have evaluated a total of 2,160 interfaces. We can easily see the time of switch from one automated user to another in Figure 2. In each case the program was able to catch the difference and converge to the preferred interface. In this experiment the user would spend one minute per interface evaluation and total experiment time would result in more than sixteen hours of evaluation. This clearly shows why we have time constraints for real user and why we have designed the automated user for the initial test phase. But our results can be validated for a prolonged time as well. We should add that, in a given time we store only forty different interfaces collected in consecutive temporal intervals of

Figure 2. Performance metrics

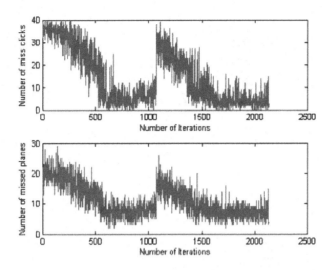

interaction. This was accounted for fast changing characteristics of user such as vigilance, attention, etc. Every time a new interface is generated we delete the oldest interface from the population to maintain a fixed number of interface populations. Figure 3 show a snapshot during the evolution.

Figure 3. Sample interface appearance at different iterations

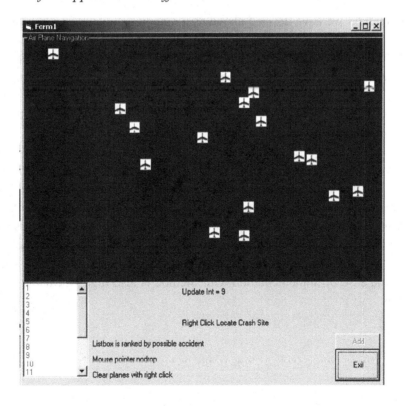

Figure 4. Euclidean distance between interface and preference vector

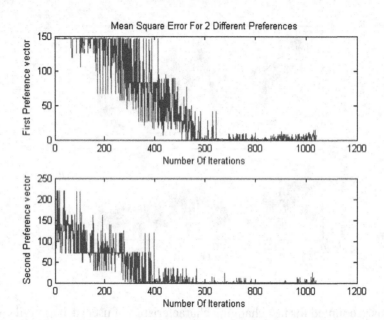

We would also like to see if we were able to find the preference of the automated user (in psychological space). The euclidean distance between the interface and the preference vector was calculated and plotted in Figure 4. Figure 4 depicts three things;

1. The ranking method we have defined above as a mapping strategy is a valid mapping between feature space and psychological space.
2. Stochastic behavior, at least for the automated user's behavior, can be modeled using this technique and the interface adapts to user preferences in order to enhance the performance of the human-computer interaction.
3. The user model defined earlier was effective in localizing the search since, by the end of Figure 4, the variance of the interface is very small.

All of these improvements were established using least knowledge about the domain and the user. The evaluation for GA was done only for one interface for a given period of time. The interface has not interrupted the user and asked to give preferences between couple of interfaces. All processes were handled online. Improvements to this technique are possible. But the best part of this method is that its flexibility is not inversely related with its feasibility. That is, we can easily incorporate more explicit domain knowledge to guide the search and still the interface will be feasible in the sense of collecting extra information and ease of implementation. Our method is also highly scalable for more complex domain interactions.

Human Users

This subsection is dedicated to the results reported by the human user. The main purpose of this subsection is to show the validity of the approach in real life situations. However there is one difference between the interface model used under this subsection and the subsection "Automated User Model." We have employed a smaller number of parameters. There are two reasons for this difference. First and the most important reason is the burden on the user. Real time adaptation lasts approximately thirty seconds for every evaluation. We have collected eighty data points for eighty iterations. Simple calculation shows that this results in forty minutes of interaction. It is hard for the user to sit in front of the computer and interact with the interface longer than that amount of time. However prolonged interaction, which is the case in real environments, may lead to the convergence of the search in the case of a bigger space and this was shown in the subsection "Automated user Model." The second reason for less number of parameters is the constraint on the interface model as given in Assumption 1.

Our interface parameters are selected using some background knowledge from the HCI domain. The first parameter is related to peripheral vision. Interface switches between four different types of airplane representations when the airplanes reach a critical zone. The critical zone is defined as a frame across the interface borders with predefined thickness. Implemented representations are small white planes, small red planes, large white planes, and large red planes. These parameters are coded into the gene as 0, 1, 2, and 3, respectively. Use of color is rooted from the well known fact about the peripheral vision of humans. The ergonomics field has shown that peripheral vision is sensitive to changes in its vicinity. Change of color is supposed to alert the user about the endangered plane which is on the edge of destruction. The reason for changing the size of the plane comes from the HCI field, specifically Fitts' law. Fitts' Law is a model to account for the time it takes to point at something, based on the size and distance of the target object. The formula is given as $T = k \log_2(D / S + 0.5)$, where $k \approx 100m \sec$ and T is the time to move the hand to a target, D is the distance between the hand and the target and S is the size of the target. According to the formula, an increase in size will decrease the response time, hence leading to an increase in performance.

The second parameter is the update interval for the plane's positions. The assumption behind the different updates comes from cognitive science. If the plane's positions are to be updated with every change in their positions, movement will be smooth and will not rely on short term memory hence decreasing the cognitive load. However, it will be harder for the user to click on the planes due to the rapid change of the plane position. On the other hand, update of the plane's position on the interface at longer intervals will give more response time to the user, yet result in higher cognitive load since the user should estimate the next position of the plane. Change in the update interval does not change the speed of the planes.

The new position of the plane is calculated. However, the position on the interface is updated in intervals defined by the update interval parameter. The update interval parameter spans an interval [1-20] and is coded respectively. When we put these two together, we have a search space of eighty which is a fairly large number of alternatives to be evaluated in a small amount of time and iterations. These parameters are also selected because they justify Assumption 1. The genome to be used under evaluation with these features will be the possible combinations of these features. For example $\left\{ A \middle| A = \begin{bmatrix} 10 & 1 \end{bmatrix} \in \mathring{A} \right\}$ is interpreted as: 1) update interval will be 10 sample times and 2) change plane appearance to small size red at possible crash site.

Figure 5. User model

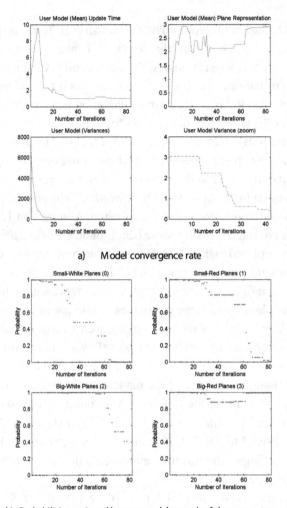

a) Model convergence rate

b) Probabilities assigned by user model to each of the parameters

Results will be given under two categories. The first category will give the convergence of the user model and performance value as well as interface shown to the user. We are not able to give the distance between the interface model and user preference since user preference vector is not available for the real user. Figure 5a) depicts the user model which was able to converge to a value our intuition about the best interface suggested. The upper left portions of Figure 5a) show the convergence of the update time. The update time converged to one. The upper right parts of Figure 5a) show the plane's representation. Interfaces with the large sized planes were better in response time since they take advantage of the Fitt's rule. The user model converged to the interface model with large planes and final variance of the user model converged to a small value. The dotted line in the bottom portion of Figure 5a) is the variance of the update interval and the dashed line is the variance of the plane's representation. The final value of the user model shows that the user model has a bias towards large red planes instead of small red planes which is logical since color and size together improve both response time and accuracy. Figure 5b) shows the probabilities assigned to candidate interfaces by the Gaussian user model. It is easier to

Figure 6. Statistical distributions of parameters at every 20 iterations

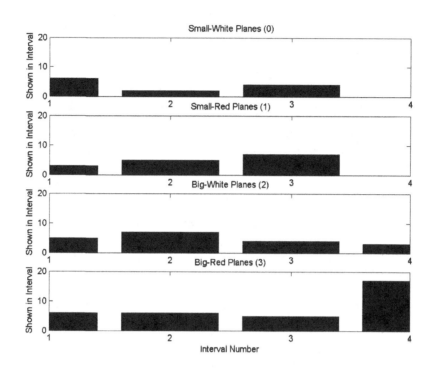

see from this figure that preferences assigned to small size planes get smaller and smaller while prefer-ences given to large size planes preserve their initial level. The equal preference in the beginning phase was due to large variance of the user model.

In order to show that the convergence of the user model was able to localize the search, we show the statistical distribution of the interfaces evaluated. Figure 6 can be interpreted in two ways. Look at Figure 6 horizontally; we can see the number of times a given parameter is shown to the user throughout the interaction. This shows the change of bias of the user model for a given parameter and is consistent with the findings of Figure 5.

Look at Figure 6 vertically and we can inspect the distribution of the shown parameters for every twenty interactions. This shows the proposed algorithm was able to converge to the interface type with large size planes. Figure 7 depicts the performance index collected during interaction. The bottom part of Figure 7a) is the ratio of destroyed planes to shown planes. The top part of Figure 7a) presents the ratio of off-clicks to total clicks. It can be seen that by the end of the adaptation, the ratio of destroyed planes to shown planes converges to zero (no destroyed planes). Figure 7b) depicts another perspective of the evaluation. Results in Figure 7a) are added and the minimum points are connected with a dashed line. Change in the dashed line indicates the update of the user model as explained in Equation (2). These results show that interface adaptation was successful in decreasing the error rate and it eventually converges at least to some local minima.

Second category of results is the subjective evaluation of the adaptation supplied by the users after the interaction with the interface. We have done statistical tests using the subjective results assessed from the questionnaires. These results correspond to the results of the distance between the preferred

Figure 7. Performance index collected during interaction

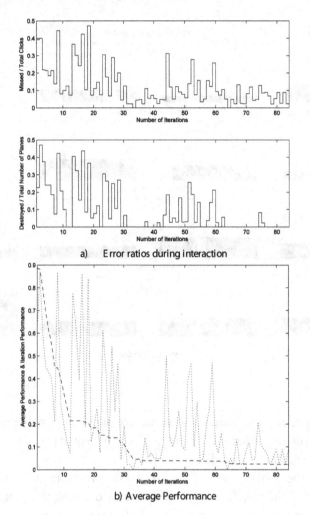

a)   Error ratios during interaction

b) Average Performance

interface and the interface model, shown under the subsection "Automated User Model." We have employed seven individuals in order to test the algorithm.

The first two questions were meant to measure the difference between user preference and user model. We have calculated the correlation coefficient between the subjective ranking of the user for the interface parameters and bias of the user model. Correlation coefficient calculated for plane representation is 0.93 and for the update interval is 0.89. This shows that the interface was able to find the preferred interface. Questions three and four were asked to retrieve the subjective performance index and workload level. The results are given in percentiles. The user evaluation for the improvement of their efficiency results in a mean and standard deviation of $\mu = 4$, $\sigma = 0.89$ respectively and the evaluation for the decrease of their workload results in a mean and standard deviation of $\mu = 3$, $\sigma = 1.26$ respectively. The upper quartile for question three is 5 and for question four is 4. These results show that human users are affected by the adaptation and parameters were able to span the user psychology space. Questions five and six were designed to assess the consistency of the adaptation. These questions were asked because it is important that the adaptation is smooth and consistent, otherwise it may distract the user. User evaluation for the consistency of the adaptation results in a mean and standard deviation of $\mu = 2.8$, $\sigma = 1.17$, respectively and the evaluation for the comfort of using interface results in a mean and standard deviation of $\mu = 3.8$, $\sigma = 1.47$ respectively. The upper quartile for question five is 4 and for question six is 5. The results for question five and six show that adaptation is smooth and easy to handle. Finally, question seven was asked to collect more data about the importance of the parameters. Two users thought that the update interval was more important than the plane's appearance (the other five thought otherwise). Overall, subjective evaluation shows that the proposed algorithm was able to improve the interaction performance and that adaptation did not disturb the users.

CONCLUSION

We have shown in this chapter that non-parametric methods can be employed for evaluating the interface under uncertain environments. Especially if a human is in the loop then statistical methods may prove to show better performance at estimating the user's characteristic. The importance of this work is to define a general framework for adaptation under ill-defined situations. In our case, we have unobservable system states, namely users' preferences. User is stochastic so is the fitness evaluation. There is no explicit objective function as of now that interprets user performance perfectly. Overall uncertainty in the system is very high even in a very simple implementation.

The algorithm is flexible enough to handle any kind of heuristic. Domain dependent knowledge can be regarded as another measurement. Ranking scheme will handle the situation as if another data is collected. In addition to that, other methods can be used to solve this optimization problem, such as multiobjective evolutionary algorithm (Lu and Yen, 2003; Yen and Lu 2003) and particle swarm optimization (Leong and Yen, 2008). However, GA is best fit for this kind of adaptation due to its easy use in highly constrained problems. GA is also scalable to higher dimensions. This is important because in more complex systems the search space can grow exponentially with the number of features considered. More involved and complicated architectures can be developed into this idea. Using this approach also enables interaction of multi-disciplinary knowledge in the field of HCI. As shown, statistical approach, machine learning and rule based systems can easily go together and can easily be incorporated into a general framework.

REFERENCES

Adelman, L., Miller, S. L., & Yeo, C. (2004). Testing the effectiveness of icons for supporting distributed team decision making under time pressure. *IEEE Transactions on Systems, Man and Cybernetics- Part A, 34*, 179-189.

Benyon, D. R., & Murray, D. M. (1993). Applying user modeling to human-computer interaction design. *Artificial Intelligence Review, 6*, 43–69.

Bi, S., & Salvendy, G. (1994). Analytical model and experimental study of human workload in scheduling of advanced manufacturing systems. *International Journal of Human Factors in Manufacturing, 4*, 205–234. doi:10.1002/hfm.4530040207

Billings, C. E. (1997). *Aviation automation: The search for a human-centered approach.* New York: Lawrence Erlbaum.

Brusilovsky, P. (1996). Methods and techniques of adaptive hypermedia. *User Modeling and User-Adapted Interaction, 6,* 87–129. doi:10.1007/BF00143964

Claude-Nicolas, F., & Seth, R. (2000). Learning subjective functions with large margins. In *Proceedings of the International Conference on Machine Learning,* Stanford, CA (pp. 287-294).

Endsley, M. R. (1998). Situation awareness global assessment technique (SAGAT). In *Proceedings of the National Aerospace and Electronics Conference,* Dayton, OH (pp. 789-795).

Fitts, P. M. (1951). *Human engineering for an effective air-navigation and traffic-control system.* Columbus, OH: Ohio State University Press.

Francisco-Revilla, L., & Shipman, F. M. (2000). Adaptive medical information delivery combining user, task, and situation model. In *Proceedings of International Conference on Intelligent User Interfaces,* New Orleans, LA (pp. 94-97).

Gervasio, T. M., Iba, W., & Langley, P. (1999). Learning user evaluation functions for adaptive scheduling assistance. In *Proceedings of the International Conference on Machine Learning,* Bled, Slovenia (pp. 121-126).

Hart, S. G., & Staveland, L. E. (1988). Development of NASA-TLX: Results of experimental and theoretical research. In *Human mental workload.* Amsterdam, The Netherlands.

Horvitz, E. (1999). Principles of mixed-initiative user interfaces. In *Proceedings of Human Factors in Computing Systems,* Pittsburgh, PA (pp. 159-166).

Kaber, B. D., Prinzel, L. J., Wright, C. M., & Clamann, M. P. (2002). *Workload-matched adaptive automation support of air traffic controller information processing stages* (NASA/TM 2002-211932).

Kaber, B. D., & Riley, J. M. (1999). Adaptive automation of a dynamic control task based on workload assessment through a secondary monitoring task. In *Automation technology and human performance: Current research trends* (pp. 55-78). Mahwah, NJ.

Laois, L., & Giannacourou, M. (1995). Perceived effects of advanced ATC functions on human activities: Results of a survey on controllers and experts. In *Proceedings of International Symposium on Aviation Psychology,* Columbus, OH (pp. 392-397).

Leong, W. F., & Yen, G. G. (2008). PSO-based multiobjective optimization with dynamic population size and adaptive local archives. *IEEE Transactions on Systems, Man, and Cybernetics. Part B, Cybernetics, 38,* 1270–1293. doi:10.1109/TSMCB.2008.925757

Lu, H., & Yen, G. G. (2003). Rank-density-based multiobjective genetic algorithm and benchmark test function study. *IEEE Transactions on Evolutionary Computation, 7,* 325–343. doi:10.1109/TEVC.2003.812220

Masui, T. (1994). Evolutionary learning of graph layout constraints from examples. In *Proceedings of Symposium on User Interface Software and Technology,* Marina del Rey, CA (pp. 103-108).

Mathe, N., & Chen, J. (1996). User driven and context basis adaptation. *User Modeling and User-Adapted Interaction, 3*, 145–154.

Norcio, A. F., & Stanley, J. (1989). Adaptive human-computer interfaces: A literature survey and perspective. *IEEE Transactions on Systems, Man, and Cybernetics, 19*, 399–408. doi:10.1109/21.31042

Pazzani, M., & Billsus, D. (1997). Learning and revising user profiles: The identification of interesting WEB sites. *Machine Learning, 27*, 313–331. doi:10.1023/A:1007369909943

Pew, R. W. (1979). Secondary tasks and workload measurement. In N. Moray (Ed.), *Mental workload: It's theory and measurement* (pp. 23-28). New York: Plenum Press.

Prinzel, J. L. (2003). *Team-centered perspective for adaptive automation design* (NASA/TM 2003-212154).

Prinzel, J. L., Pope, A. T., Freeman, G. F., Scerbo, M. W., & Mikulka, P. J. (2001). Empirical analysis of EEG and ERPs for psychophysical adaptive task allocation. *Engineering Psychology, 52*, 124–135.

Reid, G. B., & Nygren, T. E. (1988). The subjective workload assessment technique: A scaling procedure for measuring mental workload. In *Human mental workload* (pp. 183-201). Amsterdam, The Netherlands.

Rothrock, L., Koubek, R., Fuchs, F., Haas, M., & Salvendy, G. (2002). *Review and reappraisal of adaptive interfaces: Toward biologically-inspired paradigms*. New York: Taylor and Francis.

Rouse, W. B., Geddes, N. D., & Curry, R. E. (1988). Architecture for intelligent interface: Outline of an approach to support operators of complex systems. *Human-Computer Interaction, 3*, 87–122. doi:10.1207/s15327051hci0302_1

Sanderson, P., Pipingas, A., Danieli, F., & Silberstein, R. (2003). Process monitoring and configural display design: A neuroimaging study. *Theoretical Issues in Ergonomics Science, 4*, 151–174. doi:10.1080/1463922021000020909

Sheridan, T. B. (1993). Space teleoperation through time delay: Review and prognosis. *IEEE Transactions on Robotics and Automation, 9*, 592–606. doi:10.1109/70.258052

Suchak, R. P., & Lacovou, N. (1994). GroupLens: An open architecture for collaborative filtering for netnews. In *Proceedings of Conference on Computer Supported Cooperative Work,* Chapel Hill, NC (pp. 175-186).

Takagi, H. (2001). Interactive evolutionary computation: Fusion of the capabilities of EC optimization of EC optimization and human evolution. *Proceedings of the IEEE, 89*, 1275–1296. doi:10.1109/5.949485

Terrell, G. R. (1999). *Mathematical statistics: A unified introduction*. New York: Springer.

Thathachar, M. A., & Sastry, P. S. (2002). Varieties of learning automata: An overview. *IEEE Transactions on Systems, Man, and Cybernetics, 32*, 711–721. doi:10.1109/TSMCB.2002.1049606

Viano, G., Parodi, A., Alty, J., & Khalil, C. (2000). Adaptive user interface for process control based on multi-agent approach. In *Proceedings of the Working Conference on Advanced Visual Interfaces,* Palermo, Italy (pp. 201-204).

Wickens, C. D. (1985). Engineering psychology and human performance. *Engineering Psychology, 36,* 307–348.

Wilson, G. F., & Lambert, J. D. (2000). Performance enhancement with real-time physiologically controlled adaptive aiding. In *Proceedings of the Human Factors and Ergonomics Society Annual Meeting,* Dayton, OH (pp. 61-64).

Wu, K., Aggarwal, C. C., & Yu, P. S. (2001). Personalization with dynamic profiler. In *Proceedings of the International Workshop on Advanced Issues of E-Commerce and Web-Based Information Systems,* San Jose, CA (pp. 12-21).

Yen, G. G., & Lu, H. (2003). Dynamic multiobjective evolutionary algorithm: Adaptive cell-based rank and density estimation. *IEEE Transactions on Evolutionary Computation, 7,* 253–274. doi:10.1109/TEVC.2003.810068

Chapter 8
Synthesis of Analog Circuits by Genetic Algorithms and their Optimization by Particle Swarm Optimization

Esteban Tlelo-Cuautle
Instituto Nacional de Astrofísica Óptica y Electrónica, México

Ivick Guerra-Gómez
Instituto Nacional de Astrofísica Óptica y Electrónica, México

Carlos Alberto Reyes-García
Instituto Nacional de Astrofísica Óptica y Electrónica, México

Miguel Aurelio Duarte-Villaseñor
Instituto Nacional de Astrofísica Óptica y Electrónica, México

ABSTRACT

This chapter shows the application of particle swarm optimization (PSO) to size analog circuits which are synthesized by a genetic algorithm (GA) from nullor-based descriptions. First, a historical description of the development of automatic synthesis techniques to design analog circuits is presented. Then, the synthesis of analog circuits by applying a GA at the transistor level of abstraction is demonstrated. After that, the authors present the proposed multi-objective (MO) PSO algorithm which makes calls to the circuit simulator HSPICE to evaluate performances until optimal sizes of the transistors are found by using standard CMOS technology of 0.35 μm of integrated circuits. Finally, the MO-PSO algorithm is compared with NSGA-II, and some open problems oriented to circuit synthesis and sizing are briefly discussed.

DOI: 10.4018/978-1-60566-798-0.ch008

INTRODUCTION

Recently, some research on the application of evolutionary algorithms has been conducted to synthesize practical electronic circuits. As mentioned by Koza et al. (2004), Liu et al. (2009), and Mattiussi and Floreano (2007), many electronic systems of technical and scientific interest can be seen as collections of devices connected by links characterized by a numeric value. Furthermore, the synthesis or design of analog circuits can be viewed as the focus of the engineering activity (Martens and Gielen, 2008; McConaghy and Gielen, 2006; Tlelo-Cuautle and Duarte-Villaseñor, 2008a; Unno and Fujii, 2007). In electronics, an analog designer has several design strategies at his disposal to synthesize electronic circuits (Eeckelaert et al., 2005; Koza et al., 2004; Mattiussi and Floreano, 2007; McConaghy et al., 2005; Rutenbar et al., 2007; Smedt and Gielen, 2003; Stehr et al., 2007; Tlelo-Cuautle and Duarte-Villaseñor, 2008a; Van der Plas et al., 2001). However, as mentioned by Martens and Gielen (2008), the chosen strategy mainly depends on the complexity of the system with respect to size and performance demands (Guerra-Gómez et al., 2008). On the other hand, the design process starts with the selection of a topology, where systematic exploration methodologies are very much needed to automatically generate new topologies (McConaghy et al., 2007; Rutenbar et al., 2007; Smedt et al., 2003; Tlelo-Cuautle and Duarte-Villaseñor, 2008a). Afterwards, for a selected topology, the next problem consists of searching different values for the parameters until optimal performances are found. Although Stehr et al. (2007) presented a simulation-based method for the calculation of the feasible performance values of amplifier-based circuits by computing the Pareto-optimal trade-offs of competing performances at full simulator accuracy, there are new circuits which include multi-ports, such as current conveyors (Fakhfakh et al., 2007; Sánchez-López et al., 2007; Smith and Sedra, 1968; Tlelo-Cuautle et al., 2008c; Trejo-Guerra et al., 2008) which also present trade-offs among their port's characteristics. Therefore an appropriate optimization method must be used to find optimal parameters for a particular circuit topology.

In summary, the synthesis process of electronic circuits is known as the problem of finding the correct circuit topology (a collection of interconnected devices), and the problem of finding numeric values of the circuit elements is considered as a sizing problem (Fakhfakh, 2008; Liu et al., 2009; McConaghy et al., 2007; Mattiussi and Floreano, 2007). The selection of a circuit topology can be done during sizing (Matens and Gielen, 2008), where topological options are stored in a library as entire architectures, thus making a larger set of valid topologies available for sizing exploration. Therefore, since this is a complex process, the automatic synthesis of analog circuits is a problem which can be solved by applying either or both swarm intelligence (Coello and Lechuga, 2002; Kennedy et al., 2001) and evolutionary techniques (Deb et al., 2002; Lamont and Coello, 2007). For instance, analog computer-aided design (CAD) tools based on evolutionary algorithms have been developed to find the optimal parameters of various systems (Koza et al., 2004; Liu et al., 2009; Martens and Gielen, 2008; McConaghy and Gielen, 2006; Mattiussi and Floreano, 2007). Besides that, to find optimal performances of an electronic circuit, it is desired that the proposed algorithm allows multi-objective optimization including multiple constraints (Coello and Lechuga, 2002; Lamont and Coello, 2007; Liu et al., 2009; Santana-Quintero et al., 2008). More recently, Liu et al. (2009) have introduced a hybrid evolutionary-based design system to size analog integrated circuits by combining MATLAB and HSPICE (Synopsys, 2007), once a circuit topology has been selected. Following this direction, this chapter describes the application of Particle Swarm Optimization (PSO) to size analog electronic circuits which are synthesized by the Genetic Algorithm (GA) as described in the following section. The proposed system also combines MATLAB and HSPICE,

Figure 1. Model of the voltage follower using nullators

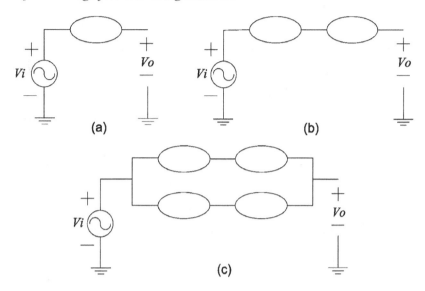

and the PSO algorithm allows multi-objective (MO) optimization. It is compared with NSGA-II (Deb et al., 2002) to size current conveyors.

SYNTHESIS OF ANALOG CIRCUITS BY GENETIC ALGORITHMS

Analog circuit synthesis can be performed by starting with simplified or ideal models (Unno and Fuji, 2007), which can be modeled by using the pathological element called nullor (Kumar and Senani, 2002). In a similar manner, Tlelo-Cuautle et al. (2008b) have introduced the synthesis of basic unity-gain cells (UGCs) such as voltage followers (VFs) and voltage mirrors (VMs) by beginning with abstract descriptions using nullors (Kumar and Senani, 2002; Tlelo-Cuautle and Duarte-Villaseñor, 2008a). The topology to be generated is created by starting from a lower abstraction level, by connecting individual circuit elements in a systematic way until the genotype is formed, which is decoded to obtain already known and several new circuit topologies.

As described in Tlelo-Cuautle et al. (2007), the nullor consists of two elements: the nullator and the norator. The voltage and the current in the nullator are zero, whereas in the norator the voltage and the current are arbitrary. By using these properties, one can use one, two or four nullators to model the ideal behavior of the voltage follower, as shown in Figure 1, where the output voltage is equal to the input voltage, $V_o = V_i$. In the same manner, one can use one, two or four norators to model the ideal behavior of the current follower, as shown in Figure 2, where the output current is equal to the input current, $I_o = I_i$.

Basically, the GA introduced in Tlelo-Cuautle et al. (2007) and Tlelo-Cuautle and Duarte-Villaseñor (2008a) manipulates nullators and norators, which must always exist in a pair to form the nullor (Kumar and Senani, 2002). Therefore, the nullator-norator (O-P) pair can be connected in three ways: in parallel (see Figure 3(a)), both connected at node i (see Figure 3(b)), and both connected at node j (see Figure 3(c)). Further, the nullator-norator pair can be synthesized by a transistor, e.g. the MOSFET, as

Figure 2. Model of the current follower using norators

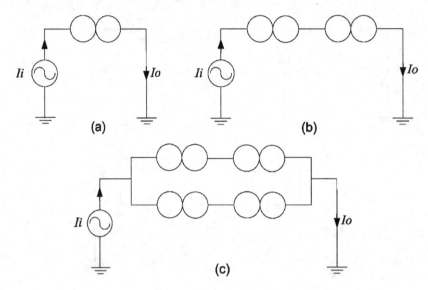

shown in Figure 3(c) and Figure 3(d). By beginning with the voltage follower shown in Figure 1(c), the equivalent nullator-norator circuit is shown in Figure 4, where ideal voltage biases (Vdd, Vss), and ideal current biases (Idd, Iss) have been added mainly to the norators (P). Finally, the nullator-norator pairs are synthesized by MOSFETs, and the ideal current sources are synthesized by current mirrors (Tlelo-Cuautle and Duarte-Villaseñor 2008a), leading to the genotype and phenotype of the voltage follower shown in Figure 5.

The process described above can be encoded by four genes, and they can be used for the automatic circuit synthesis of the four unity-gain cells described in Tlelo-Cuautle et al. (2008a):

Gene of the small-signal circuitry (genSS): Codifies the combinations in connecting nullator-norator pairs using two bits for each pair. Therefore, in Figure 4, genSS=8 bits.

Gene of synthesis of the MOSFETs (genSMos): Each nullator-norator combination is synthesized by a MOSFET which can be type N or type P. This is codified by genSMos using one bit for each pair. In Figure 4, genSMos=4 bits.

Gene of addition of the bias circuitry (genBias): The addition of voltage and current biases (Vdd, Vss, Idd and Iss) is codified by genBias using two bits for each nullator-norator pair. In Figure 4, gen-Bias=8 bits.

Figure 3. Connection of a nullator-norator pair in: (a) parallel, (b) at node i, and (c) at node j, and (d) synthesis of an O-P pair by a MOSFET

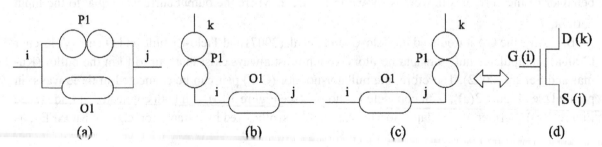

Figure 4. Voltage follower described by nullator-norator pairs and ideal current sources (Idd, Iss)

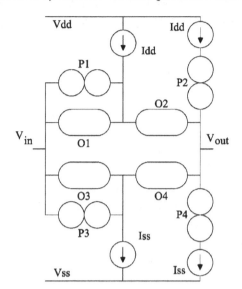

Gene of synthesis of the bias circuitry (genCM): Each current source (Idd, Iss) is synthesized by a current mirror, so that this gene consists of a library of different kinds of current mirrors, and its size depends on their number in the library.

As a result, the genotype and phenotype of the voltage follower are as shown in Figure 5, where the chromosome is 22 bits long when genCM=2 bits. An important aspect of the GA is that it generates simple topologies which are suitable to be evolved to more complex circuits. For example, Tlelo-Cuautle et al. (2008b) demonstrated the synthesis of voltage mirrors by GAs from the evolution of the voltage follower whose chromosome is augmented by one gene. The synthesis of the current follower is similar to the above process for the voltage follower, but we begin from Figure 2, instead of Figure 1 (Tlelo-Cuautle and Duarte-Villaseñor, 2008a).

The flow diagram of the GA for the synthesis of voltage followers and its behavior according to the fitness evaluation and number of generations can be found in Tlelo-Cuautle et al. (2007). The proposed

Figure 5. The genotype and phenotype of the voltage follower shown in Figure 4

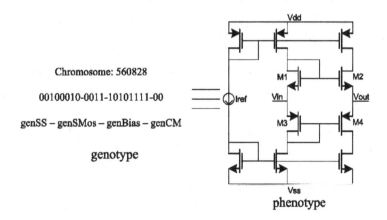

GA begins with the creation of random solutions according to the chromosome of each unity-gain cell (see Figure 5 for the voltage follower) and it ends its search after selecting a circuit which accomplishes Equation (1), where $0.7 \leq gain \leq 1.2$ in order to select practical unity-gain cells.

$$\left. \begin{array}{c} v_{out} \\ i_{out} \end{array} \right\} \geq gain * \left\{ \begin{array}{c} v_{in} \\ i_{in} \end{array} \right.$$

(1)

The main steps of the GA are the following:

1. A start-population is randomly created (generation 0).
2. Each genotype, describing a valid topology, will create an HSPICE file (phenotypes).
3. The phenotypes files are run in HSPICE (Synopsys 2007).
4. Each chromosome is evaluated according to Equation (1) to calculate the fitness. If one or more individuals satisfy equation (1), the program stops.
5. A new population is generated using the operations of crossover and mutation (Reyes-García et al., 2008).
6. The program continues from step 2, creating HSPICE files, until a specified number of generations is reached.

Crossover Operator

A circuit is represented by an ordered set of genes (for the voltage follower: genSS*genSMos*genBias*genCM (Tlelo-Cuautle et al., 2007)). The crossover operator is defined by the interchange of the genes of parent chromosomes. If the parent chromosomes are parents 1 and 2 as shown in Figure 6, there are 14 new offspring chromosomes possible. This is analogous to the standard 'one-point crossover' algorithm used in many GA applications. By applying equal probability, only two of the children chromosomes are selected for the new generation to maintain an average population.

Mutation Operator

The mutation randomly changes the value of a bit in a chromosome; e.g. in Figure 7 the chromosome '110000011011' is changed to '111000011011'. In the GA all the chromosomes are evaluated with the crossover operator and only 5% of them are mutated.

By combining unity-gain cells, more complex circuits can be generated. For example, Tlelo-Cuautle et al. (2008c) have introduced the synthesis of the negative-type second generation current conveyor (CCII-) by superimposing a voltage follower with a current follower, by performing genetic operations (Reyes-García et al., 2008). In the same manner, Fakhfakh et al. (2007) have introduced the synthesis of the positive-type second generation current conveyor (CCII+) by searching for the interconnection among a voltage follower and current mirrors. It is worthy to mention that in analog signal processing, both the CCII+ and CCII- are quite useful for implementation in practical applications, such as amplifiers (Koza et al., 2004; Mattiussi and Floreano, 2007; McConaghy and Gielen, 2006; Unno and Fujii, 2007), filters and oscillators (Fakhfakh et al., 2007; Tlelo-Cuautle and Duarte-Villaseñor, 2008a). Figure 8 shows the CCII+ and CCII- synthesized by evolving the voltage follower as shown in Figure 5.

Figure 6. Crossover operator

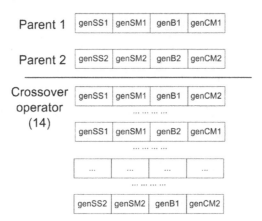

MULTI-OBJECTIVE PARTICLE SWARM OPTIMIZATION ALGORITHM

In analog electronics, circuit synthesis is a challenging problem because the analog design process is characterized by a combination of experience and intuition, and requires creativity to deal with the large number of free parameters such as gain, band-width, offset, impedances, noise, distortion, etc (Eeckelaert et al., 2005; Liu et al., 2009; Rutenbar et al., 2007; Stehr et al., 2007). Additionally, these parameters sometimes present obscure interactions among them, because each kind of circuit topology presents different trade-offs between two or more parameters. For example, in circuits processing either voltages or currents, when the gain is improved the impedances can be degraded, so that the noise might become greater than it is desired. However, when a circuit can process both voltage and current, as is case for CCII+ and CCII-, the optimization problem for accomplishing the device parameters through sizing is not known or deterministic. Therefore, the optimization process should be solved by re-simulations. In this case, circuit synthesis begins by selecting a topology and its design is generated by finding parameter values (e.g. transistors lengths and widths) to satisfy a set of performance specifications (Guerra-Gómez et al., 2008).

Some analog design automation tools oriented to circuit sizing are: AMGIE (Van der Plas *et al.*, 2001), WATSON (Smedt and Gielen, 2003), CAFFEINE (McConaghy *et al.*, 2005) and MOJITO (McConaghy *et al.*, 2007). The optimization techniques search for the optimal design solution according to the given

Figure 7. Mutation operator

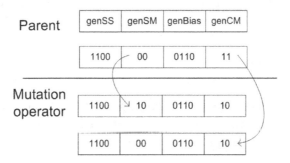

Figure 8. (a) CCII+ and (b) CCII-

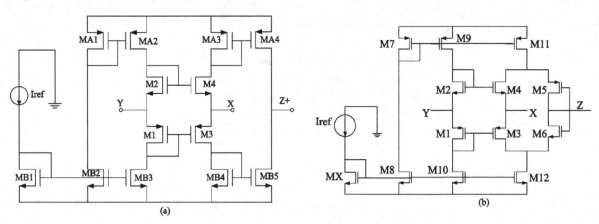

(a)   (b)

specifications (Eeckelaert *et al.*, 2005), but at different levels of abstraction (Martens and Gielen, 2008). Besides that, only few methods have been presented which apply evolutionary computation (Liu et al., 2009; Mattiussi and Floreano, 2007). In this chapter, the proposed optimization technique is based on the concept of swarm intelligence (Kennedy et al., 2001), and is compared to NSGA-II (Deb et al., 2002) to show that our proposed Multi-Objective PSO (MO-PSO) (Coello and Lechuga, 2002) algorithm is suitable for circuit sizing and that it can achieve better performance in the case of CCII+s and CCII-s. The MO-PSO has been programmed in MATLAB, and HSPICE is linked to it to evaluate the circuit performances (Guerra-Gómez et al., 2008). The MO-PSO algorithm evaluates the circuits in terms of Pareto optimality (Stehr et al., 2007): a solution is considered optimal if it cannot be improved without deteriorating at least one of its components in which case it is probable that there will be more than one Pareto optimal solution (Deb et al., 2002).

In the MO-PSO algorithm there are *n* particles denoted by X_i, where i =1,…*n*, and represented by their positions in the search space. Each particle $X_i = (x_i^1, x_i^2, ..., x_i^k)$ represents a position in the space and depends on its previous local best position (*Pbest*), and the previous global best position (*Gbest*). To compute the speed of each particle the following expression is used:

$$V_i = k_w V_i + R_1 (\mathrm{P}best_i - P_i) + R_2 (\mathrm{G}best - P_i) \tag{2}$$

where V_i is the current velocity of the particle *i*, k_w is the inertia weight which takes typical values less than 1, $Pbest_i$ is the best position of particle *i*, P_i is the position of the current particle and *Gbest* is a global best selected among the global best solutions. The new position of each particle is computed as follows:

$$P_i = P_i + V_i \tag{3}$$

The algorithm ensures that the current position is not beyond the bound limits. Algorithm 1 (see Figure 9) shows the pseudo-code for the proposed MO-PSO. Step 1 is the initialization procedure where the bound limits are set, and the particles are initialized randomly inside these bound limits. The velocities are initialized with zero values. In step 2, the population is evaluated to update the best position (P*best*) at step 3, for each particle. Afterwards, the non-dominated particles are evaluated to randomly select a global best (G*best*) into that repository (steps 4 and 5). Then the velocity and position of each particle are updated by using Equations (2) and (3) while staying within the bound limits (steps 7 to 11). Once all the particles are updated, then an evaluation process is applied to update the best position for each particle. Also, the non-dominated particles are selected, and one is selected randomly to set it as the global best for the next loop (steps 12 to 15). This process continues until a determined number of loops have been completed.

Dominance and Constraints

The selection of non-dominated particles is done by taking into account some constraints, so that each solution can be either feasible or infeasible. Thus, there may be at most three situations: solutions are feasible, one is feasible and the other is not, or both are infeasible. Then a solution j is said to be constraint-dominated by a solution i, if any of the following conditions is true (Deb *et al.*, 2002):

1. Solution i is feasible and solution j is not.
2. Solutions i and j are both infeasible, but solution i has a smaller overall constraint violation.
3. Solutions i and j are both feasible and solution i dominates solution j.

Figure 9.

Algorithm 1 Psuedocode for MOPSO
1: Initialize NoLoops, bound limits, population (N) and velocities
2: Evaluate population
3: Update P*best*
4: Select non-dominated particles
5: Select G*best* randomly among non-dominated particles
6: **for** i= 1 to NoLoops **do**
7:    **for** j=1 to N **do**
8:       Update particle velocity
9:       Update particle position
10:      Ensuring new position is into bound limits
11:    **end for**
12:   Evaluate population
13:   Update P*best*
14:   Select non-dominated particles
15:   Select G*best* randomly among non-dominated particles
16: **end for**

MO-PSO on Test Functions

The MO-PSO algorithm was programmed and tested on the Zitzler functions (Zitzler et al., 2000), with constraint functions over 80 generations with a population of 80 particles. The non-dominated solutions for the ZDT3 are shown in Figure 10 and those for the TNK function are shown in Figure 11.

CIRCUIT OPTIMIZATION BY MO-PSO

The circuit optimization process consists of searching for the width and length sizes of all MOSFETs of the CCII+ and CCII-. To apply the MO-PSO algorithm, the evaluation procedure (lines 2 and 12 in Algorithm 1) links HSPICE to measure all performances. In this manner, a frequency analysis is performed with the statement .MEASURE (Guerra-Gómez et al., 2008), that defines results on successive simulations. The .MEASURE instruction prints user-defined electrical specifications of a circuit, and the results can be manipulated in a post-processing step. The .MEASURE basic syntax is (Synopsys, 2007):

.MEASURE <DC|AC|TRAN> resultname +TRIG ... TARG...where *resultname* is the name chosen to save the results, *TRIG* identifies the beginning of trigger specifications and *TARG* identifies the beginning of target specifications. The syntax could be different depending of the type of measurement, and it is possible to use the following syntax too:

Figure 10. Non-dominated solutions for ZDT3

$$
\text{ZDT3} \quad \begin{cases} f_1(x) = x_1 \\ f_2(x) = g(x)[1 - \sqrt{\dfrac{x_1}{g(x)}} - \dfrac{x_1}{g(x)} \sin(10\pi x)] \\ g(r) = \dfrac{9}{n-1}\sum_{i=2}^{n} x_i + 1 \quad, \text{ where } x_i \in [0,1] \text{ and } i = 2,\dots 10 \end{cases}
$$

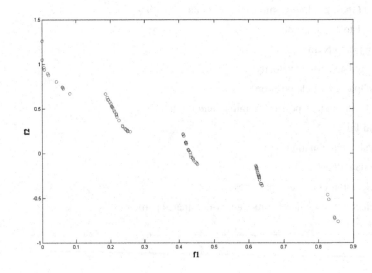

.MEASURE <DC|AC|TRAN> resultname + func out_var <FROM = val> <TO = val>where *func* is a specific function such as MIN, MAX or AVG, *out_var* is the name of any output variable whose function (*func*) is measured through simulation. In this manner, it is possible to perform an automatic circuit evaluation process.

In Figure 8(a), the CCII+ accomplishes $V_X=V_Y$ and $I_Z=I_X$, and in Figure 8(b) the CCII- accomplishes $V_X=V_Y$ and $I_Z=-I_X$ (Tlelo-Cuautle and Duarte-Villaseñor, 2008a). By applying the proposed MO-PSO, we consider three objectives for voltage mode and three objectives for current mode for both the CCII+ and CCII-:

- Voltage mode: Y-X voltage gain, voltage offset and voltage band-width
- Current mode: X-Z current gain, current offset and current band-width.

The ideal value for gain is unity, for voltage and current offset is zero, and for band-width is infinity. In real applications, gain is close to unity, offset is minimal and band-width is a high frequency (Fakhfakh, 2008).

To select the non-dominated particles, the MO-PSO takes into account the saturation condition in each MOSFET as a constraint (Guerra-Gómez et al., 2008). The CCII+ and CCII- are evaluated using an HSPICE MOSFET model Level 49 with a standard CMOS Technology of 0.35μm. The current is set to $I_{ref} = 50$μA, the load is set to 1pF, and all lengths of MOSFETs are set to L=1μm, so that the optimization process consists of finding optimal width (W) sizes within the bound limits (0.35μm and 300μm).

Figure 11. Non-dominated solutions for TNK

$$\text{TNK} \begin{cases} f_1(x) = x_1 \\ f_2(x) = x_2 \quad , \text{ where } x_i \in [0,\pi] \\ Constrains: \\ g_1(x) = 1 - x_1^2 - x_2^2 + 0.1 \cdot \cos(16 \cdot \arctan(\frac{x_1}{x_2})) \leq 0 \\ g_2(x) = (x_1 - 0.5)^2 + (x_2 - 0.5)^2 \leq 5 \end{cases}$$

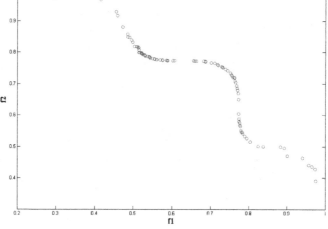

For the CCII+ shown in Figure 8(a), there are two variables: W_1 (N-MOSFETs width) and W_2 (P-MOSFETs width). For the CCII- shown in Figure 8(b), there are eight variables: W_1 (M1,M3), W_2 (M5), W_3 (M2,M4), W_4 (M6), W_5 (M7,M9), W_6 (M11), W_7 (M8,M10,MX) and W_8 (M12). In the first step the optimizer system runs under different parameters (number of generations, population size, and different inertia weights) to determine the best combination of parameters. Table 1 and Table 2 show the performance characteristics for the CCII+ and CCII- respectively. In both the CCII+ and CCII- there are two ports denoted by Vx=Vy and Iz=±Ix, and in each port the MO-PSO optimizes the three parameters: gain, offset and band-width.

Table 1 and Table 2 show the mean, standard deviation, max and min values found by MO-PSO with 80 and 50 particles respectively over 80 loops, with an inertia weight of 0.25, 0.65 and 0.4. In all the three cases for both circuits, the max and min values are closer to each other but their standard deviation is influenced by the inertia value; this behavior is evident from Equation (2). However, the last experiment has satisfactory results with a smaller population size (N=50). Therefore the next part of this chapter uses an inertia weight of 0.4.

In the second step, the optimizer is run with 80 particles over 80 loops, and an inertia weight of 0.4. The results are shown in Figures 12, 13, 14 and 15, where they are compared with NSGA-II.

Tables 3 and 4 list the results for five runs for the CCII+ and CCII- respectively. It can be seen that the experiments achieve similar results. All experiments have 80 particles over 80 generations and an inertia weight of 0.4. The mean, minimum and maximum values show how the proposed MO-PSO tends to converge to the same Pareto front and the standard deviation shows that gain and band-width results are not dispersed. However, the offset is dispersed in some cases where it reaches the global minimum (zero value).

Table 1. CCII+ performances by varying (k) the inertia weight in Equation (2)

	Voltage Mode (Vx=Vy)			Current Mode (Iz=Ix)		
	Gain (V/V)	*Offset (V)*	*Band-Width (Hz)*	*Gain (I/I)*	*Offset (A)*	*Band-Width (Hz)*
	N= 80, Generations=80 k=0.25					
Mean	9.9328E-01	1.3863E-03	9.1354E+07	9.8354E-01	5.6863E-08	1.4100E+08
Std. Dev. (σ)	4.2238E-04	4.5746E-05	5.3558E+06	1.3914E-03	7.9166E-08	5.7689E+06
Max value	9.9386E-01	1.4704E-03	1.0523E+08	9.8700E-01	2.5895E-07	1.4986E+08
Min value	9.8887E-01	9.8073E-04	7.7468E+07	9.8100E-01	7.7093E-13	1.2515E+08
	N= 80, Generations=80 k=0.65					
Mean	9.9309E-01	1.3564E-03	9.1802E+07	9.8721E-01	8.8001E-08	1.7845E+08
Std. Dev. (σ)	7.4430E-04	7.5642E-05	9.7710E+06	1.6723E-03	1.0720E-07	1.7047E+07
Max value	9.9401E-01	1.5455E-03	1.2572E+08	9.8900E-01	2.9644E-07	1.9348E+08
Min value	9.8871E-01	1.0060E-03	7.1414E+07	9.8300E-01	1.2321E-12	1.4139E+08
	N= 50, Generations=80 k=0.4					
Mean	9.9313E-01	1.3738E-03	9.4314E+07	9.8871E-01	6.5881E-08	1.8852E+08
Std. Dev. (σ)	3.5171E-04	4.7231E-05	6.1006E+06	4.6881E-04	9.0341E-08	2.9615E+06
Max value	9.9381E-01	1.5392E-03	1.1398E+08	9.8900E-01	2.7931E-07	1.9423E+08
Min value	9.9171E-01	1.1888E-03	7.8339E+07	9.8800E-01	3.1753E-11	1.8360E+08

Table 2. CCII- performances by varying (k) the inertia weight in Equation (2)

	Voltage Mode (Vx=Vy)			Current Mode (Iz=-Ix)		
	Gain (V/V)	Offset (V)	Band-Width (Hz)	Gain (|I/I|)	Offset (A)	Band-Width (Hz)
N= 80, Generations=80 k=0.25						
Mean	9.9300E-01	4.9671E-04	9.8648E+07	9.9564E-01	5.4484E-06	1.6877E+08
Std. Dev. (σ)	5.2284E-04	3.7150E-04	2.9636E+06	4.2055E-04	8.3590E-06	9.2315E+06
Max value	9.9384E-01	1.6505E-03	1.0562E+08	9.9634E-01	3.4734E-05	1.8419E+08
Min value	9.9077E-01	0	8.8745E+07	9.9484E-01	8.0738E-09	1.4362E+08
N= 80, Generations=80 k=0.65						
Mean	9.9302E-01	4.3503E-04	1.0189E+08	9.9389E-01	1.5404E-02	1.9271E+08
Std. Dev. (σ)	9.5158E-04	4.0647E-04	7.7710E+06	3.4243E-03	1.2403E-01	3.5615E+07
Max value	9.9441E-01	1.6707E-03	1.1786E+08	9.9635E-01	1.0000E+00	2.8628E+08
Min value	9.8771E-01	0	8.2801E+07	9.7736E-01	8.5575E-09	1.0181E+08
N= 50, Generations=80 k=0.4						
Mean	9.9306E-01	4.1131E-04	1.0101E+08	9.9574E-01	4.8262E-06	1.3277E+08
Std. Dev. (σ)	4.3764E-04	3.8653E-04	3.1396E+06	3.7150E-04	6.1697E-06	5.1470E+06
Max value	9.9378E-01	1.7271E-03	1.0832E+08	9.9649E-01	3.2732E-05	1.4279E+08
Min value	9.9178E-01	0	9.3395E+07	9.9488E-01	1.0025E-08	1.1884E+08

Figure 12. Voltage optimization for CCII+: (a) MO-PSO and, (b) NSGA-II results

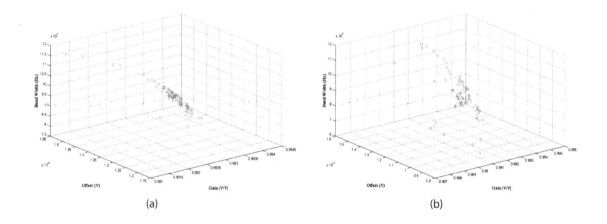

(a)   (b)

DISCUSSION ON THE RESULTS AND OPEN PROBLEMS

Tables 7 and 8 list the sizes of the CCII+ and CCII- respectively, corresponding to the best values of the three objectives found by MO-PSO. For the CCII+, the best Gain (close to unity) has different sizes with respect to the best offset (close to zero), as shown in Table 7. This is the same case for the Band-Width in both Voltage and Current modes. Additionally, it can be seen that the sizes between the Gain in Voltage mode and Current mode are also different. This is an open problem, since in an optimal CCII+, all MOSFETs must have the same width (W) and length (L), and they should also optimize the same

Figure 13. Current optimization for CCII+: (a) MO-PSO and, (b) NSGA-II results

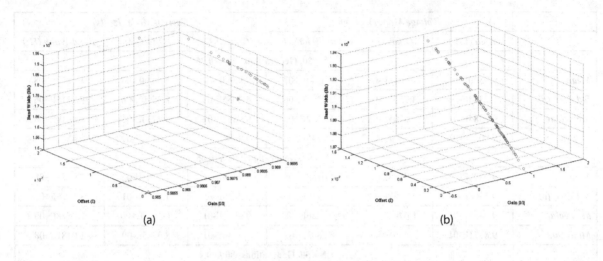

(a)   (b)

Figure 14. Voltage optimization for CCII-: (a) MO-PSO and (b) NSGA-II results

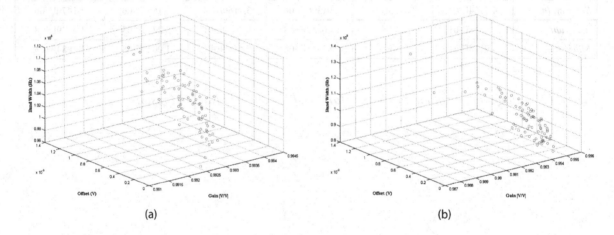

(a)   (b)

Figure 15. Current Optimization for CCII-: (a) MO-PSO and, (b) NSGA-II results

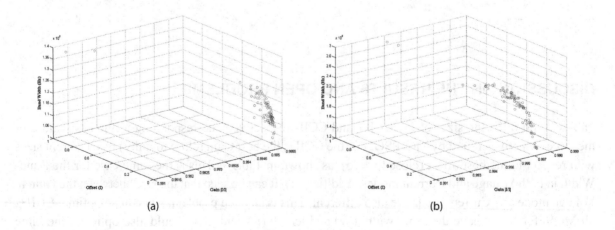

(a)   (b)

Table 3. CCII+ performances with 5 runs

	Voltage Mode (Vx=Vy)			Current Mode (Iz=Ix)		
	Gain (V/V)	Offset (V)	Band-Width (Hz)	Gain (I/I)	Offset (A)	Band-Width (Hz)
PSO Run 1						
Mean	9.9316E-01	1.4063E-03	9.3889E+07	9.8874E-01	4.9532E-08	1.8750E+08
Std. Dev. (σ)	3.6786E-04	5.0599E-05	6.6655E+06	8.1300E-04	4.8708E-08	7.7355E+06
Max value	9.9378E-01	1.5249E-03	1.1395E+08	9.8900E-01	1.8992E-07	1.9377E+08
Min value	9.9152E-01	1.2834E-03	8.0069E+07	9.8500E-01	3.7678E-11	1.5058E+08
PSO Run 2						
Mean	9.9327E-01	1.3997E-03	9.1022E+07	9.8825E-01	1.8108E-08	1.8333E+08
Std. Dev. (σ)	5.4105E-04	5.4773E-05	6.8573E+06	7.0711E-04	2.0095E-08	4.9853E+06
Max value	9.9400E-01	1.4934E-03	1.0998E+08	9.8900E-01	5.5274E-08	1.8923E+08
Min value	9.8943E-01	1.0450E-03	7.2786E+07	9.8700E-01	2.3665E-11	1.7372E+08
PSO Run 3						
Mean	9.9333E-01	1.3882E-03	9.0260E+07	9.8856E-01	6.3106E-08	1.8665E+08
Std. Dev. (σ)	3.1499E-04	4.5779E-05	6.2969E+06	5.2705E-04	9.6093E-08	3.6041E+06
Max value	9.9387E-01	1.4729E-03	1.0971E+08	9.8900E-01	2.5097E-07	1.9124E+08
Min value	9.9222E-01	1.2616E-03	7.5782E+07	9.8800E-01	4.2273E-11	1.8057E+08
PSO Run 4						
Mean	9.9332E-01	1.3917E-03	9.1104E+07	9.8861E-01	2.9193E-08	1.8523E+08
Std. Dev. (σ)	2.1357E-04	4.3213E-05	4.8165E+06	7.7754E-04	4.0790E-08	6.6570E+06
Max value	9.9379E-01	1.5206E-03	1.0240E+08	9.8900E-01	1.5913E-07	1.9354E+08
Min value	9.9275E-01	1.2682E-03	7.9679E+07	9.8600E-01	1.2121E-11	1.6342E+08
PSO Run 5						
Mean	9.9318E-01	1.3814E-03	9.3198E+07	9.8575E-01	2.9996E-08	1.6344E+08
Std. Dev. (σ)	3.9365E-04	4.5912E-05	6.3837E+06	4.0255E-03	5.2925E-08	3.3048E+07
Max value	9.9373E-01	1.5435E-03	1.1173E+08	9.8900E-01	1.5184E-07	1.9376E+08
Min value	9.9130E-01	1.2813E-03	8.0560E+07	9.7700E-01	3.3900E-11	9.4544E+07

parameters, offset, band-width, impedances, for instance. By comparing Table 3 with Table 5, and Table 4 with Table 6, it can be observed that the parameters gain, offset and band-width have similar values. The only exception is the offset, which is zero (ideal) in Table 4 for the CCII- optimized by MO-PSO, and is high in Current mode in Table 6. This is an advantage of the MO-PSO algorithm with respect to NSGA-II. On the other hand, although NSGA-II generates better Pareto Fronts (see for example Figure 12) than MO-PSO, it consumes more CPU-time and memory storage since the population is doubled. However, for the optimization of CCII+s and CCII-s (Tables 7 and 8), the MO-PSO obtains the same performance characteristics for Gain, Offset and Band-Width, making it suitable for analog circuit optimization. In addition, future research may include other Pareto domination based algorithms, other ranking methods, and other reproduction operators.

Table 4. CCII- performances with 5 runs

	Voltage Mode (Vx=Vy)			Current Mode (Iz=-Ix)		
	Gain (V/V)	*Offset (V)*	*Band-Width (Hz)*	*Gain (\I/I\)*	*Offset (A)*	*Band-Width (Hz)*
PSO Run 1						
Mean	9.9314E-01	4.3810E-04	1.0314E+08	9.9541E-01	4.8158E-06	1.4710E+08
Std. Dev. (σ)	3.5032E-04	4.1213E-04	3.6105E+06	5.9175E-04	6.2776E-06	1.0254E+07
Max value	9.9373E-01	1.8686E-03	1.1100E+08	9.9630E-01	2.7330E-05	1.6516E+08
Min value	9.9190E-01	5.8111E-07	9.4749E+07	9.9435E-01	4.6848E-09	1.1942E+08
PSO Run 2						
Mean	9.9338E-01	4.4998E-04	1.0002E+08	9.9541E-01	4.3120E-06	1.9822E+08
Std. Dev. (σ)	3.4094E-04	3.4111E-04	3.3185E+06	4.3113E-04	7.8939E-06	2.1903E+07
Max value	9.9391E-01	1.5908E-03	1.0722E+08	9.9609E-01	5.0915E-05	2.3455E+08
Min value	9.9178E-01	0.0000E+00	8.9936E+07	9.9417E-01	1.0875E-08	1.1988E+08
PSO Run 3						
Mean	9.9341E-01	3.0876E-04	1.0282E+08	9.9570E-01	4.5910E-06	1.4839E+08
Std. Dev. (σ)	3.2260E-04	3.5085E-04	4.3406E+06	5.8761E-04	6.1262E-06	9.3851E+06
Max value	9.9398E-01	1.8120E-03	1.1223E+08	9.9646E-01	2.2207E-05	1.6069E+08
Min value	9.9259E-01	0	9.0408E+07	9.9425E-01	1.5954E-09	1.2393E+08
PSO Run 4						
Mean	9.9338E-01	4.4998E-04	1.0002E+08	9.9497E-01	4.6826E-06	1.1762E+08
Std. Dev. (σ)	3.4094E-04	3.4111E-04	3.3185E+06	2.2193E-04	8.0575E-06	5.8912E+06
Max value	9.9391E-01	1.5908E-03	1.0722E+08	9.9524E-01	5.2867E-05	1.3046E+08
Min value	9.9178E-01	0	8.9936E+07	9.9425E-01	5.1860E-09	1.0305E+08
PSO Run 5						
Mean	9.9290E-01	5.1648E-04	1.0465E+08	9.9550E-01	3.7005E-06	1.4546E+08
Std. Dev. (σ)	4.7481E-04	3.8926E-04	3.3582E+06	4.0472E-04	7.1639E-06	5.3473E+06
Max value	9.9372E-01	1.6769E-03	1.1094E+08	9.9613E-01	3.1933E-05	1.5789E+08
Min value	9.9100E-01	0	9.6657E+07	9.9447E-01	1.5662E-09	1.3669E+08

Table 5. CCII+ performances with NSGA-II

	Voltage Mode (Vx=Vy)			Current Mode (Iz=Ix)		
	Gain (V/V)	*Offset (V)*	*Band-Width (Hz)*	*Gain (I/I)*	*Offset (A)*	*Band-Width (Hz)*
Mean	9.9278E-01	1.2900E-03	8.3939E+07	9.8900E-01	6.6260E-08	1.9023E+08
Std. Dev. (σ)	1.5832E-03	1.5768E-04	1.2574E+07	2.2345E-16	3.5279E-08	1.6192E+06
Max value	9.9414E-01	1.4955E-03	1.1827E+08	9.8900E-01	1.5242E-07	1.9367E+08
Min value	9.8754E-01	8.8840E-04	6.4375E+07	9.8900E-01	7.0867E-09	1.8715E+08

Table 6. CCII- performances with NSGA-II

	Voltage Mode (Vx=Vy)			Current Mode (Iz=-Ix)		
	Gain (V/V)	*Offset (V)*	*Band-Width (Hz)*	*Gain (|I/I|)*	*Offset (A)*	*Band-Width (Hz)*
Mean	9.9358E-01	2.8556E-04	1.0123E+08	9.9575E-01	2.5027E-02	2.2907E+08
Std. Dev. (σ)	1.1712E-03	2.2930E-04	1.2645E+07	1.0416E-03	1.5711E-01	4.1664E+07
Max value	9.9458E-01	1.3240E-03	1.3165E+08	9.9716E-01	1.0000E+00	2.9488E+08
Min value	9.8769E-01	9.4485E-06	8.1722E+07	9.9188E-01	9.8556E-08	1.3281E+08

Table 7. CCII+ sizes for the best performance of each parameter

	Best Value	**W1 (μm)**	**W2 (μm)**
	Voltage Mode		
Gain (V/V)	0.994	247.26	244.74
Offset (V)	1.0450E-03	142.75	184.26
Band-Width (Hz)	1.14730E+08	58.969	107.92
	Current Mode		
Gain (I/I)	0.989	17.937	15.981
Offset (A)	1.2121E-11	22.515	25.5
Band-Width (Hz)	1.9377E+08	19.646	12.865

Table 8. CCII- sizes for the best performance of each parameter

	Best Value	**W1 (μm)**	**W2 (μm)**	**W3 (μm)**	**W4 (μm)**	**W5 (μm)**	**W6 (μm)**	**W7 (μm)**	**W8 (μm)**
	Voltage Mode								
Gain (V/V)	0.99341	258.94	71.218	186.09	118.99	68.549	180.51	78.501	221.21
Offset (V)	0	197.53	95.759	140.92	123.25	61.652	201.71	59.207	231.64
Band-Width (Hz)	1.1310E+08	105.52	94.629	123.79	124.4	61.227	193.66	66.462	215.15
	Current Mode								
Gain (I/I)	0.99646	128.07	158.61	1.3677	169.98	82.895	223.05	62.88	187.76
Offset (A)	1.5662E-09	117.57	248.87	27.004	151.81	66.106	206.03	75.153	241.61
Band-Width (Hz)	2.38990E+08	9.1229	194.62	26.676	86.317	32.589	219.16	64.553	219.7

CONCLUSION

A GA for the synthesis of analog circuits was described in the chapter. Further, two synthesized current conveyors CCII+ and CCII- were optimized by applying a proposed MO-PSO algorithm which has been implemented by combining MATLAB and HSPICE. This optimization algorithm was compared with NSGA-II, and from the optimization results, we conclude that the MO-PSO algorithm is able to find optimal sizes of analog circuits, since the performances of the CCII+ and CCII- have been improved compared to the already reported ones in the literature.

ACKNOWLEDGMENT

This work is supported by CONACyT/MEXICO under the project 48396-Y.

REFERENCES

Coello, C. A., & Lechuga, M. S. (2002). MOPSO: A proposal for multiple objective particle swarm optimization. In *Proceedings of the Congress on Evolutionary Computation* (pp. 1051-1056).

Deb, K., Pratap, A., Agarwal, S., & Meyarivan, T. (2002). A fast and elitist multiobjective genetic algorithm: NSGA-II. *IEEE Transactions on Evolutionary Computation*, 6(2), 182–197. doi:10.1109/4235.996017

Eeckelaert, T., McConaghy, T., & Gielen, G. (2005). Efficient multiobjective snthesis of analog circuits using hierarchical pareto-optimal performance hypersurfaces. *Design, Automation and Test in Europe*, (2), 1070-1075.

Fakhfakh, M. (2008). A novel alienor-based heuristic for the optimal design of analog circuits. *Microelectronics Journal*, 40(1), 141–148. doi:10.1016/j.mejo.2008.07.007

Fakhfakh, M., Loulou, M., & Tlelo-Cuautle, E. (2007). Synthesis of CCIIs and design of simulated CCII based floating inductances. In *Proceedings of the IEEE ICECS*, Marrakech, Morocco (pp. 379-382).

Guerra-Gómez, I., Tlelo-Cuautle, E., Li, P., & Gielen, G. (2008). Simulation-based optimization of UGCs performances. In *Proceedings of the IEEE ICCDCS*, Cancun, México (pp. 1-4).

Kennedy, J., Eberhart, R. C., & Shi, Y. (2001). *Swarm intelligence*. Menlo Park, CA: Morgan Kaufmann.

Koza, J. R., Jones, L. W., Keane, M. A., Streeter, M. J., & Al-Sakran, A. H. (2004). Toward automated design of industrial-strength analog circuits by means of genetic programming. In *Genetic programming theory and practice II* (pp. 121-142). Amsterdam: Kluwer Academic Publishers.

Kumar, P., & Senani, R. (2002). Bibliography on nullors and their applications in circuit analysis, synthesis and design. *Analog Integrated Circuits and Signal Processing*, 33(1), 65–76. doi:10.1023/A:1020337229998

Lamont, G. B., & Coello, C. A. (2007). *Evolutionary algorithms for solving multi objective problems*. Berlin, Germany: Springer-Verlag.

Liu, B., Wang, Y., Yu, Z., Liu, L., Li, M., Wang, Z., Lu, J., & Fernández, F. V. (2009). Analog circuit optimization system based on hybrid evolutionary algorithms. *INTEGRATION, the VLSI journal*, 42(2), 137-148.

Martens, E., & Gielen, G. (2008). Classification of analog synthesis tools based on their architecture selection mechanisms. *INTEGRATION, the VLSI journal*, 41, 238-252.

Mattiussi, C., & Floreano, D. (2007). Analog genetic encoding for the evolution of circuits and networks. *IEEE Transactions on Evolutionary Computation, 11*(5), 596–607. doi:10.1109/TEVC.2006.886801

McConaghy, T., Eeckelaert, T., & Gielen, G. (2005). CAFFEINE: Template-free symbolic model generation of analog circuits via canonical form functions and genetic programming. In *Proceedings of the Solid-State Circuits Conference* (pp. 243-246).

McConaghy, T., & Gielen, G. (2006). Genetic programming in industrial analog CAD: Applications and challenges. In T. Yu et al. (Eds.), *Genetic programming theory and practice III* (pp. 291-306). Berlin, Germany: Springer-Verlag.

McConaghy, T., Palmers, P., Gielen, G., & Steyaert, M. (2007). Simultaneous multitopology multi-objective sizing across thousands of analog circuit topologies. In *Proceedings of the Design Automation Conference* (pp. 944-947).

Reyes-García, C. A., Barajas, S. E., Tlelo-Cuautle, E., & Reyes-Galaviz, O. F. (2008). A hybrid system for automatic infant cry recognition II. In J. R. Rabuñal, J. Dorado, & A. Pazos (Eds.), *Encyclopedia of artificial intelligence* (pp. 867-872). Hershey, PA: Information Science Reference.

Rutenbar, R. A., Gielen, G., & Roychowdhury, J. (2007). Hierarchical modeling, optimization, and synthesis for system-level analog and RF designs. *Proceedings of the IEEE, 95*(3), 640–669. doi:10.1109/JPROC.2006.889371

Sánchez-López, C., Tlelo-Cuautle, E., Fakhfakh, M., & Loulou, M. (2007). Computing simplified noise-symbolic-expressions in CMOS CCs by applying SPA and SAG. In *Proceedings of the IEEE ICM*, Cairo, Egypt (pp. 159-162).

Santana-Quintero, L. V., Ramírez-Santiago, N., & Coello, C. A. (2008). Towards a more efficient multi-objective particle swarm optimizer. In L. T. Bui & S. Alam (Eds.), *Multi-objective optimization in computational intelligence* (pp. 76-105). Hershey, PA: Information Science Reference.

Smedt, B., & Gielen, G. E. (2003). WATSON: Design space boundary exploration and model generation for analog and RF IC design. *IEEE Transactions on Computer-Aided Design of Integrated Circuits and Systems, 22*(2), 213–224. doi:10.1109/TCAD.2002.806598

Smith, K., & Sedra, A. (1968). The current-conveyor - a new circuit building block. *Proceedings of the IEEE, 56*(8), 1368–1369. doi:10.1109/PROC.1968.6591

Stehr, G., Graeb, H. E., & Antreich, K. J. (2007). Analog performance space exploration by normal-boundary intersection and by Fourier-Motzkin elimination. *IEEE Transactions on Computer-Aided Design of Integrated Circuits and Systems, 26*(10), 1733–1748. doi:10.1109/TCAD.2007.895756

Synopsys. (2007). *HSPICE RF user guide Z-2007.3* (pp. 95-104).

Tlelo-Cuautle, E., & Duarte-Villaseñor, M. A. (2008a). Evolutionary electronics: Automatic synthesis of analog circuits by GAs. In A. Yang, Y. Shan, & L.T. Bui (Eds.), *Success in evolutionary computation* (pp. 165-188). Berlin, Germany: Springer-Verlag.

Tlelo-Cuautle, E., Duarte-Villaseñor, M. A., & Guerra-Gómez, I. (2008b). Automatic synthesis of VFs and VMs by applying genetic algorithms. *Circuits . Systems and Signal Processing, 27*(3), 391–403. doi:10.1007/s00034-008-9030-2

Tlelo-Cuautle, E., Duarte-Villaseñor, M. A., Reyes-García, C. A., & Reyes-Salgado, G. (2007). Automatic synthesis of electronic circuits using genetic algorithms. *Computación y Sistemas, 10*(3), 217–229.

Tlelo-Cuautle, E., Moro-Frías, D., Sánchez-López, C., & Duarte-Villaseñor, M. A. (2008c). Synthesis of CCII-s by superimposing VFs and CFs through genetic operations. *IEICE Electronics Express, 5*(11), 411–417. doi:10.1587/elex.5.411

Trejo-Guerra, R., Tlelo-Cuautle, E., Cruz-Hernández, C., Sánchez-López, C., & Fakhfakh, M. (2008). Current conveyor realization of synchronized Chua's circuits for binary communications. In *Proceedings of the IEEE DTIS*, Tozeur, Tunisia (pp. 1-4).

Unno, N., & Fujii, N. (2007). Automated design of analog circuits accelerated by use of simplified MOS model and reuse of genetic operations. *IEICE Transactions on Electronics . E (Norwalk, Conn.), 90-C*(6), 1291–1298.

Van der Plas, G., Debyser, G., Leyn, F., Lampaert, K., Vandenbussche, J., & Gielen, G. G. E. (2001). AMGIE-a synthesis environment for CMOS analog integrated circuits. *IEEE Transactions on Computer-Aided Design of Integrated Circuits and Systems, 20*(9), 1037–1058. doi:10.1109/43.945301

Zitzler, E., Deb, K., & Thiele, L. (2000). Comparison of multi-objective evolutionary algorithms: Empirical results. *IEEE Transactions on Evolutionary Computation, 8*(2), 173–195.

Chapter 9
Statistical Analysis of Computational Intelligence Algorithms on a Multi-Objective Filter Design Problem

Flávio Teixeira
University of Victoria, Canada

Alexandre Ricardo Soares Romariz
University of Brasilia, Brazil

ABSTRACT

This chapter presents the application of a comprehensive statistical analysis for both algorithmic performance comparison and optimal parameter estimation on a multi-objective digital signal processing problem. The problem of designing optimum digital finite impulse response (FIR) filters with the simultaneous approximation of the filter magnitude and phase is posed as a multi- objective optimization problem. Several computational-intelligence-based algorithms for solving this particular optimization problem are presented: genetic algorithms (GA), particle swarm optimization (PSO) and simulated annealing (SA) with multi-objective scalarization methods. Algorithms with Pareto sampling methods, namely non-dominated sorting genetic algorithm II (NSGA-II) and multi-objective simulated annealing (MOSA) are also applied as a way of dealing with multi-objective optimization. Instead of using a process of trial and error, a statistical exploratory analysis is used to estimate optimal parameters. A comprehensive statistical comparison of the applied algorithms is addressed, which indicates a particularly strong performance of NSGA-II and pure GA with weighting scalarization.

INTRODUCTION

This chapter addresses the application of several computational-intelligence-based algorithms for solving a nonlinear multi-objective digital signal processing problem. Also, this work develops multi-objective extensions to existing single-objective statistical exploratory analysis. The developed methodology is

DOI: 10.4018/978-1-60566-798-0.ch009

primarily intended to obtain an estimate of best parameter values for the adaptive algorithms and also to effectively compare performance. In this regard, a binary quality indicator will be used for comparison of the Pareto front approximations obtained.

The rest of the chapter is organized as follows: in the next section, the digital signal processing problem is described – more specifically, it is a multi-objective optimization problem on digital filter design. Optimization theory to better analyze the problem at hand is subsequently discussed. Following which, the optimization algorithms that will be applied to the signal processing problem are addressed. After that, the statistical exploratory analysis and its extensions to the multi-objective case are developed. The results on the digital signal processing problem are then presented, and finally, the last section presents conclusions about the work.

DIGITAL FILTER DESIGN THEORY

Introduction

In a strict sense, the term frequency selective filter suggests a system that passes certain frequency component and totally rejects all others, but in a broader context, any system that modifies certain frequencies relative to others is also classified as a filter (Oppenheim & Schafer, 1999).

A digital filter can be uniquely characterized on the time-domain by its impulse response $h(n)$. Alternatively, a digital filter can also be uniquely characterized on the frequency domain by its frequency response $H\left(e^{j\omega}\right)$, which is also the DTFT (Discrete-Time Fourier Transform) of the sequence $h(n)$ (Madisetti & Williams, 1999).

Digital filters can be classified into two main classes:

- FIR (Finite Impulse Response), also known as non-recursive filters.
- IIR (Infinite Impulse Response), also known as recursive filters.

For the FIR filters, $h(n)$ is nonzero for a finite number of samples while on the IIR filters, $h(n)$ has an infinite number of nonzero samples. Additionally, particularly for the FIR filters, $h(n)$ sequence samples are also known as the filter coefficients. For the IIR filters, the filter coefficients include feedback terms in the filter difference equation (Diniz, da Silva, & Lima, 2004).

Digital filter design has been extensively addressed within the last 25 years. The design and realization of digital filters involve a blend of theory, applications, and technologies (Madisetti & Williams, 1999). On most applications, the filter design specifications are given on the frequency domain by the filter desired frequency response $D\left(e^{j\omega}\right)$. It is important to note that $D\left(e^{j\omega}\right)$ is in general a complex-valued function. This work focuses on the simultaneous arbitrary approximation, in the optimum sense, of both the magnitude and the phase of the response.

Given that the frequency response of a digital filter is always periodic on the frequency variable ω with period equal to 2π, the filter design specifications need only be defined on a period of the frequency variable, usually in the frequency region $[-\pi, \pi]$. Besides that, when the filter frequency response is conjugate symmetric $D^{*}\left(\omega\right) = D\left(e^{-j\omega}\right)$, it suffices to specify the frequency response on positive frequencies $[0, 2\pi]$ (Madisetti & Williams, 1999). This symmetric-conjugate condition on the filter frequency response is the most usual situation, given that it generates filters with real coefficients. This chapter will investigate the design of real coefficient filters only.

The simplest digital filter magnitude specification is given by the ideal low-pass, high-pass, band-pass and band-stop responses. As an example, the low-pass ideal filter magnitude response is given by:

$$\left| H\left(e^{j\omega}\right) \right| = \begin{cases} 1, & \text{for } \omega \le \omega_c \\ 0, & \text{for } \omega_c \le \omega \le \pi \end{cases} \tag{1}$$

In addition to the four basic ideal filters above, other common ideal filters found in the digital signal processing literature include the differentiators and the Hilbert transform filters.

The ideal digital filters discussed above include discontinuities on the magnitude of the frequency response, and for this reason cannot be directly implemented. They must be approximated by a physically feasible system, i.e., the discontinuity on the cut-off frequency ω_c for the low-pass ideal filter should be replaced by a transition band over which the filter magnitude changes smoothly from the pass band $\omega \le \omega_c$ to the reject band $\omega \ge \omega_c$.

In general, the design of digital filters is composed of the following stages:

- Specification of the desired frequency response.
- Approximation of the specifications by means of a discrete-time causal system.
- Realization of the system

This chapter focuses on the approximation of the filter specification only.

Traditionally, most digital filters designed for practical applications are specified in terms of restrictions on the magnitude of the frequency response, although no restrictions on the phase of the filter frequency response are posed besides those implicitly required by stability and/or causality (Madisetti & Williams, 1999). As an example, the linear phase of the frequency response is generally imposed for FIR filters (constant phase slope) by the following relation:

$$\Theta\left(\omega\right) = -M\omega \tag{2}$$

where $\Theta(\omega)$ denotes the phase of the frequency response $\angle D(e^{j\omega})$ and the parameter M equals the filter's desired delay.

However, for some specialized applications, it is necessary to meet both magnitude and phase specifications, giving rise to different design approaches than those commonly used, i.e., the window design technique, the Parks-McClellan optimization approach, etc. In these specialized applications, the phase of the frequency response is generally specified in terms of the filter group delay $\tau(\omega)$ by the following relation:

$$\tau\left(\omega\right) = -\frac{d\Theta\left(\omega\right)}{d\omega} \tag{3}$$

In equation (4), the filter group delay is defined as the negative derivative of the phase of the frequency response. Also, the group delay $\tau(\omega)$ gives the filter delay, in samples, added by a system on a sine wave with frequency ω (Diniz, da Silva, & Lima, 2004).

Nonlinear-Phase FIR Filter Design

One common design principle for FIR filters is that the phase of the filter frequency response is linear. Although this characteristic is desired in most situations, in some specialized applications this can be more restrictive than desirable. The following scenarios motivate the use of nonlinear phase FIR filters (Madisetti & Williams, 1999):

- For some applications, phase linearity is necessary only on some predefined frequency bands. In this case, it is desirable to sacrifice exact linear phase in exchange for reduction or control of the filter delay.
- For some applications, the filter frequency response $H\left(e^{j\omega}\right)$ should approximate a desired non-linear frequency response $D\left(e^{j\omega}\right)$. Examples include equalizer design.

In this work, we focus on low group delay on the pass bands. As a comparison, for the FIR linear phase filters, the group delay introduced is constant and independent of the frequency of the entire band, but it can still be quite large. In practice, a variable group delay in stop bands is of little concern, and by allowing the phase response to be nonlinear in stop bands, FIR filters can be designed with constant group delay with respect to the pass bands. This significantly reduces the constant group delay relative to that achieved with filters that have a constant group delay throughout the entire frequency band (Antoniou & Lu, 2007).

IIR filters can meet the specification of linear phase and constant group delay on the pass bands combined with nonlinear phase on the reject bands. As is widely known in the digital signal processing literature, IIR filters offer better frequency selectivity, smaller computational complexity and smaller system delay compared to FIR filters of the same size (Antoniou & Lu, 2007). However, a main disadvantage of IIR filter design is that an exact linear phase can only be approximately achieved and the design must explicitly deal with the stability problem unlike the FIR design where a filter is always stable (Antoniou & Lu, 2007).

The stability problem can be handled in several ways. A popular approach is to impose stability constraints that establish a class of stable IIR filters from which the best solution for the design problem can be obtained. Obviously, this leads to a constrained optimization formulation for the design. However, technical difficulties can often occur if we attempt to implement a stability constraint that is explicitly related to the design variables. Linear stability constraints that depend on the design variables were also proposed. It should be mentioned, however, that constraints of this class are sufficient conditions for stability and are often too restrictive to permit a satisfactory design (Antoniou & Lu, 2007).

Classical Approximation Problem

The problem of designing nonlinear phase digital filters may be regarded as a classical approximation problem (Deczky, 1972). In general terms the problem may be stated as:

"Let $f(x)$ be a given real-valued function defined on a set X, and F (A, x) be a real-valued approximation function depending continuously on $x \in X$ and on N parameters A. Given a distance function ρ, determine the N parameters $A^* \in P$ such that:" (Deczky, 1972, pp.1)

$$\rho \left[F\left(A^*, x\right), f\left(x\right) \right] \leq \rho \left[F\left(A, x\right), f\left(x\right) \right],$$

for all $A \in P$.

$$(4)$$

To apply this general approximation problem to the nonlinear phase FIR filter design problem, let the filter transfer function $H(z)$ be a function of N parameters (e.g., the filter coefficients) ordered in a vector A. The independent variable x is converted to the digital frequency ω and the set X is $(\omega: 0 \leq \omega \leq \pi)$.

Also, the frequency response of the filter, including the magnitude and group delay, may be expressed as a real-valued function of A and ω, $F(A, \omega)$, while the desired frequency response becomes $f(\omega)$.

Given the approximation problem, an important aspect of the optimization relates to the distance function. In this work, the distance function used is the L_p norm, as this function has been extensively studied, and its properties are well known (Deczky, 1972):

$$\left\| L\left(A\right) \right\|_p = \left(\int_0^\pi W\left(\omega\right) \left| F\left(A, \omega\right) - f\left(\omega\right) \right|^p d\omega \right)^{\frac{1}{p}}$$

$$(5)$$

Common error criteria such as the minimum square and the minimax error are special cases of the distance function in equation (5).

Transfer Function and Frequency Response Forms

The FIR filter transfer function, in this work, is defined in the pole-zero-gain form as:

$$H\left(z\right) = k_0 \prod_{i=1}^n z - z_{zi}$$

$$(6)$$

where z_{zi} are the transfer function zeros, in real or complex conjugate form and k_0 is a constant gain.

The parameter vector A is defined as the transfer function zeros in polar coordinates:

$$A = \left[\phi_{z1}, r_{zi}, \phi_{z2}, r_{z2}, \ldots, \phi_{zN}, r_{zN}, p_N \right]$$

$$(7)$$

with a total of $N = n + 1$ parameters. The transfer function zeros in polar coordinates are defined as:

$$z_{zi} = r_{zi} \exp^{j\phi_{zi}}$$

$$(8)$$

The filter frequency response $F(A, \omega)$ is expressed as the magnitude attenuation $\eta(\omega)$ in dB and the group delay $\tau(\omega)$ in samples:

$$\eta\left(\omega\right) = -20\log_{10}\left|H\left(\exp^{j\omega}\right)\right|\text{dB}$$

$$\tau\left(\omega\right) = -\frac{d}{d\omega}\left(\measuredangle H\left(\exp^{j\omega}\right)\right) \tag{9}$$

As such, given the FIR filter transfer function in pole-zero-gain form, the filter magnitude attenuation is given by (Deczky, 1974):

$$\eta\left(A,\omega\right) = -\sum_{i=1}^{n}10\log_{10}\left(1 - 2r_{zi}\cos\left(\omega - \phi_{zi}\right) + r_{zi}^{2}\right) - p_{N} \tag{10}$$

And the group delay by (Deczky, 1974):

$$\tau\left(A,\omega\right) - \sum_{i=1}^{n}\frac{1 - r_{zi}\cos\left(\omega - \phi_{zi}\right)}{1 - 2r_{zi}\cos\left(\omega - \phi_{zi}\right) + r_{zi}^{2}} - p_{N} \tag{11}$$

where $p_{N} = \log_{10}k_{0}$, for the filter attenuation and $p_{N} = \tau_{0}$ for the group delay.

Objective Function for Optimization

For the simultaneous approximation of the magnitude and group delay of the filter, the weighted L_{p} norm in equation (5) is simplified for discrete approximation:

$$L_{2p,2q}^{\eta,\tau}\left(A\right) = \delta\sum_{i=1}^{I}W_{\eta}\left(\omega_{i}\right)\left(\eta\left(A,\omega_{i}\right) - \eta_{d}\left(\omega_{i}\right)\right)^{2p} + \left(1 - \delta\right)\sum_{i=1}^{I}W_{\tau}\left(\omega_{i}\right)\left(\tau\left(A,\omega_{i}\right) - \tau_{d}\left(\omega_{i}\right)\right)^{2q} \tag{12}$$

where W_{η} is the filter magnitude discrete weighting function, η is the designed filter discrete magnitude response, η_{d} is the desired discrete magnitude response, W_{τ} is the filter discrete group delay weighting function, τ is the designed filter discrete group delay and τ_{d} is the desired discrete group delay.

All functions are specified over the discrete digital frequencies ($\omega : 0 \leq \omega \leq \pi$).

It is worth noting that the function in equation (12) is also called an objective function f in the optimization literature, given that the filter design's main goal is to attain a minimum functional value of equation (12), consequently leading to a better approximation of the filter design specifications.

OPTIMIZATION THEORY APPLIED TO THE NONLINEAR PHASE FIR DESIGN PROBLEM

Introduction

Optimization can be defined as the science of obtaining the best solutions for certain mathematically well-defined problem. Optimization theory involves the study of optimum criteria for problems, algorithmic methods for its solution, the study of the structure of these methods and computational experimentation on real problems (Fletcher, 1980).

One measure of the complexity of the optimization problem relates to the mathematical function that expresses the problem and the constraints imposed on the variables. Basically, two classes can be distinguished in this subject: linear and nonlinear optimization.

First, in linear optimization, both the objective function and the constraints are linear functions of the problem variable. When the objective function and at least one of the constraints are nonlinear functions of the problem variable, then the problem is regarded as a nonlinear optimization problem. In this problem class, an important concept is that of convexity. The term convex can be applied both for sets and the functions (Nocedal & Wright 2006).

It can be said that a function f is convex if its domain S is a convex set and for any two points x and y in S, the following relation is satisfied (Nocedal & Wright 2006):

$$f\big(\alpha x + (1-\alpha)y\big) \le \alpha f(x) + (1-\alpha)f(y) \quad \text{for all } \alpha \in [0,1] \tag{13}$$

The concept of convexity for a function has direct connection with the problem resolution complexity. An important result of the optimization theory is that if both the objective and the constraint functions are convex, then any local solution is also a global solution (Nocedal & Wright 2006).

In general, nonlinear functions do not have the convexity property of equation (13). This observation significantly increases the optimization complexity, since for nonlinear functions with many local minima it is hard to find a global minimum. Generally, optimization algorithms tend to be trapped at local minima (Nocedal & Wright 2006).

It is worth noting that there exists no mathematical proof, for all algorithms that will be discussed in the section on optimization algorithms, of obtaining global solutions for the nonlinear objective functions with many local minima. However, when comparing the solutions obtained by the gradient-based optimization algorithms with those of the algorithms based on computational intelligence theory, much of the literature has shown better performance for the latter, especially for nonlinear optimization problems with many local minima (Engelbrecht, 2007).

Optimization Problem Definition

According to Bonnans, Gilbert, Lemaréchal, & Sagastizábal (2006), the optimization problem can be defined as:

For a given set X and a function $f\colon X \circledR \mathrm{R}$, also called the objective function, find a point $\mathbf{x}^* \in X$ in which, for all $\mathbf{x} \in X$, the relation $f(\mathbf{x}) \ge f(\mathbf{x}^*)$ is valid. The variable $\mathbf{x}$ is generally called the decision or control variable. Given this statement, the optimization problem is given by the following relation:

$$\begin{aligned}
&\min f(\mathbf{x}) \quad \mathbf{x} \in \mathbb{R}^n \\
&\text{subject to} \\
&c_j(\mathbf{x}) \ge 0 \quad j \in I \\
&c_j(\mathbf{x}) = 0 \quad j \in E
\end{aligned} \tag{14}$$

where, for the optimization problem in equation (14), the control variable is defined in the n-dimensional Euclidian space $\mathbf{x} \in R^n$, c_j:$R^n \circledR R$ denotes the constraint functions and I and E are two disjoint integer sets that represent the inequality and equality constraints function indices respectively.

Optimization Problem Categories

From the optimization problem definition in equation (14), four major problem classes can be derived. The first two classes relate to the constraints imposed on the control variable $\mathbf{x}$. In this chapter, only the unconstrained optimization problem will be analyzed.

The last two important classes of optimization problems relate to the number of objective functions simultaneously minimized during the optimization. The problem shown in equation (14) defines only one objective function f. For this reason, it is also regarded as a single optimization problem. However, real problems generally involve decision making, choices and trade-offs between several conflicting objectives. All these objectives should then be considered simultaneously, and optimally (Miettinen, 1999). These problems are also regarded as multi-objective optimization problems. Unlike the single-objective problems, a unique optimal solution that simultaneously minimizes all objective functions does not necessarily exist. In this chapter, only the multi-objective optimization problem will be addressed and as such, the nonlinear phase FIR filter design problem defined in the previous section will also be formulated as a multi-objective problem later in this section.

Multi-Objective Problems

Problem Definition

The multi-objective problem can be defined as (Miettinen, 1999):

$$
\min \left\{ f_1\left(\mathbf{x}\right), f_2\left(\mathbf{x}\right), \ldots, f_k\left(\mathbf{x}\right) \right\}
$$
$$
\text{subject to}
$$
$$
\mathbf{x} \in S \tag{15}
$$

where the number of objective function is $k \geq 2$ with f_i: $R^n \rightarrow R$, $i = 1, \ldots, k$. The objective function vector is defined as $\mathbf{f}(\mathbf{x}) = [f_1(\mathbf{x}), f_2(\mathbf{x}), \ldots, f_k(\mathbf{x})]^T$ belonging to the feasible region S, which is a subset of the decision variable space R^n.

Optimal Solutions Characterization: The Pareto Optimal Front

It is generally not possible to find a unique problem solution for equation (15) that minimizes all objective functions simultaneously. However, some objective function vectors $\mathbf{f}(\mathbf{x})$ can be selected for inspection. These vectors are those whose components $f_i(\mathbf{x})$ cannot be made better without the deterioration of at least one other component. This solution is generally called Pareto optimal, a term developed by the French-Italian engineer-economist Vilfredo Pareto (Miettinen, 1999). The formal definition for the Pareto optimal concept, according to Miettinen (1999), is:

An objective vector $\mathbf{f}^* \in F$ is Pareto optimal if no other decision vector exists $\mathbf{f} \in F$ for which:

$$\begin{cases} f_i \leq f_i^* & \text{for all } i = 1, \ldots, k \\ f_j < f_j^* & \text{for at least one index } j \end{cases} \tag{16}$$

In the formal Pareto definition in equation (16), $\mathbf{f}^*$ is Pareto optimal if the corresponding decision vector $\mathbf{x}^*$ is also Pareto optimal.

Another equivalent name for the Pareto optimal front is non-dominance set. The decision vectors $\mathbf{x}^*$ included in the Pareto optimal set are also called non-dominated vectors (Ehrgott & Gandibleaux, 2002).

The Pareto optimal concept in equation (16) was actually defined on a global context. As already outlined for the single-objective optimization problem, finding an optimal problem solution is a hard task. The same statement is also true for finding a Pareto optimal global set, especially if this set is non-convex.

Mathematically, each Pareto optimal point is an equally acceptable solution to the multi- objective optimization problem. However, a unique point is generally desired as solution, and its choice usually requires information not explicitly found in the objective functions (Miettinen, 1999). Generally, a decision maker, supposed to have a better knowledge of the problem, and better insight on trade-off relations between different solutions, is responsible for selecting the problem's final solution (Miettinen, 1999) from the ones in the Pareto front.

Generation Methods for Pareto Optimal Fronts

Several methods have been developed in the literature to generate the Pareto optimal front on the multi-objective optimization problem in equation (15). One of the strategies used in this chapter consists of transforming the multi-objective problem to an equivalent single-objective problem through its scaling. Another strategy consists of Pareto sampling methods like the NSGA-II and MOSA. In the next section, several single-objective algorithms, including the Quasi-Newton algorithm, the Genetic Algorithm, Simulated Annealing and the Particle Swarm Optimization algorithms will be applied to the multi-objective digital filter design optimization problem. This application is possible since the multi-objective problem will be scaled through the weighting method discussed below.

Among the several existing strategies for scaling the multi-objective optimization problem in equation (15), the weighting method (Chankong & Haimes, 1983) is worth mentioning:

Make $\mathbf{W} = \left\{ \mathbf{w} \mid \mathbf{w} \in \mathbb{R}^n, w_j \geq 0 \text{ e} \sum_{j=1}^{n} w_j = 1 \right\}$ a nonnegative weight set. The weighting method

must solve the following single-objective problem $P(\mathbf{w})$ for some weight vector $\mathbf{w} \in W$:

$$P\left(\mathbf{w}\right) = \min_{\mathbf{x} \in S} \sum_{j=1}^{n} w_j f_j\left(\mathbf{x}\right) \tag{17}$$

In general, even though the weighting method is the most straightforward strategy for scaling the multi-objective optimization problem, it is not always successful in generating the entire Pareto optimal front for the non-convex situation (Li, 1996).

In this chapter, only the weighting scalarization method will be used in conjunction with the single-objective optimization algorithms of the next section. Even though the authors are aware that this method is not able to generate the entire Pareto optimal front on non-convex cases, it is worth using it as a means of comparison with newer methods based on Pareto sampling, i.e., NSGA-II and MOSA.

Analysis of the Nonlinear FIR Filter Design Problem

The original formulation of the classical approximation problem applied to the design of nonlinear FIR filters, where the L_p norm is used as the approximation distance metric between the desired magnitude and group delay responses, was pioneered by Deczy (1972). This chapter follows this design approach for implementing the single-objective optimization algorithms in the minimization of the approximation distance in the L_p norm.

Even though there is no mention in Deczy (1972) of the multi-objective nature of the digital filter design problem, it is straightforward to show that the filter magnitude and group delay simultaneous approximation in equation (12) has similar functional form to the weighting scalarization method. For this, let $\mathbf{W} = \left\{ \mathbf{w} \mid \mathbf{w} \in \Re^n, w_j \geq 0 \text{ e} \sum_{j=1}^{n} w_j = 1 \right\}$ be a non-negative weight set. The weighting method must solve the single-objective problem $P(\mathbf{w})$ defined in equation (17).

On the multi-objective problem formulation, there are two distinct functions for minimization: first, the filter magnitude attenuation approximation distance:

$$f_1(\mathbf{x}) = \left(\int_0^\pi W_\eta(\omega) \left| \eta(A, \omega) - \eta_d(\omega) \right|^p d\omega \right)^{\frac{1}{p}}$$

(18)

and second, the filter group delay approximation distance:

$$f_2(\mathbf{x}) = \left(\int_0^\pi W_\tau(\omega) \left| \tau(A, \omega) - \tau_d(\omega) \right|^p d\omega \right)^{\frac{1}{p}}$$

(19)

where the decision variable $\mathbf{x}$ in equation (18) and equation (19) represents the transfer function zeros vector A on polar coordinates.

Given the two distinct objective functions, the multi-objective problem formulation is given by:

$$\min \left\{ f_1(\mathbf{x}), f_2(\mathbf{x}) \right\}$$
$$\text{subject to}$$
$$\mathbf{x} \in S$$

(20)

A direct consequence of the multi-objective formulation in equation (20) is that it is not possible to obtain a unique problem solution. Instead, we can obtain the Pareto-optimal front, the decision vector set $\mathbf{x}^*$ for which equation (16) holds.

Additionally, it is important to note that given the nonlinear objective function's form in equation (18) and equation (19), one can only guarantee a local Pareto optimal front. Unfortunately, there is no theory available at the moment to predict the characteristics of the Pareto-optimal filters, in terms of the pole patterns or magnitude and group-delay behaviors (Cortelazzo & Lightner, 1984).

Given the local Pareto-optimal front of the multi-objective problem in equation (20), it is the decision maker's (filter designer's) task to choose one solution from the Pareto front that meets the specifications. This choice is based on the decision-maker's knowledge of the existing Pareto front solution's trade-offs.

A number of algorithms in the literature have been used to solve the multi-objective optimization problem in equation (20). The first solution was reported by Deczky (1972). In this work, a Quasi-Newton algorithm was used to solve the simultaneous approximation of the magnitude and group delay of a Infinite Impulse Response (IIR) filter design problem.

In Cortelazzo & Lightner (1984), the problem in equation (20) was solved using the weighting method with a Sequential Quadratic Programming (SQP) algorithm. Following that work, in Calvagno, Cortelazzo, & Mian (1995), the same weighting method was used in conjunction with a differential correction algorithm. With this algorithm, a better performance was obtained compared to the results of Cortelazzo & Lightner (1984).

Ahmad & Antoniou (2007) used a different approach. Specifically, Pareto sampling methods were used to solve the multi-objective optimization problem with an Elitist Non-dominated Sorting Genetic Algorithm (ENSGA). In Teixeira & Romariz (2007), the multi-objective problem in equation (20) was solved with the weighting method in conjunction with three computational- intelligence-based algorithms: genetic algorithms, simulated annealing and particle swarm optimization. Performance comparisons were made and the particle swarm optimizer was reported as the algorithm with the best quality solutions attained.

A fundamental question on using black-box algorithms such as evolutionary algorithms, particle swarm optimization and simulated annealing on these applications concerns parameter selection. Examples include population size, mutation and crossover rates, elite group size, acceleration constants, step sizes, and so on. Values for these parameters are most commonly set through a process of trial and error, or based on recommendations from related problems in the literature, rather than through statistically sound analysis of their effects on the algorithm's performance (Czarn, MacNish, Vijayan, Turlach, & Gupta, 2004). Given that, in Teixeira & Romariz (2008), a statistical exploratory analysis for the computational-intelligence-based algorithms was made. With this approach, optimal algorithm parameters were obtained for solving the multi-objective problem in equation (20). Performance comparisons between the algorithms were made once more and the particle swarm optimizer was again the best performer.

Given these results in the literature, an important question is how to effectively compare these algorithms. The notion of performance includes both the quality of the outcome as well as the computational resources needed to generate this outcome. Concerning the latter aspect, it is common practice to monitor either the number of fitness evaluations or the overall run-time on a particular computer. In this sense, there is no difference between single and multi- objective optimization. As to the quality aspect, however, there is a difference. In single-objective optimization, we can define quality by means of the objective function: the smaller the value, the better the solution. If we compare two solutions in the presence of multiple optimization criteria, the concept of Pareto dominance can be used.

The problem of effectively comparing the algorithms' performance on multi-objective optimization problems is addressed by Zitler *et al.* (2003) through the use of binary quality measures. With this mathematical framework, correct and fair comparisons between the algorithms are made possible.

In the section on statistical exploratory analysis that will be presented later in this chapter, multi-objective extensions of the original statistical exploratory analysis in Czarn *et al.* (2004) will be made, allowing the generation of statistical experiments with the purpose of firstly, estimating the optimal parameter values for the black-box algorithms, and secondly, effectively comparing the different optimization algorithms through the use of the binary quality measures.

OPTIMIZATION ALGORITHMS

Gradient-Based Algorithms

In their general form, gradient-based optimization algorithms have the following structure in the kth iteration (Fletcher, 1980):

- Determine the direction of search $s^{(k)}$.
- Find $\lambda^{(k)}$ to minimize $(x^{(k)} + \lambda s^{(k)})$ with respect to λ.
- Set $x^{(k+1)} = x^{(k)} + \lambda^{(k)} s^{(k)}$.

In this form, an initial estimate point $x^{(1)}$ in the hyperspace is required. Different gradient-based optimization algorithms correspond to different ways of choosing $s^{(k)}$ in each iteration.

In Newton-like methods, each new direction of search is generated with information of the Hessian matrix $G = \nabla^2 f(x)$ and the gradient vector $g = \nabla f(x)$ by the following relation:

$$s^{(k)} = -\left(G^{(k)}\right)^{-1} g^{(k)} \tag{21}$$

The main disadvantage of Newton-like methods is that the implementer must supply a formula from which the second derivative matrix G can be evaluated (Fletcher, 1980). This disadvantage is especially true for the filter L_p norm in equation (12), as it is already quite complicated to express the first order partial derivatives in closed form.

Quasi-Newton Algorithm

The above disadvantage is avoided with a class of optimization algorithms known as Quasi-Newton methods, which have the following basic structure:

- Set $s^{(k)} = - H^{(k)} g^{(k)}$.
- Line search along $s^{(k)}$ giving $x^{(k+1)} = x^{(k)} + \lambda^{(k)} s^{(k)}$.
- Update $H^{(k)}$ giving $H^{(k+1)}$.

The most commonly used updating formula for $H^{(k)}$ which, in general, yields the best results (Nocedal & Wright, 2006) is known as the Broyden-Fletcher-Goldfarb-Shanno - BFGS formula given by:

$$H^{(k+1)} = H + \left(1 + \frac{\gamma^T H \gamma}{\delta^T \gamma}\right)\frac{\delta\delta^T}{\delta^T \gamma} - \left(\frac{\delta\gamma^T H + H\gamma\delta^T}{\delta^T \gamma}\right)$$

(22)

where $\delta^{(k)} = x^{(k+1)} - x(k)$ and $\gamma(k) = g^{(k+1)} - g^{(k)}$.

With the Quasi-Newton approach, only first order partial derivatives are needed. The quantity $\lambda^{(k)}$ in the general structure of the gradient-based optimization algorithms defined above is calculated by a class of algorithms known as line-search methods, as they solve a one-dimensional function minimization problem at each iteration of the optimization algorithm. Typical line search algorithms try out a sequence of candidate values for λ, accepting one of those values when certain conditions are satisfied. The line search is done in two stages: a bracketing phase finds an interval containing desirable step lengths, and a bisection or interpolation phase computes a good step length within this interval (Nocedal & Wright, 2006). Sophisticated line search algorithms can be quite complicated. The implementation of the line search algorithm in this chapter was based on the algorithm developed by Dennis & Schnabel (1983).

Computational-Intelligence-Based Single-Objective Algorithms

Genetic Algorithm

Difficult search problems such as the nonlinear function minimization in equation (12) can often benefit from an effective use of parallelism, in which many different possibilities are explored simultaneously. Biological evolution is an appealing source of inspiration for addressing these problems. Evolution is, in effect, a method of searching among an enormous number of possibilities for solutions (Melanie, 1999).

Based on the features described above, the genetic algorithm can be basically described as follows:

- Population: The population of the genetic algorithm consists of a given number of individuals representing one possible optimum FIR filter. Each individual chromosome is represented by the coefficients set in equation (7), with real-valued encoding for the magnitude and phase of the filter zeros in polar coordinates.
- Fitness Function: At each new generation of the genetic algorithm, the offspring are created based on the fitness function. For the optimum FIR filter design, the filter design error is already defined in equation (12). As the objective of the optimization is the minimization of equation (12), the fitness, function of the chromosome (FIR filter coefficients), is defined as:

$$f(x) = \frac{1}{1 + L_{2p,2q}^{\eta,\tau}}$$

(23)

- Selection: Based on the fitness function, each individual is selected using a roulette-wheel selection method, meaning that the probability of being selected for the next generation is proportional to the individual's fitness. In addition, the algorithm uses elitism in selection, meaning that a pre-defined number of best individuals are always selected for the next population.

- Crossover: The crossover genetic operation is defined for the current implementation as follows: a single crossover position is chosen at random and the genes (filter zeros) of two parents, after the crossover position, are exchanged to form two offspring.
- Mutation: With a predefined probability, a real Gaussian random number is added to each gene, (magnitude and phase of the filter zeros z_{zi}).

Following the statistical methodology that will be developed in the next section, the implementation of the genetic algorithm is deliberately simple. In this regard, parameters such as the population size were not varied but fixed at the values shown below. The only parameters statistically analyzed and optimized were the crossover and the mutation rates.

The details of implementation for the genetic algorithm are given below:

- Population size: *40* individuals.
- Stopping criteria: Stall generations. The algorithm stops if there is no improvement in the best fitness value for *50* generations.

Simulated Annealing Algorithm

The development of the simulated annealing algorithm was motivated by studies in statistical mechanics that deal with the equilibrium of a large number of atoms in solids and liquids at a given temperature. In order to reach a more stable, globally minimum energy state, a process analogous to annealing, applied in metallurgy, is used: the exploration of the solution space is, at first, highly random (a high "temperature") and then becomes increasingly more deterministic, thus increasing the probability of finding a better local minima (Haftka & Gürdal, 1992).

One important topic about the simulated annealing optimization deals with the cooling schedule of the algorithm. In the current implementation, the Boltzmann annealing (Ingber, 1989) is used. This cooling schedule represents how the system's temperature is decreased, when new energy states are generated, and when these new energy states are accepted or rejected during optimization.

The only parameter in the implementation of simulated annealing that needed adjustment is the system initial temperature. In this regard, the statistical exploratory analysis experiment described in the next section, developed to generate an estimation of the black-box algorithms' best parameter values, was not implemented for this algorithm. For a fair performance comparison with the other optimization algorithms, the system's initial temperature was given a high value and an extended annealing time was allowed. More specifically, the optimization was halted only when the current atom's energy state had not changed its temperature for *50* consecutively iterations.

The implementation details of simulated annealing are given below:

- The probability density function of the atom states $g(z_{zi})$ - the filter zeros' (z_{zi}) deviation in equation (6) is defined as:

$$g(z_{zi}) = (2\pi t)^{\frac{-(N-1)}{2}} e^{-\frac{\Delta z_{zi}^2}{2T}}$$

(24)

where $\Delta z_{zi} = z_{zi}^{(j+1)} - z_{zi}^{(j)}$ is the deviation from state (filter) j to $j+1$, and T is a measure of the fluctuations of the Boltzmann distribution g in the N dimension of the filter zeros.

- The probability density for acceptance of a new cost-function (energy state) given the previous value - this cost function, in the filter design problem, is defined by the filter error function of equation (12). The probability density function is defined as:

$$f(z_{zi}) = \frac{1}{1 + e^{\frac{\Delta E}{T}}}$$

(25)

where ΔE represents the energy difference between the present and the previous values of the cost-function, $\Delta E = E_{(k+1)} - E_k$.

- The annealing schedule of the temperature T in annealing-time steps k, $T(k)$, is defined as:

$$T(k) = \frac{T_0}{\ln k}$$

(26)

Particle Swarm Optimization Algorithm

A swarm can be described as a population of interacting elements that is able to optimize some global objective through collaborative search of a space. Interactions that are relatively local (topologically) are often emphasized. There is a general stochastic (or chaotic) tendency in a swarm of individuals to move toward a center of mass in the population on critical dimensions, resulting in the convergence to an optimum (Kennedy, Eberhart, & Shi, 2001).

Given this, the technique called Particle Swarm Optimization, which has its roots in artificial life and social psychology as well as engineering and computer science, defines population members, called particles, whose positions in solution space are changed according to a dynamic system. When the population is initialized, in addition to the variables being given random values, they are stochastically accelerated toward a neighborhood best position (the position of highest fitness for any particle in its neighborhood) (Kennedy, Eberhart, & Shi, 2001).

The particle swarm optimization operation can be described by the following set of operations:

```
- Loop
- For i =1 to number of individuals
- If G(xᵢ) > G(pᵢ) then do
-   pᵢd = xᵢd
- End do
- g=i
```

```
- For j = indexes of neighbors
- If G(pⱼ) > G(pₘ)   then g=j
- Next j
- vᵢ_d(t) = vᵢ_d(t-1) + φ₁(pᵢ_d - xᵢ_d(t-1)) + φ₂( pₘ_d - xᵢ_d(t-1))
- vᵢ_d ∈ (-Vₘₐₓ, Vₘₐₓ)
- xᵢ_d (t) = xᵢ_d(t-1) + vᵢ_d(t)
- Next i
- Until termination criterion.
```

- Individual (or particle) in the particle swarm optimization is represented by the coefficients set in equation (7), with real-valued encoding for the magnitude and phase of the filter zeros in polar coordinates,
- The particle's neighborhood is defined by the particles to its left and right in a ring topology,
- x_i is the current particle (FIR filter) of the loop,
- p_i is the x_i particle with best fitness value (filter with less error),
- p_g is the x_i neighborhood particle with best fitness value (filter with less error),
- $G(\vec{x_i}) = \dfrac{1}{1 + L_{2p,2q}^{\eta,\tau}}$ is a modified filter inverse error, or in the particle swarm optimization nomenclature, the particle's fitness value,
- The dimension subscript d is represented by the filter length, the number of coefficients of the FIR filter,
- v_i is the particle's velocity term,
- φ_1, φ_2 are random numbers drawn from a uniform distribution with predefined up and down limits,
- V_{max} is a limiting term to prevent explosion in the particle movement through the hyperspace, keeping the velocity term convergent.

The implementation of the particle swarm optimization, following the implementation approach in the genetic algorithm, was also deliberately simple. Again, parameters such as the population size were not varied but fixed at the values shown below. The only parameters statistically analyzed were the control parameter ϕ and the inertia weight α.

The details of implementation for the particle swarm optimization are given below:

- Population size: *40* particles.
- Control parameter φ: Determines the type of trajectory the particle travels. If $\varphi \approx 0$ then the particle's trajectory simply increases linearly. As φ increases, the particle's trajectory has a tendency to an increased oscillatory behavior. Generally $\varphi = \varphi_1 + \varphi_2$ and $\varphi_1 = \varphi_2 \approx 2$.
- Inertia weight α: In the classical particle swarm optimization, generally, particle's position oscillations have a tendency to grow unbounded. One approach to control the oscillations is to use the inertia weight in the particle's velocity. Usually (Kennedy, Eberhart, & Shi, 2001), α is chosen in the range $0 \leq \alpha \leq 1$.

- Stopping criteria: Stall generations. The algorithm stops if there is no improvement in the best particle fitness value for *50* generations.

STATISTICAL EXPLORATORY ANALYSIS OF OPTIMIZATION ALGORITHMS

Introduction

This section aims at developing a comprehensive methodology for both the estimation of optimal parameter values for black-box algorithms and effective performance comparison. The first methodology feature, optimal parameter value estimation, will be addressed by a statistical exploratory analysis, originally developed by Czarn *et al.* (2004).

There is an issue regarding whether this technique is applicable to multi-objective optimization problems, given that in Czarn et *al.* (2004), single-objective quality indicators are used for performance comparison between the black-box algorithms runs. With regards to the quality, it can be said that in single-objective optimization, we can define quality by means of the objective function: the smaller the value, the better the solution. If we compare two solutions in the presence of multiple optimization criteria, the possibility of two solutions being incomparable, i.e., neither dominates the other, complicates the situation (Zitzler, Laumanns, Fonseca, & da Fonseca, 2003).

To address this issue, latter in this section, the binary ϵ-indicator originally developed by Zitzler *et al.* (2003) will be the chosen method to effectively compare different multi-objective algorithm runs, for reasons explained latter in this section.

As a final remark, multi-objective extensions of the original statistical exploratory analysis developed in Czarn, MacNish, Vijayan, Turlach, & Gupta (2004) will be addressed later in this section, setting up the statistical experiments to effectively estimate black-box optimal parameter values, and to compare performance. The results of these statistical experiments will be presented in the next section.

Single-Objective Statistical Exploratory Analysis

Currently, there is no generally accepted methodology for analyzing the relationship between parameters and the performance of the computational-intelligence-based optimization algorithms. For this reason, statistical analysis methods have been used in the literature to address this issue. One of the main drawbacks of the early statistical methods is that the general results of different methods have varied significantly. The main reasons for these remarkable result variations between different methods are the lack of the following desirable features (Czarn, MacNish, Vijayan, Turlach, & Gupta, 2004):

1. Blocking of seeds as a source of variation: Blocking of seeds by grouping experimental units into homogenous blocks, so that each run of the black-box algorithm for differing parameter values occurs with the same seeds, thus limiting the variation of the parameters within the blocks.
2. Calculation of power and sample sizes: Without calculating the power of the number of samples, it is not clear whether the statistical method has adequate power and, thus, sample size to detect noteworthy differences.
3. Detailed response curve analysis: It is important to undertake a detailed response curve analysis as it allows one to study the behavior of the parameter over the range of values that were used.

In order to identify the most appropriate type of experimental design and statistical test, the statistical exploratory analysis developed in Czarn *et al.* (2004) addressed five main features.

The first feature is blocking for variation or noise due to the seed. In such a design, every combination of parameter values appears the same number of times in the same block and the blocks are defined through seeds. For example, if there are *i* values for parameter A and *j* values for parameter B, then each block contains all *ij* combinations (Czarn, MacNish, Vijayan, Turlach, & Gupta, 2004). An increase in the sample size is handled by replicating the blocks identically except for the seeds.

The second feature is the choice of an appropriate statistical test. Czarn *et al.* mainly use the Analysis of Variance (ANOVA) to compare performances for two or more parameters using a randomized complete block design.

The third feature is a statistical test for individual parameters and their interactions. First, ANOVA supports the testing of the significance of individual parameters to be statistically demonstrated. Second, it supports the testing of the interaction between the parameters.

The fourth feature is a response curve analysis. Once a parameter is demonstrated to be statistically significant in ANOVA, the effect of the parameter may be modeled through an appropriate polynomial. Once the shape of the response curve is established, polynomial regression can be carried out to obtain estimates of the coefficients of the various parameters in the response-curve equation.

Finally, the last feature, power calculation, can be done in ANOVA by using the effect size index *f*.

Quality Indicators on Multi-Objective Problems

As already outlined in the previous section, several algorithms for solving the multi-objective FIR filter design optimization problem exist, and certainly, we are interested in the technique that provides the best approximation for the given problem. However, in order to reveal the strengths and weaknesses of certain approaches and to identify the most promising techniques, existing algorithms have to be compared. This, in turn, directly leads to the issue of assessing the performance of multi-objective optimizers. As already outlined in this chapter before, if we compare two solutions in the presence of multiple optimization criteria, the concept of Pareto dominance can be used, although the possibility of two solutions being incomparable complicates the situation. However, it gets even more complicated when we compare two sets of solutions because some solutions in either set may be dominated by solutions in the other set, while others may be incomparable (Zitzler, Laumanns, Fonseca, & da Fonseca, 2003). Accordingly, it is not clear what quality means with respect to the approximations of the Pareto-optimal front: closeness to the optimal solutions in objective space, or the coverage of a wide range of diverse solutions, etc (Zitzler, Laumanns, Fonseca, & da Fonseca, 2003).

Several studies can be found in the literature that address the problem of comparing approximations of the Pareto optimal front in a quantitative manner. Most popular are unary quality measures, i.e., the measure that assigns each approximation set a number that reflects a certain quality aspect; and usually a combination of such measures is used. Other methods are based on binary quality measures, which assign numbers to pairs of approximation sets. Zitzler *et al.* (2003) developed a mathematical framework to assess the different methodologies found in the literature and the following statements are proven for two arbitrary Pareto approximation sets **A** and **B** (Zitzler, Laumanns, Fonseca, & da Fonseca, 2003):

- Unary measures are able to detect whether **A** is better than **B**, but their use is generally restricted.

- Binary quality measures overcome the limitations of unary measures and, if properly designed, are capable of indicating whether **A** is better than **B**.

With these results, the binary quality class of indicators have been chosen as the quality indicators for this chapter. More specifically, in Zitzler, Laumanns, Fonseca, & da Fonseca (2003), the binary ε-indicator, I_ε (**A,B**), is given by:

$$I_\epsilon\left(\mathbf{A},\mathbf{B}\right) = \max_{\mathbf{z}^2 \in \mathbf{B}} \min_{\mathbf{z}^1 \in \mathbf{A}} \max_{1 \leq i \leq n} \frac{z_i^1}{z_i^2}$$

(27)

It can be said that the binary ε-indicator in equation (27) implies one of the following properties when I_ε (**A,B**) >1:

1. **A** ◁ **B**.
2. **A** ∥ **B**,

where the operator ∥ means that sets **A** and **B** are incomparable and operator ◁ means that set **A** is better than set **B**.

However, by using the following test $F : \mathbf{R}^n \times \mathbf{R}^n \rightarrow \left\{false, true\right\}$:

$$F = \left(I_\epsilon\left(\mathbf{A},\mathbf{B}\right) \leq 1 \wedge I_\epsilon\left(\mathbf{B},\mathbf{A}\right) > 1\right)$$

(28)

we are actually able to conclude that **A** is better than **B**, **A** ◁ **B**, as proved by Zitzler *et al.* (2003).

Multi-Objective Extensions to the Statistical Exploratory Analysis

Optimal Parameter Estimation

With the single-objective statistical exploratory analysis and the binary quality indicator, we are now able to define a statistical exploratory analysis to estimate the best parameter values for the black-box algorithms applied to the multi-objective FIR filter design problem. The steps to accomplish the optimal parameter estimation are:

1. Create a complete, randomized design for the black-box algorithm under study.
2. Generate a dot diagram to minimize the occurrence of censoring.
3. Define the parameters' starting ranges for the exploratory statistical exploratory analysis.
4. Generate an initial data set consisting of an arbitrary number of replicates.
5. Calculate power post hoc based upon a chosen effect.
6. Conduct ANOVA analysis and determine which parameters are statistically significant.
7. For parameters that are statistically significant, partition the sum of squares into polynomial contrast terms. Determine which polynomial terms are statistically significant.

8. Use polynomial regression to obtain the coefficients for the overall response curve.
9. Differentiate and solve the response curve for each parameter to obtain the best values and calculate confidence intervals.

Regarding the complete, randomized design, experiments will be conducted in this chapter for each optimization algorithm applied to the multi-objective FIR filter design problem.

In the first experiment conducted, genetic algorithm with the weighting scalarization method, a complete, randomized block design is used to estimate the optimal parameter values. Parameter A is defined as the mutation rate and Parameter B is the crossover rate. In the second experiment, particle swarm optimization with the weight scalarization method, parameter A is defined as the control parameter and Parameter B is the inertia weight α.

As mentioned above, only two parameters for each algorithm were statistically analyzed and optimized. The main reason is that with more than two parameters the statistical analysis gets more complicated and computationally expensive.

The second step in the methodology consists of generating a dot diagram to minimize the occurrence of censoring. To accomplish this, we must conduct an experiment with 10 arbitrary replicates (Czarn, MacNish, Vijayan, Turlach, & Gupta, 2004) using the black-box algorithms' full range of parameter values, i.e., for the genetic algorithm complete randomized design, using the crossover parameter p_{cr} in $0 < p_{cr} < 1$ and the mutation parameter p_{mu} in $0 < p_m < 1$. An instance of censoring is identified in this experiment when the difference between the best individual quality indicator's value and the worst individual quality indicator's value is less than or equal to an arbitrary threshold value. When this situation occurs, a dot is plotted on the dot diagram, as can be seen in the example of Figure 1 taken from Teixeira & Romariz (2008).

Regarding the quality indicator, in this chapter we use the binary quality indicator of equation (27). Given that this quality indicator must be compared with another approximation set, this chapter proposes the use of an arbitrary reference set $\mathbf{Z}^*$, where all black-box algorithms should be compared. More specifically, the reference set is composed of only one single point, an estimate of the ideal objective vector

Figure 1. Genetic algorithm dot diagram example

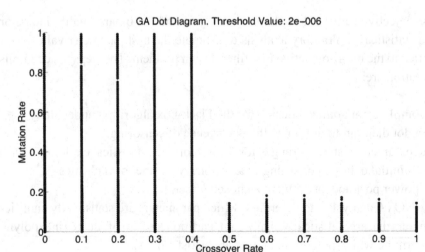

$\mathbf{z}^*$. This reference point $\mathbf{z}^*$ is defined by the vector that individually minimizes each one of the objective function values. It is worth noting that for the nonlinear phase digital filter design problem, the filter magnitude attenuation approximation distance f_1 in equation (18), and the filter group delay approximation distance f_2 in equation (19) are non-convex functions. Given that the ideal objective vector definition assumes that we have global knowledge of both individual objective functions (Miettinen, 1999), $\mathbf{z}^*$ is only an estimate of the ideal objective vector, since we cannot guarantee the global minimum of these objective functions. We have taken this comparison approach with the reference set $\mathbf{Z}^*$ since most of the time we can obtain a valid comparison for the binary ε-indicator I$_\varepsilon$($\mathbf{Z}^*$,$\mathbf{A}$), i.e., $\mathbf{Z}^* \lhd \mathbf{A}$.

Comparison between the reference set $\mathbf{Z}^*$ and an arbitrary approximation set $\mathbf{A}$ generated by an optimization algorithm is defined through the following algorithm:

$$If \left(I_\epsilon \left(\mathbf{Z}^*, \mathbf{A} \right) \leq 1 \wedge I_\epsilon \left(\mathbf{A}, \mathbf{Z}^* \right) > 1 \right) = \text{TRUE}$$

- indicatorValue = I$_\varepsilon$ ($\mathbf{Z}^*$,$\mathbf{A}$)
- else
- *discard approximation set*$\mathbf{A}$

With this test, we are able to compute a single value that quantifies by how much the reference set $\mathbf{Z}^*$ is better than the approximation set $\mathbf{A}$.

The next step in the methodology consists of defining the parameters' starting ranges for the statistical exploratory analysis. To accomplish this, the best parameter values for each of the ten arbitrary experiments of one hundred replicates each (Czarn, MacNish, Vijayan, Turlach, & Gupta, 2004) are found, using the dot diagram's uncensored parameter values as starting ranges. The combination of the parameters resulting in the best performance is found in each experiment. When these ten combinations are collated, they demonstrate the lowest and highest parameter values associated with the best performance.

After finding the parameters' starting ranges, an initial complete randomized design experiment of 100 replicates (Czarn, MacNish, Vijayan, Turlach, & Gupta, 2004) must be generated for the black-box algorithms. For these two factor factorial experiments, instead of separately computing the sum of squares for the main effects and for the total sum of squares, a statistical software package is usually employed to conduct the ANOVA on this kind of experiment (Montgomery, 2001). The result of this procedure is generally an ANOVA table where the partitioned sum of squares for each factor are shown, e.g., for the genetic algorithm: crossover, mutation and interaction of both. As outlined by Czrarn *et al.* (2004), the values of the partitioned sum of squares factors are necessary to evaluate the degree of the polynomials used in the linear regression for the general response surface of the experiment. With this general response surface, optimal parameter values can be estimated. Also, the resulting ANOVA table shows the level of significance of the parameters. This level should be inspected to see if the interaction parameter is highly statistically significant, i.e., $\mathbf{Pr}$ (F) ≤ 0.01, so no further increase in the sample size would be necessary.

Given the partitioned sum of squares, linear regression should be used to estimate the general response surface for each black-box experiment. Finally, the last step in the methodology would be to obtain the best parameter value estimates, minimizing the response surface found.

Performance Comparisons between Black-Box Algorithms

Additionally, we are certainly interested in the technique that provides the best approximation for the given problem. For that, an additional complete, randomized design is set up, with i observations for each block-replicate, where i is the number of algorithms under comparison.

To effectively compare the optimization algorithms' performance using the binary quality indicator, the following steps should be taken:

1. Create a complete, randomized design for the black-box algorithms under study.
2. Calculate binary quality indicators statistics, i.e., the first and the second order moments of I_ε ($\mathbf{Z}^*$,$\mathbf{A}$).
3. The best algorithm is the one that has the highest statistical moments of I_ε ($\mathbf{Z}^*$,$\mathbf{A}$), i.e., the highest mean value $\overline{I_\varepsilon\left(\mathbf{Z}^*,\mathbf{A}\right)}$.

Finally, it is worth discussing one last question regarding the experiment to effectively compare the algorithms' performance. Clearly, the most we can say about the statistical experiment is that the best obtained algorithm is the best performer only for the filter specification set under study. For example, if we run a statistical experiment for an arbitrary band-stop filter and the genetic algorithm is hypothetically the best performer, we cannot, a priori, generalize this result to the comparison of the best algorithm for a high-pass filter. This is due to the fact that the objective function changes from one specification set to the other.

Regarding the question of the best algorithm that can be found for an application domain, a number of interesting works have already been published. More specifically, the no-free-lunch theorem - NFL, establishes that for any pair of algorithms a_1 and a_2, the following relation is true (Wolpert & Macready, 1997):

$$\sum_f P\left(d_m^y \mid f, m, a_1\right) = \sum_f P\left(d_m^y \mid f, m, a_2\right) \tag{29}$$

where d_m^y denotes all samples of the objective function f and the operator P denotes the conditional probability of obtaining a particular sample d_m under the imposed conditions.

In other words, equation (29) states that the average performance of any pair of algorithms for all possible optimization problems is identical. This means that if algorithm a_1 is better than algorithm a_2 for a problem set, then the inverse must be true for all possible remaining optimization problems (Wolpert & Macready, 1997).

The NFL theorem assumes a uniform probability distribution over objective functions, and closure under permutation. It appears that naturally occurring classes of problems are unlikely to be closed under permutation. Igel & Toussaint (2005) show that the fraction of non-empty subsets that are closed under permutation rapidly approaches zero as the cardinality of the search space increases, and that constraints on the steepness and the number of local minima lead to subsets that are not closed under permutation (MacNish, 2007).

These results can be a motivation to investigate the fact that, for practical problems, i.e., nonlinear phase FIR filter design problem, it is expected that some algorithms are better, and that a generalization of which is the best algorithm for this problem domain can be made. This important question is not addressed in this chapter and further investigation is necessary.

RESULTS

FIR Filter Design Problem Specification

As a specific problem, we have defined a band-stop FIR filter design with reduced group delay on the pass bands with the following specifications:

$$W_\eta(\omega) = 1 \qquad \begin{cases} 0 \le \omega \le 0.25 \\ 0.3 \le \omega \le 0.65 \\ 0.7 \le \omega \le \pi \end{cases}$$

$$W_\eta(\omega) = 0 \qquad \begin{cases} 0.25 < \omega < 0.3 \\ 0.65 < \omega < 0.7 \end{cases}$$

$$W_\tau(\omega) = 1 \qquad \begin{cases} 0 \le \omega \le 0.25 \\ 0.7 \le \omega \le \pi \end{cases}$$

$$W_\tau(\omega) = 0 \qquad \begin{cases} 0.25 < \omega < 0.7 \end{cases}$$

$$\eta_d(\omega) = \begin{cases} 0\mathrm{dB} & 0 \le \omega \le 0.25 \, and \, 0.7 \le \omega \le \pi \\ -30\mathrm{dB} & 0.3 \le \omega \le 0.65 \end{cases}$$

$$\tau_d(\omega) = \begin{cases} 0 \mathrm{samples} & 0 \le \omega \le 0.25 \, and \, 0.7 \le \omega \le \pi \end{cases}$$

$$N = 8 \qquad p = 2 \qquad q = 2 \qquad n = 10 \tag{30}$$

where for the specification set in equation (30), N is the filter order, p is the L_p norm value for the filter magnitude approximation, q is the L_q norm for the filter group delay approximation and n is the weight vector $\mathbf{W}$ dimension for the weighting scalarization method (number of points of the Pareto front approximation). Note that for the desired group delay $\tau_d(\omega)$, a value of zero is used. Even though this requirement is not physically implementable for a filter with finite number of coefficients, this requirement forces the optimization to find the minimum group delay value over the desired frequency bands.

Figure 2 shows the graph of the magnitude of the frequency response and the group delay for the specification set in equation (30).

The number of objective function evaluations in the statistical exploratory analysis was restricted to *200000* evaluations for each minimization (realization) of the algorithm under study. This restriction was imposed to speed up the generation of the results given the high computational complexity and runtime requirement of the statistical experiments. In regard to the single-objective algorithms in conjunction with the weighting scalarization method, the number of function evaluations was subdivided, equally, for each weight vector $\mathbf{w} \in \mathbf{W}$ of the weight set; *(200000 evaluations)/(10 points of the Pareto front approximation)=20000* function evaluations. This restriction was imposed for a fair comparison of the Pareto sampling multi-objective algorithms, NSGA-II and MOSA, each restricted to *200000* function evaluations.

Additionally, for each statistical experiment, the reference vector $\mathbf{Z}^*$ for the calculation of the binary ε-indicator $I_\varepsilon(\mathbf{Z}^*,\mathbf{A})$ of each observation is rigorously the same.

Figure 2. Frequency response specification of the reject-band filter. (a) Magnitude Specification. (b) Group Delay Specification

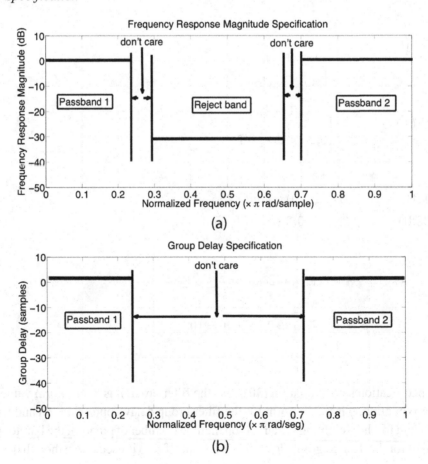

Results for Optimal Parameter Estimates

Results for the Genetic Algorithm in Conjunction with the Weighting Scalarization Method

Following the steps presented in the statistical exploratory analysis of the previous section, for optimal parameter estimation of the crossover p_{cr} and mutation p_{mu} rate of the genetic algorithm, first, we created a complete, randomized block design with 10 replicates and parameter values $0 \leq p_{mu} \leq 1$ and $0 \leq p_{cr} \leq 1$ in equally spaced intervals of length *0.1*. An instance of censoring was identified in this experiment when the difference between the binary ε-indicator of the best individual $I_{\varepsilon}(\mathbf{Z^*},\mathbf{A})$ and the binary ε-indicator of the worst individual $I_{\varepsilon}(\mathbf{Z^*},\mathbf{A_w})$ in the observation was less than or equal to 0.94. The dot diagram for this threshold can be seen in Figure 3.

Regarding the chosen threshold value in this experiment, it was adjusted to match the dot diagram to a desired configuration. If, for example, the dot diagram for a chosen threshold value resulted in all dots, then this meant that the threshold was too high, i.e., the threshold was never reached. This way, the threshold was decreased, i.e., 0.9 to 0.8, which resulted in some areas of the diagram having no points.

Figure 3. Process of choosing a threshold on the dot diagram. (a) Threshold 1. (b) Threshold 0.99. (c) Threshold 0.94

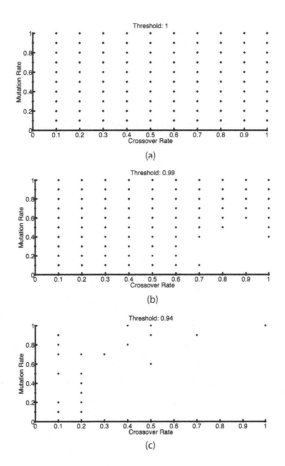

If there was a threshold value that we could test, then this would become the chosen threshold value for the dot diagram generation. This process can be graphically visualized in Figure 3, for the threshold values 1, 0.99 and 0.94, where for each threshold value reduction, more test levels are generated.

To define the parameters' starting ranges, we generated *10* experiments of *100* replicates each using the no-censure parameter values of the dot diagram in Figure 3 as test levels in the experiments. The combination resulting in the best performance, i.e., highest $I_e(\mathbf{Z^*,A})$ value shows the lower and higher values of the parameters associated with the best performance. The resulting starting range for Crossover was from 0.7 to 1, and for Mutation rate was for 0.1 to 0.5.

After obtaining the final parameters' intervals, a complete, randomized block design of *100* replicates was generated with the parameters' values given above. The ANOVA table for this experiment is given in Table 1.

In Table 1, the column *df* represents the degree of freedom associated with each parameter, *SS* represents the sum of squares and *MS* represents the mean squares for each parameter.

Additionally, as seen on Table 1, the interaction parameter is highly significant $\mathbf{Pr}\,(F)=0.0000000$, so it was not necessary to increase the sample size (number of replicates in the experiment).

Still, in regard to the ANOVA results, Table 1 shows the partitioned sum of squares for each factor (mutation and crossover). These values are necessary to evaluate the degree of the polynomials used in the linear regression for the generation of the experiment response surface. The statistically significant values were selected for the equation of the fitted response surface of the experiment:

$$S_{ga} = -0.5128 + 1.7206 x_{cr} + 0.8005 x_{cr}^3 + 0.0904 x_{mu}^2 - 0.0915 x_{mu}^3$$
$$-2.0377 x_{cr}^2 - 0.0185 x_{mu} - 0.0072 x_{cr}^2 x_{mu} - 0.0069 x_{cr}^3 x_{mu}^3 \tag{31}$$

The *3*-dimensional response surface in equation (31) can be seen in Figure 4.

Finally, to obtain the optimal parameter value estimates, the maximum point of this surface must be found. This problem is posed as a constrained optimization problem by:

Table 1. ANOVA Table with the partitioned sum of squares for the genetic algorithm experiment

Parameter	df	SS	MS	F	Pr(F)
Crossover	3	0.00081081	0.0002702687	15.94334	0.0000000
Power of 1	1	0.00017910	0.0001790981	10.56512	0.0011735
Power of 3	1	0.00053700	0.0005370030	31.67817	0.0000000
Mutation	4	0.00096178	0.0002404441	14.18396	0.0000000
Power of 2	1	0.00024277	0.0002427656	14.32091	0.0001591
Power of 3	1	0.00046401	0.0004640082	27.37216	0.0000002
Interaction	12	0.00145158	0.0001209646	7.13579	0.0000000
Power2:Power1	1	0.00021802	0.0002180192	12.86110	0.0003443
Power3:Power3	1	0.00017644	0.0001764378	10.40819	0.0012769

$$\max_x S_{ga}\left(x_{mu}, x_{cr}\right)$$
$$\text{subject to}$$
$$0.7 \leq x_{cr} \leq 1$$
$$0.1 \leq x_{mu} \leq 0.5 \tag{32}$$

Even though the optimization problem in equation (32) is nonlinear, particularly for polynomial functions, i.e., the response surface function in equation (31), algorithms for global optimization of polynomial functions are developed through a novel technique that involves the use of the sum of squares and semi-definite programming (Parrilo & Sturmfels, 2003). With this technique, global values for this optimization problem were obtained with a MATLAB library in (Seiler & Parrilo, 2004):

$$x_{cr}^{*} = 0.7701 \qquad x_{mu}^{*} = 0.4639 \tag{33}$$

The response surface value for the optimal parameters in equation (33) is:

$$S_{ga}\left(x_{mu}^{*}, x_{cr}^{*}\right) = 0.9944 \tag{34}$$

Results for the Particle Swarm Optimization Algorithm in Conjunction with the Weighting Scalarization Method

Following the steps of the methodology of the previous section, with the aim of obtaining optimal parameter values for the particle swarm optimization algorithm, the first step consists of generating a complete, randomized block design of *10* replicates and parameter values $0 \leq \alpha < 1$ and $0 < \phi < 4$. The selected threshold value for the experiment's dot diagram was 0.9. Figure 5 illustrates the resulting dot diagram.

Figure 4. Genetic algorithm experiment response surface

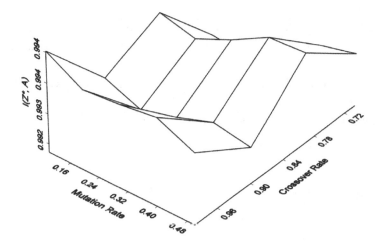

Figure 5. Particle swarm optimization dot diagram with threshold of 0.9

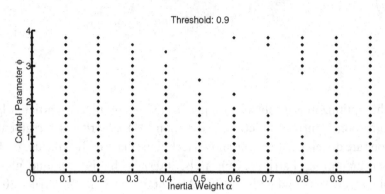

Table 2. ANOVA Table with the partitioned sum of squares for the particle swarm optimization experiment

Parameter	df	SS	MS	F	Pr(F)
Inertia α	2	3.956673	1.978336	15.94334	0.000000
Power of 1	1	1.080438	1.080438	1232.871	0.000000
Power of 2	1	2.876234	2.876234	3282.025	0.000000
Control φ	8	4.045458	0.505682	577.026	0.000000
Power of 1	1	0.315420	0.315420	359.921	0.000000
Power of 2	1	0.364443	0.364443	415.861	0.000000
Interaction	16	6.585366	0.411585	469.653	0.000000
Power1:Power1	1	0.058580	0.058580	66.844	4.440892×10−16
Power2:Power1	1	0.505633	0.505633	576.969	0.000000
Power1:Power2	1	0.105872	0.105872	120.809	0.000000
Power2:Power2	1	0.434902	0.434902	496.260	0.000000

The resulting interval for Parameter Control was between 2 to 3.6, and the interval for Weight Inertia was between 0.6 and 0.8.

After obtaining the final parameter values, a complete, randomized block design of *100* replicates was generated with the parameter values above. The ANOVA table for this experiment is illustrated in Table 2.

Again, as can be seen in Table 2, the interaction parameter is highly significant. **Pr** $(F) = 0.0000000$, so no increase in the sample size was necessary.

The statistically significant values were selected for the equation of the fitted response surface of the experiment:

$$S_{pso} = 6.3771 - 15.5283x_\alpha + 11.0608x_\alpha^2 - 5.1732x_\phi + 0.8695x_\phi^2 \\ + 15.1011x_\alpha x_\phi - 10.9736x_\alpha^2 x_\phi - 2.5361x_\alpha x_\phi^2 + 1.8406x_\alpha^2 x_\phi^2 \tag{35}$$

Figure 6. Particle swarm optimization experiment response surface

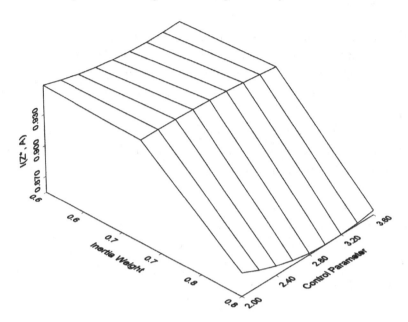

The *3*-dimensional response surface in equation (35) can be seen in Figure 6.

Finally, to obtain the optimal parameter value estimates, the maximum point of this surface must be found. This problem is posed as a constrained optimization problem by:

$$\max_x S_{\text{pso}}\left(x_\phi, x_\alpha\right)$$
$$\text{subject to}$$
$$2 \leq x_\phi \leq 3.6$$
$$0.6 \leq x_\alpha \leq 0.8$$

(36)

Global values for this optimization problem were obtained with the MATLAB library in (Seiler & Parrilo, 2004):

$$x_\phi^* = 2.5448 \qquad x_\alpha^* = 0.6550$$

(37)

The response surface value for the optimal parameters in equation (37) is:

$$S_{\text{pso}}\left(x_\phi^*, x_\alpha^*\right) = 0.9642$$

(38)

Results for the NSGA-II

Again, following the steps of the methodology of the previous section, for optimal parameter estimation of the crossover p_{cr} and mutation p_{mu} rate of the NSGA-II, the first step consists of generating a complete, randomized block design of 10 replicates and parameter values $0 \leq p_{mu} \leq 1$ and $0 \leq p_{cr} \leq 1$. The selected threshold value for the experiment's dot diagram was 2.5×10^{-2}. Figure 7 illustrates the resulting dot diagram.

For the next step of finalizing the initial starting ranges, we generated 10 experiments of 100 replicates each using the uncensured values of the dot diagram in Figure 7 as the test levels in the experiment. The combination resulting in the best performance, i.e., highest $I_\varepsilon (\mathbf{Z^*}, \mathbf{A})$ value shows the lower and higher values of the parameters associated with the best performance. The resulting starting range for crossover was from 0 to 1, and for mutation rate, it was from 0.6 to 0.9.

After obtaining the final parameter values, a complete, randomized block design of 100 replicates was generated with the parameter values above. The ANOVA table for this experiment is given in Table 3.

Again, as can be seen in Table 3, the interaction parameter is highly significant. $\mathbf{Pr}\,(F) = 0.0000000$, so no increase in the sample size was necessary.

The statistically significant values were selected for the equation of the fitted response surface of the experiment:

$$
\begin{aligned}
S_{nsga-ii}\left(\mathrm{x}_{cr},\mathrm{x}_{mu}\right) = {} & -34.3 + 128.2\mathrm{x}_{cr} - 1290.6\mathrm{x}_{cr}^{2} + 12154.8\mathrm{x}_{cr}^{3} - 59121.7\mathrm{x}_{cr}^{4} \\
& + 162714\mathrm{x}_{cr}^{5} - 267623.8\mathrm{x}_{cr}^{6} + 259609.4\mathrm{x}_{cr}^{7} - 137009.8\mathrm{x}_{cr}^{8} + 30457.6\mathrm{x}_{cr}^{9} \\
& + 141.9\mathrm{x}_{mu} - 189.5\mathrm{x}_{mu}^{2} + 83\mathrm{x}_{mu} - 344.7\mathrm{x}_{cr}\,\mathrm{x}_{mu} + 1378.1\mathrm{x}_{cr}^{2}\mathrm{x}_{mu}^{3} - 13455.2\mathrm{x}_{cr}^{3}\mathrm{x}_{mu} \\
& + 67278.7\mathrm{x}_{cr}^{4}\,\mathrm{x}_{mu} - 185461.7\mathrm{x}_{cr}^{5}\mathrm{x}_{mu} + 308553.7\mathrm{x}_{cr}^{6}\mathrm{x}_{mu} - 302604.2\mathrm{x}_{cr}^{7}\,\mathrm{x}_{mu} \\
& 160566.7\mathrm{x}_{cr}^{8}\mathrm{x}_{mu} - 35987\mathrm{x}_{cr}^{9}\mathrm{x}_{mu} + 368.2\mathrm{x}_{cr}\mathrm{x}_{mu}^{2} - 4172.9\mathrm{x}_{cr}^{5}\,\mathrm{x}_{mu}^{2} + 3905.8\mathrm{x}_{cr}^{6}\mathrm{x}_{mu}^{2} \\
& - 151.2\mathrm{x}_{cr}\mathrm{x}_{mu}^{3} - 416.6\mathrm{x}_{cr}^{4}\mathrm{x}_{mu}^{3} + 2328.8\mathrm{x}_{cr}^{5}\mathrm{x}_{mu}^{3} - 3798.6\mathrm{x}_{cr}^{7}\mathrm{x}_{mu}^{3} + 2376.1\mathrm{x}_{cr}^{8}\mathrm{x}_{mu}^{3} \\
& - 382.3\mathrm{x}_{cr}^{9}\mathrm{x}_{mu}^{3}
\end{aligned}
\tag{39}
$$

The 3-dimensional response surface in equation (39) can be seen in Figure 8.

Figure 7. NSGA-II dot diagram with threshold of 2.5×10^{-2}

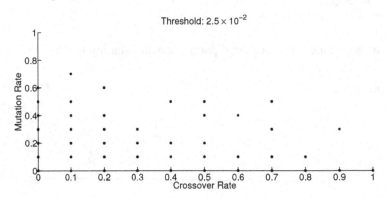

Finally, to obtain the optimal parameter value estimates, the maximum point of this surface must be found. This problem is posed as a constrained optimization problem by:

Table 3. ANOVA Table with the partitioned sum of squares for the NSGA-II experiment

Parameter	df	SS	MS	F	Pr(F)
Crossover	10	15.47	1.54	43.3	0.0000000
Power of 1	1	7.1719	7.1719	200.9774	0.0000000
Power of 2	1	1.3922	1.39223	39.0140	0.0000000
Power of 3	1	1.5187	1.51874	42.5594	0.0000000
Power of 4	1	0.9867	0.98667	27.6492	0.0000002
Power of 5	1	0.6360	0.63602	17.8231	0.0000247
Power of 6	1	0.5348	0.53476	14.9854	0.0001099
Power of 7	1	0.3304	0.33040	9.2588	0.0023577
Power of 8	1	1.2476	1.24763	34.9621	0.0000000
Power of 9	1	0.6052	0.60515	16.9580	0.0000389
Mutation	3	26.3204	8.77346	245.8563	0.0000000
Power of 2	1	2.0494	2.04936	57.4288	0.0000000
Power of 3	1	24.2650	24.26502	679.9726	0.0000000
Interaction	30	37.5786	1.25262	35.1019	0.0000000
Power1:Power1	1	2.1433	2.14334	60.0623	0.0000000
Power2:Power1	1	0.8025	0.80249	22.4879	0.0000022
Power3:Power1	1	0.2518	0.25185	7.0575	0.0079222
Power4:Power1	1	2.0960	2.09597	58.7349	0.0000000
Power5:Power1	1	0.8949	0.89487	25.0766	0.0000006
Power6:Power1	1	2.9068	2.90677	81.4557	0.0000000
Power7:Power1	1	0.7086	0.70860	19.8569	0.0000086
Power8:Power1	1	1.7869	1.78694	50.0749	0.0000000
Power9:Power1	1	1.7547	1.75475	49.1729	0.0000000
Power1:Power2	1	2.8649	2.86490	80.2823	0.0000000
Power5:Power2	1	1.4258	1.42580	39.9547	0.0000000
Power6:Power2	1	0.2857	0.28571	8.0065	0.0046824
Power1:Power3	1	1.6519	1.65191	46.2910	0.0000000
Power3:Power3	1	2.1267	2.12675	59.5974	0.0000000
Power4:Power3	1	1.5590	1.55904	43.6887	0.0000000
Power5:Power3	1	1.6700	1.67004	46.7992	0.0000000
Power7:Power3	1	0.5973	0.59729	16.7377	0.0000437
Power8:Power3	1	1.0543	1.05434	29.5455	0.0000001
Power9:Power3	1	5.7858	5.78583	162.1349	0.0000000

Figure 8. NSGA-II experiment response surface

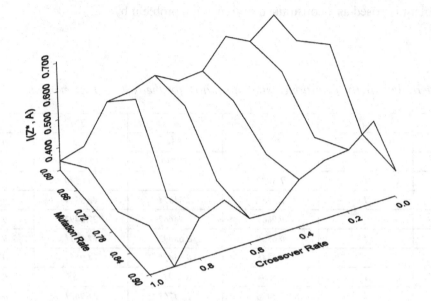

$$\max_x S_{\text{nsga-ii}}\left(x_{cr}, x_{mu}\right)$$
$$\text{subject to}$$
$$0 \leq x_{cr} \leq 1$$
$$0.6 \leq x_{mu} \leq 0.9$$

(40)

Global values for this optimization problem were obtained with the MATLAB library in (Seiler & Parrilo, 2004):

$$x_{cr}^* = 0.0377 \qquad x_{mu}^* = 0.6490$$

(41)

The response surface value for the optimal parameters in equation (41) is:

$$S_{\text{nsga-ii}}\left(x_{cr}^*, x_{mu}^*\right) = 0.9283$$

(42)

Results for the Comparison of Performance between Algorithms

Following the statistical methodology of the previous section, for the effective comparison between the different algorithms applied to the design of a reject-band filter with the specification set of equation (30), we created a complete, randomized block design of 100 replicates with the four single-objective optimization algorithms (Quasi-Newton, genetic algorithm, simulated annealing, particle swarm optimization) in conjunction with the weighting scalarization method, and also the two multi-objective algorithms with Pareto sampling methods (NSGA-II and MOSA).

Table 4. ANOVA Table for the algorithm performance comparison

Parameter	df	SS	MS	F	Pr(F)
Optimization Algorithm	5	32.8273	6.56545	123.06	0

Table 5. $I_\varepsilon(\mathbf{Z^*}, \mathbf{A})$ statistics for algorithm performance comparison

Algorithm	Max	Min	Mean	Variance
NSGA-II	0.9998	0.0170	0.7593	0.0625
Simulated Annealing	0.9978	0.0030	0.9757	0.0160
Quasi-Newton	0.9973	0.0011	0.6663	0.1485
Genetic Algorithm	0.9968	0.9466	0.9924	4.0226×10^{-4}
Particle Swarm Optimization	0.9919	0.8935	0.9563	2.5054×10^{-4}
MOSA	0.9621	0.0147	0.3973	0.0928

The genetic algorithm, particle swarm optimization and NSGA-II were adjusted with the optimal parameter values from the three previous statistical experiments of this section. The number of objective function evaluations in this experiment was restricted to 200000 evaluations for each algorithm under study. Again, for the single-objective algorithms in conjunction with the weighting scalarization method, the number of function evaluations for each single-objective problem was equally divided for each weight vector $\mathbf{w} \in \mathbf{W}$ of the weight set, 20000 function evaluations. The ANOVA table of this experiment can be seen in Table 4.

As seen in Table 4, the variation of the parameter *Optimization Algorithm* has a high statistical significance in the experiment response (binary ε-indicator value). Table 5 shows the minimum, maximum and the first and second order moments of the binary ϵ-indicator for each optimization algorithm.

As seen in Table 5, the NSGA-II was the algorithm that obtained the best approximation of the Pareto front, with a $I_\varepsilon(\mathbf{Z^*}, \mathbf{A})$ value of *0.998*. However, on average, the best performer in the statistical experiments was the genetic algorithm in conjunction with the weighting scalarization method, with a $I_\varepsilon(\mathbf{Z^*}, \mathbf{A})$ value of *0.9924*. The statistics in Table 5 are graphically illustrated in Figure 9, which shows the box plot of the statistical experiment.

Comments on the Pareto Front's Approximations Obtained and on the Frequency Response of the Optimal Filters

To illustrate the approximation of the Pareto front obtained by each algorithm, Figure 10 shows the approximation set obtained by each single-objective optimization algorithm in conjunction with the weighting scalarization method on a typical realization of the comparisons between the optimization algorithms. Again, the number of objective function evaluations was restricted to 200000 evaluations for each algorithm under study.

Figure 10 also shows the binary ϵ-indicator for each approximation of the Pareto front. Additionally, we can see that in this typical realization, the particle swarm optimization obtained the filter with the

Figure 9. Box plot of the statistical experiment of comparison of performance

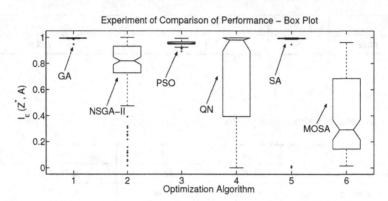

Figure 10. Pareto front comparison for the FIR reject-band filter

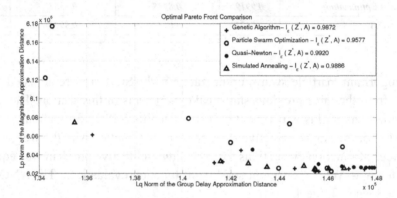

best group delay approximation distance $\cong 1.35 \times 10^5$ and the filter with the best magnitude approximation distance $\cong 6.02 \times 10^6$. Even though the best extreme values were obtained with the particle swarm optimization, some points of the Pareto front have very high values for the magnitude and group delay approximation distance. For this reason, considering the Pareto front as a whole, the algorithm obtained the worst binary ε-indicator value in this realization. The Quasi-Newton algorithm obtained the best binary ε-indicator value, and the Pareto front's shape appears to be of a quadratic convex set.

With these filters, each point of the Pareto front approximation we can clearly see the trade-off between the simultaneous approximation of the magnitude and group delay. If the magnitude approximation distance is decreased, the group delay approximation distance is consequently increased and vice-versa.

CONCLUSION

Goals Achieved in this Work

In conclusion, this chapter has applied a statistical methodology to evaluate the performance of different optimization algorithms applied to a nonlinear digital filter design problem. Based on the single-objective statistical exploratory analysis, multi-objective extensions by means of binary quality indicators were developed, allowing the estimation of the best parameter values for the adaptive algorithms and, additionally, making an effective performance comparison among the different optimization approaches.

With the developed statistical methodologies, we were able to obtain statistically sound Pareto optimal solution sets of good quality applied to a digital filter design problem.

Comments on the Performance of the Algorithms

The NSGA-II obtained the best approximation of the Pareto front in the statistical comparison of the performance of different optimization algorithms, using the binary ϵ-indicator as a measure of quality of the Pareto front approximation.

Even though the multi-objective NSGA-II obtained the best approximation of the Pareto front in the experiment, considering the average performance of the optimization algorithms, the best performer in the experiment was surprisingly the genetic algorithm in conjunction with the weighting scalarization method. This is despite the bad reputation of the weighting scalarization method in the multi-objective community.

Future Work

Regarding the comparison of the algorithms' performances, it is worth noting that the results obtained are, in principle, only valid for the specific reject-band specification set under test. In view of the results of the NFL theorem and its extensions in the literature, the results of this work are motivating for a possible generalization to other filter specification sets, and a possible conclusion regarding which optimization approach is the best for this problem domain.

REFERENCES

Ahmad, S. U., & Antoniou, A. (2007). A multiobjective genetic algorithm for asymmetric FIR filters. In *Proceedings of the IEEE International Symposium on Signal Processing and Information Technology* (pp. 525-530). Piscataway, NJ: IEEE Press.

Antoniou, A., & Lu, W. S. (2007). *Practical optimization, algorithms and engineering applications.* Berlin, Germany: Springer Science+Business Media, LLC.

Bonnans, J. F., Gilbert, J. C., Lemaréchal, C., & Sagastizábal, C. A. (2006). *Numerical optimization – theoretical and practical aspects.* Berlin, Germany: Springer-Verlag.

Calvagno, G., Cortelazzo, G. M., & Mian, G. A. (1995). A technique for multiple criterion approximation of fir filters in magnitude and group delay. *IEEE Transactions on Signal Processing, 43*(2), 393–400. doi:10.1109/78.348122

Chankong, V., & Haimes, Y. Y. (1983). *Multiobjective decision making theory and methodology.* Amsterdam: Elsevier Science.

Cortelazzo, G., & Lightner, M. (1984). Simultaneous design in both magnitude and group-delay of IIR and FIR filters based on multiple criterion optimization. *IEEE Transactions on Acoustics, Speech, and Signal Processing, 32*(5), 949–967. doi:10.1109/TASSP.1984.1164426

Czarn, A., MacNish, C., Vijayan, K., Turlach, B., & Gupta, R. (2004). Statistical exploratory analysis of genetic algorithms. *IEEE Transactions on Evolutionary Computation, 8*(4), 405–421. doi:10.1109/TEVC.2004.831262

Deczky, A. (1972). Synthesis of recursive digital filters using the minimum p-error criterion. *IEEE Transactions on Audio and Electroacoustics, 20*(4), 257–263. doi:10.1109/TAU.1972.1162392

Deczky, A. (1974). Equiripple and minimax (Chebyshev) approximations for recursive digital filters. *IEEE Transactions on Acoustics, Speech, and Signal Processing, 22*(2), 98–111. doi:10.1109/TASSP.1974.1162556

Dennis, J. E., & Schnabel, R. B. (1983). *Numerical methods for unconstrained optimization and nonlinear equations*. Upper Saddle River, NJ: Prentice-Hall.

Diniz, P. S. R., da Silva, E. A. B., & Lima Netto, S. (2004). *Processamento digital de sinais - projeto e análise de sistemas*. Porto Alegre, Brazil: Bookman.

Ehrgott, M., & Gandibleaux, X. (Eds.). (2002). *Multiple criteria optimization: State of the art*. Amsterdam: Kluwer Academic Publishers.

Engelbrecht, A. (2007). *Computational intelligence: An introduction*. New York: John Wiley & Sons.

Fletcher, R. (1980). *Practical methods of optimization: Volume 1 – unconstrained optimization*. New York: John Wiley & Sons.

Haftka, R. T., & Gürdal, Z. (1992). *Elements of structural optimization*. Amsterdam: Kluwer Academic Publishers.

Igel, C., & Toussaint, M. (2005). A no-free-lunch theorem for non-uniform distributions of target functions. *Journal of Mathematical Modelling and Algorithms, 3*(4), 313–322. doi:10.1007/s10852-005-2586-y

Ingber, L. (1989). Very fast simulated re-annealing. *Mathematical and Computer Modelling, 12*(8), 967–973. doi:10.1016/0895-7177(89)90202-1

Kennedy, J., Eberhart, R. C., & Shi, Y. (2001). *Swarm intelligence*. San Francisco: Morgan Kaufmann Publishers.

Li, D. (1996). Convexification of a noninferior frontier. *Journal of Optimization Theory and Applications, 88*(1), 177–196. doi:10.1007/BF02192028

MacNish, C. (2007). Towards unbiased benchmarking of evolutionary and hybrid algorithms for real-valued optimisation. *Connection Science, 19*(4), 361–385. doi:10.1080/09540090701725581

Madisetti, V. K., & Williams, D. (1999). *Digital signal processing handbook*. Boca Raton, FL: CRC Press.

Melanie, M. (1999). *An introduction to genetic algorithms*. Cambridge, MA: The MIT Press.

Miettinen, K. (1999). *Nonlinear multiobjective optimization*. Amsterdam: Kluwer Academic Publishers.

Montgomery, D. (2001). *Design and analysis of experiments*. New York: John Wiley & Sons.

Nocedal, J., & Wright, S. (2006). *Numerical optimization*. Berlin, Germany: Springer-Verlag.

Oppenheim, A., & Schafer, R. (1999). *Discrete-time signal processing*. Upper Saddle River, NJ: Prentice-Hall.

Parrilo, P. A., & Sturmfels, B. (2003). Minimizing polynomial functions. In S. Basu & L. Gonzalez-Vega (Eds.), *Algorithmic and quantitative real algebraic geometry* (pp. 83-99). AMS.

Seiler, P., & Parrilo, P. A. (2004). *SOSTOOLS: Sum of squares optimization toolbox for MATLAB* (Tech. Rep.). Pasadena, CA: CALTECH. Retrieved from http://www.cds.caltech.edu/sostools

Teixeira, F., & Romariz, A. R. S. (2007). Optimum finite impulse response digital filter design using computational intelligence based optimization algorithms. In *Proceedings of the Seventh International Conference on Intelligent Systems Design and Applications* (pp. 635-640). Washington, DC: IEEE Computer Society.

Teixeira, F., & Romariz, A. R. S. (2008). Digital filter arbitrary magnitude and phase approximations: Statistical analysis applied to a stochastic-based optimization approach. In *Proceedings of the IEEE World Congress on Computational Intelligence* (pp. 4088-4095). Piscataway, NJ: IEEE Press.

Wolpert, D. H., & Macready, W. G. (1997). No free lunch theorems for optimization. *IEEE Transactions on Evolutionary Computation, 1*(1), 67–82. doi:10.1109/4235.585893

Zitzler, E., Thiele, L., Laumanns, M., Fonseca, C. M., & da Fonseca, V. G. (2003). Performance assessment of multiobjective optimizers: an analysis and review. *IEEE Transactions on Evolutionary Computation, 7*(2), 117–132. doi:10.1109/TEVC.2003.810758

Section 3
Adaptive Collective Systems

Chapter 10
Diffusion and Emergence in Social Networks

Akira Namatame
National Defense Academy, Japan

ABSTRACT

Diffusion is the process by which new products and practices are invented and successfully introduced into society. Numerous studies on the diffusion of individual innovations have been conducted, many exhibiting common features such as the famous S-shaped diffusion curve. One basic question posed by innovation diffusion is why there is often a long lag time between an innovation's first appearance and the time when a substantial number of people have adopted it. An extensive amount of theoretical and empirical literature has been devoted to this phenomenon and the mechanisms behind it. New ideas, products, and innovations often take time to diffuse, a fact that is often attributed to the heterogeneity of human populations. In this chapter, we provide an overview of the research examining how the structure of social networks impacts the diffusion process. The diffusion process enhances innovations via feedback of information about the innovation's utility—which can be used to make future improvements—to many different users. This aspect of the diffusion process is similar to the micro-macro loop, which is an essential part of emergence. The aim of this research is to understand how the structure of social networks determines the dynamics of various types of emergent properties occurring within those networks. For emergence at the social level, patterns of social interactions are critical.

INTRODUCTION

For decades, social scientists, economists and physicists have been interested in the fundamental and widespread question of how infectious diseases, new technological practices, or the latest trends spread through society. When a new technology appears, society's members have the chance to become aware

DOI: 10.4018/978-1-60566-798-0.ch010

of the innovations of the new technology and incorporate those innovations into their lives. The main study on diffusion modeling is based on the Bass model (Bass, 1969). The Bass diffusion model describes the process by which new products are adopted as an interaction between users and potential users. When an innovation is a product to be consumed by individuals, a single consumer can decide whether or not to adopt it.

More specifically, the Bass model formalizes the aggregate level of penetration of a new product, emphasizing two processes: external influence via advertising and mass media as well as internal influence via word-of-mouth. The decision of a consumer is described as the probability of the consumer adopting the new product at a specific time, and it is assumed to depend on both external and internal influences. The Bass model displays a cumulative S curve of adopters: when the number of users of a new product is plotted against time, the resulting curve shows an S-shaped distribution—adoption proceeds slowly at first, accelerates as it spreads throughout the potential adopting population, and then slows down as the relevant population becomes saturated. The S-shape is a natural implication of the observation that adoption is usually an absorbing state. The fast growth of diffusion is generated by the interaction between early adopters and late adopters. The Bass model, however, does not specify the consumer's decision-making process or how consumers communicate with and influence one another at the micro level. The Bass model assumes the population of consumers to be homogeneous—such diffusion models are referred to as aggregate models.

Rosenberg (1972) observed two dominant characteristics of the diffusion process: the overall slowness of the process, on one hand, and the wide variations in the rates of acceptance of different inventions on the other. Empirical measurements and studies have since confirmed his view. Why is diffusion sometimes slow? Why is it faster in some regions than others? Why do rates of diffusion differ among different types of innovations? What factors govern the wide variation in diffusion rates? Hall (2003) provides a comparative historical perspective on diffusion that looks at the broad economic, social, and institutional determinants. In the modern world, markets occasionally accept innovations very slowly, despite technological advances. Chakravorti (2004) also provides many examples of the slow pace of fast change.

New ideas, products, and innovations often take time to diffuse, a fact that is often attributed to the heterogeneity of human populations. Global markets are now larger and more complex than ever before. As such, the amount of information available to consumers has considerably increased; as a result, consumers spend much more time thinking and hesitating before making a decision. Thus, consumers require more time to make personal decisions about matters such as whether to use a certain new product or participate in the latest technology.

Consumers may realize different aspects of the benefits and costs of a particular innovation, have different beliefs regarding benefits and costs, hear about the innovation at different times, or delay in acting on the information they receive. Young (2007) analyzes the effects of incorporating heterogeneity into three broad classes of models: contagion, social influence, and social learning. In addition, when a consumer has many neighbors, these represent many potential sources of information, and the consumer may have problems effectively handling such a large amount of information. Clarification of this relationship calls for analysis of the types of social interactions linking various individuals within a society.

Societies consist of individuals and the social systems that largely determine how individuals behave and interact. Individuals' actions are influenced by friends, acquaintances, and neighbors, and relationships between individuals form the basis of social networks. One of the cardinal rules of human behavior is: "birds of a feather flock together"—friends of friends become friends, and this property fosters the development of dense clusters of connections throughout social networks. However, little is known about the dynamic processes of networks and how these processes depend on the network's properties. Among the research concerning dynamic diffusion processes, the diffusion of diseases has received the most attention (Colizza, 2006).

An *emergent pattern* or an emergent property can appear when a number of simple entities operate in an environment, forming more complex patterns collectively. In this sense, many insights can be derived from the study of biology. Many biological systems appear to demonstrate emergent behavior, such as the sudden dispersion of a flock of animals in the presence of a predator (Reynolds, 1987). Emergent properties in biological systems appear to govern behaviors that are advantageous to the group as a whole. A natural interest in the behavior of animals and individuals, coupled with the possibility of utilizing these behaviors to design desirable systems, has prompted the study of self-organization in adaptive systems (Namatame, 2006). In adaptive systems with a large number of entities, global behavior emerging from localized interactions is a critical concept. Understanding and shaping emergence may be essential to the survival of social systems.

Emergent patterns are not the property of any single entity, nor can they easily be predicted or deduced from behavior in lower-level entities. Having a large number of interactions alone is not enough to guarantee emergent patterns—a system may need to reach a certain critical mass before it can self-generate emergent patterns. In some cases, a system must reach a combined threshold of diversity, organization, and connectivity before emergent properties appear. Unintended consequences and side effects are closely related to emergent properties. In other words, the global or macroscopic functionality of a system is the sum of the side effects of all emergent properties.

Social network structures are also related to emergent properties that cannot be trivially derived from the properties of their components. Simple rules concerning individual behavior can result in very complex phenomena at the societal level. Emergent macroscopic patterns throughout the social space can be divided into dense intra-connected clusters with sparse inter-connectivity between the clusters (Newman, 2003). In turn, emergent stylized facts or regularities observed at the societal level also influence individual behaviors and interactions. On the other side, individual behaviors create the social networks to which individuals belong. This bi-directional causal relationship is an essential component of the study of social complexity, including diffusion process from the viewpoint of emergence.

Understanding the relationship between the different levels at which macroscopic phenomena can be observed has been made possible by the tools and insights generated in complex network research. In particular, much is known about measuring the topological properties of social networks. Recently, a number of works have focused on the rules of network formation and the relationship between the network creation process and the structure of the resulting network (Barabasi, 2000).

We begin by discussing several examples of studies that illustrate how the structure of social networks impacts macroscopic diffusion patterns. The discussions are divided into three classes. First, we discuss progressive diffusion processes. Many diffusion processes are progressive in the sense that once a node switches from one state to another, it remains in the same state in all subsequent time steps. For this type of diffusion, we focus on the correlations between social interaction patterns and the observable transmission rate at the individual level.

The second class consists of non-progressive diffusion processes where, as time progresses, nodes can switch from one state to the other or vice versa, depending on the states of their neighbors. For non-progressive diffusion processes, we focus on decision making at the individual level. This class ties individuals to the analysis of the underlying games among a network of agents.

The third class consists of bi-directional diffusion process. In this class, individuals require proper interaction rules regulating information exchange among individuals so that all individuals in the social network eventually share the same information or internal states. Consensus problems have a long history in computer science and control theory (Olfati-Saber, 2007). Such problems form the foundation of the field of distributed systems since they have a tradition in systems and control theory on asynchronous agreement problems. In networks of agents, consensus means to reach an agreement regarding a certain quantity of interest depending on the state of all agents. A consensus algorithm is an interaction rule concerning the information exchange between an agent and all of its neighbors within the network.

STUDY OF DIFFUSION AND EMERGENCE

Diffusion is the process by which new products and practices are successfully introduced into society. The Bass model formalizes the aggregate level of penetration of a new product, emphasizing two processes: external influence via advertising and mass media and internal influence via word-of-mouth. The Bass model assumes all consumer populations to be homogeneous—such diffusion models are referred to as aggregate models. However, an individual decision rule can also be derived from the Bass model: the number of individuals who adopt a new product at a given time is a function of the number of individuals who have already adopted the product. If we calculate the expected number of adopters at a given time, the aggregate model displays a cumulative S curve of adopters (Katona, Zubcsek & Sarvary, 2007). The probability of an individual adopting a product, then, is a function of the number of that individual's neighbors who have already adopted the product. Naturally, if a person has more friends already using a certain product or service, he or she will be more likely to adopt the product or service. The familiar Bass model does not formalize this complex emergent aspect of the diffusion process.

The diffusion of innovations, new ideas or rumors can be modeled after the spread of infectious diseases (Meyers, 2005). However, because epidemiological models describe infection in terms of transmissibility and susceptibility, such models cannot adequately describe diffusion processes that usually involve individual information processing and decision-making. People are usually affected by word-of-mouth, which is referred to as a social influence. What influences people to participate in the diffusion process? How do consumers choose which items to buy? These questions are constant in the minds of many scientists in different fields. Various models of human behavior span the extremes from simple and easily influenced behavior to interdependent and complex behavior where nothing is easily controlled or predicted.

Spielman defines an innovation system as "a network of agents, along with the institutions, organizations, and policies that condition their behavior and performance with respect to generating, exchanging, and utilizing knowledge" (Spielman, 2005). An innovation system reflects one aspect of the value chain analysis by bringing the actors in the application of knowledge together within a value chain. This definition highlights the need for a holistic view of the nature and structure of interactions among agents linked to one another within networks. The adoption of an innovation by one agent in a network can have positive or negative impact on the behavior of other agents, which is often unintentional or unpredictable.

The growing literature on social interactions has examined how decision-making by an agent is influenced by the decisions of others in the context of a multitude of social phenomena. Examples include studies on the diffusion of new technologies (Arthur, 1989), herding behavior in stock markets (Banerjee, 1992) and the diffusion of conventions and social norms (Ellison, 1993; Morris, 2000). While the research on diffusion recognizes the importance of complex interactions among agents, it rarely explains or measures unintended impacts, both positive and negative, on agents within a network. More to the point, current methodologies provide insufficient explanation of the concept of network externalities. This suggests the need for alternative tools to provide a more enhanced understanding of these interactions.

In social systems that involve a large number of interacting agents, emergent global stylized facts that arise from local interactions are a critical concept. The emergence of the Internet, for instance, marked the appearance of totally new forms of social and economic exchange (Sole, 2003). As a technological innovation, the Internet provided a new stage for communication and information processing within societies, leading to the creation of previously non-existent system structures.

Everyday, billions of people worldwide make billions of decisions about many things. The aggregation of these unmanaged individual decisions often leads to unpredictable outcomes. People constantly interact with each other in different ways and for different purposes. Somehow, these individual interactions exhibit some degree of coherence at the aggregate level, and therefore aggregation may reveal structure and regularity. The individuals involved may have a very limited view of the whole system, but their activities are coordinated to a large extent and produce desirable outcomes at the aggregate level, often exhibiting the features of emergent properties—system's properties that individual components do not have. These emergent properties are the result of not only the behavior of individuals but the interactions between them (Ball, 2004).

Important processes that take place within social networks, such as the spreading of opinions and innovations, are influenced by the topological properties of those networks. In turn, the opinions and practices of individuals can have a clear impact on network topology, for instance, when conflicting opinions lead to the breakup of social interaction. From an application point of view, it is desirable to compose an inventory of the types of microscopic dynamics that have been investigated in social networks and their impact on emergent properties at the network level. Such an inventory could provide researchers with specific guidelines concerning the kinds of phenomena present in social systems where similar diffusion processes are at work.

A large number of interactions is not enough to guarantee emergent patterns in a system; in some cases, a certain critical mass must be reached before emergent patterns can be generated—a system must reach a combined threshold of diversity, organization, and connectivity before emergent properties appear. Topological network properties should be derived from the dynamics by which the networks are created. Formation of new links, for example, may occur when individuals introduce their friends to new people, creating new connections between existing nodes. In reality, social networks are formed by social processes in which individuals create and maintain social relationships; in turn, these social processes influence the dynamics of social networks. This process results in the self-organization of social systems, in which social relations depend on—and, in turn, influence—the relationship between individuals and groups within society. The aim of this research is to understand how the structure of social networks determines the dynamics of various types of emergent properties occurring within those networks. For emergence at the social level, patterns of social interactions are critical.

One of the major focuses of this research is the dynamics of networks. Here, the topology of the network itself is regarded as a dynamic system—it changes in time according to specific, often local rules. Investigations in this area have revealed that certain evolutionary rules give rise to peculiar network topologies with special properties. For instance, let us consider a graph $G(n, p)$ that consists of n nodes (or vertices) joined by links (or edges) with some probability p. Specifically, each possible edge between two given nodes occurs with a probability p. The average number of links (also called the average degree) of a given node will be $z = np$, and it can be easily shown that the probability $p(k)$ that a vertex has a degree k follows a Poisson distribution. This model displays a phase transition at a given critical average degree $z_c = 1$. At this critical point a giant component forms and for $z > z_c$ a large fraction of nodes are connected in a web, whereas for $z < z_c$ the system is fragmented into small sub-webs (Durrent, 2007).

The second major line of network research focuses on the dynamics of networks. Here, each node of the network represents a dynamic system. Individual systems are coupled according to the network topology. Thus, the topology of the network remains static while the states of the nodes change dynamically. Important processes studied within this framework include synchronization of the individual dynamic systems and contact processes, such as opinion formation and epidemic spreading. Studies like these have clarified that certain topological properties have a strong impact on the dynamics of networks.

TYPES OF SOCIAL INTERACTION AND NETWORK TOPOLOGIES

Human interactions are governed by formal and informal social networks. The approach of social networks formalizes the description of networks of relations in a society. In social networks individuals can be represented as nodes, and relations or information flows between individuals can be represented as links. These links can represent different types of relations between individuals, including exchange of information, transfers of knowledge, collaboration, mutual trust, etc.

Types of Social Interaction

Here, we present a brief overview of some forms of social interaction, divided into the following three categories:

<Information transmission> Individuals pass information to other individuals. An individual who has a piece of information will share this information with friends or colleagues. A form of this process may be described as a gossip algorithm (Boyd, Ghosh, Prabhakar & Shah, 2006), the process underlying the spread of information in social groups and societies. The fundamental question is under what conditions the information will diffuse throughout society. Whether the information will diffuse throughout a society depends primarily on the probability that it will be passed from one individual to that individual's interaction partners. Many stylized facts on the role of social network structure on information transmission are well understood in the literature on the diffusion of disease. For instance, dynamics of information transmission is also a threshold phenomenon, where below a certain value the information will spread only in a limited group; however, above the threshold it will penetrate throughout the entire society.

<Interaction with externalities> Social interdependence defines another type of interaction among individuals. Social interdependence can be understood as a dependence of outcomes of one individual's decision on another individual's decision. Such a relationship among individuals is described as payoffs for the choices of individuals. This is usually described with the formalism of the game theory. In game theory, the payoff of one agent depends on the choices of other agents, and, in turn, the choice of one agent changes the payoff structure of other agents.

<Consensus formation> Interaction between individuals does not involve merely sharing information; its function is to construct a shared reality consisting of agreed-upon opinions. In this process of consensus formation, individuals must influence one another to arrive at a common interpretation of their shared reality. Social influence is usually observed by the change in an individual's thoughts, feelings or actions resulting from the presence of others. Social influence concerns not only the formation of opinions but also a variety of other social phenomena, such as learning from others and changes in attitude.

Interaction Topology

<Global or random network> All individuals have a certain probability of interacting with everyone else in the social group. Such interaction consists of interfaces such as communication through mass media, densely connected social networks, and posts on message boards, among others. Epidemic models of phenomena like the spread of diseases, rumors, or gossip belong to this class. Epidemic models have autocatalytic properties since everybody who becomes infected becomes a new source of infection.

<Local network> Individuals may not interact with everyone—space imposes important constraints on interaction. Individuals have the highest probability of interaction with those who are nearby. Cellular automata are the models of choice for investigating the emergence of patterns from local interactions among individuals in various spatial configurations. Individuals are arranged in a discrete space such as a 2D lattice, and time proceeds in discrete states. Interaction rules are local—the state of each cell depends on the state of its neighboring cells in a way governed by a specified rule (Nowak, 2006).

<Small-world network> The path linking any two nodes has to go though only a small number of other nodes, meaning that, in principle, messages can spread throughout the entire society in very few steps. This type of network is known as a small-world network with short paths (Watts, 1999).

<Scale-free network> Formation of new links may happen when individuals introduce their friends to new people; by this process, the most connected individuals acquire most new links. By extension, power is distributed according to the number of links (Barabási, Albert & Jeong, 2000). Emergent network properties do not depend on the size of the network. A small number of individuals have many links, while many individuals have few links.

PROGRESSIVE DIFFUSION PROCESS

Many diffusion processes are progressive in the sense that once a node switches from state A to state B, it remains with B in all subsequent time steps. This type of diffusion process is progressive. The other type of diffusion is a non-progressive process in which, as time progresses, nodes can switch from A to B or from B to A depending on the states of their neighbors. In this section, we discuss the progressive diffusion process; the next two sections are devoted to the non-progressive diffusion process.

The diffusion of information, rumors, or gossip through social networks can be modeled after the spread of infectious diseases. Clearly, becoming infected is not an individual's choice, and contagion in this case is not a strategic phenomenon. In the spread of a disease, some nodes (individuals) get infected initially through some exogenous sources, and consequently some of these individual's neighbors are infected through contact. There is a possibility that a given node is immune; however, if a node is not immune, then it is sure to catch the disease if one of its neighbors is infected.

The basic diffusion model is the SIR model, in which nodes are initially susceptible to the disease and can become infected from infected neighbors. Once infected, a node continues to infect its neighbors until it is randomly removed from the system. The SIR model presumes that, once infected, a node will eventually infect all of its susceptible neighbors. Infected nodes can either recover and stop transmitting the disease or die and completely disappear from the network.

The other model is the SIS model, in which nodes, once infected, can randomly recover; however, after recovery, they are once again susceptible to infection. The SIS model corresponds well with many real-world viral infections that may cause individual's transition back and forth between health and illness.

We can view disease propagation as a dynamical birth-death process with self-recovery. An infected node i propagates the disease to another node j in a single step with probability β, while at the same time an infected node i may recover with some probability δ. The ratio of the two factors $\lambda = \beta/\delta$ defines the relative infection rate of the disease. From this, it is known that the diffusion process is governed by the threshold phenomenon, and therefore infection spreads throughout the entire network only if

$$\beta/\delta > <k>/<k^2> \tag{1}$$

where $<k>$ is the average connectivity and $<k^2>$ is the average of the square of the connectivity (Meyers, 2005). Therefore, higher infection rates lead to the possibility of positive infection, as do degree distributions with high variances. The rationale behind high-variance distribution is that there will be some hub nodes with a high degree of infection, which may foster the contagion, accelerating the spread of the disease.

Note that while this analysis correctly observes that highly linked nodes are more likely to become infected, the aggregate behavior does not exhibit the S-shape common to many real-world diffusion processes. Beyond these empirical studies, this analysis provides some insight into what kinds of social structures are necessary for infection to spread; however, it does not provide an accurate figure of how extensive infection will be and how network structure affects infection rate.

Given a social network topology described with the adjacency matrix among nodes and infection and recovery rates, the epidemic dynamics is also characterized by the relative infection rate and the inverse of the largest eigenvalue of the adjacency matrix $A = (a_{ij})$ (Wang & Chakrabarti, 2003). We denote the largest eigenvalue of the adjacency matrix A by $\lambda_1(A)$. If an epidemic dies out, then it is necessarily true that

$$\beta/\delta < 1/\lambda_1(A) \tag{2}$$

For homogeneous networks, the largest eigenvalue is

$$\lambda_1(A) = <k> \tag{3}$$

Figure 1. Basic scheme of spread of disease

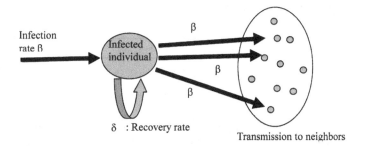

For star networks, the largest eigenvalue is

$$\lambda_1(A) = k^{1/2} \tag{4}$$

For scale-free networks with infinite variance, the largest eigenvalue is

$$\lambda_1(A) = \infty \tag{5}$$

Therefore, the disease may spread widely throughout scale-free networks, since this type of network has no threshold (See Figure 1).

Equation 2 is also critical in determining how quickly a society may recover from epidemic diffusion. The number of infected nodes decays exponentially over time. While it can be very useful to identify correlations between nodes identifying causation is more complicated without the right exogenous variation.

NON-PROGRESSIVE DIFFUSION PROCESS

Epidemiological models describe infection in terms of transmissibility and recovery. These are extended diffusion models that explicitly include decisions influenced by social situations and word-of-mouth processes at the individual level (Jackson, 2008).

A fundamental question in the social sciences is to understand the ways in which new ideas, behaviors, and practices diffuse throughout human populations; for example, in the adoption of new technologies, the emergence of new social norms or organizational conventions, or the spread of languages. An active line of research in economics and mathematical sociology is concerned with modeling these types of diffusion processes as a coordination game played in a social network.

In most of the settings that form the motivation for diffusion models, coexistence is the typical outcome. An important piece, however, that is arguably missing from the basic game-theoretic models of diffusion is a more detailed picture of what is happening at the coexistence boundary, where the basic form of the model posits nodes that adopt A linked to nodes that adopt B.

Another big part of the research on innovation diffusion has focused on empirical studies showing the crucial elements of the structure of social interactions and on computational models that investigate patterns of innovation diffusion through social networks (Rogers, 2005).

Table 1. Payoff matrix of a coordination game

Other's choices Own choice	A(p)	B(1 – p)
A	1 - θ	0
B	0	θ

For simple diffusion such as the spread of disease or rumors—in which a single active node is efficient to trigger the activation of its neighbors, hub nodes with many connections or random links connecting distant nodes allow dramatic diffusion as discussed in the previous section. However, not all propagations are the simple activation of nodes after exposure to multiple active neighbors. This type of cascade model is called a threshold model. Each agent has a threshold that determines the proportion of neighbors required to activate it.

Threshold models become structurally equivalent to coordination games on networks. This approach builds on work investigating the diffusion of innovations in the economics literature, which seeks to model how a new technology A might spread through a social network of individuals who are currently users of technology B. We consider several ways of capturing the compatibility of A and B, focusing primarily on a model in which users can choose to adopt either A or B. We characterize how the ability of A to spread depends on its quality relative to B (Ellison, 1993).

There are many social interactions with positive externalities in which the underlying game is formulated as a coordination game with multiple equilibria. We begin by discussing one of the most basic game-theoretic diffusion models proposed by Morris (Morris, 2000). Morris provided a set of elegant game-theoretic characterizations for when these qualitatively different types of equilibria arise in terms of the underlying network topology and the quality of A relative to B (i.e., the relative sizes of $1 - \theta$ and θ). There can be a cascading sequence of nodes switching to A, such that a network-wide equilibrium is reached in the limit; with all nodes adopting A or it may involve coexistence with the nodes partitioned into a set adopting A and a set adopting B.

More specifically, we describe, in terms of the following technology, adoption scenario proposed by Immorica (2007). Suppose there are two technologies A and B and agents must use the same technologies in order to communicate. There is a social network G on the agents which governs who talks to whom. Each edge (v, w) of G plays a coordination game with strategies A or B: if v and w each choose A, then they each receive a payoff of $1 - \theta$ (since they can talk to each other using system A); if they each choose B, then they each receive a payoff of θ. However if they choose opposite technologies, then they each receive a payoff of 0, reflecting the lack of interoperability.

The binary decision itself can be considered a function solely of the relative number of other agents who are observed to choose one alternative over the other. The outcome depends on the strategy choices of all the agents. Fortunately, in certain strategic situations, interactions among multiple agents can be analyzed by decomposing the game into the underlying 2 × 2 games. We consider strategic interactions in which agents are identically situated in the sense that every agent's outcome, regardless of the choice made, depends on the number of agents who choose A or B. Each agent faces a binary problem between two choices: A or B. For any agent, the payoff for a choice of A or B depends on which other agents choose. This strategic situation is modeled as the 2 × 2 games with payoffs shown in Table 1. Note that *A* is the better technology if $\theta < 1/2$, while *A* is the worse technology if $\theta > 1/2$.

Let us suppose that all agents (nodes) initially adopt B. Thereafter, a small number of agents begin adopting new strategy A instead of B. If we apply best-response updates to the nodes in the network, then nodes will in effect be repeatedly applying the following simple rule: switch to A if the proportion of neighbors who have already adopted A is larger than the threshold θ.

We propose a diffusion model that explicitly includes individual decisions influenced by social situations. In the model described above, agents decide according to their own preferences, but are at the same time influenced by other agents' decisions. This interdependence is described as a threshold rule (Watts, 2007).

Next, let us consider a population of N agents. Each faces a binary problem between two choices: A or B. For any agent, the payoff for a choice of A or B depends on how many other agents also choose A or B. The payoff for each agent is given as an explicit function of the actions of all other agents; for this reason, agents have an incentive to pay attention to the collective decision. The payoffs for each agent choosing A or B are given as:

$$U(A) = (1 - \theta)p,$$

$$U(B) = \theta(1 - p) \tag{6}$$

where p ($0 \leq p \leq 1$) is the proportion of the neighbors' agents who have chosen A.

The binary decision itself can be considered a function solely of the relative number of other agents who are observed to choose one alternative over the other. The outcome depends on the choices of all agents. We have two stable Nash equilibria at the end points, where all agents choose either A or B. If everyone chooses A or B, no one is motivated to switch. In this case with multiple equilibria, the problem is to get a concerted choice. Since $\theta < 1/2$, there is no ambiguity about which equilibrium is the superior one; the problem is then how to achieve the most efficient situation where all agents choose A. The direction in which the collective behavior will move depends on the point where the proportion of agents choosing A is θ. If only a few choose A, they will subsequently switch to B, but if most agents choose A, the few agents who choose B will soon switch to A. If many agents choose B, no agent is motivated to choose A unless enough other agents make the switch to take the ratio of A-choosers beyond the point p = θ, which is known as a crucial mass parameter (threshold). It is enough merely to get agents to make the right choice at the beginning for the selection of A as collective efficiency.

López-Pintado and Watts (2005) studied the problem of spreading a particular behavior among agents located in a random social network. In each period of time, neighboring agents interact strategically, playing the 2×2 coordination game shown in Table 1. Assuming myopic-best response dynamics, they showed that there exists a threshold for the degree of risk dominance of an action such that below the threshold, the action spreads. This threshold depends on the network's connectivity distribution. Based on this threshold concept, we show that the well-known scale-free networks (which are extremely popular in epidemiology) do not properly support this type of contagion, which is better accomplished by a more intermediate variance network.

López-Pintado and Watts also compared a homogeneous, an exponential and a scale-free random network with connectivity distributions $P_H(k)$, $P_E(k)$ and $P_{SF}(k)$, respectively. The exponential network had the highest threshold and the homogeneous network had the lowest, as follows:

Figure 2. Basic scheme showing the spread of innovation

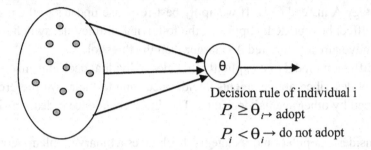

Decision rule of individual i

$P_i \geq \theta_i \rightarrow$ adopt

$P_i < \theta_i \rightarrow$ do not adopt

Pi : Ratio of neighbors who have already adopted

$$\theta_H^* \leq \theta_{SF}^* \leq \theta_E^* \tag{7}$$

Notice that, as in the previous example, the network with intermediate variance is the most successful for contagion (Figure 2). Also, the higher the average connectivity of the network, the lower the threshold. Again, the reason for this has to do with the existence of a giant component of vulnerable nodes. This result differs from the standard contagion models proposed to describe epidemic dynamics shown in the previous section.

CONSENSUS AND SYNCHRONIZATION ON SOCIAL NETWORKS

Consensus problems have a long history in computer science and control theory. In networks of agents, consensus means to reach an agreement regarding a certain quantity of interest that depends on the state of all agents. A consensus algorithm is an interaction rule that specifies the information exchange between an agent and all of its neighbors in the network. The theoretical framework for solving consensus problems for networked systems was introduced by Olfati-Saber and colleagues (Olfati-Sabe, Fax & Murray, 2007).

The analysis of consensus problems relies heavily on matrix theory and spectral graph theory. The interaction topology of a network of agents is represented using a directed graph G with the set of nodes and edges. We denote neighbors of agent i with N_i. Consider a network of agents with the following dynamics:

$$\dot{x}_i(t) = \sum_{j \in N_i} a_{ij} \left(x_j(t) - x_i(t) \right) \tag{8}$$

Here, reaching a consensus means asymptotically converging to the same internal state by way of an agreement characterized by the following equation:

$$x_1 = x_2 = \ldots = x_N = \alpha \tag{9}$$

Assuming that the underlying graph G is undirected ($a_{ij}=a_{ji}$ for all i, j), the collective dynamics converge to the average of the initial states of all agents:

$$\alpha = \frac{1}{N}\sum_{i=1}^{N} x_i(0) \tag{10}$$

The dynamics of system (8) can be expressed as

$$\dot{\mathbf{x}}(t) = -\mathbf{L}\mathbf{x}(t) \tag{11}$$

L is the graph Laplacian of the network G; the graph Laplacian is defined as

$$\mathbf{L} = D - A \tag{12}$$

where $D = \mathrm{diag}(d_1, d_2,...,d_N)$ is the diagonal matrix with elements $d_i = \sum_{j \neq i} a_{ij}$ and A is the N × N matrix with elements a_{ij} for all i, j.

We now consider directed networks where $a_{ij} \neq a_{ji}$ for some i, j. In this case, the underlying graph G is called balanced if $\sum_{j \neq i} a_{ij} = \sum_{j \neq i} a_{ji}$ for all i. In a balanced graph, the total weight of edges entering a node (agent) and leaving the same node are equal for all nodes. Assuming that the underlying graph G is directed but balanced, the collective dynamics in (8) converge to the average of the initial states of all agents as shown in (12).

A consensus protocol is an iterative method that provides the group with a common coordination variable. Network design problems for achieving faster consensus algorithms have attracted considerable attention from a number of researchers. The graph Laplacians and their spectral properties are important graph-related matrices that play a crucial role in the convergence analysis of consensus algorithms. The distributed consensus algorithm in (8) guarantees convergence to an agreement if the underlying network topology G is a connected graph; however, in a disconnected network, it is impossible for all nodes to reach an agreement.

It is worth mentioning that the second smallest eigenvalue λ_2 of the graph Laplacian L, called algebraic connectivity, quantifies the quality of the consensus algorithm. Therefore, network connectivity affects the performance and the robustness of a system of networked agents. It is important for the agents to act in coordination with the other agents. To achieve coordination, individual agents do not need to share information; rather, they must be aware of the actions of other agents. In order to achieve a certain level of convergence and robustness in a dynamically changing environment, an appropriate network protocol must, therefore, be designed. A consensus protocol is an interactive method that satisfies this need by providing the group with a common coordination variable.

A challenging issue is to analyze the diffusion process with a dynamic network topology that is time-varying, including subjects such as ad-hoc networks and synchronization of mobile agents. In the last several years, flocks of mobile agents have attracted significant attention (Vicsek, 1995). Efforts have been made to understand how a group of autonomous moving agents, such as flocks of birds or crowds of people, can form clustered groups without centralized coordination.

Such research is motivated by recent advances in communication and computation, as well as links to problems in social dynamics. Some problems have also been studied in ecology and theoretical biology, in the context of animal aggregation and social cohesion (Buchanam, 2007). The role of consensus algorithms in particle-based flocking is for an agent to achieve matching velocity with respect to its neighbors. Flocks are networks of dynamic systems with a dynamic topology. This topology is a proximity graph that depends on the state of all agents and is determined locally for each agent; i.e., the topology of flocks is a stated dependent graph.

It has been shown that flocking behavior results from a class of local control laws for the collection of agents. Flocking can occur when local action exploits the network properties of the underlying interconnections among agents. Exploiting modern results from algebraic graph theory, these properties are directly related to the topology of the network through the eigenvalues of the graph Laplacian; such an algorithm is possible using local control action agents that exploit the network properties of the underlying interconnection among agents. Network connectivity affects the performance and the robustness of a system of networked agents.

One approach is to keep the weights fixed and design the topology of the network to achieve a relatively high degree of algebraic connectivity. A randomized algorithm for network design is proposed based on random rewiring that led to creation of the celebrated small-world model. The random rewiring of existing links of a network gives rise to considerably faster consensus algorithms, due to a multiple orders of magnitude increase in the algebraic connectivity of the network compared to a lattice type nearest-neighbor graph (Jackson & Yariv, 2008).

A reasonable conjecture is that a small-world network should result in a good convergence speed for self-organization consensus problems due to its low average pair-wise path length, which should increase the speed of information diffusion in the system. This leads to a slight increase in the algebraic connectivity of the network, which is a measure of the speed of convergence of consensus algorithms (Figure 3) (Motter, 2005).

SUMMARY

The diffusion process enhances an innovation via the feedback of information about the innovation's utility across different users; this feedback can then be used to improve the innovation. This aspect is similar to the micro-macro loop, which is an essential part of emergence. In this chapter, we provided an overview of research that examines how social network structure impacts emergent properties in diffusion processes. Most human social activities are substantially free of centralized management, and although people may care about the end result of the aggregate, individuals' decisions and behaviors are typically motivated by self-interest. To make the connection between microscopic behavior and macroscopic

Figure 3. Basic scheme of consensus formation

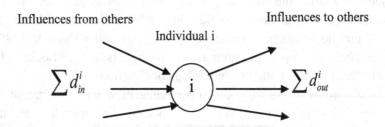

patterns of interest, we should look at the system of interactions among agents—this can be described as the interaction topology. We focused on the stylized facts of macroscopic emergent phenomena that are results of the bi-directional interactions. Social network topologies determine a basic and important form of social interaction among agents, and microscopic behaviors of agents largely determine the diffusion patterns observed at the macroscopic level.

Many diffusion processes are progressive in the sense that once a node switches from state A to state B, it remains with B in all subsequent time steps. It was shown that scale-free networks with hub nodes foster diffusion. The other type of diffusion is a non-progressive process in which, as time progresses, nodes can switch from state A to B or from B to A, depending on the states of their neighbors. In the case of a non-progressive process such as innovation, diffusion processes largely determine individual decisions. In this case, exponential networks with many mid-size hub nodes foster diffusion, as demonstrated by the epidemic and rumor models. We also gave a brief overview of the consensus and synchronization processes that relate to the emergence of coherent patterns by emphasizing the underlying network topology. In this case, a network with a balanced underling network topology is necessary for the emergence of coordination.

As a result, we now have a better understanding of the emergent properties of desirable aggregate process. How humans act is often influenced by friends, acquaintances or neighbors; social networks, in other words, are an important form of social interaction. We conclude that topological properties of networks should be derived from the dynamics from which the networks were created. A large number of interactions is not enough to guarantee emergence. In some cases, the diffusion process may need to reach a certain critical mass—a combined threshold of diversity, organization and connectivity—before desirable emergent properties appear.

REFERENCES

Arthur, W. (1989). Competing Technologies, Increasing Returns, and Lock-In By Historical Events. *The Economic Journal, 99*, 116–131. doi:10.2307/2234208

Ball, P. (2004). *Critical Mass*, Farrar, Straus and GirouxBanerjee, A. (1992). A Simple Model of Herd Behavior. *The Quarterly Journal of Economics, 110*, 797–817.

Banerjee, A. (1992). A Simple Model of Herd Behavior. *The Quarterly Journal of Economics, 107*, 797–817. doi:10.2307/2118364

Barabási, A., Albert, R., & Jeong, H. (2000). Scale-free characteristics of random networks: the topology of the World-Wide Web. *Physica A, 281*, 69–77. doi:10.1016/S0378-4371(00)00018-2

Bass, F. M. (1969). A New Product Growth Model for Consumer Durables. *Management Science, 13*(5), 215–227. doi:10.1287/mnsc.15.5.215

Boyd, S., Ghosh, A., Prabhakar, B., & Shah, D. (2006). Randomized Gossip Algorithms. *IEEE Transactions on Information Theory, 52*(6), 2508–2530. doi:10.1109/TIT.2006.874516

Buchanam, M. (2007). *The Social Atoms*, Reed Elsevier, Inc.

Chakravorti, B. (2003). *The Slow Pace of Fast Change: Bringing Innovations to Market in a Connected World*. Boston, Harvard Business School Press.

Chatterjee, K., & Susan, H. (2004). Technology Diffusion by Learning from Neighbors. *Advances in Applied Probability*, *36*, 355–376. doi:10.1239/aap/1086957576

Colizza, B., Barrat, A., Barthelemy, M., & Vespignamic, D. (2006). The role of the airline transportation network in the prediction and predictability of global epidemics . *Proceedings of the National Academy of Sciences of the United States of America*, *103*, 2015–2020. doi:10.1073/pnas.0510525103

Durrent, R. (2007). *Random Graph Dynamics*, Cambridge University Press.

Ellison, G. (1993). Learning, Local Interaction, and Coordination. *Econometrica*, *61*(5), 1047–1071. doi:10.2307/2951493

Hall, B. (2004). Innovation and Diffusion, *Handbook of Innovation*, In Fagerberg, J., D. Mowery, and R. R. Nelson (eds.), Oxford University Press.

Immorica, N., Kleinberg, M., & Mahdian, M. (2007). The Role of Compatibility in the Diffusion of Technologies through Social Networks. *Proceedings of the 8th ACM conference on Electronic commerce*, pages 75-83, ACM Press, New York.

Jackson, M., & Yariv, L. (2008). *Diffusion, Strategic Interaction and Social Structure*, TR-Stanford University.

Katona, Z., Zubcsek, P., & Sarvary, M. (2007). *Joining the Network: Personal Influences as Determinants of Diffusion*, Technical Report, UC Berkeley.

Lopetz-Pintado, D. (2006). Contagion and coordination in random networks . *International Journal of Game Theory*, *34*, 371–382. doi:10.1007/s00182-006-0026-5

López-Pintado, D., & Watts, D. J. (2005). *Social influence and random networks*. Mimeo, Columbia University.

Meyers, L., Pourbohloul, D., & Newman, M. E. J. (2005). Network Theory and SARS: prediciting outbreak diversity. *Journal of Theoretical Biology*, *232*, 71–81. doi:10.1016/j.jtbi.2004.07.026

Morris, S. (2000). Contagion . *The Review of Economic Studies*, *67*, 57–78J. doi:10.1111/1467-937X.00121

Motter, A., Zhou, C., Kutth, J. (2005). Network synchronization, Diffusion, and the Paradox of Heterogeneity, *Physical Review E.*, 71, 016116–1–9.

Namatame, A. (2006). *Adaptation and Evolution in Collective Systems*, World Scientific.

Newman, M. E. J. (2003). The structure and function of complex networks. *Society for Industrial and Applied Mathematics*, *45*(2), 167–256.

Nowak, M. (2006). *Evolutionary Dynamics*, Harvard University Press.

Olfati-Saber, R., Fax, J. A., & Murray, R. M. (2007). Consensus and Cooperation in Networked Multi-Agent Systems. *Proceedings of the IEEE*, *95*(1), 215–233. doi:10.1109/JPROC.2006.887293

Reynolds, C. (1987). Flocks, Herds, and Schools: A Distributed Behavioral Model. *Computers & Graphics*, *21*, 25. http://www.red3d.com/cwr/papers/1987/boids.html. doi:10.1145/37402.37406

Rogers, E., Media, U., Rivera, M., & Wiley, C. (2005). Complex Adaptive Systems and The Diffusion of Innovations . *The Innovation Journal*, *10*(3), 1–26.

Rosenberg, N. (1972). Factors Affecting the Diffusion of Technology . *Explorations in Economic History*, *10*(1), 3–33. doi:10.1016/0014-4983(72)90001-0

Sole, R., Ferrrer-Cancho, P., & Montota, R. (2003). Selection, Tinkering, and Emergence in Complex Networks. *Complexity*, *8*(1), 20–33. doi:10.1002/cplx.10055

Spielman, D. J. (2005). Systems of Innovation: Models, methods, and future directions. *Innovation Strategy Today*, *2*(1), 55–66.

Vicsek, T. (1995). Novel Type of Phase Transition in a System of Self-Driven Particles. *Physical Review Letters*, *75*(6), 1226–1229. doi:10.1103/PhysRevLett.75.1226

Wang, Y., & Chakrabarti, D. (2003). Epidemic Spreading in real Networks: An Eigenvalue Viewpoint. *Proceedings of the 22nd Symposium on Reliable Distributed Computing*, pp. 242–262.

Watts, D. (1999) *Small World*. The Princeton University Press.

Watts, D. (2007). Influentials, Networks, and Public Opinion Formation. *The Journal of Consumer Research*, *34*(4), 441–458. doi:10.1086/518527

Young, P. (2007) *Innovation Diffusion in Heterogeneous Populations: Contagion, Social Influence, and Social Learning*, CSED Working Paper No. 51, Center on Social and Economic Dynamics, Brookings.

Chapter 11
Ant Colony Programming:
Application of Ant Colony System to Function Approximation

Mariusz Boryczka
University of Silesia, Poland

ABSTRACT

Automatic programming is the method in which a computer program is constructed automatically based on the specification of goals which are to be realized. This chapter describes one of the methods for automatic function approximation (as a form of automatic programming) – ant colony programming (ACP). It is based on ant colony system (ACS) as a new method for solving approximation problems. While solving these problems by ACP two approaches are used: the expression approach and the program approach. Several improvements of this method are presented, including the elimination of introns, the use of a structure similar to the candidate list introduced in ACS, and parameter-tuning. The chapter first describes ACS and introduces the problem of symbolic regression. Then, ACP is defined. After that, improvements of ACP are presented. The main objective of the chapter is to give an overview of the published results of studies carried out on ACP, while at the same time present a new idea in the process of parameter-tuning.

INTRODUCTION

Automatic programming makes it possible to avoid the tedious task of creating computer programs. In automatic programming, the program is obtained by first specifying the goals which are to be realized by the program. Then, based on this specification, the program is constructed automatically.

This chapter describes the idea of one of the methods for automatic function approximation (as a form of automatic programming) – Ant Colony Programming (ACP). ACP is based on Ant Colony System (ACS). It has been introduced in Boryczka (2002), Boryczka & Czech (2002) and Boryczka,

DOI: 10.4018/978-1-60566-798-0.ch011

Czech & Wieczorek (2003), and was mentioned in Engelbrecht (2005) as a new approach for solving approximation problems. While solving these problems by ACP two approaches are used. In the first, the expression approach, an approximating function in the form of an arithmetic expression written in the Polish (prefix) notation, is constructed. In the second, the program approach, the desired approximating function is built as a computer program, i.e. a sequence of assignment instructions which evaluates the function. In many cases, this method may outperform other ones (see Boryczka (2006)).

There are several similar proposals on the use of ACS for symbolic regression, but they deal with this problem in a different way. In Ant Programming (Roux, 2000; Chen, 2004), each ant builds and modifies expressions using a tree structure. Each node of the tree stores pheromone for all symbols (terminals and functions) and expressions are constructed based on the amount of pheromone for individual symbols. A second method, AntTAG (Abbass, 2002), combines ACS with Grammar-Guided Genetic Programming (GGGP). This is a hybrid approach which takes advantages of Tree-adjunct Grammar (TAG) representation and the search strategy of ACS. It uses a pheromone table, which is a two-dimensional table with entries containing the amount of pheromone deposited by ants while they construct their solutions. Finally, the Generalized Ant Programming (GAP) (Keber, 2002) uses a formal language specified by the context-free grammar. Expressions of the language are paths visited by the ants (sequences of terminal symbols and the corresponding derivation steps), where ants deposit their pheromone.

The chapter presents ACP as well as several improvements of the standard method. One of them is eliminating the so called introns which arise while generating solutions (Boryczka, 2005). As introns are the excerpts (sequences of symbols or instructions) which do not influence the quality of approximation, they should be eliminated, because they complicate the structure of solutions and increase the evaluation time.

The second improvement is the use of the specimen list, a structure similar to the candidate list, introduced in ACS. It allows the reduction of the algorithm's execution time and improves the quality of the results (Boryczka, 2008).

Another problem lies in the process of parameter-tuning of ACP. There are two kinds of parameters: quantitative parameters inherited from ACS, and qualitative parameters, characteristic of the described method. All of them should be tuned as fine as possible to obtain good (maybe exact) solutions.

The chapter gives a summary of the results of studies carried out on ACP (Boryczka, 2002; Boryczka & Czech, 2002; Boryczka, Czech & Wieczorek, 2003; Boryczka, 2005; Boryczka, 2006; Boryczka, 2008), while at the same time presents a new idea in the process of parameter-tuning. The organization of the chapter is as follows. First, ACS is described and the problem of symbolic regression is introduced. Then, ACP is defined as a method adapting ACS to solve the problem of function approximation (symbolic regression). After that, improvements of ACP are presented. They are: eliminating of introns, the use of the specimen list and finally – automatic tuning of the parameters of ACP. Conclusions recapitulate the chapter.

ANT COLONY SYSTEM

Ant Colony System (ACS), nowadays a part of the ant colony optimization metaheuristic (Cordón, Herrera & Stützle, 2002), is derived from the research on systems inspired by the behavior of real ants. It was originally proposed by Dorigo, Maniezzo and Colorni (1991) as an ant system for solving the traveling salesman problem. ACS is inspired by the behavior of colonies of real ants, therefore artificial ants used in ACS have some features similar to the behavior of real ants, e.g.:

- Choice of a route for an artificial ant depends on the amount of pheromone – a chemical substance deposited by an ant,
- Artificial ants co-operate in order to achieve the best result,
- Artificial ants move in a random fashion.

Additionally, in the artificial ACS the following assumptions are made:

1) Each artificial ant in the ACS has a limited memory, called the tabu list, in which e.g. a set of visited cities for the traveling salesman problem is stored.
2) Artificial ants are not completely blind. They move in accordance with some probability function determining the next move. Like in real ant colonies, it depends on the parameters corresponding to the distance of the colony's nest from a source of food, and the amount of (artificial) pheromone deposited on the route.
3) Artificial ants live in an environment in which time is discrete.

The aim of a single ant in the traveling salesman problem is to find a salesman's tour in the graph, whose nodes are the cities and with the edges connecting the cities initialized with some amount of pheromone trail, τ_0. Each ant located at time t at city i makes the decision regarding the next city on its tour using a probability rule of transfer. For this goal it generates a random number q, $0 \leq q \leq 1$. If $q \leq q_0$, where q_0 is a parameter of the algorithm, then the best available edge is chosen. Otherwise the edge is chosen in a random fashion:

$$
j = \begin{cases} \arg \max\{\tau_{ij}(t)[\eta_{ij}]^{\beta}\} & \text{if } q \leq q_0 \text{ (exploitation)}, \\ S & \text{otherwise (exploration)}, \end{cases}
$$

where $\tau_{ij}(t)$ is the amount of pheromone trail on edge (i, j) at time t, η_{ij} is the visibility of city j from city i and equals $\dfrac{1}{d_{ij}}$, where d_{ij} is the distance between cities i and j, β is a parameter which controls the relative weight of the pheromone trail and visibility, and S is a city drawn by using the probabilities:

$$
p_{ij}^{k}(t) = \begin{cases} \dfrac{\tau_{ij}(t)\cdot[\eta_{ij}]^{\beta}}{\sum\limits_{r \in J_i^k}[\tau_{ir}(t)]\cdot[\eta_{ir}]^{\beta}} & \text{if } j \in J_i^k, \\ 0 & \text{otherwise}, \end{cases}
$$

where J_i^k is the set of the cities to which ant k can move when being located in city i (i.e. the set of unvisited neighbor cities).

After having found a salesman's tour, an ant deposits pheromone information on the edges through which it travelled. It constitutes a local update of the pheromone trail, which also comprises partial evaporation of the trail. The local update proceeds according to the formula:

$$\tau_{ij}(t+1) = (1-\rho)\cdot\tau_{ij}(t) + \rho\cdot\tau_0 ,$$

where $1-\rho$, $\rho \in (0,1\rangle$, is the pheromone decay coefficient, and τ_0 is the initial amount of pheromone on edge (i,j).

After all ants have completed their tours, a global update of pheromone trail takes place. The level of pheromone is then changed as follows:

$$\tau_{ij}(t+n) = (1-\rho)\cdot\tau_{ij}(t) + \rho\cdot\frac{1}{L} ,$$

where edges (i,j) belong to the shortest tour found so far, and L is the length of this tour.

On the updated graph, the consecutive cycles of the ant colony algorithm are carried out. The number of cycles is the parameter of the algorithm. The output of the algorithm is the shortest salesman tour found by the ants during the whole experiment.

SYMBOLIC REGRESSION

Symbolic regression (i.e. function identification) (Koza, 1992) involves finding a mathematical expression, in a symbolic form, that provides a good, best, or perfect fit between a given finite sampling of values of the independent variables and the associated values of the dependent variables. That is, symbolic regression involves finding a model that fits a given sample of data. When the variables are real-valued, symbolic regression involves finding both the functional form and the numeric coefficients for the model.

The object of the search is a symbolic description of a model, not just a set of coefficients in a pre-specified model. This is in sharp contrast with other methods of regression, where a specific model is assumed and often only the complexity of this model can be varied. Thus, symbolic regression differs from conventional linear, quadratic, or polynomial regressions, which merely involve finding the numeric coefficients for a function whose form (linear, quadratic, or polynomial) has been pre-specified.

The regression task can be specified with a set of input, independent variables X and a desired output, dependent variable, y. The object of the search is then to approximate y using X and coefficients W such that:

$$y = f(X,W) + \varepsilon$$

where ε represents a noise term. With standard regression techniques the functional form f is pre-specified. Using linear regression for example, f would be:

$$f(X, W) = w_0 + w_1 x_1 + \ldots + w_n x_n$$

where the coefficients W are found using least square regression.

In contrast with these techniques, genetic programming, ACP and similar methods applied to the task of symbolic regression do not use a pre-specified functional form. They use low-level primitive functions. These functions can be combined to specify the full function. Given a set of primitive functions $h_1, \ldots, h_u$ taking one argument, and a set of functions $g_1, \ldots, g_b$ taking two arguments, the overall functional form induced by the mentioned methods can take a variety of forms. The functions H and G are usually standard arithmetic functions such as addition, subtraction, multiplication and division but could also include trigonometric, logical, and transcendental functions. An example function could be:

$$f(X, W) = h_1(g_2(g_1(x_3, w_1), h_2(x_1)))$$

However, any legal combination of functions and variables can be obtained. This particular function filled with some concrete primitive functions for the abstract symbols h and g can lead to the expression:

$$f(X, W) = \log((x_3 + w_1) \cdot \sin(x_1))$$

The object of the search is then a composition of the input variables, coefficients and primitive functions such that the error of the function with respect to the desired output is minimized. The shape and the size of the solution is not specified at the outset of the optimization (although typically a maximum size is given) and is another object of the search. The number of coefficients to use and the values they take is another issue that is determined in the search process itself.

Thus, the advantage of methods inducing symbolic expressions on data over standard regression methods is that the search process works simultaneously on both the model specification problem and the problem of fitting coefficients. Symbolic regression would therefore appear to be a particularly valuable tool for the analysis of experimental data where the specification of the strategic function used is often difficult and may even vary over time.

The main automated method for symbolic regression is Genetic Programming (Koza, 1992). This is one of the techniques in the field of genetic and evolutionary computation which also includes other techniques such as genetic algorithms, evolution strategies, evolutionary programming, grammatical evolution, and machine code (linear genome) genetic programming.

ANT COLONY PROGRAMMING

Ant Colony Programming (ACP) is based on the idea of ACS (Dorigo & Gambardella, 1997; Dorigo, Maniezzo & Colorni, 1991) for solving the problem of symbolic regression (in the meaning of Koza

(1992)). ACP has been described in several works, e.g. Boryczka (2002), Boryczka (2005), Boryczka (2006), and Boryczka (2008), and is also considered by Engelbrecht (2005). There are two approaches in ACP, referred to as the expression approach and the program approach. In the first, ants create arithmetic expressions in the prefix (Polish) notation, while in the second, expressions are built in the form of a sequence of simple assignment instructions.

Expression Approach

In the expression approach, ACP is applied for generating arithmetic expressions which are represented in the prefix notation. ACS as the basis of ACP is modified in the way given below:

1. The components of graph $G = (N, E)$ have the following meaning: N is the set of nodes, where each node represents either a terminal symbol (including variables), or a function of an arithmetic expression; E is the set of edges representing branches between the parts of an arithmetic expression given in the form of the tree.
2. The probability of moving ant k located in node r to node s in time t equals:

$$p_{rs}^{k}(t) = \frac{\tau_{rs}(t) \cdot [\gamma_s]^{\beta}}{\sum_{i \in J_r^k} [\tau_{ri}(t)] \cdot [\gamma_i]^{\beta}}$$

Here, $\gamma_s = \left(\dfrac{1}{2 + \pi_s}\right)^d$, where π_s is the power (arity) of symbol s which can be either a terminal symbol ($\pi_s = 0$) or a function ($\pi_s = 1$ for functions with one argument, $\pi_s = 2$ for operators and functions with two arguments), and d is the current length of the arithmetic expression. The consequence of the definition of γ_s is that in the process of generating an expression, symbols of large power π_s are preferred when the expression is short. Otherwise, when the expression is long, i.e. of large d, symbols of small power are preferred – this guarantees that the generated expression closes shortly (this protects expressions from growing too much).

During the creation process, one has to determine if the expression is closed, i.e. if it can be evaluated. An expression is closed if all its functions have their arguments in the form of terminal symbols or closed expressions; otherwise it is open. For example, the expression:

$$+ * - x / - 1\, x\, 5\, x\, 5$$

is closed and can be evaluated (it represents $\left(x - \dfrac{1 - x}{5}\right) \cdot x + 5$ in the infix notation), whereas the expression:

$$+ * - x / - 1\, x\, 5\, x$$

is open, since the function (operator) " + " does not have its right argument, so evaluation of this expression is unfeasible.

There are two versions of this approach: with or without the tabu list. If the tabu list is used, it holds the information about the path pursued in the graph. It prevents the ants from visiting the nodes of the graph more than once. If the list is absent, multiple occurrences of a node in the expression are not prohibited. Thus, in the first version of ACP, N is, in fact, a multi-set. A terminal symbol or a function must be represented in N several times because these symbols may occur in a generated expression several times as well.

For example, using the set of functions:

$$\{1, 2, 10, x, +, -, {}^{*}, /\}$$

the following result may be obtained:

$$/ - + + 10\ x\ *\ +\ *\ x\ *\ 1\ *\ 1\ -\ 10\ 1\ 2\ 1\ 2\ +\ *\ x\ x\ *\ 2\ 1$$

which (after optimization) represents the expression:

$$y = 10 \cdot \frac{x+1}{x^2 + 2}$$

Program Approach

In the program approach, the ACP system creates an approximating function in the form of a sequence of assignment instructions. The elements of the system are as follows:

1. The nodes of the graph $G = (N, E)$ represent the assignment instructions out of which the desired program is built. The instructions comprise the terminal symbols, i.e. constants, input and output variables, temporary variables and functions. The edges of the graph, $(i, j) \in E$, indicate the instructions (represented by nodes j) which can expand the program, while its last instruction is the one represented by the node i.
2. The probability of moving ant k located in node r to node s in time t equals:

$$p_{rs}^k(t) = \frac{\tau_{rs}(t) \cdot [\psi_s]^\beta}{\sum_{i \in J_r^k} [\tau_{ri}(t)] \cdot [\psi_i]^\beta} .$$

Here, $\psi_s = \frac{1}{e}$, where e is an approximation error given by the program after being expanded by the instruction represented by node s. The approximation error is computed based on the raw fitness function $r_i = \sum_{j=1}^{n} |W_{i,j} - C_j|$, where $W_{i,j}$ is the value returned by the i-th program for the j-th test, C_j is the correct answer for test j, and n is a number of tests.

As in the expression approach, the tabu list may be present or absent. If it is used, set N of instructions must include several nodes representing the same instruction. The process of program generation consists of expanding the program by consecutive instructions taken from set N. When the tabu list is exploited, not all instructions from set N need to be used. If the current program gives the approximation error equal to 0, the generation process completes. If all the instructions from set N have been exhausted and no exact solution has been found, one may accept a current program, or repeat the generation process with the modified values of the parameters, including, perhaps, the set N of instructions.

When the tabu list is absent, a program is generated as long as its quality (the approximation error) is not satisfactory and the assumed length of the program is not achieved.

A sample set of instructions used for program generation is shown in Table 1 (as mentioned before, each instruction may appear in set N more than once; e.g. if every instruction appeared 5 times, this sample set N would contain 100 instructions).

The instructions consist of constants, input variable x, the temporary variables a, b and c, the output variable y, and functions. A sample program generated by using set N is shown in Table 2a) and this program after optimization is shown in Table 2b). It represents the expression:

$$y = 10 \cdot \frac{x+1}{x^2+2}.$$

EXPERIMENTS

This section briefly describes some illustrative examples comparing the results obtained by ACP with other approaches. The detailed description of the experiments can be found in several previous works

Table 1. Exemplary set of instructions

1	$a = x + 1$	8	$y = a \;/ b$	15	$y = a * b$
2	$b = x + 1$	9	$y = b + c$	16	$a = x * c$
3	$c = a * b$	10	$a = 10 * x$	17	$y = c + 2$
4	$a = b + 1$	11	$b = a * x$	18	$c = b + 2$
5	$b = 10 * a$	12	$c = 2 * x$	19	$a = c + 2$
6	$c = a + 2$	13	$y = b \;/ c$	20	$b = c \;/ a$
7	$y = a * b$	14	$a = b + c$		

(e.g. Boryczka (2002) and Boryczka (2006)). The experiments considered different functions and methods published by their authors, e.g. Koza (1992), Jankowski (1999), Roux & Fonlupt (2000) and Sałustowicz (2003).

The exemplary functions are:

- $F_1 = x^3 \cdot e^{-x} \cdot \cos x \cdot \sin x \cdot (\sin^2 x \cdot \cos x - 1)$,
- $F_2 = (1 + x^{0.5} + y^{-1} + z^{-1.5})^2$.

These functions were approximated using the following methods:

- F_1 — ACP, Genetic Programming (GP), the method by Sałustowicz (2003) called Probabilistic Incremental Program Evolution (PIPE), and Ant Programming (AP) by Roux & Fonlupt (2000),
- F_2 — ACP, GP, PIPE, and Incremental Neural Network by Jankowski (1999).

All methods were first run on a training set (101 equidistant points in the interval $\langle 0.0; 10.0 \rangle$ for F_1 and 216 randomly generated points of range $\langle 1.0; 6.0 \rangle$ for F_2), and then the results were verified on a testing set (101 equidistant points in the interval $\langle 0.05; 10.05 \rangle$ for F_1 and 115 randomly generated points

Table 2. a) Program generated by the ACP; b) Program after optimization

	a)									b)	
1	$c = 2 * x$	12	$a = b + 1$	23	$y = a * b$	34	$c = 2 * x$	1	$b = x * x$		
2	$c = a * b$	13	$a = x * c$	24	$y = a * b$	35	$c = a + 2$	2	$a = x + 1$		
3	$c = b + 2$	14	$b = x * x$	25	$y = a * b$	36	$c = 2 * x$	3	$c = b + 2$		
4	$a = b + 1$	15	$y = b + c$	26	$y = b + c$	37	$a = c + 2$	4	$b = 10 * a$		
5	$y = a / b$	16	$y = c + 2$	27	$y = c + 2$	38	$b = x * x$	5	$y = b / c$		
6	$y = c + 2$	17	$b = x + 1$	28	$y = a * b$	39	$a = x + 1$				
7	$b = x * x$	18	$a = 10 * x$	29	$a = b + c$	40	$c = b + 2$				
8	$y = a * b$	19	$a = x + 1$	30	$a = 10 * x$	41	$y = b / c$				
9	$y = a * b$	20	$y = a / b$	31	$b = a * x$	42	$b = 10 * a$				
10	$a = b + c$	21	$y = a / b$	32	$b = a * x$	43	$b = 10 * a$				
11	$a = b + 1$	22	$y = b + c$	33	$b = a * x$	44	$y = b / c$				

of range $\langle 1.0; 6.0 \rangle$ for F_2). Such a setting, adopted by other researchers, allowed the comparison of our results with the results cited in the literature. For every experiment the absolute error (AE):

$$\mathrm{AE}_i = \sum_{j=1}^{n} \left| W_{ij} - C_j \right|,$$

and/or the average percentage error (APE):

$$\mathrm{APE}_i = \frac{1}{n} \sum_{j=1}^{n} \left| \frac{W_{ij} - C_j}{C_j} \right| \cdot 100\%,$$

Table 3. ACP parameters' values

Function F_1				
Parameter	Expression approach		Program approach	
	without TABU	with TABU	without TABU	with TABU
τ_0	0.0001	0.00001	0.0001	0.001
β	1	9	5	5
q_0	0.1	0.1	0.5	0.9
ρ	0.1	0.1	0.1	0.1
Function F_2				
Parameter	Expression approach		Program approach	
	without TABU	with TABU	without TABU	with TABU
τ_0	0.0001	0.00001	0.00001	0.00001
β	1	9	5	7
q_0	0.1	0.1	0.9	0.9
ρ	0.1	0.1	0.1	0.1
Common parameters				
No. of ants	100	100	100	100
No. of cycles	100000	100000	100	100
No. of steps	—	—	100	—

(where W_{ij} is the value returned by the i-th solution for the j-th test, C_j is the correct answer for test j, and n is the number of tests) were computed (according to the literature). The parameters' values of ACP were computed during the initial experiments and are presented in Table 2. The sets of functions, operators, variables and constants were:

- $F_1: \{x, N, \sin, \cos, \exp, \ln, +, -, *, /\}$,
- $F_2: \{x, y, z, 1, (\ )^2, (\ )^3, \sqrt{(\ )}, \dfrac{1}{(\ )}, +, -, *, /\}$,

and, in the program approach, 3 temporary variables were used (Table 3).

The results of the experiments are summarized in Table 4. The methods are abbreviated as follows: GP — Genetic Programming, AP — Ant Programming, PIPE — Probabilistic Incremental Program Evolution, IncNet — Incremental Neural Network, ACPET — ACP with expression approach and with tabu list, ACPENT — ACP with expression approach and without tabu list, ACPPT, ACPPNT — ACP with program approach with and without tabu list respectively.

The experiments showed that ACP gives good results and, in many cases, outperforms other methods. It is very important that ACP is able to construct exact solutions (errors equal to 0.0007 and 0.0006 are floating-point round-off error).

Table 4. Results of experiments

Function F_1		
Method	AE (training)	AE(testing)
GP	17.87	—
AP	14.82	—
ACPPNT	8.98	8.97
PIPE	0.90	1.18
ACPENT	0.78	0.81
ACPET	0.27	0.27
ACPPT	0.00	0.00
Function F_2		
Method	APE (training)	APE(testing)
ACPPNT	8.48	7.68
ACPENT	2.70	3.10
GP	0.074	0.155
PIPE	0.058	0.99
IncNet	0.053	0.061
ACPET	0.0007	0.0006
ACPPT	0.0007	0.0006

INTRONS

Introns are sections of DNA within a gene that do not encode part of the protein that the gene produces, and are spliced out of the mRNA that is transcribed from the gene before it is exported from the cell nucleus. The regions of a gene that remain in the spliced mRNA are called exons (Lakatos, 1978). Therefore, introns are defined as non-coding DNA sequences performing (probably but not certainly) control and stabilizing functions. Moreover, they are devoid of any piece of information concerning the protein structure (Solomon, Berg, Martin & Villee, 1996).

The benefits and vices of introns in evolutionary computation have been widely debated (Carbajal & Martinez, 2001; Eggermont, Kok & Kosters, 2004; Iba & Terao, 2000; Luke, 2000; O'Neill & Nicolau, 2001; Smith 2000). Also, the taxonomy of introns in genetic programming is defined. It includes hierarchical introns, horizontal or transient introns and asymptotic introns including the subcategory of incremental fitness introns.

ACP is not an evolutionary approach, but the similarities in the methods can be observed. In ACP, from the resulting expressions and programs, one can find excerpts (sequences of symbols or instructions) which do not influence the quality of approximation. This situation may be observed both in the expression and program approaches.

In the expression approach, ants attach consecutive elements (operators or terminals) using the transition rule which takes into consideration the actual length of the expression without possibility of evaluation (commonly, expressions are opened so they cannot be evaluated at all). Thus, the resulting expressions may include fragments, whose utility may be judged only after the expression is completed (closed) and may be evaluated. Very often, these fragments may be superfluous, similar to introns, e.g. multiplication or division by 1, the occurrence of an even number of unary minuses or negations, etc. The example of introns in the expression approach of ACP is shown in Figure 1.

In the program approach, there are stepwise changes in error while attaching instructions to the generated program (a new value of the error arises when an instruction assigning a value to the output variable is attached). Therefore, between these changes one is not able to determine the meaning of attached instructions, i.e. their influence on the quality of the generated program. So, within the generated programs, one can observe the structures similar to introns known from nature (Figure 2).

Furthermore, sub-expressions with the constant value (e.g. "$+1\,2$"), expressions of value 0 (e.g. "$*\,0\,x$", "$-\,x\,x$") may occur within generated solutions in the expression approach, and a similar situation may be observed in the program approach. All these superfluous fragments should be identified

Figure 1. Introns in ACP with the expression approach

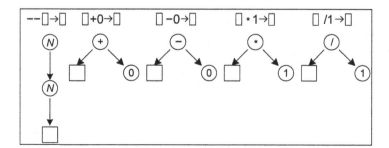

and removed, and such a process may be called post-processing as it may be executed after the set of solutions (expressions or programs) has been found.

Many experiments with functions of different form and different number of variables were performed. The benefit of eliminating introns was evaluated and the results show that the introns may be observed in expressions and programs generated by ACP very often – they constitute a significant part of the solutions' code. Table 5 shows how profitable it is to eliminate introns and perform post-processing (Boryczka, 2005). For example, in the program approach about 96% instructions may be eliminated from the solution generated by an ant, and the evaluation time of such an expression is reduced by about 75% after its optimization.

Introns may be observed as a typical (general) case both in the expression approach and the program approach, and they constitute a significant part of the generated expressions and programs. The elimination of introns improves readability of the solutions and decreases their evaluation time. Additionally, introns are an important part of solutions while local and global pheromone updating rules are executed. Therefore, as in nature, introns may influence the overall performance of ACP, so they should be eliminated after the main ACP algorithm finishes.

THE SPECIMEN LIST

In solving the traveling salesman problem with ACS, the set of cities that each ant chooses from may become excessively large. This causes ACS to devote much execution time to evaluating the transition rule (which city to add to the solution). Computational time can be significantly reduced by using a candidate list (Gambardella & Dorigo, 1996). It contains for ant N at node $a = x + 1$, a set of promising nodes (of size cl – the algorithm's parameter) and these nodes are evaluated first. Only when this list is empty, the other nodes are evaluated.

Figure 2. Introns in ACP with the program approach

$a = b + 1$	$a = a + b$	$a = 0$	$a = 1$
$a = x$	$a = a - b$	$b = b - a$	$b = b * a$
$a = -x$	$a = a * b$	$a = 0$	$a = 1$
$a = x$	$a = a / b$	$b = a + b$	$b = b / a$

Table 5. Profits gained from eliminating introns and performing post-processing (solutions' size and their evaluation time)

Expression approach		Program approach	
introns	introns and post-processing	introns	introns and post-processing
SIZE			
14%	40%	76%	96%
EVALUATION TIME			
25%		75%	

ACP with the tabu list may exploit a similar idea. If, in the program approach, the tabu list is present, each instruction must be represented in set + several times, because it may occur in a generated program several times as well. An ant completing a program does not have to distinguish elements within this set of identical instructions. Therefore, the ant may calculate the transition rule for the set of unique instructions only. This idea is similar to the candidate list mentioned before. Such a list includes only unique instructions (promising nodes) so that computational time can be reduced as in ACS with the candidate list.

In the expression approach, a similar structure, i.e. the specimen list, may be exploited. Here, each ant puts together its solution completing the expression in prefix notation using elements from set $b = x + 1$ of terminals and functions. If the tabu list is present, set (multi-set) 1 must contain more than one copy of each element, because the sets of expressions built from unique components are extremely small. So, similar to the program approach, the specimen list contains unique instances of terminals and functions.

ACP with the specimen list is shown from Figure 3 and Table 6. When it is used, an ant chooses elements needed to construct a solution from the set of unique instructions (functions), whereas, while the specimen list is not concerned, the ant takes into consideration all available elements.

Experiments performed with the use of the specimen list showed that it causes a significant reduction in the number of tests performed by the ants, even though, in some cases, the number of cycles needed to obtain the best solution grows. It also improves the quality of results generated by the ants: the minimal APE as well as the average APE are of smaller values. This may be observed especially in the expression approach. Table 7 shows the results of the experiments performed for exemplary functions:

$$F_1 : y = x^3 - 3x^2 - 4x + 3$$

$$F_2 : y = (1 + \sqrt{u} + \frac{1}{v} + \frac{1}{\sqrt{w^3}})^2$$

Figure 3. ACP without and with the specimen list

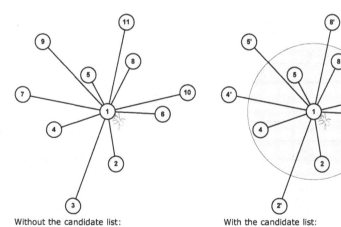

Without the candidate list:

Ant chooses from all
instructions/functions: {2, 3, ..., 11}

With the candidate list:

Ant chooses from unique
instructions/functions: {2, 4, 5, 6, 8}

In summary, the specimen list is very useful. It reduces the time of constructing solutions and may help to generate solutions with smaller values of errors as well.

Table 6. Set of instructions/operators with the specimen list

No.	Instructions	Operators
1	$b = x + 1$	1
2	$a = b + 1$	x
3 (2')	$b = 10 * a$	$*$
4	$c = a + 2$	2
5	$a = b + 1$	x
6	$y = b\,/\,c$	$/$
7 (4')	$b = 10 * a$	$*$
8	$c = a + 2$	2
9 (5')	$y = b\,/\,c$	$/$
10 (6')	$F_1 : y = x^3 - 3x^2 - 4x + 3$	$F_2 : y = (1 + \sqrt{u} + \dfrac{1}{v} + \dfrac{1}{\sqrt{w^3}})^2$
11 (8')	F_1	F_2

Table 7. Results of using the specimen list for exemplary functions

Function	Candidate list	Average number of test		Number of cycles		Error (APE)	
		cycle	experiment	minimal	average	minimal	average
EXPRESSION APPROACH							
τ_0	absent	339	2979175	2918	16382	0	0.0
	present	148	1803916	1209	23726	0	0.0
q_0	absent	543	15480377	4086	64826	0	0.9
	present	198	3551677	7653	37035	0	0.2
PROGRAM APPROACH							
τ_0	absent	717	17366	2	18	0.0	0.0
	present	212	5458	2	19	0.0	0.0
q_0	absent	945	52878	10	46	11.5	15.4
	present	268	20375	14	55	7.9	14.0

TUNING OF THE PARAMETERS OF ACP

ACP, as an algorithm, is controlled by a set of parameters. They may be divided into two main groups:

- Parameters inherited from ACS; they may be described as quantitative parameters,
- Additional parameters, specific for ACP; they may be described as qualitative parameters.

The parameters of ACS (quantitative) are as follows:

$\alpha \in \langle 0; 1 \rangle$ – the initial pheromone trail,
$x'_1 = \alpha \cdot x_1 + (1 - \alpha) \cdot x_2$ – the parameter controlling the choice: exploitation/exploration,
$x'_2 = \alpha \cdot x_2 + (1 - \alpha) \cdot x_1$ – the pheromone decay coefficient,
τ_0 – the relative importance of the pheromone trail and the heuristic information.

The parameters describing the performance of ACP (qualitative) are:

- for the expression approach: the set of constants, variables and functions (including operators),
- for the program approach: the set of simple assignment instructions built from the set of constants, variables (input variables, temporary variables, an output variable) and functions (including operators).

The values of these parameters determine decidedly the quality of solutions produced by ants. Therefore, they should be precisely tuned (quantitative parameters) and the qualitative parameters should be carefully defined. For this reason, different methods are used for tuning the parameters. Several of these methods may be applied to ACP, and some of them will be described:

- Tuning the quantitative parameters of ACP by means of the genetic algorithm (GA),
- Dynamic tuning of quantitative parameters on the run of the ACP algorithm,
- Determining the set of instructions for ACP (program approach) using ACS – double ACP.

TUNING OF THE PARAMETERS OF ACP USING GA

In this approach classic GA is used to solve the problem of tuning the ACP's quantitative parameters. It may be described as follows:

```
procedure GeneticAlgorithm
begin
  t := 0
  CreationOfInitialPopulation( P(t) )
  EvaluationOfPopulation( P(t) )
 while ( not terminationCondition ) do
```

```
begin
  t := t + 1
  P(t) := Selection( P(t-1) )
  Crossover( P(t) )
  Mutation( P(t) )
  EvaluationOfPopulation( P(t) )
end
```
end

The genome (individual) of GA represents a combination of parameters' values (one value for each parameter) in a floating-point representation. The preferred values for parameters according to Boryczka (2006) are:

- β q_0 {0.5, 1, 3, 5, 7, 9, 15},
- ρ $\alpha \in \langle 0; 1 \rangle$ {0.1, 0.3, 0.5, 0.7, 0.9},
- τ_0 $x' = x \pm \alpha \cdot x$ {0.00001, 0.0001, 0.001, 0.01, 0.1},
- q_0 $Fit_k = \dfrac{1}{1 + err_k}$ {0.1, 0.3, 0.5, 0.7, 0.9},

but any value from the featured range for the specific parameter is acceptable.

The crossover operator is implemented as arithmetical crossover performed in the following way:

1) Draw a pair of individuals.
2) Draw a parameter (err_k, Fit_k, τ_0 or q_0).
3) Draw a number β.
4) Swap chosen parameter between parents producing offspring:
   - first individual: ρ,
   - second individual: τ_0.

If the preferred values of the parameters are required then replace the computed value with the nearest value from the appropriate set of values.

5) Replace parents with the produced offspring.

The mutation operator also exploits the floating-point representation of the chromosome. This operator acts as follows:

1) Draw an individual.
2) Draw the parameter that is to be mutated (q_0, $y = x^2$, $y = x$ or $y = \sqrt{x}$).
3) Draw a number $y = -x^2 + 1$.
4) Decide (randomly) if a parameter should be increased or decreased.
5) Perform the operation: $y = -x + 1$ depending on the decision taken at step 4).

If the preferred values of parameters are required then replace the computed value with the nearest value from the appropriate set of values.

Evaluation of individuals (and the selection process — roulette-wheel selection) exploits a fitness function which is a crucial part of this approach. The value of the fitness function is computed by the ACP algorithm. The individual being subject to evaluation represents (contains) the set of parameters' values, and these values in turn control the performance of the ACP algorithm. The error computed by ACP is used to evaluate the fitness function:

$$y = -\sqrt{x} + 1,$$

where τ_0 is the average error returned by ACP (after a defined number of experiments have been performed) for individual q_0, and $\{x, u, v, 1, +, -, *, /, \mathrm{sqr}(), \mathrm{sqrt}(), \sin(), \cos(), \ln(), \exp(), ...\}$ is the value of its fitness function. Thus, ACP is in fact involved in the main loop of GA as a tool used by the fitness function.

Experiments (see Table 8) showed that this method generates values of essential parameters ($\leq$, ε and $\geq$) similar to those achieved using manual tuning in Boryczka (2006). Figure 4 presents how the approximation error of ACP diminishes and the population fitness of GA increases.

Table 8. Exemplary results of experiments (derived parameters' values)

Tuned parameter	Preferred values used	Whatever values used	Manual tuning
I_y	7	10	5
$y = a_0 + a_1$	0,3	0,05	0,1
I_{x_k}	0,001	0,001	0,001
$k = 1, 2, ..., IZ$	0,9	0,85	0,9

Figure 4. Exemplary results of experiments (approximation error and fitness)

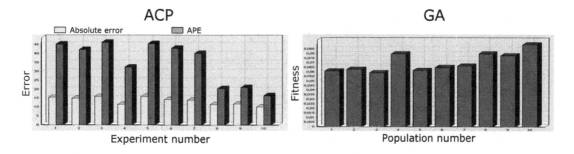

DYNAMIC TUNING OF PARAMETERS

The second method concerning the tuning process of ACP's quantitative parameters involves changing their values during an experiment. In order to do that, some functions describing the directions of changes are required. The functions are:

1) Increasing functions:
   ◦ IZ,
   ◦ $a_0 = a_0 + x_1$,
   ◦ I_{a_k},
2) decreasing functions:
   ◦ $k = 1, 2, \ldots, IA$,
   ◦ IA,
   ◦ $a_0 = a_0 + a_1$.

As in the method described in the previous section, a wide range of experiments were performed. The experiments confirmed some conclusions as described in several papers, e.g. Birattari, Stützle, Paquete & Varrentrapp (2002); Cordón, Herren & Stützle (2002); Boryczka (2006), concerning the meaning and the significance of parameters. Figure 5 shows the ways the parameters change to achieve the best results of approximation by ACP. The conclusions of the process of dynamic tuning of the parameters are the following:

Figure 5. The ways of parameters' changes

Parameter	Way of changing	
τ_0	$y = \sqrt{x}$	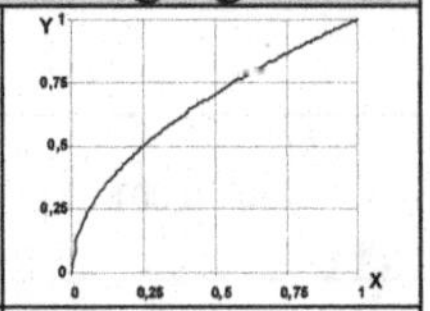
q_0	$y = x$	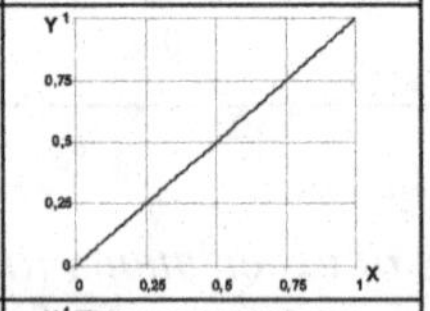
ρ	$y = -\sqrt{x} + 1$	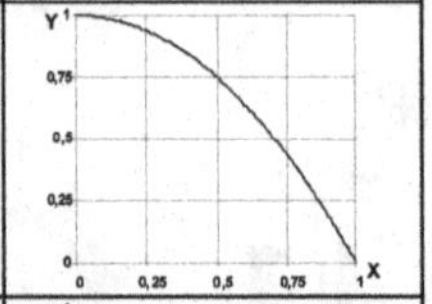
β	$y = -x + 1$	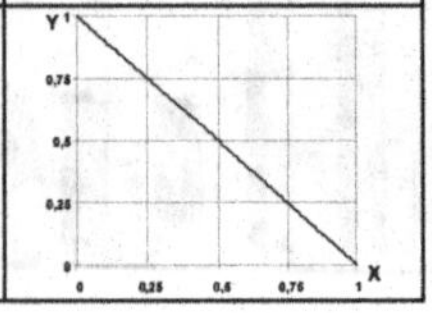

- Monotonicity of parameters I_c, $a_1 = a_1 + 1$ and η_j shows the growing significance of the pheromone trail with the progress in ants' learning process,
- Parameter

$$
\eta_j = \begin{cases} \max\left\{ d(P^m, \mathcal{I}_k) \cdot \dfrac{1}{\text{APE}_{\mathcal{I}_k}} \right\} + \left(p_{T(I_j)} - \dfrac{Hits(T(I_j))}{n} \right) & \text{when } I_j \in \mathcal{I}_k \wedge \exists_{\mathcal{I}_k} I_j \in \mathcal{I}_k \\ \eta_0 & \text{otherwise} \end{cases}
$$

changes according to the expectations described in the mentioned publications – the role of exploitation (relative to exploration) grows along with the running of the ACP algorithm.

DOUBLE ACP

Previous methods of tuning concerned the quantitative parameters of ACP, inherited from ACS. On the other hand, there are the qualitative parameters which should also be tuned, but in a different way. As it turns out, an appropriate method to do this is double ACP (DACP). It may be used to determine the appropriate set of instructions for ACP with the program approach.

Generally, in both the expression and the program approaches of ACP, a base set of elements used by ants to generate the solutions (expressions) should be determined. In particular, there are:

- In the expression approach:
  - input variables,
  - constants,
  - operators,
  - functions,
- In the program approach – assignment instructions are built from:
  - input variables,
  - temporary variables,
  - the output variable,
  - constants,
  - operators,
  - functions.

While in the expression approach the set of basic elements is relatively small, e.g.: P^m, in the program approach, even though the set of elements is small, the number of instructions built from these elements may be very large (e.g. for 20 elements, over 500 unique instructions). Therefore, in this approach, it is very hard to determine a relatively small but adequate set of instructions which guarantee that ants will find exact (very good) solutions.

As mentioned before, the appropriate approach to determine the adequate set of assignment instructions for the program approach of ACP is DACP. Here, apart from the main colony of ants solving the approximation problem, there is a second colony, cooperating with it. This colony generates subsets of instructions exploited by the main colony. More exactly, the goals of both colonies are the following:

- The generating colony:
  - creating the subsets of instructions,
  - evaluating the subsets of instructions based on the approximation error returned by the computing colony.
- The computing colony:
  - the main ACP system solving the approximation problem, working with the sets of instructions sent by the generating colony.

The architecture of DACP is presented in Figure 6, and the pseudo-code of DACP can be described as follows:

```
procedure DoubleACP
begin
    Initialization
    // including constructing the main instruction set
    while ( not terminationCondition ) do
      begin
        iterationNumber := iterationNumber + 1
        instructionList := GeneratingColony.Generate
        solution        := ComputingColony.Compute(instructionList)
        GeneratingColony.EvaluateInstructionSet(solution.error, in-
```

Figure 6. The architecture of DACP

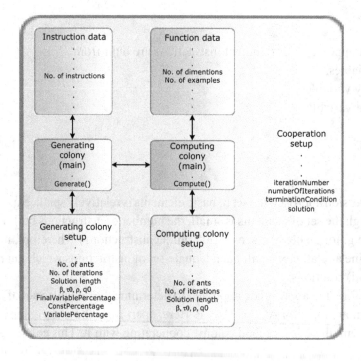

```
structionList)
        if ( solution.error  𝓘ₖ d(·) ) or
            ( iterationNumber  APE_{𝓘ₖ}  numberOfIterations )
            then terminationCondition := true
    end
end
```

To provide a suitable diversity of instructions returned by the generating colony, the following division of instructions is predefined:

- Instructions containing an output variable ($\mathcal{I}_k$), e.g. $T(I_j)$,
- Instructions containing an input variable (I_j, p, where $Hits(T(\cdot))$ is the number of input variables), e.g. $T(\cdot)$,
- Instructions containing a temporary variable (P^m), η_0, where IA is the number of input variables), e.g. $a_0 = a_0 + a_1$,
- Instructions containing a constant (I_c), e.g. $a_1 = a_1 + 1$.

It is obvious that one instruction may belong to several groups presented above.

Using the types of instructions mentioned above, the generating colony exploits the following expression describing the "appeal" (η_j) of j-th instruction:

$$\eta_j = \begin{cases} \max\left\{d(P^m, \mathcal{I}_k)\cdot\dfrac{1}{\text{APE}_{\mathcal{I}_k}}\right\} + \left(p_{T(I_j)} - \dfrac{Hits(T(I_j))}{n}\right) & \text{when } I_j \in \mathcal{I}_k \wedge \exists_{\mathcal{I}_k} I_j \in \mathcal{I}_k \\ \eta_0 & \text{otherwise} \end{cases}$$

where:

P^m – the set of instructions generated by ant m,
$\mathcal{I}_k$ – the subset of instructions evaluated by the computing colony at k-th iteration,
$d(\cdot)$ – the similarity of sets based on the Hamming distance,
$\text{APE}_{\mathcal{I}_k}$ – approximation error for the set of instructions $\mathcal{I}_k$,
$T(I_j)$ – the type of instruction I_j,
p – the assumed probability of appearance of an instruction of a given type,
$Hits(T(\cdot))$ – the number of copies of an instruction of type $T(\cdot)$,
n – the cardinal number (the number of elements) of set P^m,
η_0 – the default value of the "appeal" of an instruction.

This expression is used by the ants' transition rule to determine which instruction should be added to the set of instructions being created.

Experiments performed show that this method produces solutions with approximation error comparable to those achieved with sets of instructions constructed in the manual way. When problems are of small or medium size, the adequate set of instructions is obtained in a very short time. For large problems, the process of constructing such a set is very time-consuming, but it runs automatically without user control (of course, the user may interfere with the work of the generating colony if there are some reasons, e.g. he/she knows which or what instructions should or must be used).

Recapitulating, the main advantage of DACP is its ability to produce adequate set of instructions independently, replacing the trial and error approach.

CONCLUSION

Ant Colony Programming (ACP) is a new method for function approximation based on the Ant Colony System (ACS). This method has two approaches: the expression approach, in which solutions are constructed in the Polish (prefix) notation, and the program approach, where mathematical expressions are denoted as programs built from simple assignment instructions. The experiments described in previous works show that this method is effective and, in many cases, outperforms the other ones.

This chapter described the main features of ACP as well as its improvements by eliminating introns and the use of specimen list. The different methods of tuning the parameters (quantitative and qualitative) for ACP show that this process may be automated without the loss in the quality of approximation.

Elimination of introns improves readability of solutions and decreases their evaluation time. As in nature, introns may influence the overall performance of ACP. Also, the specimen list is very useful. It allows reducing the time of constructing solutions, and it may help to generate better solutions as well.

Tuning the ACP's parameters is another very important problem. The results obtained depend largely on the values of the quantitative parameters. The issue of establishing the set of instructions, which defines the solution space explored by ACP, is also very important. On one hand, this set should be as small as possible so that the searching process is fast. On the other hand, it should be large enough for the best (exact) solutions to be found.

The described method seems to be able to solve not only the problem of approximation, but also other problems, such as finding the perfect hash functions or different problems from the game theory. As an example of the nature-inspired algorithm, this method may be interesting for researchers and academics and may also be developed towards automatic programming.

REFERENCES

Abbass, H. A., Hoai, X., & McKay, R. I. (2002). AntTAG: A new method to compose computer programs using colonies of ants. In *Proceedings of the IEEE Congress on Evolutionary Computation* (pp. 1654-1659). Washington, DC: IEEE Press.

Birattari, M., Stützle, T., Paquete, L., & Varrentrapp, K. (2002). A racing algorithm for configuring meta-heuristics. In W. Langdon, E. Cantu-Paz, & K. Mathias (Eds.), *GECCO'02: Proceedings of the Genetic and Evolutionary Computation Conference* (pp. 11-18). San Francisco: Morgan Kaufmann.

Boryczka, M. (2002). Ant colony programming for approximation problems. In *Proceedings of the Eleventh International Symposium on Intelligent Information Systems,* Sopot, Poland (pp. 147-156).

Boryczka, M. (2005). Eliminating introns in ant colony programming. *Fundamenta Informaticae*, *68*(1/2), 1–19.

Boryczka, M. (2006). *Ant colony programming in the process of approximation* (in Polish). Katowice, Poland: University of Silesia.

Boryczka, M. (2008). Ant colony programming with the candidate list. In N. T. Nguyen, G.-S. Jo, R. J. Howlett, & L. C. Jain (Eds.), *Proceedings of the KES-AMSTA* (LNCS 4952, pp. 302-311). Berlin, Germany: Springer-Verlag.

Boryczka, M., & Czech, Z. (2002). Solving approximation problems by ant colony programming. In W. Langdon, E. Cantu-Paz, & K. Mathias (Eds.), *GECCO-2002: Proceedings of the Genetic and Evolutionary Computation Conference* (p. 133). San Francisco: Morgan Kaufmann.

Boryczka, M., Czech, Z., & Wieczorek, W. (2003). Ant colony programming for approximation problems. In E. Cantu-Paz (Ed.), *GECCO-2003: Proceedings of the Genetic and Evolutionary Computation Conference* (LNCS 2723-2724, pp. 142-143). Berlin, Germany: Springer-Verlag.

Carbajal, S., & Martinez, F. (2001). Evolutive introns: A non-costly method of using introns in GP. *Genetic Programming and Evolvable Machines*, *2*(2), 111–122. doi:10.1023/A:1011548229751

Chen, Y., Yang, B., & Dong, J. (2004). Evolving flexible neural networks using ant programming and PSO algorithm. In *Advances in Neural Networks — ISNN 2004* (LNCS 3173, pp. 211-216). Berlin, Germany: Springer-Verlag.

Cordón, O., Herrera, F., & Stützle, T. (2002). A review on the ant colony optimization metaheuristic: Basis, models and new trends. *Mathware & Soft Computing*, *9*(2/3), 141–175.

Dorigo, M., & Gambardella, L. (1997). Ant colony system: A cooperative learning approach to the traveling salesman problem. *IEEE Transactions on Evolutionary Computation*, *1*, 53–66. doi:10.1109/4235.585892

Dorigo, M., Maniezzo, V., & Colorni, A. (1991). *Positive feedback as a search strateg.* (Tech. Rep. 91–016). Milano, Italy: Politechnico di Milano.

Eggermont, J., Kok, J., & Kosters, W. (2004). Detecting and pruning introns for faster decision tree evolution. In X. Yao, E. Burke, J. Lozano, J. Smith, J. Merelo-Guervós, J. Bullinaria, J. Rowe, P. T. A. Kabán, & H.-P. Schwefel (Eds.), *Parallel Problem Solving from Nature — PPSN VIII* (LNCS 3242, pp. 1068-1077). Berlin, Germany: Springer-Verlag.

Engelbrecht, A. (2005). *Fundamentals of computational swarm intelligence*. New York: John Wiley & Sons.

Gambardella, L., & Dorigo, M. (1996). Solving symmetric and asymmetric TSPs by ant colonies. In *Proceedings of the IEEE Conference on Evolutionary Computation* (pp. 622-627). Washington, DC: IEEE Press.

Iba, H., & Terao, M. (2000). Controlling elective introns for multi-agent learning by genetic programming. In D. Whitley, D. Goldberg, E. Cantu-Paz, L. Spector, I. Parmee, & H.-G. Beyer (Eds.), *GECCO-2000: Proceedings of the Genetic and Evolutionary Computation Conference* (pp. 419-426). San Francisco: Morgan Kaufmann.

Jankowski, N. (1999). Approximation and classification with RBF-type neural networks using flexible local and semi-local transfer functions In *Proceedings of the Fourth Conference on Neural Networks and Their Applications* (pp. 77-82).

Keber, C., & Schuster, M. G. (2002). Option valuation with generalized ant programming. In *GEC-CO-2002: Proceedings of the Genetic and Evolutionary Computation Conference* (pp. 74-81). San Francisco: Morgan Kaufmann.

Koza, J. (1992). *Genetic programming: On the programming of computers by natural selection.* Cambridge, MA: The MIT Press.

Lakatos, I. (1978). History of science and its rational reconstructions. In J. Worrall & G. Currie (Eds.), *The methodology of scientific research programmes: Philosophical research papers vol. I* (pp. 102-138). Cambridge, UK: The Press Syndicate of the University of Cambridge.

Lobo, F., Deb, K., Goldberg, D., Harik, G., & Wang, L. (1998). Compressed introns in a linkage learning genetic algorithm. In J. Koza, W. Banzhaf, K. Chellapilla, K. Deb, M. Dorigo, D. Fogel, M. Garzon, D. Goldberg, H. Iba, & R. Riolo (Eds.), *Genetic Programming 1998: Proceedings of the Third Annual Conference* (pp. 551-558). San Francisco: Morgan Kaufmann.

Luke, S. (2000). Code growth is not caused by introns. In D. Whitley (Ed.), *Late Breaking Papers at the 2000 Genetic and Evolutionary Computation Conference,* Las Vegas, USA (pp. 228-235).

O'Neill, M., & Nicolau, M. (2001). Grammar defined introns: An investigation into grammars, introns, and bias in grammatical evolution. In L. Spector, E. Goodman, A. Wu, W. Langdon, H.-M. Voigt, M. Gen, S. Sen, M. Dorigo, S. Pezeshk, M. Garzon, & E. Burke (Eds.), *GECCO-2001: Proceedings of the Genetic and Evolutionary Computation Conference* (pp. 97-103). San Francisco: Morgan Kaufmann.

Roux, O., & Fonlupt, C. (2000). Ant programming: Or how to use ants for automatic programming. In . *Proceedings of ANTS, 2000,* 121–129.

Sałustowicz, R. P. (2003). *Probabilistic incremental program evolution.* Unpublished doctoral dissertation, Technical University of Berlin, Germany.

Smith, P. (2000). Controlling code growth in genetic programming. In R. John & R. Birkenhead (Eds.), *Advances in soft computing* (pp. 166-171). Heidelberg, Germany: Physica-Verlag.

Solomon, E., Berg, L., Martin, D., & Villee, C. (1996). *Biologia.* Warszawa, Poland: Oficyna Wydawnicza.

Chapter 12

A Performance Comparison between Efficiency and Pheromone Approaches in Dynamic Manufacturing Scheduling

Paolo Renna
University of Basilicata, Italy

ABSTRACT

This chapter proposes an innovative coordination mechanism in manufacturing systems by pheromone approach in a multi-agent architecture environment. A pheromone-based coordination mechanism can reduce the communication among agents and decision-making complexity. The chapter focuses on job shop scheduling problem in cellular manufacturing systems. The principal aim is the evaluation of the performance of the proposed approaches compared with the approaches proposed in the literature (benchmark) in order to evidence the improvements. A simulation environment developed in ARENA® package was used to investigate the influence of several parameters on the manufacturing performance. The proposed approaches are tested in a dynamic environment; the simulation scenarios are characterized by the following parameters: inter-arrival, machine breakdowns and processing time efficiency. The simulation results highlighted that the performance of the proposed approaches are very competitive to the benchmark.

INTRODUCTION

These days competition is played in an environment characterized by high market shifting, rapid development as well as introduction of new technologies, global competition and customer needs focalization. Therefore, manufacturing environments are becoming more dynamic and turbulent than ever before. Traditional manufacturing facilities, however, are not able to cope with such environments, as no single

DOI: 10.4018/978-1-60566-798-0.ch012

Copyright © 2010, IGI Global. Copying or distributing in print or electronic forms without written permission of IGI Global is prohibited.

facility can be flexible enough to cope with such a large magnitude of change in products and production requirements.

Szelke et al. (1999) identify that in the field of manufacturing, agility and reactivity can be achieved by operating both at system and control level. At the system level, the most common solution is the decomposition of the manufacturing system into smaller units, e.g. manufacturing cells, in order to achieve simplicity, specialization, scalability, fault tolerance, etc. At the control level, there are two ways to guide the complexity of operation management problems to simplicity, reactivity, scalability and fault tolerance: a) to enhance the reactivity and pro-activity of the scheduling and control systems by sophisticated new control techniques; b) to take advantages of distributed control.

Autonomous Agents Systems (AAS) are becoming very popular in several industries, such as manufacturing, telecommunications, medicines and so forth because of their ability to build very reactive, fast-learning and efficient distributed systems. In AAS, the focus is on the coordination and negotiation among intelligent autonomous agents. In manufacturing, such systems have demonstrated their ability to build up very agile and reactive systems from several viewpoints: enterprise integration and supply chain management (Swaminathan *et al.*, 1996); dynamic system reconfiguration (Shen *et al.*, 1998); learning in agent-based manufacturing systems (Monostori *et al.*, 1996; Shen *et al.*, 2000; Shen, 2002); distributed dynamic scheduling (Chiuc *et al.*, 1995; Vancza *et al.*, 2000); factory control architectures (Brennan *et al.*, 1997); and implementation tools and standards.

In particular, the scheduling problem in real time is a difficult task in a dynamic environment. In order to operate in such an environment, a reactive scheduling or adaptive control needs to be developed.

The problem of scheduling in manufacturing systems concerns the allocation of resources to jobs over time. It is a decision-making process with the goal of optimizing one or more objectives (Pinedo, 2008). The objectives can be: minimization of the mean throughput time, tardiness of the jobs, minimization of the work in process, etc. Scheduling in Flexible Manufacturing Systems differs from other conventional job shop because each job can have alternative process plans and each operation can be performed on alternative machines. The scheduling problem is known to be NP-hard, i.e., the time required to solve the problem optimally increases exponentially with increasing problem size.

Most manufacturing systems operate in dynamic environments where, usually, inevitable and unpredictable real-time events may cause changes in scheduled plans. Examples of such events include machine breakdowns, demand changes in mix and volume, operational time of the manufacturing operations, etc.

MacCarthy and Liu (1993) addressed the nature of the gap between the scheduling theory and scheduling practice, and the failure of the classical scheduling theory to respond to the needs of practical environments. A decade later, Cowling and Johanson (2002) also addressed an important gap between scheduling theory and practice, and stated that scheduling models and algorithms are unable to make use of real-time information.

Manufacturing environments are subject to various exceptions, which can change system status and affect its performance. They can be classified into two categories:

- **Internal exceptions**: these exceptions are caused by the equipments, material handling, and resources of the manufacturing system. Examples of exception include machine breakdowns, efficiency of the manufacturing machine, operator errors, etc.
- **External exceptions**: these exceptions are caused by external changes to the manufacturing system. Examples of exception include changes in volume and mix demand products, rush orders, due date changes, etc.

In dynamic environments, scheduling problem can be solved by using the following techniques:

- Mathematical programming approach;
- Dispatching rules approach;
- Heuristic approach;
- Artificial intelligence approach.

Moreover, most of the scheduling systems developed in industrial environments are centralized and hierarchical, but these approaches present a number of drawbacks. The most important drawbacks are the following:

- A central computer: it constitutes a bottleneck with a limit of capacity and it is a single point of failure that can bring down the entire manufacturing system.
- It is more difficult to extend and modify the configuration of the scheduling system;
- A slow response to disturbance because the information has to flow to the high level and then a reaction is planned.

Therefore, a centralized scheduling is inefficient in a very dynamic environment where the exceptions are more frequent. For the above reasons, a decentralized control method is more efficient in a dynamic environment. Multi-Agent Systems (MAS) approaches are more suitable to develop agile and robust distributed control, but their performance is more dependent on the coordination mechanism. The most common coordination mechanisms used are the Contract net protocol (Smith, 1980), market based, auction based (Siwamogsatham and Saygin, 2004), and game theory.

MAS are a network of problem solvers that work together to solve problems that are beyond their individual capabilities (O'Hare and Jennings, 1996). These approaches have limitations such as: communication overhead and the reduction in the reactivity of the agents due to constant exchange of information.

Recently, many authors have developed several approaches inspired by the behavior of social insects like ants, bees, termites and wasps to propose an alternative method for coordination in complex systems. The most promising approach is based on ant colony; ant colony coordination refers to the cooperative ant foraging behavior. Ant colonies can always find shorter paths from a nest to a food source by laying and following pheromone trails. Dorigo et al. (1991) first introduced Ant Systems (AS) for solving the Traveling Salesman Problem, which is based on ant foraging. In the manufacturing scheduling problem, this approach can be used to coordinate the MAS architecture.

This chapter concerns agent-based approach to scheduling in dynamic manufacturing systems. The focus is to propose a MAS architecture and further develop a pheromone based coordination mechanism. Moreover, two pheromone formulations are compared and finally, the performances of the proposed approaches are compared with those of the benchmark approaches proposed in the literature.

The structure of the chapter is as follows: in Section 2 an overview of the literature is presented. The manufacturing context is described in Section 3 and its MAS architecture is implemented in Section 4. In Section 5 the proposed pheromone-based coordination mechanisms are explained. The simulation environment and the experiments conducted are given in Section 6, while in Section 7, the simulation results are presented. Finally, conclusions and future research path are presented in Section 8.

OVERVIEW OF THE LITERATURE

Many authors have proposed research on dynamic manufacturing scheduling by MAS architecture. Sousa and Ramos (1999) proposed a multi-agent architecture for dynamic scheduling in manufacturing systems which involves job and resource agents. The job agents negotiate the operations of the job with the resource agents using the contract net protocol. When a resource agent detects a malfunction, it sends a machine fault message to every job agent that has contracted its operations. On receiving the machine fault message, the job agent renegotiates the failed operations with other resource agents capable of performing the operations.

Renna et al. (2001a; 2001b) proposed decision making strategies for autonomous agents in cellular manufacturing systems. The proposed approach is implemented with Multi-Agent Architecture in order to obtain a robust scheduling. For each manufacturing cell, an efficiency index based on processing time, breakdowns machine and workload is computed. A simulation environment is developed to test the proposed approach in dynamic conditions. The simulation results show that the proposed approach performs better than market-like approaches when the manufacturing system becomes more dynamic.

Cowling et al. (2001; 2003: 2004) and Ouelhadj et al. (2003a; 2003b) proposed a novel multi-agent architecture for integrated and dynamic scheduling in steel production. Each steel production process is represented by an agent including the continuous caster agents, the hot strip mill agent, the slab yard agent, and the user agent. The hot strip mill and continuous caster agents perform the robust predictive–reactive scheduling of the hot strip mill and the continuous caster respectively. Robust predictive–reactive scheduling generates robust predictive–reactive schedules in the presence of real-time events using utility, stability, and robustness measures and a variety of rescheduling heuristics.

Wang et al. (2003) proposed a multi-agent and distributed ruler based approach to production scheduling in agile manufacturing systems. Three classes of agents which populate the production-scheduling environment are defined: management agents, resource agents and part agents. All these agents are arranged on the heterarchical framework. Consequently, with the distribution of agents, the complicated scheduling problem is divided into several sub-problems, such as the self-supporting and decision-making activities of each agent for generating local near-optimal schedules, and the cooperation and coordination between agents for system global performance. A ruler-based decision making mechanism is proposed to ensure orderly management of agents, and the ability to respond to customer's needs or environmental changes rapidly. Meanwhile the heterarchical MAS architecture offers regrouping capabilities that support those rulers to be reconfigured and reused flexibly. Case studies illustrated the feasibility and efficiency of the approach.

Aydin and Fogarty (2004) proposed a parallel implementation of the modular simulated annealing algorithm for classical job-shop scheduling. A multi-agent system based on java technology is proposed. The empirical results obtained show that the method proposed is scalable and consumes less CPU time compared with other approaches proposed in the literature.

Wonga et al. (2006) proposed an agent-based approach for the dynamic integration of the process planning and scheduling functions. The agents are to negotiate on a fictitious cost with the adoption of a currency function. Two MAS architectures were evaluated in this paper. One is a simple MAS architecture that comprises part-agents and machine-agents only; the other one involves the addition of a supervisor agent to establish a hybrid-based MAS architecture. A hybrid contract net protocol is developed to support both types of MAS architectures. This new negotiation protocol enables multi-task many-to-many negotiations; it also incorporates global control into the decentralized negotiation. Simulation runs are conducted to evaluate the proposed approaches. The simulations show that the hybrid-based MAS, with the introduction of supervisory control, is able to provide integrated process planning and job shop scheduling solutions with a better global performance.

Renna et al. (2008) proposed an innovative decision making strategy for autonomous agents in a cellular manufacturing environment by introducing a budget assigned to each job in order to purchase manufacturing cell services. The budget is managed as a market-like approach among agents to coordination the multi-agent system. Moreover, a fuzzy tool has been proposed to assign the budget to each job. A simulation environment is developed in order to test the proposed approach. The simulations show that the proposed approach is robust and is able to select jobs that have provided better performance.

Zhou et al. (2008) proposed an agent-based Decision Support System (DSS) for the effective dynamic scheduling of a Flexible Manufacturing System (FMS). The proposed DSS mainly includes six components: User Interface Agent (UIA), Criteria and Rules Selection Agent (CRSA), Performance Evaluation Agent (PEA), Scheduling Decision Selection Agent (SDSA), FMS database and Scheduling Knowledge Base (SKB). Functions of each component are discussed and a corresponding prototype system is developed. Finally, some examples are used to illustrate the decision process and to study the performance of the FMS under different dynamic disturbances.

Recently, a few studies have been conducted on ant colony inspired scheduling in shop floor control. Most of the applications proposed concern the shop floor routing and permutation flow-shop sequencing problem. Among them, Bellen et al. (2004), Sastra et al. (2006), Chen and Ting (2006), and Rossi and Dini (2007) proposed Ant Colony Optimization (ACO) techniques for vehicle routing problem. Meanwhile, Ying and Liao (2004), Rajendran and Ziegler (2005), Alaykýran et al. (2007), and Yagmahana and Yeniseyb (2008) proposed Ant Colony approaches to solve flow shop scheduling problem.

Few works have been conducted on job shop manufacturing scheduling problem. Peeters et al. (2001) developed a concept control system based on coordination mechanism of insect colonies; in particular, a pheromone based control scheme is introduced. Basic principles of the pheromone concept, the control system architecture and a layered approach for decision-making have been discussed. Test beds of industrial scale have been used to demonstrate the properties and benefits of this approach. The main advantages that emerged for the pheromone approaches are: a simple coordination mechanism, the automatic guidance to the optimized solution, and the capability to handle dynamic situations.

Yu and Ram (2006) proposed a multi-agent approach designed for dynamic job shops with routing flexibility and sequence-dependent setup. A bio-inspired strategy based on division of labor in insect societies is presented for coordination among agents. The strategy is accomplished using a computational model, which is composed of response threshold, response intention, and machine-centered reinforcement learning. The bio-inspired scheduling is compared with an agent-based approach and a dispatching rule-based approach. The experiments were performed using simulation and statistical analysis. Results show that the proposed bio-inspired scheduling model performs better than the other two methods on all eight common scheduling metrics.

Xiang and Lee (2008) developed a dynamic scheduling by MAS, introducing agent coordination that is inspired by Ant Colony. The proposed approach is tested in a shop floor model characterized by multiple job types and parallel multi-purpose machines with dependent setup times. Moreover, the machine breakdown is included as a disturbance of the manufacturing system. In this research, the Ant Colony is used to find an appropriate machine agent for processing and helps the machine agent to determine the next job to be processed in the current queue.

Scholz-Reiter et Al. (2008) proposed a pheromone-based autonomous control method to a mix model of a shop floor and tested it in different dynamic demand situations.

All the above research works have the following limitations:

- A benchmark based on MAS architecture with complex coordination mechanism was not used in order to evaluate the advantages and disadvantages of Ant Colony coordination mechanism;
- The proposed approaches are tested in manufacturing environment with exceptions (breakdown, demand scenario, etc.), but a very dynamic environment was not developed;
- The proposed approaches are tested using only a few performance measures (for example only throughput performance);
- In some researches, the dynamism is limited to demand changes; this change is simulated by a sinusoidal function. A continuous demand is not realistic in a manufacturing environment.

This chapter proposes a scheduling approach on pheromone based control mechanism in a very dynamic manufacturing system environment. Two pheromone formulations will be proposed and compared. Then, the proposed approaches are benchmarked with an efficiency based coordination mechanism in Agent-based manufacturing system. In order to highlight the advantages and disadvantages of pheromone-based approach, the performance measures used are: throughput, throughput time, machine utilization, due date delay and work in process.

The simulations are conducted in several degrees of dynamism; specifically, the dynamism concerning both internal (machine breakdowns and machine efficiency) and external exceptions (demand changes). The research presented here differs from previous research in the following aspects:

- The development of a simulation environment in order to test the pheromone approaches in a very dynamic environment;
- The pheromone approaches have been compared with a complex MAS approach in order to determine the environment where the proposed approach can be competitive;
- The research concerns a wide range of performance measures;
- Several manufacturing dynamism levels are tested.

MANUFACTURING SYSTEM CONTEXT

The manufacturing system consists of a given number of cells; each cell is able to perform any kind of manufacturing operation so that the resulting manufacturing system is a pure general-purpose one. In such a system, the scheduling decision consists of deciding what manufacturing operation each cell will perform in the next operation, therefore a pure dispatching problem. The manufacturing system has the following characteristics:

- Several part types have to be manufactured by the manufacturing system. Each part type has a predefined number of operations performed by the manufacturing cell and a due date is assigned to it.
- Orders for production of different parts arrive randomly.

Figure 1. Manufacturing system

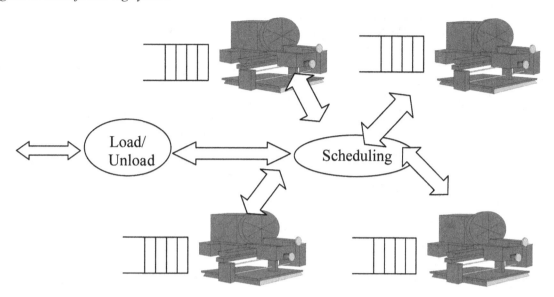

- Each machine performs the manufacturing operation with an efficiency, which sets the speed of the operation.
- The queues are managed by the First In First Out policy in order to investigate only the pheromone approaches policy.
- Each machine can breakdown randomly.

In this work, the material handling time is included in the machining time, and the handling resources are always available.

Figure 1 shows the manufacturing system.

MULTI-AGENT ARCHITECTURE

The Multi-Agent Architecture consists of two types of agents: resource agents, and part agents. A resource agent associated to each workstation is an intelligent entity whose principle aim is to schedule the resource tasks in order to improve the resource efficiency. Moreover, when a new part enters the system, the corresponding part agent is created which analyzes the part status locating the following activities to be scheduled.

The coordination mechanism among the agents consists of the following steps (see Figure 2):

- The part agent analyzes the part status and it locates the technological operation required by the part;
- It sends a message to the resource agents informing them that a part is available for operations and waits for the resource agents' answer;
- The resource agent evaluates the workstation status at the negotiation time t and provides an estimation of a given set of performances based on its productive engine;

Figure 2. Multi-agent activity diagram interaction

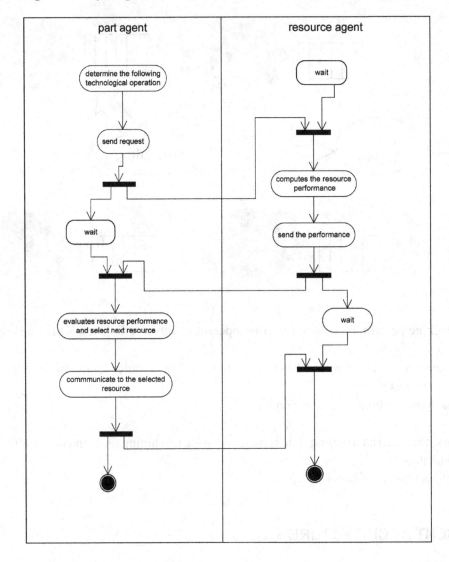

- The part agent receives such evaluations from all the resources, and, based on its productive engine, it builds up an index for evaluating each resource's offer; if, at this stage, the part agent does not receive any offer from a given resource, it assigns the part to the poorest performance index resource (deadlock avoidance);
- Finally, the part is assigned to the resource that provides the best offer at time *t*.

As the reader can notice, the above procedure defines the environmental relations of the autonomous agents involved in the network, but no indication about the agent's decision making behavior (productive function) is given. This means that the above protocol can be adapted to different productive functions of the agents involved in the MAS. The productive function defines agent's objectives and decision-strategies.

Figure 3. Ant colony path choice

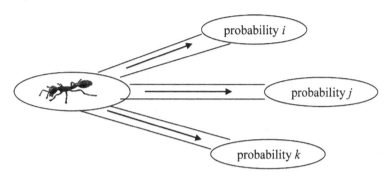

COORDINATION BY PHEROMONE APPROACH

The coordination approach is inspired by the behavior of foraging ants that leave a pheromone trail on their way to the food. In the real world, ants (initially) wander randomly, and upon finding food return to their colony while laying down pheromone trails. If other ants find such a path, they are likely not to keep traveling at random, but to instead follow the trail, returning and reinforcing it if they eventually find the food. Over time, however, the pheromone trail starts to evaporate, thus reducing its attractive strength. The more time it takes an ant to travel down the path and back again, the faster the pheromones evaporate. A short path, by comparison, gets marched over faster, and thus the pheromone density remains high as it is laid on the path as fast as it can evaporate. Pheromone evaporation also has the advantage of avoiding the convergence to a locally optimal solution. If there were no evaporation at all, the paths chosen by the first ants would tend to be excessively attractive to the following ones. In that case, the exploration of the solution space would be constrained (see http://en.wikipedia.org/wiki/Ant_colony_optimization for more details).

Figure 3 shows the choice of the path by the ant based on a probability that is correlated to the pheromone deposited by the other ants. The simplicity of each individual ant allows modeling the ant colony as a Multi-Agent System; therefore an ant colony is an example of a highly distributed natural Multi-Agent System.

The advantages of a pheromone approach are the following:

- A simple coordination mechanism, because the ants do not communicate directly to each other. In fact, the communication is performed by the pheromone in the environment. Therefore, the ants have to know how to put information and how to get information from the environment.
- Capability to handle dynamic situations; the pheromone approach with the evaporation mechanism can adapt to changing environmental conditions.

The main disadvantage of the pheromone approach is the delay in passing the information. There is a significant time delay between the spreading of new information in the environment and when the information is taking into account by other ants. Another disadvantage is the tuning of the evaporation parameter that affects the performance of the approach.

The procedure of selecting paths is the following. The ant selects a path with a probability obtained by the following expression:

$$p_{i,j} = \frac{(\tau_{ij}^{\varepsilon}) \cdot (\eta_{ij}^{\beta})}{\sum (\tau_{ij}^{\varepsilon}) \cdot (\eta_{ij}^{\beta})} \tag{1}$$

where,

τ_{ij} is the amount of pheromone on arc i,j (between node i and node j)
ε is a parameter to control the influence of τ_{ij}
η_{ij} is the desirability of arc i,j (a priori knowledge, typically $1/d_{i,j}$), where $d_{i,j}$ is the distance between node i and j
β is a parameter to control the influence of η_{ij}

Pheromone Update

$$\tau_{i,j} = \rho\tau_{i,j} + \Delta\tau_{i,j} \tag{2}$$

where,

$\tau_{i,j}$ is the amount of pheromone on a given arc i,j
ρ is the rate of pheromone evaporation
and $\Delta\tau_{i,j}$ is the amount of pheromone deposited, typically given by:
$1/L_k$ if ant travels on arc i,j

$$\Delta\tau_{i,j}^{k} = \tag{3}$$

0 otherwise

where L_k is the cost of the k_{th} ant's tour (typically length).

In the manufacturing scheduling context, this behavior can be imitated by the part that leaves a manufacturing cell. It deposits a pheromone as information about processing time and waiting time in queue. Therefore, there are two main problems:

- How the pheromone information is formalized, what type of information can be included;
- The methodology of pheromone evaporation.

From the above formulation of general ant colony optimization the following adjustment has been proposed. Figure 4 shows the activities of an ant colony algorithm for scheduling in manufacturing systems.

Pheromone Formulation I

In manufacturing system the ants are the parts that flow through the manufacturing cell; the manufacturing cells are the nodes that ants must visit. When a part leaves a manufacturing cell, it deposits a pheromone

Figure 4. Diagram of ant colony scheduling in manufacturing systems

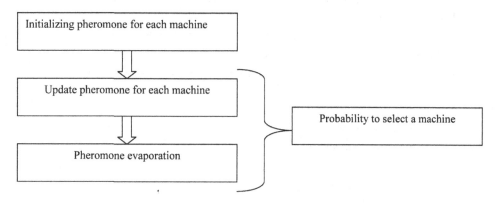

based on the throughput time in the manufacturing cell. In particular, the pheromone is computed by the following expression:

$$value = \frac{QPh}{tnow - tin}$$ (4)

where,

tnow is the time when the part leaves the manufacturing cell;
tin is the part's arrival time in the manufacturing cell;
QPh is the maximum value of pheromone that the part can deposit.

From the above expression, the difference *(tnow-tin)* concerns the throughput time of the part in the manufacturing cell. Therefore, if the throughput time is low then the pheromone deposited by the part is high. The value *QPh* is a fixed positive value; if the value *QPh* increases, the difference among the manufacturing cells' pheromone is amplified. However, the proportion among the manufacturing cells' pheromone is unchanged by the value of *QPh*.

The value of pheromone at start time of the simulation is obtained by the following expression:

$$value = \frac{QPh}{Working\ time}$$ (5)

where *Working time* is the value of processing time performed by the manufacturing cell.

Then, an evaporation strategy has to be implemented; each manufacturing cell is characterized by a pheromone computed by the following expression:

$$pheromone_j(t) = (1 - \alpha) \bullet pheromone_j(t-1) + \alpha \bullet value$$ (6)

The above expression is the average between the last value memorized (*pheromone$_j$(t-1)*) and the value computed by the part that leaves the manufacturing cell (*value*). The value $\alpha \in [0-1]$ simulates the evaporation of the pheromone. In particular, a high value of α leads to high evaporation because the *value (*see expression 6*)* is more significant and vice versa for low value of α.

Therefore, according to the scheme of Figure 4, the activities are the following:

- Initialize pheromone (expression 5);
- Update pheromone (expression 4);
- Pheromone evaporation (expression 6).

The probability to select a manufacturing cell by the part agent, is directly proportional to the value of *pheromone$_j$(t)*; specifically, the probability to select a manufacturing cell *j* is:

$$\frac{pheromone_j(t)}{\sum_j pheromone_j(t)} \text{, with j=1,....,number of } \textit{manufacturing cells.}$$

This formulation of pheromone is a look-back methodology, because the pheromone value is computed with the knowledge of past events. For example, if a machine is in breakdown status, the pheromone is reduced with a delay time that the other parts can "*sniff*".

Pheromone Formulation II

The second approach proposed is based on the queues of the manufacturing cells. Each part that is in queue releases a pheromone; the pheromone evaporation rate is directly proportional to the part's time in the queue. When the part agent sends a request to the manufacturing cell agents, the manufacturing cell agent *j* computes the pheromone according to this expression:

$$pheromone_j = \frac{1}{Working\ time} + nq \bullet \sum_{i=1}^{nq} \frac{1}{(tnow - tin)} \tag{7}$$

where *nq* is the number of part in queue.

The pheromone computed in expression (7) evaluates the working time of the manufacturing cell and the average queue time of the parts. Therefore, when the manufacturing cell computes the *pheromone* (*tnow*), if the parts are in queue for a long time, the value of the pheromone decreases (evaporation).

The evaporation is obtained by the inverse of the average queue time of the parts:

$$\frac{1}{nq} \bullet \sum_{i=1}^{nq} tnow - tin) \text{ (second component in expression 7).}$$

This formulation of pheromone is a look-ahead methodology, because the pheromone value is computed based on the manufacturing cells' status that leads to obtaining a level of queue. Moreover, pheromone approach II is simpler than pheromone approach I because no parameters have to be set (α in pheromone approach I).

The above proposed approaches will be evaluated in the next section in terms of performance measures in order to compare with the efficiency approach.

Benchmark Efficiency Approach (Renna et al. 2001)

Following this approach, the productive function of the resource agent consists of evaluating and providing the following three parameters to the part agent: Expected Part Throughput Time (*ETT*), Resource Failure Index (*RFI*), and Resource Processing Time Index (*RPTI*).

The activities of the efficiency approach are the following:

- The part agent sends a message to the resources agent about the technological operation requested;
- The resource agent computes the following parameters:

$$StdFlowTime_k(t) = \frac{medwtime}{medwtime + FlowTime_k(t)} \tag{8}$$

where *medwtime* is the average service time of the part in the resource. The real service time is obtained by multiplying this value by the efficiency of the resource.

FlowTime$_k$(t) is the expected resource *k-th* throughput time computed by summing up the processing times of the parts waiting in the resource queue plus the residual service time of the part being operated in the manufacturing cell at the negotiation time *t*. This index is the measure of workload of the generic manufacturing cell. The index value is 1 if no parts are in queue and the resource is in idle state; it decreases with the increase of parts in queue. Then, a *Resource Failure Index* is computed:

$$RFI_k(t) = 1 - \frac{FT_k(t)}{t} \tag{9}$$

where $FT_k(t)$ is the total time of failure status of the resource until the negotiation time *t*. The *RFI* in (9) is an index of the reliability of the manufacturing cell. The index value is 1 if no failure occurs and decreases with the increase of the failure time.

A *Resource Processing Time Index* is computed:

$$RPTI_k(t) = 1 - eff_k(t) \tag{10}$$

where *eff$_k$(t)>0* is the efficiency of the resource *k* at time *t*. The value of *eff$_k$(t)* multiplied per *medwtime* leads to the real working time of the resource.

These indices are related only to the manufacturing cell. The *RPTI$_k$(t)* is the efficiency of the manufacturing cell. In particular, a lower value of *eff$_k$(t)* leads to lower time in manufacturing a generic part.

Therefore, $RPTI_k(t)$ is the reciprocal of the $eff_k(t)$.

Then, an *Internal Resource Index* is computed by the following expression as a combination of the two indices above:

$$IRI_k(t) = \frac{RPTI_k(t) + RFI_k(t)}{2} \tag{11}$$

and an *External Resource Index*

$$ERI_k(t) = StdFlowTime_k(t) \tag{12}$$

The *IRI* is the average of the index related to the resource, while the *ERI* is the index related to the manufacturing system's status.

The index of the manufacturing cell is the following (Resource Efficiency Index):

$$REI_k(t) = \beta \cdot ERI_k(t) + (1 - \beta) \cdot IRI_k(t) \tag{13}$$

where β is the weight between the internal and external efficiency. The part agent selects the resource with high *REI* index value, i.e., the manufacturing cell with high performance.

As the reader can notice, the efficiency approach is more complex and takes into account a resource index to select the resource with high performance while the pheromone approaches are simpler in terms of computational time and information required. The simulation environment described in the next section is used to verify the performance measures of the pheromone approaches benchmarked to a more complex approach like the efficiency based approach.

SIMULATION ENVIRONMENT

The objective of the simulation experiments is to measure the performance of the proposed approaches (pheromone-based) benchmarked to the efficiency approach in a very dynamic environment. Arena® discrete event simulation platform by Rockwell Software Inc. has been selected for developing the simulation model of the presented approaches.

Discrete event simulation – these days, in many commercial tools and simulation packages, the simulation model is automatically created from high level modeling languages and notations – allows not only the validation and optimization of dynamic and discrete systems such as production systems, but also workflows such as negotiation mechanisms. These models facilitate evaluating different coordination scenarios and maximizing their potential output and benefits. Arena®, based on the known SIMAN simulation language, is well suited for modeling shop floors of production systems in which each entity (part) follows a manufacturing route through production resources (servers, material handling systems, buffers, and so forth) (Law and Kelton, 2000).

The simulation model, therefore, consists of servers (representing manufacturing cells), circulating entities (representing parts to be processed), and a number of modeling blocks representing the Resource

Agents, the Part Agents, and the changing stages. Figure 5 shows a sketch of the simulation model which has been built into the Arena® environment for the four Resource Agents.

Figure 5 shows the simulation model of the resource agents. The SIMAN blocks "arrive", "wait" and "assign" implement the agent's activities. The block "arrive" activates the agent with local information about the manufacturing cell controlled by the agent. The block "wait" keeps the agent in standby until a part agent sends a request. Finally, the block "assign" implements the productive function of the resource agent and transmits the answer to the part agent.

Figures 6a and b show the simulation model of the part agent. The part agent is more complex than the resources agent because it collects the resource agents' answer and it has to select the manufacturing cell to perform the next technological operation. The activities simulated by the SIMAN blocks are the following:

- "create" activates the part agent;
- "wait" keeps the agent in standby until the part terminates a technological operation;
- "signal" sends a signal to resources agent because the part has to perform the next technological operation;
- "assign", "while" and "choose" implement the computation of the index that the part agent assigns to each manufacturing cell.
- "branch" and "assign" select the next manufacturing cell to perform the technological operation of the part.

Figure 7 shows the simulation model of the stages. Setting the stage length, the SIMAN block "create" creates a new entity that assigns the new values of the stage. The second block "create" initializes the pheromone values of each manufacturing cell at the beginning of the simulation.

The manufacturing system consists of four general-purpose cells that are called to manufacture a set of four different parts. Each part needs several disjointed visits to a manufacturing cell; the number of visits for each part is reported in Table 1, where the production mix is also provided. In order to emulate a dynamic environment the proposed approaches have been tested through a production run consisting of several alternating stages; each stage is characterized by different internal attributes.

Figure 5. Resource agents

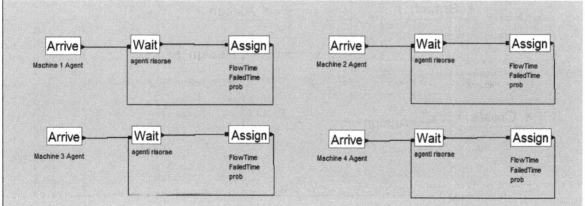

Figure 6. Part agent

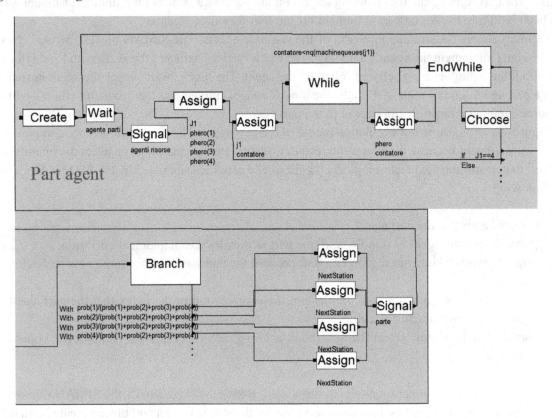

Figure 7. Stages simulation

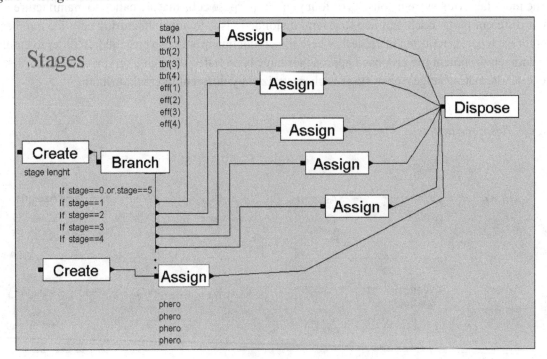

Table 1. Mix part

	Part 1	Part 2	Part 3	Part 4
Mix	30%	40%	15%	15%
Number of visit	3	3	3	2

Table 2. Manufacturing system's data

	Stage 1	Stage 2	Stage 3	Stage 4	Stage 5
MTBF (1)	10	8	6	4	2
MTBF (2)	8	6	4	2	10
MTBF (3)	6	4	2	10	8
MTBF (4)	4	2	10	8	6
Eff (1)	0.9	0.7	0.5	0.3	0.1
Eff (2)	0.7	0.5	0.3	0.1	0.9
Eff (3)	0.5	0.3	0.1	0.9	0.7
Eff (4)	0.3	0.1	0.9	0.7	0.5

The working time of a manufacturing cell is characterized by an efficiency parameter (*eff*); in particular, the working time is obtained by the following expression:

$$working\ time = eff_j \bullet ePT \tag{14}$$

where *ePT* is the expected Process Time (medwtime) for all the parts equal to 30 unit times. The *Mean Time To Repair = 1.5*ePT*.

The evaporation parameter a of the pheromone approach I is fixed to α=0.5 and the *QPh*=10. The value α set to 0.5 means that the weights of the last pheromone value memorized and the pheromone value computed by the part that leaves the manufacturing cell are the same (see expression 6). However, the simulations performed for various values of α do not improve the performance significantly.

As reported above, the *QPh* is a scale factor; therefore it is unimportant for the manufacturing cell's selection.

The Mean Time Between Failure (MTBF (*resource*)) and efficiency (eff (*resource*)) for each stage are reported in Table 2.

Parts enter the system following an exponential arrival stream whose inter-arrival times are reported in Table 3. The simulations are performed for three congestion levels of the manufacturing system (low, medium and high).

Table 3. Inter-arrival stream

	low	medium	high
Inter-arrival	10	20	25

Table 4. Experiment classes

Class experiment	Stage length factor	Inter-arrival congestion	Simulation run length
1	10	Low	12400
2	40	Low	12400
3	1000	Low	12400
4	10	Medium	12400
5	40	Medium	12400
6	1000	Medium	12400
7	10	High	12400
8	40	high	12400
9	1000	high	12400

SIMULATION RESULTS

The proposed approaches are tested in static and highly dynamic situations; the dynamism of the manufacturing system is characterized by the stage length factor. The simulation length is fixed to 12400 time units, and the length of each stage characterizes the dynamism of the manufacturing system. Three stage lengths and three congestion levels (see Table 4) are performed. By combining the stage length and the congestion level, nine experiment classes are obtained, as reported in Table 4, where the simulation lengths are also reported.

The stage length is obtained by the following expression:

$$stage\,lenght = stage\,lenght\,factor \bullet ePT \tag{15}$$

As the reader can notice, for stage length factor 10 time units, by expression (15) the stage length is 300 time units. Over the simulation time the manufacturing system is more dynamic and the stages alternate about 41 times. For stage length factor 40 time units, the stage length is 1200 time units and over the simulation time the manufacturing system is less dynamic and the stages alternate only about 10 times. Finally, for stage length factor 1000 time units, the stage length is 30000 time units; then over the simulation time, the manufacturing system is static and only one stage is performed. In this case, the simulation data are the "stage 1" of Table 2.

Furthermore, because of the random input and in order to guarantee a statistical validity of the results, for each run, the number of executed replications guarantees, for the output performance measures, that the length of confidence intervals (95% level) of the mean among replications is lower than 5% of the mean

Table 5. Simulation results pheromone approach I

	Throughput time	throughput	WIP	Average utilization	delay
1	722.27%	- 34.07%	747.31%	3.42%	1164.74%
2	61.50%	-5.45%	68.43%	-0.68%	61.44%
3	0.36%	0.86%	2.04%	-0.64%	0.10%
4	98.70%	0%	99.25%	- 4.32%	2034.41%
5	55.69%	0%	55.75%	-13.90%	758.19%
6	79.46%	-0.67%	79.66%	-3.03%	806.47%
7	80.68%	0.42%	82.29%	-1.54%	1548.88%
8	42.72%	0%	42.36%	-14.34%	677.08%
9	61.08%	-0.42%	60.98%	-5.98%	703.25%
average	115.95%	-4.37%	137.56%	-4.56%	861.62%

Table 6. Simulation results pheromone approach II

	Throughput time	throughput	WIP	Average utilization	delay
1	2.27%	0%	1.98%	1.70%	-4.43%
2	-3.03%	0.51%	-2.81%	1.03%	-0.32%
3	-1.35%	-0.29%	0.59%	-0.66%	-1.36%
4	79.32%	-0.33%	78.57%	24.23%	278.99%
5	69.46%	-0.33%	68.64%	20.67 &	180.20%
6	41.12%	0%	41.11%	2.83%	125.55%
7	83.49%	0%	84.38%	28.70%	355.19%
8	76.10%	-0.42%	75.37%	24.36%	288.97%
9	47.99%	0%	48.20%	9.73%	199.20%
average	43.93%	-0.10%	44.00%	11.49%	158.00%

itself. The performance measures are: throughput time, throughput, Work In Process (WIP), the average manufacturing system utilization, and the average number of delay time units of the parts (delay).

Tables 5 and 6 report the percentage difference between the pheromone approaches I and II respectively and the efficiency approach. By the analysis of the results the following conclusions can be drawn:

- The pheromone approach I leads to worse performance for all measures; in particular, the average delay time is the performance that is more penalized.
- The pheromone approach II performs better than the pheromone approach I for all performance measures, and this confirms the advantage of pheromone approach II.
- The pheromone approach II leads to performance measures very close to the efficiency approach for the experiment classes with low inter-arrival time and therefore, high manufacturing congestion. This means the pheromone approach II is a competitive approach in high congestion condition.

- For medium and high inter-arrival time, the pheromone approach II leads to worse performance measures compared to the efficiency approach.
- From the point of view of the manufacturing dynamism, the efficiency based approach improves the manufacturing performance, particularly on low stage length, and therefore highly suitable for dynamic manufacturing system.
- From the point of view of manufacturing congestion, the difference of performance measures is inversely proportional to the level of congestion.

The pheromone approach II leads to better performance measures than the pheromone approach I, therefore for this approach further simulations are conducted. The above simulations are conducted in a dynamic environment in which the manufacturing cell attributes vary (internal manufacturing changes). The dynamism of the manufacturing system is extended to external change such as the demand variation. The stream of the demand change for each stage is reported in Table 7.

The stages reported in Table 7 report the inter-arrival parameter for each stage in order to simulate the dynamism of product's orders. The pheromone approach II is tested both for external and internal changes.

Table 8 reports the simulation results for both internal (breakdown and efficiency) and external (inter-arrival time) changes and for several values of stage length factor. The pheromone approach II leads to performance very close to the efficiency based approach. Therefore, in a very dynamic (internal and external changes) environment the proposed pheromone approach II is competitively benchmarked to a complex approach. The average differences between pheromone approach II and the efficiency approach are very minor.

Figure 8 shows the trend of the performance measures over the stage length factor.

From the analysis of Figure 8, the following issues can be drawn:

Table 7. Demand stages

	Stage 1	Stage 2	Stage 3	Stage 4	Stage 5
Inter-arrival	25	5	25	5	25

Table 8. Simulation results

Stage length factor	Throughput time	throughput	WIP	Average utilization	delay
10	9.57%	0%	9.55%	4.10%	19.92%
40	- 8.86%	1.17%	-8.97%	-0.37%	-10.85%
60	-12.52%	0.18%	-12.01%	-0.46%	-12.58%
100	-9.49%	0.92%	-7.47%	-0.08%	-8.20%
200	-2.06%	0.73%	1.89%	1.55%	-4.07%
300	3.18%	-0.31%	3.23%	3.15%	0.20%
average	**-3.36%**	**0.45%**	**-2.30%**	**1.32%**	**-2.60%**

- The performance measures like average utilization and throughput are the measures that are less affected by the stage length changes and therefore by the environment's dynamism;
- The other performance measures like throughput time, WIP and delay are more affected and they follow the same trend;
- In high dynamism state, the efficiency based approach leads to better performance and in particular for delay performance.
- In medium dynamism state, the pheromone approach II leads to better performance with percentage difference about 10%.
- Finally, in static state, the efficiency and pheromone approaches lead to similar performances.

CONCLUSION AND FUTURE DEVELOPMENT

Dynamic scheduling is an important issue in manufacturing systems where exceptions may occur dynamically and unpredictably. The exceptions can be classified into two categories: internal exceptions such as manufacturing breakdowns; and external exceptions such as demand changes. The research presented in this chapter proposes a dynamic scheduling by a coordination mechanism inspired by the collective intelligence of ant colonies and, in particular, by the pheromone approach. This approach is simpler than the traditional approaches based on MAS coordination.

Two approaches have been proposed to formulate the pheromone in manufacturing systems: one is based on the past information of a part (throughput time of the manufacturing cell); and the other on the queue of a manufacturing cell. In order to test the proposed approaches, a generic flexible manufacturing system has been developed and the topologies of two exceptions are considered: internal and external.

Figure 8. Performance measures trend

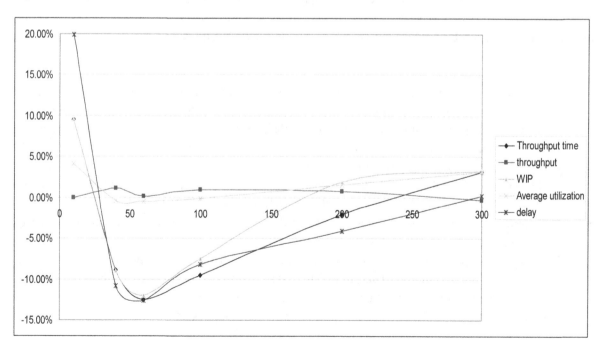

The internal exceptions are the efficiency and the failure distribution of the manufacturing cell, whereas the external exception is the demand changes over the time simulation.

Moreover, the proposed approaches are compared to an approach from the literature based on efficiency indexes. Then, a simulation environment by Rockwell Arena package is developed in order to test the proposed approaches.

The results of this research can be summarized as it follows:

- The pheromone approach I based on the throughput of the manufacturing cell leads to worst performance measures. Therefore, an approach based on past information is inefficient in a very dynamic environment.
- When the dynamic environment concerns only internal changes (machine breakdowns and efficiency of the manufacturing operation), the pheromone approaches lead to worse performance measures compared to the efficiency based approach. In particular, the performance measures with greater percentage reduction are, in decreasing order: delay, WIP and throughput time.
- The simulation results are also conducted in different levels of congestion and dynamism of the manufacturing system. The performances are similar in case of high congestion and low dynamism and the difference increases with the reduction of congestion and the increase in dynamism.
- The pheromone approach II is tested in the simulation environment with internal and external changes. In this case, the pheromone approach II performs better than the efficiency based approach in some cases. In particular, with a high level of dynamic changes the efficiency based approach is better, while for medium level, the pheromone approach II performs better. Finally, for the low level of dynamism, the efficiency based is again the better approach.

In the case of high dynamism, the delay information of pheromone approach is higher than the stage length, so the pheromone approach is unable to compete with the efficiency approach. With medium dynamism, the delay information of pheromone approach is comparable with the stage length, and the pheromone approach leads to better results. Finally, in static environment, the simulation results of the two approaches are similar because the environment conditions are fixed.

Future work of this chapter can be the following:

- The influence of the manufacturing system size on the performance measure: the study of the performance measures when a high number of manufacturing cells characterizes the manufacturing system. The increase of the manufacturing cells leads to a more complex scheduling problem; therefore a more thorough investigation of the pheromone approach's responsiveness to the complexity of larger scheduling problem can be performed.
- An investigation into the impact of the dispatching rules on the performance measures; how the queue policy management can impact on the pheromone approach.
- The extension of the research to the material handling system and the development of the pheromone approach for both scheduling and routing of the parts.
- The development of hybrid approach; in this case, the dynamic scheduling approach can be adapted to the environment conditions. Therefore, when dynamism is high, complex method is activated. Otherwise, the pheromone approach can be performed. This allows reducing the computational time and complexity to dynamic scheduling in manufacturing systems.

REFERENCES

Alaykýran, K., Engin, O., & Döyen, A. (2007). Using ant colony optimization to solve hybrid flow shop scheduling problems. *International Journal of Advanced Manufacturing Technology, 35,* 541–550. doi:10.1007/s00170-007-1048-2

Aydin, M. E., & Fogarty, T. C. (2004). A simulated annealing algorithm for multi-agent systems: A job shop scheduling application. *Journal of Intelligent Manufacturing, 15,* 805–814. doi:10.1023/B:JIMS.0000042665.10086.cf

Bell, J. E., & McMullen, P. R. (2004). Ant colony optimization techniques for the vehicle routing problem. *Advanced Engineering Informatics, 1*(8), 41–48. doi:10.1016/j.aei.2004.07.001

Brennan, R. W., Balasubramanian, S., & Norrie, D. H. (1997). Dynamic control architecture for advanced manufacturing system. In *Proceedings of the International Conference on Intelligent Systems for Advanced Manufacturing,* Pittsburgh, PA (pp. 213-223).

Chen, C. H., & Ting, C. J. (2006). An improved ant colony system algorithm for the vehicle routing problem. *Journal of the Chinese Institute of Industrial Engineers, 23*(2), 115–126.

Chiuc, C., & Yih, Y. (1995). A learning based methodology for dynamic scheduling in distributed manufacturing systems. *International Journal of Production Research, 33*(11), 3217–3232. doi:10.1080/00207549508904870

Cowling, P. I., & Johansson, M. (2002). Using real time information for effective dynamic scheduling. *European Journal of Operational Research, 139*(2), 230–244. doi:10.1016/S0377-2217(01)00355-1

Cowling, P. I., Ouelhadj, D., & Petrovic, S. (2001). A multi-agent architecture for dynamic scheduling of steel hot rolling. In *Proceedings of the 3rd International ICSC World Manufacturing Congress,* Rochester, NY (pp. 104-111).

Cowling, P. I., Ouelhadj, D., & Petrovic, S. (2003). A multi-agent architecture for dynamic scheduling of steel hot rolling. *Journal of Intelligent Manufacturing, 14,* 457–470. doi:10.1023/A:1025701325275

Cowling, P. I., Ouelhadj, D., & Petrovic, S. (2004). Dynamic scheduling of steel casting and milling using multi-agents. *Journal of Production Planning and Control, 15*(2), 178–188. doi:10.1080/09537280410001662466

Dorigo, M., Maniesco, V., & Colorni, A. (1991). Distributed optimization by ant colonies. In *Proceedings of the European Conference on Artificial Life,* Paris, France (pp. 134-142).

Law, A. M., & Kelton, W. D. (2000). *Simulation modeling and analysis* (3rd ed.). New York: McGraw Hill.

MacCarthy, B. L., & Liu, J. (1993). Addressing the gap in scheduling research: A review of optimization and heuristic methods in production scheduling. *International Journal of Production Research, 31*(1), 59–79. doi:10.1080/00207549308956713

Monostori, L., Markus, A., Van Brussels, H., & Westkaemper, E. (1996). Machine learning approaches to manufacturing. *Annals of CIRP, 45*(2), 675–712.

O'Hare, G., & Jennings, N. (1996). *Foundations of distributed artificial intelligence*. New York: Wiley-Interscience.

Ouelhadj, D., Cowling, P. I., & Petrovic, S. (2003a). Contract net protocol for cooperative optimisation and dynamic scheduling of steel production. In A. Ibraham, K. Franke, & M. Koppen (Eds.), *Intelligent systems design and applications* (pp. 457-470). Berlin, Germany: Springer-Verlag.

Ouelhadj, D., Cowling, P. I., & Petrovic, S. (2003b). Utility and stability measures for agent-based dynamic scheduling of steel continuous casting. In *Proceedings of the IEEE International Conference on Robotics and Automation,* Taipei, Taiwan (pp. 175-180).

Peeters, P., Van Brussel, H., Valckenaers, P., Wyns, J., Bongaerts, L., Kollingbaum, M., & Heikkila, T. (2001). Pheromone based emergent shop floor control system for flexible flow shops. *Artificial Intelligence in Engineering, 15*(4), 343–352. doi:10.1016/S0954-1810(01)00026-7

Pinedo, M. (2008). *Scheduling: Theory, algorithms, and systems* (3rd ed.). Berlin, Germany: Springer-Verlag.

Rajendran, C., & Ziegler, H. (2005). Two ant-colony algorithms for minimizing total flowtime in permutation flowshops. *Computers & Industrial Engineering, 48*(4), 789–797. doi:10.1016/j.cie.2004.12.009

Renna, P., Padalino, R., & Vancza, J. (2008). A multi-agent architecture for budget-based scheduling in dynamic environments. In *Proceedings of the 6th CIRP International Conference on Intelligent Computation in Manufacturing Engineering*, Naples, Italy.

Renna, P., Perrone, G., Amico, M., & Bruccoleri, M. (2001). A new decision making strategy for distributed control of cellular manufacturing systems. In C. H. Dagli et al. (Eds.), *Intelligent engineering through artificial neural networks* (pp. 975-980). New York: ASME Press.

Renna, P., Perrone, G., Amico, M., Bruccoleri, M., & Noto La Diega, S. (2001). A performance comparison between market like and efficiency based approaches in agent based manufacturing environment. In *Proceedings of the 34th International Seminar for Manufacturing Systems,* Athens, Greece (pp. 93-98).

Rossi, A., & Dini, G. (2007). Flexible job-shop scheduling with routing flexibility and separable setup times using ant colony optimisation method. *Robotics and Computer-integrated Manufacturing, 23*(5), 503–516. doi:10.1016/j.rcim.2006.06.004

Sastra, J. J., Asokan, P., Saravanan, R., & Delphin, A. (2005). Simultaneous scheduling of parts and AGVs in an FMS using non-traditional optimization algorithms. *International Journal of Applied Management and Technology, 3*(1), 305–316.

Scholz-Reiter, B., De Beer, C., Freitag, M., & Jagalski, T. (2008). Bio-inspired and pheromone-based shop floor control. *International Journal of Computer Integrated Manufacturing, 21*(2), 201–205. doi:10.1080/09511920701607840

Shen, W., Maturana, F., & Norrie, D. (2000). Metaphor II: An agent-based architecture for distributed intelligent design and manufacturing. *Journal of Intelligent Manufacturing, 11*(3), 237–251. doi:10.1023/A:1008915208259

Shen, W., Xue, D., & Norrie, D. (1998). An agent-based manufacturing enterprise infrastructure for distributed integrated intelligent manufacturing system. In *Proceedings the 3rd International Conference on Practical Application of Intelligent Agents and Multi-Agent Systems,* London, UK (pp. 533-548).

Shen, W. M. (2002). Distributed manufacturing scheduling using intelligent agents. *IEEE Intelligent Systems, 17*(1), 88–94. doi:10.1109/5254.988492

Siwamogsatham, V., & Saygin, C. (2004). Auction-based distributed scheduling and control scheme for flexible manufacturing systems. *International Journal of Production Research, 42,* 547–572. doi:10.1080/00207540310001613683

Smith, R. G. (1980). The contract net protocol: High level communication and control in a distributed problem solver. *IEEE Transactions on Computers, 29*(12), 1104–1113. doi:10.1109/TC.1980.1675516

Sousa, P., & Ramos, C. (1999). A distributed architecture and negotiation protocol for scheduling in manufacturing systems. *Computers in Industry, 38*(2), 103–113. doi:10.1016/S0166-3615(98)00112-2

Swaminathan, J. M., Smith, S. F., & Sadeh, N. M. (1996). A multi-agent framework for modeling supply chain dynamics. In *Proceedings of the NSF Research Planning Workshop on Artificial Intelligence and Manufacturing*, Albequerque, NM.

Szelke, E., & Monostori, L. (1999). Real scheduling in real time production control. In P. Brandimarte & A. Villa (Eds.), *Modelling manufacturing systems: From aggregate planning to real-time control* (pp. 65-114). Berlin, Germany: Springer-Verlag.

Vancza, J., & Markus, A. (2000). An agent model for incentive-based production scheduling. *Computers in Industry, 43,* 173–187. doi:10.1016/S0166-3615(00)00066-X

Wang, Y. H., Yin, C. W., & Zhang, Y. (2003). A multi-agent and distributed ruler based approach to production scheduling of agile manufacturing systems. *International Journal of Computer Integrated Manufacturing, 16*(2), 81–92. doi:10.1080/713804987

Wonga, T. N., Leunga, C. W., Maka, K. L., & Fungb, R. Y. K. (2006). Dynamic shop floor scheduling in multi-agent manufacturing systems. *Expert Systems with Applications, 31*(3), 486–494. doi:10.1016/j.eswa.2005.09.073

Xiang, W., & Lee, H. P. (2008). Ant colony intelligence in multi-agent dynamic manufacturing scheduling. *Engineering Applications of Artificial Intelligence, 21,* 73–85. doi:10.1016/j.engappai.2007.03.008

Yagmahana, B., & Yeniseyb, M. M. (2008). Ant colony optimization for multi-objective flow shop scheduling problem. *Computers & Industrial Engineering, 54*(3), 411–420. doi:10.1016/j.cie.2007.08.003

Ying, K.-C., & Liao, C.-J. (2004). An ant colony system for permutation flow-shop sequencing. *Computers & Operations Research, 31,* 791–801. doi:10.1016/S0305-0548(03)00038-8

Yu, X., & Ram, B. (2006). Bio-inspired scheduling for dynamic job shops with flexible routing and sequence-dependent setups. *International Journal of Production Research, 44*(22), 4793–4813. doi:10.1080/00207540600621094

Zhou, B., Wang, S., & Xi, L. (2008). Agent-based decision support system for dynamic scheduling of a flexible manufacturing system. *International Journal of Computer Applications in Technology*, *32*(1), 47–62. doi:10.1504/IJCAT.2008.019489

Compilation of References

Abbass, H. A., Hoai, X., & McKay, R. I. (2002). AntTAG: A new method to compose computer programs using colonies of ants. In *Proceedings of the IEEE Congress on Evolutionary Computation* (pp. 1654-1659). Washington, DC: IEEE Press.

Abuali, F. N., Schoenefeld, D. A., & Wainwright, R. L. (1994). Terminal assignment in a communications network using genetic algorithms. In *Proceedings of the 22nd Annual ACM Computer Science Conference on Scaling Up: Meeting the Challenge of Complexity in Real-World Computing Applications,* Phoenix, AZ (pp. 74-81).

Adelman, L., Miller, S. L., & Yeo, C. (2004). Testing the effectiveness of icons for supporting distributed team decision making under time pressure. *IEEE Transactions on Systems, Man and Cybernetics- Part A, 34,* 179-189.

Ahmad, S. U., & Antoniou, A. (2007). A multiobjective genetic algorithm for asymmetric FIR filters. In *Proceedings of the IEEE International Symposium on Signal Processing and Information Technology* (pp. 525-530). Piscataway, NJ: IEEE Press.

Aiyarak, P., Saket, A. S., & Sinclair, M. C. (1997). Genetic programming approaches for minimum cost topology optimisation of optical telecommunication networks. In *Proceedings of the 2nd International Conference on Genetic Algorithms in Engineering Systems: Innovations and Applications,* Glasgow, UK (pp. 415-420).

Alayкýran, K., Engin, O., & Döyen, A. (2007). Using ant colony optimization to solve hybrid flow shop scheduling problems. *International Journal of Advanced Manufacturing Technology, 35,* 541–550. doi:10.1007/s00170-007-1048-2

Alba, E., & Chicano, J. F. (2006). Evolutionary algorithms in telecommunications. In *Proceedings of the IEEE Mediterranean Electrotechnical Conference,* Málaga, Spain (pp. 795-798).

Albertini, M. K., & Mello, R. F. (2007). A self-organizing neural network for detecting novelties. In *Proceedings of the ACM symposium on Applied Computing (SAC '07)* (pp. 462-466). New York: ACM.

Alizadeh, A. A., Eisen, M. B., Davis, E. E., Ma, C., Lossos, I. S., & Rosenwald, A. (2000). Distinct types of diffuse large B-cell lymphoma identified by gene expression profiling. *Nature, 403*(6769), 503–511. doi:10.1038/35000501

Al-Subaie, M., & Zulkernine, M. (2006). Efficacy of hidden Markov models over neural networks in anomaly intrusion detection. In *Proceedings of the 30th Annual International Computer Software and Applications Conference (COMPSAC '06)* (pp. 325-332). Washington, DC: IEEE Computer Society.

Angeline, P. J. (1998). A historical perspective on the evolution of executable structures. *Fundamenta Informaticae, 35*(1-4), 179–195.

Antoniou, A., & Lu, W. S. (2007). *Practical optimization, algorithms and engineering applications.* Berlin, Germany: Springer Science+Business Media, LLC.

Arabshahi, P., Choi, J. J., Marks, R. J., & Caudell, T. P. (1992). Fuzzy control of backpropagation. In *Proceedings of the IEEE International Conference on Fuzzy Systems,* San Diego, CA (pp. 967-972).

Arthur, W. (1989). Competing Technologies, Increasing Returns, and Lock-In By Historical Events. *The Economic Journal, 99*, 116–131. doi:10.2307/2234208

Asuncion, A., & Newman, D. J. (2007). *UCI repository of machine learning databases.* Retrieved September 25, 2008, from http://archive.ics.uci.edu/ml/

Aydin, M. E., & Fogarty, T. C. (2004). A simulated annealing algorithm for multi-agent systems: A job shop scheduling application. *Journal of Intelligent Manufacturing, 15*, 805–814. doi:10.1023/B:JIMS.0000042665.10086.cf

Bäck, T. (1996). *Evolutionary algorithms in theory and practice: Evolution strategies, evolutionary programming, genetic algorithms.* Oxford, UK: Oxford University Press.

Bäck, T., Fogel, D. B., & Michalewicz, Z. (Eds.). (1997). *Handbook of evolutionary computation.* London: Taylor & Francis.

Bäck, T., Hammel, U., & Schwefel, H.-P. (1997). Evolutionary computation: Comments on the history and current state. *IEEE Transactions on Evolutionary Computation, 1*(1), 3–17. doi:10.1109/4235.585888

Baeza-Yates, R. A., & Ribeiro-Neto, B. A. (1999). *Modern information retrieval.* New York: ACM Press / Addison-Wesley.

Bagley, J. D. (1967). *The behavior of adaptive systems which employ genetic and correlation algorithms.* Unpublished doctoral dissertation, The University of Michigan, Ann Arbor, MI, USA.

Ball, P. (2004). *Critical Mass,* Farrar, Straus and Giroux-Banerjee, A. (1992). A Simple Model of Herd Behavior. *The Quarterly Journal of Economics, 110*, 797–817.

Baluja, S. (1994). *Population-based incremental learning: A method for integrating genetic search based function optimization and competitive learning* (Tech. Rep. CMU-CS-94-163). Pittsburgh, PA, USA.

Banerjee, A. (1992). A Simple Model of Herd Behavior. *The Quarterly Journal of Economics, 107*, 797–817. doi:10.2307/2118364

Barabási, A., Albert, R., & Jeong, H. (2000). Scale-free characteristics of random networks: the topology of the World-Wide Web. *Physica A, 281*, 69–77. doi:10.1016/S0378-4371(00)00018-2

Barnett, V., & Lewis, T. (1994). *Outliers in statistical data.* New York: John Wiley & Sons.

Barricelli, N. A. (1954). Esempi numerici di processi di evoluzione. *Methodos, 6*(21-22), 45–68.

Barricelli, N. A. (1957). Symbiogenetic evolution processes realized by artificial methods. *Methodos, 9*(35-36), 143–182.

Barricelli, N. A. (1963). Numerical testing of evolution theories. Part II. Preliminary tests of performance, symbiogenesis and terrestrial life. *Acta Biotheoretica, 16*(3/4), 99–126. doi:10.1007/BF01556602

Bass, F. M. (1969). A New Product Growth Model for Consumer Durables. *Management Science, 13*(5), 215–227. doi:10.1287/mnsc.15.5.215

Baumgarte, V., Ehlers, G., May, F., Nückel, A., Vorbach, M., & Weinhardt, M. (2003). PACT XPP - a self-reconfigurable data processing architecture. *The Journal of Supercomputing, 26*(2), 167–184. doi:10.1023/A:1024499601571

Belhumeur, P. N., Hespanha, J. P., & Kriegman, D. J. (1997). Eigenfaces vs. fisherfaces: Recognition using class specific linear projection. *IEEE Transactions on Pattern Analysis and Machine Intelligence, 19*(7), 711–720. doi:10.1109/34.598228

Bell, J. E., & McMullen, P. R. (2004). Ant colony optimization techniques for the vehicle routing problem. *Advanced Engineering Informatics, 1*(8), 41–48. doi:10.1016/j.aei.2004.07.001

Bensalah, Y. (2000). *Steps in applying extreme value theory to finance: A review* (Working Notes 00-20). Bank of Canada. Retrieved from http://ideas.repec.org/p/bca/bocawp/00-20.html

Benyon, D. R., & Murray, D. M. (1993). Applying user modeling to human-computer interaction design. *Artificial Intelligence Review, 6*, 43–69.

Bertarelli, S., & Censolo, R. (2000). Preference for novelty and price behaviour (Working Papers 383). Dipartimento Scienze Economiche, Università di Bologna.

Bi, S., & Salvendy, G. (1994). Analytical model and experimental study of human workload in scheduling of advanced manufacturing systems. *International Journal of Human Factors in Manufacturing, 4,* 205–234. doi:10.1002/hfm.4530040207

Billings, C. E. (1997). *Aviation automation: The search for a human-centered approach.* New York: Lawrence Erlbaum.

Birattari, M., Stützle, T., Paquete, L., & Varrentrapp, K. (2002). A racing algorithm for configuring metaheuristics. In W. Langdon, E. Cantu-Paz, & K. Mathias (Eds.), *GECCO'02: Proceedings of the Genetic and Evolutionary Computation Conference* (pp. 11-18). San Francisco: Morgan Kaufmann.

Birgmeier, M. (1995). A fully Kalman-trained radial basis function network for nonlinear speech modeling. In *Proceedings of the IEEE International Conference on Neural Networks,* Perth, Australia (pp. 259-264).

Bishop, C. M. (1995). *Neural networks for pattern recognition.* Oxford, UK: Oxford University Press.

Bishop, C. M. (2006). *Pattern recognition and machine learning (Information science and statistics).* Berlin, Germany: Springer-Verlag.

Bledsoe, W. W. W. (1961). *Lethally dependent genes using instant selection* (Tech. Rep. No. PRI 1). Palo Alto, CA, USA: Panoramic Research Inc.

Bledsoe, W. W. W. (1961). *The use of biological concepts in the analytical study of systems* (Tech. Rep. No. PRI 2). Palo Alto, CA, USA: Panoramic Research, Inc.

Bledsoe, W. W. W. (1962). *An analysis of genetic populations.* (Tech. Rep.). Palo Alto, CA, USA: Panoramic Research Inc.

Bledsoe, W. W. W. (1962). *The evolutionary method in hill climbing: Convergence rates.* (Tech. Rep.). Palo Alto, CA, USA: Panoramic Research Inc.

Bledsoe, W. W. W., & Browning, I. (1959). Pattern recognition and reading by machine. In *Proceedings of the Eastern Joint Computer Conference (EJCC) – Papers and Discussions Presented at the Joint IRE-AIEE-ACM Computer Conference,* Boston, MA (pp. 225-232).

Bobis, C. F., Gonezalez, R. C., Cancelas, J. A., Alvarez, I., & Enguita, J. M. (1999). Face recognition using binary thresholding for features extraction. In *Proceedings of the IEEE International Conference on Image Analysis and Processing,* Venice, Italy (pp. 1077-1080).

Bonnans, J. F., Gilbert, J. C., Lemaréchal, C., & Sagastizábal, C. A. (2006). *Numerical optimization – theoretical and practical aspects.* Berlin, Germany: Springer-Verlag.

Boryczka, M. (2002). Ant colony programming for approximation problems. In *Proceedings of the Eleventh International Symposium on Intelligent Information Systems,* Sopot, Poland (pp. 147-156).

Boryczka, M. (2005). Eliminating introns in ant colony programming. *Fundamenta Informaticae, 68*(1/2), 1–19.

Boryczka, M. (2006). *Ant colony programming in the process of approximation* (in Polish). Katowice, Poland: University of Silesia.

Boryczka, M. (2008). Ant colony programming with the candidate list. In N. T. Nguyen, G.-S. Jo, R. J. Howlett, & L. C. Jain (Eds.), *Proceedings of the KES-AMSTA* (LNCS 4952, pp. 302-311). Berlin, Germany: Springer-Verlag.

Boryczka, M., & Czech, Z. (2002). Solving approximation problems by ant colony programming. In W. Langdon, E. Cantu-Paz, & K. Mathias (Eds.), *GECCO-2002: Proceedings of the Genetic and Evolutionary Computation Conference* (p. 133). San Francisco: Morgan Kaufmann.

Boryczka, M., Czech, Z., & Wieczorek, W. (2003). Ant colony programming for approximation problems. In E. Cantu-Paz (Ed.), *GECCO-2003: Proceedings of the Genetic and Evolutionary Computation Conference* (LNCS 2723-2724, pp. 142-143). Berlin, Germany: Springer-Verlag.

Box, G. E. P., & Jenkins, G. M. (1976). *Time series analysis, forecasting, and control*. San Francisco: Holden-Day.

Boyd, S., Ghosh, A., Prabhakar, B., & Shah, D. (2006). Randomized Gossip Algorithms. *IEEE Transactions on Information Theory, 52*(6), 2508–2530. doi:10.1109/TIT.2006.874516

Bremermann, H. J. (1962). Optimization through evolution and recombination. In M. C. Yovits, G. T. Jacobi, & G. D. Goldstein (Eds.), *Self-organizing systems* (pp. 93-106). Washington, DC: Spartan Books.

Brennan, R. W., Balasubramanian, S., & Norrie, D. H. (1997). Dynamic control architecture for advanced manufacturing system. In *Proceedings of the International Conference on Intelligent Systems for Advanced Manufacturing,* Pittsburgh, PA (pp. 213-223).

Brusilovsky, P. (1996). Methods and techniques of adaptive hypermedia. *User Modeling and User-Adapted Interaction, 6,* 87–129. doi:10.1007/BF00143964

Buchanam, M. (2007). *The Social Atoms*, Reed Elsevier, Inc.

Cagnoni, S., Poggi, A., & Porcari, G. L. (1999). A modified modular eigenspace approach to face recognition. In *Proceedings of the 10th International Conference on Image Analysis and Processing,* Venice, Italy (pp 490-495).

Calvagno, G., Cortelazzo, G. M., & Mian, G. A. (1995). A technique for multiple criterion approximation of fir filters in magnitude and group delay. *IEEE Transactions on Signal Processing, 43*(2), 393–400. doi:10.1109/78.348122

Cano, J. R., Herrera, F., & Lozano, M. (2003). Using evolutionary algorithms as instance selection for data reduction in KDD: An experimental study. *IEEE Transactions on Evolutionary Computation, 7*(6), 561–575. doi:10.1109/TEVC.2003.819265

Cano, J. R., Herrera, F., & Lozano, M. (2005). Stratification for scaling up evolutionary prototype selection. *Pattern Recognition Letters, 26*(7), 953–963. doi:10.1016/j.patrec.2004.09.043

Carbajal, S., & Martinez, F. (2001). Evolutive introns: A non-costly method of using introns in GP. *Genetic Programming and Evolvable Machines, 2*(2), 111–122. doi:10.1023/A:1011548229751

Cavicchio, D. J., Jr. (1970). *Adaptive search using simulated evolution*. Unpublished doctoral disseration, The University of Michigan, Ann Arbor, MI, USA.

Cavicchio, D. J., Jr. (1972). Reproductive adaptive plans. In *Proceedings of the ACM Annual Conference* (pp. 60-70). New York: ACM Press.

Cerf, V., Dalal, Y., & Sunshine, C. (1974). *Specification of Internet transmission control program* (Request for Comments (RFC) No. 675). Network Working Group.

Chakravorti, B. (2003). *The Slow Pace of Fast Change: Bringing Innovations to Market in a Connected World.* Boston, Harvard Business School Press.

Chan, P., & Stolfo, S. (1998). Toward scalable learning with non-uniform class and cost distributions: A case study in credit card fraud detection. In *Proceedings of the 4th International Conference on Knowledge Discovery and Data Mining* (pp. 164-168).

Chankong, V., & Haimes, Y. Y. (1983). *Multiobjective decision making theory and methodology.* Amsterdam: Elsevier Science.

Chatterjee, K., & Susan, H. (2004). Technology Diffusion by Learning from Neighbors. *Advances in Applied Probability, 36,* 355–376. doi:10.1239/aap/1086957576

Chellappa, R., Wilson, C. L., & Sirohey, S. (1995). Human and machine recognition of faces: A survey. *Proceedings of the IEEE, 83*(5), 705–740. doi:10.1109/5.381842

Chen, C. H., & Ting, C. J. (2006). An improved ant colony system algorithm for the vehicle routing problem. *Journal of the Chinese Institute of Industrial Engineers, 23*(2), 115–126.

Chen, J.-H., Chen, H.-M., & Ho, S.-Y. (2005). Design of nearest neighbor classifiers: Multi-objective approach. *International Journal of Approximate Reasoning, 40*(1-2), 3–22. doi:10.1016/j.ijar.2004.11.009

Chen, Y., Yang, B., & Dong, J. (2004). Evolving flexible neural networks using ant programming and PSO algorithm. In *Advances in Neural Networks — ISNN 2004* (LNCS 3173, pp. 211-216). Berlin, Germany: Springer-Verlag.

Chiuc, C., & Yih, Y. (1995). A learning based methodology for dynamic scheduling in distributed manufacturing systems. *International Journal of Production Research, 33*(11), 3217–3232. doi:10.1080/00207549508904870

Claude-Nicolas, F., & Seth, R. (2000). Learning subjective functions with large margins. In *Proceedings of the International Conference on Machine Learning,* Stanford, CA (pp. 287-294).

Coello, C. A., & Lechuga, M. S. (2002). MOPSO: A proposal for multiple objective particle swarm optimization. In *Proceedings of the Congress on Evolutionary Computation* (pp. 1051-1056).

Colizza, B., Barrat, A., Barthelemy, M., & Vespignamic, D. (2006). The role of the airline transportation network in the prediction and predictability of global epidemics . *Proceedings of the National Academy of Sciences of the United States of America, 103,* 2015–2020. doi:10.1073/pnas.0510525103

Comellas, F., & Giménez, G. (1998). Genetic programming to design communication algorithms for parallel architectures. *Parallel Processing Letters, 8*(4), 549–560. doi:10.1142/S0129626498000547

Coombs, S., & Davis, L. (1987). Genetic algorithms and communication link speed design: Constraints and operators. In *Proceedings of the 2nd International Conference on Genetic Algorithms and their Application* (pp. 257-260). Hillsdale, NJ: L. Erlbaum Associates Inc.

Cordón, O., Herrera, F., & Stützle, T. (2002). A review on the ant colony optimization metaheuristic: Basis, models and new trends. *Mathware & Soft Computing, 9*(2/3), 141–175.

Corne, D. W., Oates, M. J., & Smith, G. D. (Eds.). (2000). *Telecommunications optimization: Heuristic and adaptive techniques.* New York: John Wiley & Sons.

Cortelazzo, G., & Lightner, M. (1984). Simultaneous design in both magnitude and group-delay of IIR and FIR filters based on multiple criterion optimization. *IEEE Transactions on Acoustics, Speech, and Signal Processing, 32*(5), 949–967. doi:10.1109/TASSP.1984.1164426

Cortés Achedad, P., Onieva Giménez, L., Muñuzuri Sanz, J., & Guadix Martín, J. (2008). A revision of evolutionary computation techniques in telecommunications and an application for the network global planning problem. In A. Yang, Y. Shan, & L. T. Bui (Eds.), *Success in evolutionary computation* (pp. 239-262). Berlin, Germany: Springer-Verlag.

Cowling, P. I., & Johansson, M. (2002). Using real time information for effective dynamic scheduling. *European Journal of Operational Research, 139*(2), 230–244. doi:10.1016/S0377-2217(01)00355-1

Cowling, P. I., Ouelhadj, D., & Petrovic, S. (2003). A multi-agent architecture for dynamic scheduling of steel hot rolling. *Journal of Intelligent Manufacturing, 14,* 457–470. doi:10.1023/A:1025701325275

Cowling, P. I., Ouelhadj, D., & Petrovic, S. (2004). Dynamic scheduling of steel casting and milling using multi-agents. *Journal of Production Planning and Control, 15*(2), 178–188. doi:10.1080/09537280410001662466

Cox, L., Johnson, M., & Kafadar, K. (1982). Exposition of statistical graphics technology. In *ASA Proceedings Statistical Computation Section* (pp. 55-56).

Czarn, A., MacNish, C., Vijayan, K., Turlach, B., & Gupta, R. (2004). Statistical exploratory analysis of genetic algorithms. *IEEE Transactions on Evolutionary Computation, 8*(4), 405–421. doi:10.1109/TEVC.2004.831262

de Araújo, S. G., de Castro Pinto Pedroza, A., & de Mesquita Filho, A. C. (2003). Evolutionary synthesis of communication protocols. In *Proceedings of the 10th International Conference on Telecommunications,* Tahiti, French Polynesia (pp. 986-993).

de Araújo, S. G., de Castro Pinto Pedroza, A., & de Mesquita Filho, A. C. (2003). Uma metodologia de projeto de protocolos de comunicação baseada em técnicas evolutivas. In *Proceedings of the XX Simpósio Brasileiro de Telecomunicaçãoes*, Rio de Janeiro, Brazil.

Deb, K., Pratap, A., Agarwal, S., & Meyarivan, T. (2002). A fast and elitist multiobjective genetic algorithm: NSGA-II. *IEEE Transactions on Evolutionary Computation, 6*(2), 182–197. doi:10.1109/4235.996017

Deczky, A. (1972). Synthesis of recursive digital filters using the minimum p-error criterion. *IEEE Transactions on Audio and Electroacoustics, 20*(4), 257–263. doi:10.1109/TAU.1972.1162392

Deczky, A. (1974). Equiripple and minimax (Chebyshev) approximations for recursive digital filters. *IEEE Transactions on Acoustics, Speech, and Signal Processing, 22*(2), 98–111. doi:10.1109/TASSP.1974.1162556

Demsar, J. (2006). Statistical comparisons of classifiers over multiple data sets. *Journal of Machine Learning Research, 7*, 1–30.

Dennis, J. E., & Schnabel, R. B. (1983). *Numerical methods for unconstrained optimization and nonlinear equations*. Upper Saddle River, NJ: Prentice-Hall.

Di Caro, G. (2004). *Ant colony optimization and its application to adaptive routing in telecommunication networks*. Unpublished doctoral dissertation, Université Libre de Bruxelles, Brussels, Belgium.

Di Caro, G., & Dorigo, M. (1998a). Antnet: Distributed stigmergetic control for communications networks. [JAIR]. *Journal of Artificial Intelligence Research, 9*, 317–365.

Di Caro, G., & Dorigo, M. (1998b). Two ant colony algorithms for best-effort routing in datagram networks. In *Proceedings of the 10th IASTED International Conference on Parallel and Distributed Computing and Systems* (pp. 541-546). Calgary, Canada: ACTA Press.

Dijkstra, E. W. (1959). A note on two problems in connexion with graphs. *Numerische Mathematik, 1*, 269–271. doi:10.1007/BF01386390

Diniz, P. S. R., da Silva, E. A. B., & Lima Netto, S. (2004). *Processamento digital de sinais - projeto e análise de sistemas*. Porto Alegre, Brazil: Bookman.

Donthi, S., & Haggard, R. (2003). A survey of dynamically reconfigurable FPGA devices. In *Proceedings of the 35th Southeastern Symposium on System Theory* (pp. 422-426).

Dorigo, M., & Gambardella, L. (1997). Ant colony system: A cooperative learning approach to the traveling salesman problem. *IEEE Transactions on Evolutionary Computation, 1*, 53–66. doi:10.1109/4235.585892

Dorigo, M., Maniesco, V., & Colorni, A. (1991). Distributed optimization by ant colonies. In *Proceedings of the European Conference on Artificial Life*, Paris, France (pp. 134-142).

Dorigo, M., Maniezzo, V., & Colorni, A. (1991). *Positive feedback as a search strateg.* (Tech. Rep. 91–016). Milano, Italy: Politechnico di Milano.

Durrent, R. (2007). *Random Graph Dynamics*, Cambridge University Press.

Eeckelaert, T., McConaghy, T., & Gielen, G. (2005). Efficient multiobjective snthesis of analog circuits using hierarchical pareto-optimal performance hypersurfaces. *Design, Automation and Test in Europe*, (2), 1070-1075.

Eggermont, J., Kok, J., & Kosters, W. (2004). Detecting and pruning introns for faster decision tree evolution. In X. Yao, E. Burke, J. Lozano, J. Smith, J. Merelo-Guervós, J. Bullinaria, J. Rowe, P. T. A. Kabán, & H.-P. Schwefel (Eds.), *Parallel Problem Solving from Nature — PPSN VIII* (LNCS 3242, pp. 1068-1077). Berlin, Germany: Springer-Verlag.

Ehrgott, M., & Gandibleaux, X. (Eds.). (2002). *Multiple criteria optimization: State of the art*. Amsterdam: Kluwer Academic Publishers.

El-Fakihy, K., Yamaguchi, H., & von Bochmann, G. (1999). A method and a genetic algorithm for deriving protocols for distributed applications with minimum communication cost. In *Proceedings of 11th IASTED International Conference on Parallel and Distributed Computing and Systems* (pp. 863-868). Calgary, Canada: ACTA Press.

Ellison, G. (1993). Learning, Local Interaction, and Coordination. *Econometrica*, *61*(5), 1047–1071. doi:10.2307/2951493

Endsley, M. R. (1998). Situation awareness global assessment technique (SAGAT). In *Proceedings of the National Aerospace and Electronics Conference*, Dayton, OH (pp. 789-795).

Engelbrecht, A. (2005). *Fundamentals of computational swarm intelligence*. New York: John Wiley & Sons.

Engelbrecht, A. (2007). *Computational intelligence: An introduction*. New York: John Wiley & Sons.

Er, M. J., Chen, W. L., & Wu, S. Q. (2005). High-speed face recognition based on discrete cosine transform and RBF neural network. *IEEE Transactions on Neural Networks*, *16*(3), 679–691. doi:10.1109/TNN.2005.844909

Er, M. J., Wu, S., Lu, J., & Toh, H. L. (2002). Face recognition with radial basis function (RBF) neural networks. *IEEE Transactions on Neural Networks*, *13*(3), 697–710. doi:10.1109/TNN.2002.1000134

Ergin, S., & Gülmezoğlu, M. B. (2008). Face recognition based on face partitions using common vector approach. In *Proceedings of the 3rd International Symposium on Communications, Control and Signal Processing*, St. Julians, Malta (pp. 624-628).

Eshelman, L. J. (1991). The CHC adaptative search algorithm: How to have safe search when engaging in nontraditional genetic recombination. In G. J. E. Rawlins (Ed.), *Foundations of genetic algorithms* (pp. 265-283).

Fakhfakh, M. (2008). A novel alienor-based heuristic for the optimal design of analog circuits. *Microelectronics Journal*, *40*(1), 141–148. doi:10.1016/j.mejo.2008.07.007

Fakhfakh, M., Loulou, M., & Tlelo-Cuautle, E. (2007). Synthesis of CCIIs and design of simulated CCII based floating inductances. In *Proceedings of the IEEE ICECS*, Marrakech, Morocco (pp. 379-382).

Fisher, R. A., & Tippett, L. (1928). Limiting forms for the frequency distribution of the largest or smallest member of a sample. *Proceedings of the Cambridge Philosophical Society*, *24*, 180–190. doi:10.1017/S0305004100015681

Fitts, P. M. (1951). *Human engineering for an effective air-navigation and traffic-control system*. Columbus, OH: Ohio State University Press.

Fletcher, R. (1980). *Practical methods of optimization: Volume 1 – unconstrained optimization*. New York: John Wiley & Sons.

Flexer, A., Pampalk, E., & Widmer, G. (2005). Novelty detection based on spectral similarity of songs. In *Proceedings of 6th International Conference on Music Information Retrieval* (pp. 260-263).

Fogel, L. J., Owens, A. J., & Walsh, M. J. (1966). *Artificial intelligence through simulated evolution*. New York: John Wiley & Sons.

Folino, G., Pizzuti, C., & Spezzano, G. (2005). GP ensemble for distributed intrusion detection systems. In *Proceedings of the 3rd International Conference on Advances in Pattern Recognition* (LNCS Vol. 3686, pp. 54-62). Berlin, Germany: Springer-Verlag.

Forsyth, R. (1981). BEAGLE a darwinian approach to pattern recognition. *Kybernetes*, *10*, 159–166. doi:10.1108/eb005587

Forsyth, R. (1989). The evolution of intelligence. In R. Forsyth (Ed.), *Machine learning, principles and techniques* (pp. 65-82). Boca Raton, FL: Chapman and Hall.

Forsyth, R., & Rada, R. (1986). *Machine learning applications in expert systems and information retrieval*. Chichester, UK: Ellis Horwood.

Francisco-Revilla, L., & Shipman, F. M. (2000). Adaptive medical information delivery combining user, task, and situation model. In *Proceedings of International Conference on Intelligent User Interfaces*, New Orleans, LA (pp. 94-97).

Frantz, D. R. (1972). *Nonlinearities in genetic adaptive search*. Unpublished doctoral disseratation, The University of Michigan, Ann Arbor, MI, USA.

Fraser, A. S. (1957). Simulation of genetic systems by automatic digital computers. *Australian Journal of Biological Sciences*, *10*, 484–491.

Freitas, A. A. (2002). *Data mining and knowledge discovery with evolutionary algorithms.* Berlin, Germany: Springer-Verlag.

Freund, Y., & Schapire, R. E. (1996). Experiments with a new boosting algorithm. In *Proceedings of the 13th International Conference on Machine Learning,* Bari, Italy (pp. 148-156).

Friedberg, R. M. (1958). A learning machine: Part I. *IBM Journal of Research and Development, 2,* 2–13.

Friedberg, R. M., Dunham, B., & North, J. H. (1959). A learning machine: Part II. *IBM Journal of Research and Development, 3*(3), 282–287.

Fukunaga, K. (1990). *Introduction to statistical pattern recognition* (2nd ed.). San Diego, CA: Academic Press Professional.

Gambardella, L., & Dorigo, M. (1996). Solving symmetric and asymmetric TSPs by ant colonies. In *Proceedings of the IEEE Conference on Evolutionary Computation* (pp. 622-627). Washington, DC: IEEE Press.

Gamon, M. (2006). Graph-based text representation for novelty detection. In *Proceedings of TextGraphs: the Second Workshop on Graph Based Methods for Natural Language Processing* (pp. 17-24). New York: Association for Computational Linguistics.

García, S., Cano, J. R., & Herrera, F. (2008). A memetic algorithm for evolutionary prototype selection: A scaling up approach. *Pattern Recognition, 41*(8), 2693–2709. doi:10.1016/j.patcog.2008.02.006

García-Pedrajas, N., & Ortiz-Boyer, D. (2007). A cooperative constructive method for neural networks for pattern recognition. *Pattern Recognition, 40*(1), 80–98. doi:10.1016/j.patcog.2006.06.024

General Secretariat of the Council of the European Union. COST Secretariat. (1994). *Cost 1991–1992* (Vol. 7). Luxembourg: Office for Official Publications of the European Communities.

Gershenson, C. (2002). Classification of random Boolean networks. In *Artificial Life VIII: Proceedings of the 8th International Conference on Artificial Life* (pp. 1-8).

Gervasio, T. M., Iba, W., & Langley, P. (1999). Learning user evaluation functions for adaptive scheduling assistance. In *Proceedings of the International Conference on Machine Learning,* Bled, Slovenia (pp. 121-126).

Ghosh, A., & Jain, L. C. (Eds.). (2005). *Evolutionary computation in data mining.* Berlin, Germany: Springer-Verlag.

Ghosh, D., & Patranabis, D. (1992). Software based linearisation of thermistor type nonlinearity. *IEE Proceedings-G, Circuits, Devices and Systems, 139*(3), 339–342.

Gnutella. (2000). *The Gnutella protocol specification v0.4* [Computer software manual].

Goeke, M., Sipper, M., Mange, D., Stauffer, A., Sanchez, E., & Tomassini, M. (1997). Online autonomous evolware. In *Evolvable Systems: From Biology to Hardware* (LNCS 1259, pp. 96-106). Berlin, Germany: Springer-Verlag.

Goldberg, D. E. (1989). *Genetic algorithms in search, optimization, and machine learning.* Reading, MA: Addison-Wesley Longman Publishing Co., Inc.

Goldberg, D. E. (2002). *The design of competent genetic algorithms: Steps toward a computational theory of innovation.* Amsterdam: Kluwer Academic Publishers.

Goldberg, D. E., & Deb, K. (1991). A comparative analysis of selection schemes used in genetic algorithms. In G. J. E. Rawlins (Ed.), *Foundations of genetic algorithms* (pp. 69-93).

Goldsmith, A. (2005). *Wireless communications.* Cambridge, UK: Cambridge University Press.

Golub, T. R., Slonim, D. K., Tamayo, P., Huard, C., Gaasenbeek, M., & Mesirov, J. P. (1999). Molecular classification of cancer: Class discovery and class prediction by gene expression monitoring. *Science, 286*(5439), 531–537. doi:10.1126/science.286.5439.531

Gómez-Ballester, E., Micó, L., & Oncina, J. (2006). Some approaches to improve tree-based nearest neighbour search algorithms. *Pattern Recognition, 39*(2), 171–179. doi:10.1016/j.patcog.2005.06.007

Grace, P. (2000). *Genetic programming and protocol configuration*. Unpublished master's thesis, Lancaster University, Lancaster, UK.

Greenfield, A. (2006). *Everyware: The dawning age of ubiquitous computing*. Berkeley, CA: New Riders Publishing.

Grochowski, M., & Jankowski, N. (2004). Comparison of instance selection algorithms II. Results and comments. In *Proceedings of the International Conference on Artificial Intelligence and Soft Computing* (LNCS 3070, pp. 580-585). Berlin, Germany: Springer-Verlag.

Guerra-Gómez, I., Tlelo-Cuautle, E., Li, P., & Gielen, G. (2008). Simulation-based optimization of UGCs performances. In *Proceedings of the IEEE ICCDCS*, Cancun, México (pp. 1-4).

Gul, A. B. (2003). *Holistic face recognition by dimension reduction*. Unpublished master's thesis, the Middle East Technical University.

Haddow, P., & Tufte, G. (2000). An evolvable hardware FPGA for adaptive hardware. In *Proceedings of the IEEE Congress on Evolutionary Computation* (pp. 553-560).

Haddow, P., Tufte, G., & Remortel, P. V. (2001). Shrinking the genotype:L-systems for EHW? In *Proceedings of the 4th International Conference on Evolvable Systems: From Biology to Hardware* (pp. 128-139).

Hafed, Z. M., & Levine, M. D. (2001). Face recognition using the discrete cosine transform. *International Journal of Computer Vision*, *43*(3), 167–188. doi:10.1023/A:1011183429707

Haftka, R. T., & Gürdal, Z. (1992). *Elements of structural optimization*. Amsterdam: Kluwer Academic Publishers.

Hagan, M. T., & Menhaj, M. B. (1994). Training feedforward networks with the Marquardt algorithm. *IEEE Transactions on Neural Networks*, *5*(6), 989–993. doi:10.1109/72.329697

Hall, B. (2004). Innovation and Diffusion, *Handbook of Innovation*, In Fagerberg, J., D. Mowery, and R. R. Nelson (eds.), Oxford University Press.

Hansen, J. V., Lowry, P. B., Meservy, R., & McDonald, D. (2007). Genetic programming for prevention of cyberterrorism through previous dynamic and evolving intrusion detection. *Decision Support Systems*, *43*(4), 1362–1374. doi:10.1016/j.dss.2006.04.004

Happel, B., & Murre, J. (1994). Design and evolution of modular neural network architectures. *Neural Networks*, *7*(6/7), 985–1004. doi:10.1016/S0893-6080(05)80155-8

Harke, W. (2003). *Smart home – vernetzung von haustechnik und kommunikationssystemen im wohnungsbau*. Hüthig Verlag/C. F. Müller.

Harper, R. (Ed.). (2003). *Inside the smart home*. Berlin, Germany: Springer-Verlag.

Hart, S. G., & Staveland, L. E. (1988). Development of NASA-TLX: Results of experimental and theoretical research. In *Human mental workload*. Amsterdam, The Netherlands.

Hart, W. E. (1994). *Adaptive global optimization with local search*. Unpublished doctoral dissertation, University of California, San Diego.

Hasselmann, K. (1997). Multi-pattern fingerprint method for detection and attribution of climate change. *Climate Dynamics*, *13*(9), 601–611. doi:10.1007/s003820050185

Haykin, S. (1994). *Neural networks: A comprehensive foundation*. Upper Saddle River, NJ: Prentice Hall.

Hayton, P., Scholkopf, B., Tarassenko, L., & Anuzis, P. (2000). Support vector novelty detection applied to jet engine vibration spectra. In *Advances in Neural Information Processing Systems* (pp. 946-952).

Heady, R., Luger, G., Maccabe, A., & Servilla, M. (1990). *The architecture of a network level intrusion detection system* (Tech. Rep. No. CS90-20, LA-SUB–93-219, W-7405-ENG-36, DE97002400). Department of Computer Science, University of New Mexico, USA.

Hebb, D. O. (1949). *The organization of behavior*. New York: John Wiley.

Hecht-Nielsen, R. (1989). Theory of the backpropagation neural network. In *Proceedings of the International Joint*

Conference on Neural Networks, 1, 593–606. doi:10.1109/IJCNN.1989.118638

Hedrick, C. (1988). *Routing information protocol* (Request for Comments (RFC) No. 1058). Internet Engineering Task Force (IETF), Internet Society (ISOC).

Heitkötter, J., & Beasley, D. (Eds.). (1998). *Hitch-hiker's guide to evolutionary computation: A list of frequently asked questions (FAQ).* ENCORE (The EvolutioNary Computation REpository Network).

Heywood, M. I., & Zincir-Heywood, A. N. (2002). Dynamic page-based linear genetic programming. *IEEE Transactions on Systems, Man, and Cybernetics. Part B, Cybernetics, 32*(3), 380–388. doi:10.1109/TSMCB.2002.999814

Ho, S.-Y., Liu, C.-C., & Liu, S. (2002). Design of an optimal nearest neighbor classifier using an intelligent genetic algorithm. *Pattern Recognition Letters, 23*(13), 1495–1503. doi:10.1016/S0167-8655(02)00109-5

Hodge, V., & Austin, J. (2004). A survey of outlier detection methodologies. *Artificial Intelligence Review, 22*(2), 85–126.

Holland, J. H. (1962). Outline for a logical theory of adaptive systems. *Journal of the ACM, 9*(3), 297–314. doi:10.1145/321127.321128

Holland, J. H. (1967). *Nonlinear environments permitting efficient adaptation (Vol. II).* New York: Academic Press.

Holland, J. H. (1969). Adaptive plans optimal for payoff-only environments. In *Proceedings of the 2ⁿᵈ Hawaii International Conference on System Sciences, Periodicals,* North Hollywood, CA (pp. 917-920).

Holland, J. H. (1975). *Adaptation in natural and artificial systems: An introductory analysis with applications to biology, control, and artificial intelligence.* Ann Arbor, MI: The University of Michigan Press.

Hörner, H. (1996). *A C++ class library for GP: Vienna University of economics genetic programming kernel (release 1.0, operating instructions)* (Tech. Rep.). Vienna University of Economics.

Hornik, K., Stinchcombe, M., & White, H. (1989). Multilayer feedforward networks are universal approximations. *Neural Networks, 2,* 359–366. doi:10.1016/0893-6080(89)90020-8

Horvitz, E. (1999). Principles of mixed-initiative user interfaces. In *Proceedings of Human Factors in Computing Systems,* Pittsburgh, PA (pp. 159-166).

Hu, W., Farooq, O., & Datta, S. (2008). Wavelet based sub-space features for face recognition. In *Proceedings of the International Congress on Image and Signal Processing,* Sanya, Hainan, China (pp. 426-430).

Hubner, M., Paulsson, K., Stitz, M., & Becker, J. (2005). Novel seamless design-flow for partial and dynamic reconfigurable systems with customized communication structures based on Xilinx Virtex-II FPGAs. In *System Aspects in Organic and Pervasive Computing, Workshop Proceedings* (pp. 39-44).

Huebner, U., Klische, W., Abraham, N. B., & Weiss, C. O. (1989). Comparison of Lorenz-like laser behavior with the Lorenz model. In *Coherence and Quantum Optics VI* (p. 517). New York: Plenum Press.

Hughes, G., Murray, J., Kreutz-Delgado, K., & Elkan, C. (2002). Improved disk-drive failure warnings. *IEEE Transactions on Reliability, 51*(3), 350–357. doi:10.1109/TR.2002.802886

Iba, H. (1996). Emergent cooperation for multiple agents using genetic programming. In *PPSN IV: Proceedings of the 4ᵗʰ International Conference on Parallel Problem Solving from Nature* (pp. 32-41). Berlin, Germany: Springer-Verlag.

Iba, H. (1998). Evolutionary learning of communicating agents. *Information Sciences – Informatics and Computer Science . International Journal (Toronto, Ont.), 108*(1-4), 181–205.

Iba, H., & Terao, M. (2000). Controlling elective introns for multi-agent learning by genetic programming. In D. Whitley, D. Goldberg, E. Cantu-Paz, L. Spector, I. Parmee, & H.-G. Beyer (Eds.), *GECCO-2000: Proceedings of the Genetic and Evolutionary Computation Conference* (pp. 419-426). San Francisco: Morgan Kaufmann.

Iba, H., Nozoe, T., & Ueda, K. (1997). Evolving communicating agents based on genetic programming. In *Proceedings of the IEEE International Conference on Evolutionary Computation* (pp. 297-302). Piscataway, NJ: IEEE Press.

Igel, C., & Toussaint, M. (2005). A no-free-lunch theorem for non-uniform distributions of target functions. *Journal of Mathematical Modelling and Algorithms, 3*(4), 313–322. doi:10.1007/s10852-005-2586-y

Iles, M., & Deugo, D. L. (2002). A search for routing strategies in a peer-to-peer network using genetic programming. In *Proceedings of the 21st IEEE Symposium on Reliable Distributed Systems* (pp. 341-346). Washington, DC: IEEE Computer Society.

Ilyas, M., & Mahgoub, I. (Eds.). (2004). *Handbook of sensor networks: Compact wireless and wired sensing systems*. Boca Raton, FL: CRC Press.

Iman, R. L., & Davenport, J. M. (1980). Approximations of the critical region of the friedman statistic. *Communications in Statistics, A9*(6), 571–595. doi:10.1080/03610928008827904

Immorica, N., Kleinberg, M., & Mahdian, M. (2007). The Role of Compatibility in the Diffusion of Technologies through Social Networks. *Proceedings of the 8th ACM conference on Electronic commerce*, pages 75-83, ACM Press, New York.

Information Sciences Institute. University of Southern California, (1981). *Internet protocol, DARPA Internet program protocol specification* (RFC No. 791). Defense Advanced Research Projects Agency, Information Processing Techniques Office, Arlington, USA.

Ingber, L. (1989). Very fast simulated re-annealing. *Mathematical and Computer Modelling, 12*(8), 967–973. doi:10.1016/0895-7177(89)90202-1

Ishibuchi, H., & Nakashima, T. (1999). Evolution of reference sets in nearest neighbor classification. In *Proceedings of the Second Asia-Pacific Conference on Simulated Evolution and Learning on Simulated Evolution and Learning* (LNCS 1585, pp. 82-89). Berlin, Germany: Springer-Verlag.

ISO. (1993). Information technology – security techniques – entity authentication – part 3: Mechanisms using digital signature techniques (ISO/IEC No. 9798-3). *International Standards Organization (ISO)*. (JTC 1 Information technology. TC/SC: JTC 1/SC 27. Status: withdrawn)

Itti, L., & Baldi, P. (2005). A principled approach to detecting surprising events in video. In *Proceedings of the IEEE Computer Society Conference on Computer Vision and Pattern Recognition (CVPR'05) - Volume 1* (pp. 631-637). Washington, DC: IEEE Computer Society.

Jackson, M., & Yariv, L. (2008). *Diffusion, Strategic Interaction and Social Structure*, TR-Stanford University.

Jaeger, H., & Haas, H. (2004). Harnessing nonlinearity: Predicting chaotic systems and saving energy in wireless communication. *Science, 304*(5667), 78–80. doi:10.1126/science.1091277

Jain, L. C., Halici, U., Hayashi, I., Lee, S. B., & Tsutsui, S. (1999). *Intelligent biometric techniques in fingerprint and face recognition*. Boca Raton, FL: CRC Press.

Jang, J. S. R. (1993). ANFIS: Adaptive network based fuzzy inference system. *IEEE Transactions on Systems, Man, and Cybernetics, 23*(3), 665–685. doi:10.1109/21.256541

Jankowski, N. (1999). Approximation and classification with RBF-type neural networks using flexible local and semi-local transfer functions In *Proceedings of the Fourth Conference on Neural Networks and Their Applications* (pp. 77-82).

Jaroš, J., & Dvořák, V. (2008). An evolutionary design technique for collective communications on optimal diameter-degree networks. In *Proceedings of the Genetic and Evolutionary Computation Conference* (pp. 1539-1546). New York: ACM Press.

Javagroups – a reliable multicast communication toolkit for Java [Computer Software Manual]. (1999–2008). Cornell University and SourceForge.

Jelinek, F. (1997). *Statistical methods for speech recognition*. Cambridge, MA: MIT Press.

Kaber, B. D., & Riley, J. M. (1999). Adaptive automation of a dynamic control task based on workload assessment through a secondary monitoring task. In *Automation technology and human performance: Current research trends* (pp. 55-78). Mahwah, NJ.

Kaber, B. D., Prinzel, L. J., Wright, C. M., & Clamann, M. P. (2002). *Workload-matched adaptive automation support of air traffic controller information processing stages* (NASA/TM 2002-211932).

Kampstra, P. (2005). *Evolutionary computing in telecommunications – a likely EC success story.* Unpublished master's thesis, Vrije Universiteit, Amsterdam, the Netherlands.

Kampstra, P., van der Mei, R. D., & Eiben, Á. E. (2006). *Evolutionary computing in telecommunication network design: A survey.* Retrieved from http://www.few.vu.nl/~mei/articles/2006/kampstra/art.pdf

Katona, Z., Zubcsek, P., & Sarvary, M. (2007). *Joining the Network: Personal Influences as Determinants of Diffusion*, Technical Report, UC Berkeley.

Kaufmann, G. (2004). Two kinds of creativity - but which ones? *Creativity and Innovation Management, 13*(3), 154–165. doi:10.1111/j.0963-1690.2004.00305.x

Keber, C., & Schuster, M. G. (2002). Option valuation with generalized ant programming. In *GECCO-2002: Proceedings of the Genetic and Evolutionary Computation Conference* (pp. 74-81). San Francisco: Morgan Kaufmann.

Kecman, V. (2001). *Learning and soft computing.* Cambridge, MA: MIT Press.

Kennedy, J., Eberhart, R. C., & Shi, Y. (2001). *Swarm intelligence.* San Francisco: Morgan Kaufmann Publishers.

Kennedy, J., Eberhart, R. C., & Shi, Y. (2001). *Swarm intelligence.* Menlo Park, CA: Morgan Kaufmann.

Kershenbaum, A. (1993). *Telecommunications network design algorithms.* New York: McGraw-Hill.

Khan, S. A., Shahani, D. T., & Agarwala, A. K. (2002). Sensor calibration and compensation using artificial neural networks. *ISA Transactions, 42*(3), 337–352. doi:10.1016/S0019-0578(07)60138-4

Khuri, S., & Chiu, T. (1997). Heuristic algorithms for the terminal assignment problem. In *Proceedings of the ACM Symposium on Applied Computing* (pp. 247-251). New York: ACM Press.

Kim, J. B., & Kim, H. J. (2002). Efficient image segmentation based on wavelet and watersheds for video objects extraction. In *Developments in applied artificial intelligence* (LNCS 2358, pp. 67-76). Berlin, Germany: Springer.

Kim, S.-W., & Oommen, B. J. (2007). On using prototype reduction schemes to optimize dissimilarity-based classification. *Pattern Recognition, 40*(11), 2946–2957. doi:10.1016/j.patcog.2007.03.006

Kirby, M., & Sirovich, L. (1990). Application of the Karhunen-Loeve procedure for the characterization of human faces. *IEEE Transactions on Pattern Analysis and Machine Intelligence, 12*, 103–108. doi:10.1109/34.41390

Kirkwood, I. M. A., Shami, S. H., & Sinclair, M. C. (1997). Discovering simple fault-tolerant routing rules using genetic programming. In *Proceedings of the International Conference on Artificial Neural Networks and Genetic Algorithms,* Norwich, UK (pp. 285-288).

Klasing, R., Monien, B., Peine, R., & Stöhr, E. (1992). Broadcasting in butterfly and de Bruijn networks. In A. Finkel & M. Jantzen (Eds.), *Proceedings of 9th Annual Symposium on Theoretical Aspects of Computer Science* (pp. 351-362). Berlin, Germany: Springer-Verlag.

Ko, H., Baran, R., & Arozullah, M. (1992). Neural network based novelty filtering for signal detection enhancement. In *Proceedings of the 35th Midwest Symposium on Circuits and Systems* (Vol. 1, pp. 252-255).

Kohonen, T. (1997). *Self-organizing maps.* Berlin, Germany: Springer-Verlag.

Kosko, B. (1994). Fuzzy systems as universal approximators. *IEEE Transactions on Computers, 43*(11), 1329–1333. doi:10.1109/12.324566

Koza, J. (1992). *Genetic programming: On the programming of computers by natural selection.* Cambridge, MA: The MIT Press.

Koza, J. R. (1988). *Non-linear genetic algorithms for solving problems.* Washington, DC: United States Patent and Trademark Office.

Koza, J. R. (1989). Hierarchical Genetic Algorithms Operating on Populations of Computer Programs. *Proceedings of the 11th International Joint Conference on Artificial Intelligence* (pp. 768–774). Detroit, USA.

Koza, J. R. (1990). Evolution and co-evolution of computer programs to control independent-acting agents. In *From Animals to Animats: Proceedings of the 1st International Conference on Simulation of Adaptive Behavior,* Paris, France (pp. 366-375).

Koza, J. R. (1990). Genetic evolution and co-evolution of computer programs. In *Artificial Life II: Proceedings of the Workshop on Artificial Life,* Santa Fe, NM (pp. 603-629).

Koza, J. R. (1990). *The genetic programming paradigm: Genetically breeding populations of computer programs to solve problems.* (Tech. Rep. No. STAN-CS-90-1314). Computer Science Department, Stanford University, USA.

Koza, J. R. (1990). A hierarchical approach to learning the Boolean multiplexer function. In *Proceedings of the 1st Workshop on Foundations of Genetic Algorithms,* Indiana, USA (pp. 171-191).

Koza, J. R. (1992). *Genetic programming: On the programming of computers by means of natural selection.* Cambridge, mA: The MIT Press.

Koza, J. R., Jones, L. W., Keane, M. A., Streeter, M. J., & Al-Sakran, A. H. (2004). Toward automated design of industrial-strength analog circuits by means of genetic programming. In *Genetic programming theory and practice II* (pp. 121-142). Amsterdam: Kluwer Academic Publishers.

Krumm, J., Abowd, G. D., Seneviratne, A., & Strang, T. (Eds.). (2007). *Proceedings of the 9th International Conference on Ubiquitous Computing* (LNCS 4717). Berlin, Germany: Springer-Verlag.

Kullback, S. (1959). *Information theory and statistics.* New York: John Wiley and Sons.

Kumar, A., Pathak, R. M., Gupta, M. C., & Gupta, Y. P. (1993). Genetic algorithm based approach for designing computer network topologies. In *Proceedings of the ACM Conference on Computer Science* (pp. 358-365). New York: ACM Press.

Kumar, P., & Senani, R. (2002). Bibliography on nullors and their applications in circuit analysis, synthesis and design. *Analog Integrated Circuits and Signal Processing, 33*(1), 65–76. doi:10.1023/A:1020337229998

Kuncheva, L. I. (1995). Editing for the k-nearest neighbors rule by a genetic algorithm. *Pattern Recognition Letters, 16,* 809–814. doi:10.1016/0167-8655(95)00047-K

Kuncheva, L. I., & Bezdek, J. C. (1998). Nearest prototype classification: Clustering, genetic algorithms, or random search? *IEEE Transactions on Systems, Man, and Cybernetics, 28*(1), 160–164. doi:10.1109/5326.661099

Lakatos, I. (1978). History of science and its rational reconstructions. In J. Worrall & G. Currie (Eds.), *The methodology of scientific research programmes: Philosophical research papers vol. 1* (pp. 102-138). Cambridge, UK: The Press Syndicate of the University of Cambridge.

Lamont, G. B., & Coello, C. A. (2007). *Evolutionary algorithms for solving multi objective problems.* Berlin, Germany: Springer-Verlag.

Lane, T. (1999). Hidden Markov models for human/computer interface modeling. In *IJCAI-99 Workshop on Learning About Users* (pp. 35-44).

Langton, C. G. (1995). *Artificial life: An overview. Complex adaptive systems.* Cambridge, MA: MIT Press.

Laois, L., & Giannacourou, M. (1995). Perceived effects of advanced ATC functions on human activities: Results of a survey on controllers and experts. In *Proceedings of International Symposium on Aviation Psychology,* Columbus, OH (pp. 392-397).

LaRoche, P., & Zincir-Heywood, A. N. (2005). 802.11 network intrusion detection using genetic programming. In *Proceedings of the Workshops on Genetic and Evolutionary Computation* (pp. 170-171). New York: ACM Press.

Lau, K.-M., & Weng, H. (1995). Climate signal detection using wavelet transform: How to make a time series sing. *Bulletin of the American Meteorological Society, 76*(12), 2391–2402. doi:10.1175/1520-0477(1995)076<2391:CSDUWT>2.0.CO;2

Lauer, M. (2001). A mixture approach to novelty detection using training data with outliers. In *Proceedings of the 12th European Conference on Machine Learning (ECML '01)*, London, UK (pp. 300-311). Berlin, Germany: Springer-Verlag.

Law, A. M., & Kelton, W. D. (2000). *Simulation modeling and analysis* (3rd ed.). New York: McGraw Hill.

Lawrence, S., Giles, C. L., & Tsoi, A. C. (1996). *What size neural network gives optimal generalization? Convergence properties of backpropagation* (Tech. Rep. UMIACS-TR-96-22 & CS-TR-3617). Institute for Advanced Computer Studies, University of Maryland. Lawrence, S., Giles, C. L., Tsoi, A. C., & Back, A. D. (1997). Face recognition: A convolutional neural-network approach. *IEEE Transactions on Neural Networks, 8*, 98–113. doi:10.1109/72.554195

Lee, S., & Kil, R. M. (1991). A Gaussian potential function network with hierarchically self-organizing learning. *Neural Networks, 4*(2), 207–224. doi:10.1016/0893-6080(91)90005-P

Lehmann, K. A., & Kaufmann, M. (2005). Evolutionary algorithms for the self-organized evolution of networks. In *Proceedings of the Conference on Genetic and Evolutionary Computation* (pp. 563-570). New York: ACM Press.

Leonard, J. A., & Kramer, M. A. (1991, April). Radial basis function networks for classifying process faults. *IEEE Control Systems Magazine, 11*, 31–38. doi:10.1109/37.75576

Leong, W. F., & Yen, G. G. (2008). PSO-based multiobjective optimization with dynamic population size and adaptive local archives. *IEEE Transactions on Systems, Man, and Cybernetics. Part B, Cybernetics, 38*, 1270–1293. doi:10.1109/TSMCB.2008.925757

Li, D. (1996). Convexification of a noninferior frontier. *Journal of Optimization Theory and Applications, 88*(1), 177–196. doi:10.1007/BF02192028

Li, J. B., Chu, S. C., & Pan, J. S. (2007). Facial texture feature based face recognition with common vector analysis in the kernel space. In *Proceedings of the 2nd IEEE International Conference on Industrial Electronics and Applications,* Harbin, China (pp. 714-718).

Liang, S., Zincir-Heywood, A. N., & Heywood, M. I. (2002). The effect of routing under local information using a social insect metaphor. In *Proceedings of the Congress on Evolutionary Computation* (pp. 1438-1443). Washington, DC: IEEE Computer Society.

Liang, S., Zincir-Heywood, A. N., & Heywood, M. I. (2006). Adding more intelligence to the network routing problem: Antnet and Ga-Agents. *Applied Soft Computing, 6*(3), 244–257. doi:10.1016/j.asoc.2005.01.005

Lin, S. H., Kung, S. Y., & Lin, L. J. (1997). Face recognition/detection by probabilistic decision- based neural network. *IEEE Transactions on Neural Networks, 8*, 114–132. doi:10.1109/72.554196

Lindgren, C., & Nordahl, M. (1990). Universal computation in simple one dimensional cellular automata. *Complex Systems, 4*, 299–318.

Liu, B., Wang, Y., Yu, Z., Liu, L., Li, M., Wang, Z., Lu, J., & Fernández, F. V. (2009). Analog circuit optimization system based on hybrid evolutionary algorithms. *INTEGRATION, the VLSI journal, 42*(2), 137-148.

Liu, H., & Motoda, H. (2002). On issues of instance selection. *Data Mining and Knowledge Discovery, 6*(2), 115–130. doi:10.1023/A:1014056429969

Liu, Y., & Yao, X. (1997). Evolving modular neural networks which generalize well. In *Proceedings of the IEEE Conference on Evolutionary Computation* (pp. 605-610).

Lobo, F., Deb, K., Goldberg, D., Harik, G., & Wang, L. (1998). Compressed introns in a linkage learning genetic algorithm. In J. Koza, W. Banzhaf, K. Chellapilla, K. Deb, M. Dorigo, D. Fogel, M. Garzon, D. Goldberg, H. Iba, & R. Riolo (Eds.), *Genetic Programming 1998: Proceedings of the Third Annual Conference* (pp. 551-558). San Francisco: Morgan Kaufmann.

Lopetz-Pintado, D. (2006). Contagion and coordination in random networks . *International Journal of Game Theory, 34*, 371–382. doi:10.1007/s00182-006-0026-5

López-Pintado, D., & Watts, D. J. (2005). *Social influence and random networks.* Mimeo, Columbia University.

Lozano, M., Sotoca, J. M., Sánchez, J. S., Pla, F., Pekalska, E., & Duin, R. P. W. (2006). Experimental study on prototype optimisation algorithms for prototype-based classification in vector spaces. *Pattern Recognition, 39*(10), 1827–1838. doi:10.1016/j.patcog.2006.04.005

Lu, H., & Yen, G. G. (2003). Rank-density-based multiobjective genetic algorithm and benchmark test function study. *IEEE Transactions on Evolutionary Computation, 7*, 325–343. doi:10.1109/TEVC.2003.812220

Lu, W., & Traore, I. (2004). Detecting new forms of network intrusions using genetic programming. *Computational Intelligence, 20*(3), 475–494. doi:10.1111/j.0824-7935.2004.00247.x

Luke, S. (2000). Code growth is not caused by introns. In D. Whitley (Ed.), *Late Breaking Papers at the 2000 Genetic and Evolutionary Computation Conference,* Las Vegas, USA (pp. 228-235).

Luke, S., & Spector, L. (1996). Evolving graphs and networks with edge encoding: A preliminary report. In *Late Breaking Papers at the First Annual Conference Genetic Programming (GP-96),* Stanford University, CA, USA.

Luterbacher, J., Dietrich, D., Xoplaki, E., Grosjean, M., & Wanner, H. (2004). European seasonal and annual temperature variability, trends, and extremes since 1500. *Science, 303*(5663), 1499–1503. doi:10.1126/science.1093877

Lyapunov, A. M. (1892). *The general problem of the stability of motion.* Kharkov, Ukraine: Kharkov Mathematical Society.

Ma, J., & Perkins, S. (2003). Online novelty detection on temporal sequences. In *Proceedings of the 9th ACM SIGKDD International Conference on Knowledge Discovery and Data Mining (KDD '03)* (pp. 613-618). New York: ACM.

Maass, W., & Markram, H. (2004). On the computational power of recurrent circuits of spiking neurons. *Journal of Computer and System Sciences, 69*(4), 593–616. doi:10.1016/j.jcss.2004.04.001

Maass, W., Natschlager, T., & Markram, H. (2002). Real-time computing without stable states: A new framework for neural computation based on perturbations. *Neural Computation, 14*(11), 2531–2560. doi:10.1162/089976602760407955

MacCarthy, B. L., & Liu, J. (1993). Addressing the gap in scheduling research: A review of optimization and heuristic methods in production scheduling. *International Journal of Production Research, 31*(1), 59–79. doi:10.1080/00207549308956713

Mackin, K. J., & Tazaki, E. (1999). Emergent agent communication in multi-agent systems using automatically defined function genetic programming (ADFGP). In *Proceedings of the IEEE International Conference on Systems, Man, and Cybernetics,* Tokyo, Japan (pp. 138-142).

Mackin, K. J., & Tazaki, E. (2000). Unsupervised training of multiobjective agent communication using genetic programming. In *Proceedings of the 4th International Conference on Knowledge-Based Intelligent Information Engineering Systems & Allied Technologies,* Brighton, UK (pp. 738-741).

Mackin, K. J., & Tazaki, E. (2002). Multiagent communication combining genetic programming and pheromone communication. *Kybernetes, 31*(6), 827–843. doi:10.1108/03684920210432808

MacNish, C. (2007). Towards unbiased benchmarking of evolutionary and hybrid algorithms for real-valued optimisation. *Connection Science, 19*(4), 361–385. doi:10.1080/09540090701725581

Madisetti, V. K., & Williams, D. (1999). *Digital signal processing handbook*. Boca Raton, FL: CRC Press.

Man, Z. H., Seng, K. P., & Wu, H. R. (1999). Lyapunov stability based adaptive backpropagation for discrete time system. In *Proceedings of the 5th International Symposium on Signal Processing and Its Applications*, Brisbane, Australia (pp. 661-664).

Man, Z. H., Wu, H. R., Sophie, L., & Xinghuo, Y. (2006). A new adaptive backpropagation algorithm based on Lyapunov stability theory for neural networks. *IEEE Transactions on Neural Networks, 17*(6), 1580–1591. doi:10.1109/TNN.2006.880360

Mann, H. B., & Whitney, D. R. (1947). On a test of whether one of two random variables is stochastically larger than the other. *Annals of Mathematical Statistics, 18*(1), 50–60. doi:10.1214/aoms/1177730491

Markou, M., & Singh, S. (2003). Novelty detection: A review - part 1: Statistical approaches, part 2: Neural network based approaches. *Signal Processing, 83*(12), 2481–2497, 2499–2521. doi:10.1016/j.sigpro.2003.07.018

Marsland, S. (2002). *On-line novelty detection through self-organisation, with application to inspection robotics*. Unpublished doctoral dissertation, University of Manchester, UK.

Martens, E., & Gielen, G. (2008). Classification of analog synthesis tools based on their architecture selection mechanisms. *INTEGRATION, the VLSI journal, 41*, 238-252.

Martinez, A. (1999). Face image retrieval using HMMs. In *Proceedings of the IEEE Workshop on Content-based Access of Image and Video Libraries*, Fort Collins, CO (pp. 35-39).

Masui, T. (1994). Evolutionary learning of graph layout constraints from examples. In *Proceedings of Symposium on User Interface Software and Technology*, Marina del Rey, CA (pp. 103-108).

Mathe, N., & Chen, J. (1996). User driven and context basis adaptation. *User Modeling and User-Adapted Interaction, 3*, 145–154.

Mattiussi, C., & Floreano, D. (2007). Analog genetic encoding for the evolution of circuits and networks. *IEEE Transactions on Evolutionary Computation, 11*(5), 596–607. doi:10.1109/TEVC.2006.886801

McConaghy, T., & Gielen, G. (2006). Genetic programming in industrial analog CAD: Applications and challenges. In T. Yu et al. (Eds.), *Genetic programming theory and practice III* (pp. 291-306). Berlin, Germany: Springer-Verlag.

McConaghy, T., Eeckelaert, T., & Gielen, G. (2005). CAFFEINE: Template-free symbolic model generation of analog circuits via canonical form functions and genetic programming. In *Proceedings of the Solid-State Circuits Conference* (pp. 243-246).

McConaghy, T., Palmers, P., Gielen, G., & Steyaert, M. (2007). Simultaneous multitopology multi-objective sizing across thousands of analog circuit topologies. In *Proceedings of the Design Automation Conference* (pp. 944-947).

Medrano-Marques, N. J., & Martin-Del-Brio, B. (2001). Sensor linearization with neural networks. *IEEE Transactions on Industrial Electronics, 48*(6), 1288–1290. doi:10.1109/41.969414

Melanie, M. (1999). *An introduction to genetic algorithms*. Cambridge, MA: The MIT Press.

Mermoud, G., Upegui, A., Pena, C. A., & Sanchez, E. (2005). A dynamically-reconfigurable FPGA platform for evolving fuzzy systems. In *Computational Intelligence and Bioinspired Systems* (LNCS 3512, pp. 572-581). Berlin, Germany: Springer-Verlag.

Meyers, L., Pourbohloul, D., & Newman, M. E. J. (2005). Network Theory and SARS: prediciting outbreak diversity. *Journal of Theoretical Biology, 232*, 71–81. doi:10.1016/j.jtbi.2004.07.026

Mian, A. S., Bennamoun, M., & Owens, R. (2007). An efficient multimodal 2D-3D hybrid approach to automatic face recognition. *IEEE Transactions on Pattern Analysis and Machine Intelligence, 29*(11), 1927–1943. doi:10.1109/TPAMI.2007.1105

Michalewicz, Z. (1991). A step towards optimal topology of communication networks. In V. Libby (Ed.), *Proceedings of the Data Structures and Target Classification, the SPIE's International Symposium on Optical Engineering and Photonics in Aerospace Sensing* (pp. 112-122). SPIE – The International Society for Optical Engineering.

Middleton, E. (1996). Adaptation level and 'animal spirits'. *Journal of Economic Psychology, 17*(4), 479–498. doi:10.1016/0167-4870(96)00020-7

Midorikawa, H. (1988). The face pattern identification by backpropagation learning procedure. In *Abstracts of the First Annual INNS meeting*, Boston, MA (p. 515).

Miettinen, K. (1999). *Nonlinear multiobjective optimization*. Amsterdam: Kluwer Academic Publishers.

Mihalcea, R. (2004). Graph-based ranking algorithms for sentence extraction, applied to text summarization. In *Proceedings of the 42nd Annual Meeting of the Association for Computational Linguistics.*

Miorandi, D., Dini, P., Altman, E., & Kameda, H. (2007). *WP 2.2 – paradigm applications and mapping, D2.2.2 framework for distributed on-line evolution of protocols and services* (2nd ed.). BIOlogically inspired NETwork and Services (BIONETS) and Future and Emerging Technologies (FET) project of the EU.

Molisch, A. F. (2005). *Wireless communications*. New York: John Wiley & Sons/IEEE Press.

Monostori, L., Markus, A., Van Brussels, H., & Westkaemper, E. (1996). Machine learning approaches to manufacturing. *Annals of CIRP, 45*(2), 675–712.

Montgomery, D. (2001). *Design and analysis of experiments*. New York: John Wiley & Sons.

Moody, T. J., & Darken, C. J. (1989). Fast learning in networks of locally tuned processing units. *Neural Computation, 1*(2), 281–294. doi:10.1162/neco.1989.1.2.281

Morris, S. (2000). Contagion . *The Review of Economic Studies, 67*, 57–78J. doi:10.1111/1467-937X.00121

Motter, A., Zhou, C., Kutth, J. (2005). Network synchronization, Diffusion, and the Paradox of Heterogeneity, *Physical Review E., 71*, 016116–1–9.

Moy, J. (1989). *The OSPF specification* (Request for Comments (RFC) No. 1131). Internet Engineering Task Force (IETF), Internet Society (ISOC).

Mueller, M. (1981). Least-squares algorithms for adaptive equalizers. *The Bell System Technical Journal, 60*, 1905–1925.

Mukkamala, S., Sung, A. H., & Abraham, A. (2004). Modeling intrusion detection systems using linear genetic programming approach. In R. Orchard, C. Yang, & M. Ali (Eds.), *Proceedings of the 17th International Conference on Industrial and Engineering Applications of Artificial Intelligence and Expert Systems* (LNCS 3029, pp. 633-642). Berlin, Germany: Springer-Verlag.

Munetomo, M. (1999). Designing genetic algorithms for adaptive routing algorithms in the Internet. In *Proceedings of the GECCO'99 Workshop on Evolutionary Telecommunications: Past, Present and Future*, Orlando, FL (pp. 215-216).

Munetomo, M., Takai, Y., & Sato, Y. (1997). An adaptive network routing algorithm employing path genetic operators. In *Proceedings of the 7th International Conference on Genetic Algorithms*, East Lansing, MI (pp. 643-649).

Munetomo, M., Takai, Y., & Sato, Y. (1998). An adaptive routing algorithm with load balancing by a genetic algorithm. [IPSJ]. *Transactions of the Information Processing Society of Japan, 39*(2), 219–227.

Munetomo, M., Takai, Y., & Sato, Y. (1998). A migration scheme for the genetic adaptive routing algorithm. In *Proceedings of the IEEE Conference on Systems, Man, and Cybernetics* (pp. 2774-2779). Piscataway, NJ: IEEE Press.

Musavi, M. T., Faris, K. B., Chan, K. H., & Ahmed, W. (1991). On the implementation of RBF technique in neural network. In *Proceedings of the Conference on Analysis of Neural Network Applications*, Fairfax, VA (pp. 110-115).

Nakano, T., & Suda, T. (2004). Adaptive and evolvable network services. In *Proceedings of the Genetic and Evolutionary Computation Conference* (LNCS 3102, pp. 151-162). Berlin, Germany: Springer-Verlag.

Nakano, T., & Suda, T. (2005). Self-organizing network services with evolutionary adaptation. *IEEE Transactions on Neural Networks*, *16*(5), 1269–1278. doi:10.1109/TNN.2005.853421

Nakano, T., & Suda, T. (2007). Applying biological principles to designs of network services. *Applied Soft Computing*, *7*(3), 870–878. doi:10.1016/j.asoc.2006.04.006

Namatame, A. (2006). *Adaptation and Evolution in Collective Systems*, World Scientific.

Nazeer, S. A., Omar, N., & Khalid, M. (2007). Face recognition system using artificial neural network approach. In *Proceedings of the International Conference on Signal Processing, Communication and Networking*, Chennai, India (pp. 420-425).

Nehrotra, K., Mohan, C. K., & Ranka, S. (1996). *Element of artificial neural networks*. Cambridge, MA: The MIT Press.

Newman, M. E. J. (2003). The structure and function of complex networks. *Society for Industrial and Applied Mathematics*, *45*(2), 167–256.

Nocedal, J., & Wright, S. (2006). *Numerical optimization*. Berlin, Germany: Springer-Verlag.

Norcio, A. F., & Stanley, J. (1989). Adaptive human-computer interfaces: A literature survey and perspective. *IEEE Transactions on Systems, Man, and Cybernetics*, *19*, 399–408. doi:10.1109/21.31042

Nowak, M. (2006). *Evolutionary Dynamics*, Harvard University Press.

O'Hare, G., & Jennings, N. (1996). *Foundations of distributed artificial intelligence*. New York: Wiley-Interscience.

O'Mahony, M., Sinclair, M. C., & Mikac, B. (1993). Ultra-high capacity optical transmission network: European research project COST 239. In M. Kos (Ed.), *Proceedings of the International Conference on Telecommunications*, Zagreb, Croatia (pp. 33-45).

O'Neill, M., & Nicolau, M. (2001). Grammar defined introns: An investigation into grammars, introns, and bias in grammatical evolution. In L. Spector, E. Goodman, A. Wu, W. Langdon, H.-M. Voigt, M. Gen, S. Sen, M. Dorigo, S. Pezeshk, M. Garzon, & E. Burke (Eds.), *GECCO-2001: Proceedings of the Genetic and Evolutionary Computation Conference* (pp. 97-103). San Francisco: Morgan Kaufmann.

Olfati-Saber, R., Fax, J. A., & Murray, R. M. (2007). Consensus and Cooperation in Networked Multi-Agent Systems. *Proceedings of the IEEE*, *95*(1), 215–233. doi:10.1109/JPROC.2006.887293

Oppenheim, A., & Schafer, R. (1999). *Discrete-time signal processing*. Upper Saddle River, NJ: Prentice-Hall.

Ouelhadj, D., Cowling, P. I., & Petrovic, S. (2003). Contract net protocol for cooperative optimisation and dynamic scheduling of steel production. In A. Ibraham, K. Franke, & M. Koppen (Eds.), *Intelligent systems design and applications* (pp. 457-470). Berlin, Germany: Springer-Verlag.

Ouelhadj, D., Cowling, P. I., & Petrovic, S. (2003). Utility and stability measures for agent-based dynamic scheduling of steel continuous casting. In *Proceedings of the IEEE International Conference on Robotics and Automation*, Taipei, Taiwan (pp. 175-180).

Palit, A. K., & Babuška, R. (2001). Efficient training algorithm for neuro-fuzzy network. In *Proceedings of the 10th IEEE International Conference on Fuzzy Systems*, Melbourne, Australia (pp. 1367-1371).

Palit, A. K., & Popovic, D. (2005). *Computational intelligence in time series forecasting: Theory and engineering applications*. London: Springer-Verlag.

Palit, A. K., Anheier, W., & Popovic, D. (2009). Electrical load forecasting using neural-fuzzy approach. In R. Chiong (Ed.), *Natural intelligence for scheduling, planning and packing problems*. Heidelberg, Germany: Springer-Verlag.

Papadopoulos, A. N., & Manolopoulos, Y. (2004). *Nearest neighbor search: A database perspective*. Berlin, Germany: Springer-Verlag Telos.

Paredes, R., & Vidal, E. (2006). Learning prototypes and distances: A prototype reduction technique based on nearest neighbor error minimization. *Pattern Recognition, 39*(2), 180–188. doi:10.1016/j.patcog.2005.06.001

Park, J., & Wsandberg, J. (1991). Universal approximation using radial basis functions network. *Neural Computation, 3*, 246–257. doi:10.1162/neco.1991.3.2.246

Parrilo, P. A., & Sturmfels, B. (2003). Minimizing polynomial functions. In S. Basu & L. Gonzalez-Vega (Eds.), *Algorithmic and quantitative real algebraic geometry* (pp. 83-99). AMS.

Patranabis, D., Ghosh, S., & Bakshi, C. (1988). Linearizing transducer characteristics. *IEEE Transactions on Instrumentation and Measurement, 37*(1), 66–69. doi:10.1109/19.2666

Pazzani, M., & Billsus, D. (1997). Learning and revising user profiles: The identification of interesting WEB sites. *Machine Learning, 27*, 313–331. doi:10.1023/A:1007369909943

Pedrycz, W., & Vasilakos, A. V. (2000). Computational intelligence: A development environment for telecommunications networks. In W. Pedrycz & A. V. Vasilakos (Eds.), *Computational intelligence in telecommunications networks* (pp. 1-27). Boca Raton, FL: CRC Press.

Pedrycz, W., & Vasilakos, A. V. (Eds.). (2000). *Computational intelligence in telecommunications networks*. Boca Raton, FL: CRC Press.

Peeters, P., Van Brussel, H., Valckenaers, P., Wyns, J., Bongaerts, L., Kollingbaum, M., & Heikkila, T. (2001). Pheromone based emergent shop floor control system for flexible flow shops. *Artificial Intelligence in Engineering, 15*(4), 343–352. doi:10.1016/S0954-1810(01)00026-7

Pekalska, E., Duin, R. P. W., & Paclík, P. (2006). Prototype selection for dissimilarity-based classifiers. *Pattern Recognition, 39*(2), 189–208. doi:10.1016/j.patcog.2005.06.012

Peña Reyes, C. A. (2002). *Coevolutionary fuzzy modeling*. Unpublished doctoral dissertation, EPFL.

Perez-Uribe, A. (1999). *Structure-adaptable digital neural networks*. Unpublished doctoral dissertation, EPFL.

Perrig, A., & Song, D. X. (2000). A first step towards the automatic generation of security protocols. In *Proceedings of the Symposium on Network and Distributed Systems Security,* San Diego, CA (pp. 73-83).

Perry, J. L., & Carney, J. M. (1990). Human face recognition using a multilayer perceptron. In *Proceedings of the International Conference on Neural Networks,* Washington, DC (pp. 4-13).

Pew, R. W. (1979). Secondary tasks and workload measurement. In N. Moray (Ed.), *Mental workload: It's theory and measurement* (pp. 23-28). New York: Plenum Press.

Pincus, S. (1991). Approximate entropy as a measure of system complexity. *Proceedings of the National Academy of Sciences of the United States of America, 88*, 2297–2301. doi:10.1073/pnas.88.6.2297

Pinedo, M. (2008). *Scheduling: Theory, algorithms, and systems* (3rd ed.). Berlin, Germany: Springer-Verlag.

Priebe, C., Conroy, J., Marchette, D., & Park, Y. (2005). Scan statistics on Enron graphs. *Computational & Mathematical Organization Theory, 11*(3), 229–247. doi:10.1007/s10588-005-5378-z

Prinzel, J. L. (2003). *Team-centered perspective for adaptive automation design* (NASA/TM 2003-212154).

Prinzel, J. L., Pope, A. T., Freeman, G. F., Scerbo, M. W., & Mikulka, P. J. (2001). Empirical analysis of EEG and ERPs for psychophysical adaptive task allocation. *Engineering Psychology, 52*, 124–135.

Prototype selection and feature subset selection by estimation of distribution algorithms: A case study in the survival of cirrhotic patients treated with tips. In *Proceedings of the 8th Conference on AI in Medicine in Europe* (pp. 20-29). London: Springer-Verlag.

Raghavendra, C. S., Sivalingam, K. M., & Znati, T. (Eds.). (2004). *Wireless sensor networks* (ERCOFTAC Series). Amsterdam: Springer Netherlands.

Rajendran, C., & Ziegler, H. (2005). Two ant-colony algorithms for minimizing total flowtime in permutation flowshops. *Computers & Industrial Engineering, 48*(4), 789–797. doi:10.1016/j.cie.2004.12.009

Rappaport, T. S. (2001). *Wireless communications: Principles and practice*. Upper Saddle River, NJ: Prentice Hall.

Reed, R. (1993). Pruning algorithms - a survey. *IEEE Transactions on Neural Networks, 4*(5), 740–747. doi:10.1109/72.248452

Reid, G. B., & Nygren, T. E. (1988). The subjective workload assessment technique: A scaling procedure for measuring mental workload. In *Human mental workload* (pp. 183-201). Amsterdam, The Netherlands.

Renna, P., Padalino, R., & Vancza, J. (2008). A multi-agent architecture for budget-based scheduling in dynamic environments. In *Proceedings of the 6ᵗʰ CIRP International Conference on Intelligent Computation in Manufacturing Engineering*, Naples, Italy.

Renna, P., Perrone, G., Amico, M., & Bruccoleri, M. (2001). A new decision making strategy for distributed control of cellular manufacturing systems. In C. H. Dagli et al. (Eds.), *Intelligent engineering through artificial neural networks* (pp. 975-980). New York: ASME Press.

Renna, P., Perrone, G., Amico, M., Bruccoleri, M., & Noto La Diega, S. (2001). A performance comparison between market like and efficiency based approaches in agent based manufacturing environment. In *Proceedings of the 34ᵗʰ International Seminar for Manufacturing Systems*, Athens, Greece (pp. 93-98).

Reyes-García, C. A., Barajas, S. E., Tlelo-Cuautle, E., & Reyes-Galaviz, O. F. (2008). A hybrid system for automatic infant cry recognition II. In J. R. Rabuñal, J. Dorado, & A. Pazos (Eds.), *Encyclopedia of artificial intelligence* (pp. 867-872). Hershey, PA: Information Science Reference.

Reynolds, C. (1987). Flocks, Herds, and Schools: A Distributed Behavioral Model. *Computers & Graphics, 21*, 25. http://www.red3d.com/cwr/papers/1987/boids.html. doi:10.1145/37402.37406

Ripeanu, M., Foster, I., & Iamnitchi, A. (2002). Mapping the Gnutella network: Properties of large-scale peer-to-peer systems and implications for system design. *IEEE Internet Computing Journal, 6*(1), 50–57. doi:10.1109/4236.978369

Roberts, S. J. (1999). Novelty detection using extreme value statistics. *Vision, Image and Signal Processing . IEEE Proceedings, 146*(3), 124–129.

Rogers, E., Media, U., Rivera, M., & Wiley, C. (2005). Complex Adaptive Systems and The Diffusion of Innovations . *The Innovation Journal, 10*(3), 1–26.

Roggen, D., Federici, D., & Floreano, D. (2007, March). Evolutionary morphogenesis for multi-cellular systems. *Genetic Programming and Evolvable Machines, 8*, 61–96. doi:10.1007/s10710-006-9019-1

Ronco, E., & Gawthrop, P. (May 1995). *Modular neural networks: A state of the art* (Tech. Rep. CSC-9502). Center for System and Control, University of Glasgow.

Rosen, B. E., Soriano, D., Bylander, T., & Ortiz-Zuazaga, H. (1996). Training a neural network to recognize artifacts and decelerations in cardiotocograms. In *Proceedings of the AAAI Spring Symposium on Artificial Intelligence in Medicine: Applicat. Current Technol. Working Notes*.

Rosenberg, N. (1972). Factors Affecting the Diffusion of Technology . *Explorations in Economic History, 10*(1), 3–33. doi:10.1016/0014-4983(72)90001-0

Rossi, A., & Dini, G. (2007). Flexible job-shop scheduling with routing flexibility and separable setup times using ant colony optimisation method. *Robotics and Computer-integrated Manufacturing, 23*(5), 503–516. doi:10.1016/j.rcim.2006.06.004

Rothrock, L., Koubek, R., Fuchs, F., Haas, M., & Salvendy, G. (2002). *Review and reappraisal of adaptive interfaces: Toward biologically-inspired paradigms*. New York: Taylor and Francis.

Rouse, W. B., Geddes, N. D., & Curry, R. E. (1988). Architecture for intelligent interface: Outline of an approach to support operators of complex systems. *Human-Computer Interaction*, 3, 87–122. doi:10.1207/s15327051hci0302_1

Roux, O., & Fonlupt, C. (2000). Ant programming: Or how to use ants for automatic programming. In . *Proceedings of ANTS, 2000*, 121–129.

Rutenbar, R. A., Gielen, G., & Roychowdhury, J. (2007). Hierarchical modeling, optimization, and synthesis for system-level analog and RF designs. *Proceedings of the IEEE*, 95(3), 640–669. doi:10.1109/JPROC.2006.889371

Sałustowicz, R. P. (2003). *Probabilistic incremental program evolution*. Unpublished doctoral dissertation, Technical University of Berlin, Germany.

Samaria, F., & Harter, A. (1994). Parameterization of a stochastic model for human face identification. In *Proceedings of 2nd IEEE Workshop on Applications of Computer Vision,* Austin, TX (pp. 138-142).

Sanchez, E., Mange, D., Sipper, M., Tomassini, M., Perez-Uribe, A., & Stauffer, A. (1997). Phylogeny, ontogeny, and epigenesis: Three sources of biological inspiration for softening hardware. In *Evolvable Systems: From Biology to Hardware* (LNCS 1259, pp. 35-54). Berlin, Germany: Springer-Verlag.

Sánchez-López, C., Tlelo-Cuautle, E., Fakhfakh, M., & Loulou, M. (2007). Computing simplified noise-symbolic-expressions in CMOS CCs by applying SPA and SAG. In *Proceedings of the IEEE ICM*, Cairo, Egypt (pp. 159-162).

Sanderson, P., Pipingas, A., Danieli, F., & Silberstein, R. (2003). Process monitoring and configural display design: A neuroimaging study. *Theoretical Issues in Ergonomics Science*, 4, 151–174. doi:10.1080/1463922021000020909

Santana-Quintero, L. V., Ramírez-Santiago, N., & Coello, C. A. (2008). Towards a more efficient multi-objective particle swarm optimizer. In L. T. Bui & S. Alam (Eds.), *Multi-objective optimization in computational intel-ligence* (pp. 76-105). Hershey, PA: Information Science Reference.

Sastra, J. J., Asokan, P., Saravanan, R., & Delphin, A. (2005). Simultaneous scheduling of parts and AGVs in an FMS using non-traditional optimization algorithms. *International Journal of Applied Management and Technology*, 3(1), 305–316.

Scholz-Reiter, B., De Beer, C., Freitag, M., & Jagalski, T. (2008). Bio-inspired and pheromone-based shop floor control. *International Journal of Computer Integrated Manufacturing*, 21(2), 201–205. doi:10.1080/09511920701607840

Schoonderwoerd, R. (1996). *Collective intelligence for network control*. Unpublished master's thesis, Delft University of Technology, Delft, the Netherlands.

Schoonderwoerd, R., Holland, O. E., & Bruten, J. L. (1997). Ant-like agents for load balancing in telecommunications networks. In J. Miller (Ed.), *Proceedings of the 1st International Conference on Autonomous Agents* (pp. 209-216). New York: ACM Press.

Schoonderwoerd, R., Holland, O. E., Bruten, J. L., & Rothkrantz, L. J. M. (1996). Ant-based load balancing in telecommunications networks. *Adaptive Behavior*, 5(2), 169–207. doi:10.1177/105971239700500203

Sebban, M., & Nock, R. (2000). Instance pruning as an information preserving problem. In *Proceedings of the First Conference on Knowledge Discovery and Data Mining* (pp. 174-179).

Seiler, P., & Parrilo, P. A. (2004). *SOSTOOLS: Sum of squares optimization toolbox for MATLAB* (Tech. Rep.). Pasadena, CA: CALTECH. Retrieved from http://www.cds.caltech.edu/sostools

Sekanina, L. (2004). *Evolvable components from theory to hardware implementations*. Berlin, Germany: Springer.

Sekanina, L. (2004). Virtual reconfigurable devices. In *Evolvable Components from Theory to Hardware Implementations* (pp. 153-168). Berlin, Germany: Springer,-Verlag.

Şekercioğlu, Y. A., Pitsilides, A., & Vasilakos, A. V. (2001). Computational intelligence in management of ATM networks: A survey of current state of research. *Soft Computing, 5*(4), 257–263. doi:10.1007/s005000100099

Seng, K. P., Man, Z. H., & Wu, H. R. (1999). Nonlinear adaptive RBF neural filter with Lyapunov adaptation algorithm and its application to nonlinear channel equalization. In *Proceedings of the 5th International Symposium on Signal Processing and Its Applications,* Brisbane, Australia (pp. 151-154).

Seng, K. P., Man, Z. H., & Wu, H. R. (2002). Lyapunov theory-based radial basis function networks for adaptive filtering. *IEEE Transactions on Circuits and Systems. I, Fundamental Theory and Applications, 49*(8), 1215–1220. doi:10.1109/TCSI.2002.801255

Shakhnarovich, G., Darrel, T., & Indyk, P. (Eds.). (2006). *Nearest-neighbor methods in learning and vision: Theory and practice.* Cambridge, MA: MIT Press.

Shami, S. H., Kirkwood, I. M. A., & Sinclair, M. C. (1997). Evolving simple fault-tolerant routing rules using genetic programming. *Electronics Letters, 33*(17), 1440–1441. doi:10.1049/el:19970996

Shannon, C. (1948). A mathematical theory of communication. *The Bell System Technical Journal, 27,* 379–423, 623–656.

Sharples, N. P. (1999). Evolutionary approaches to adaptive protocol design. In D. Pearce (Ed.), *CSRP 512: The 12th White House Papers Graduate Research in Cognitive and Computing Sciences at Sussex,* Brighton, UK (pp. 60-62).

Sharples, N. P. (2001). *Evolutionary approaches to adaptive protocol design.* Unpublished doctoral dissertation, University of Sussex, Brighton, UK.

Sharples, N. P., & Wakeman, I. (2000). Protocol construction using genetic search techniques. In S. Cagnoni et al. (Eds.), *Real-world applications of evolutionary computing* (LNCS 1803, pp. 235-246). Berlin, Germany: Springer-Verlag.

Shen, W. M. (2002). Distributed manufacturing scheduling using intelligent agents. *IEEE Intelligent Systems, 17*(1), 88–94. doi:10.1109/5254.988492

Shen, W., Maturana, F., & Norrie, D. (2000). Metaphor II: An agent-based architecture for distributed intelligent design and manufacturing. *Journal of Intelligent Manufacturing, 11*(3), 237–251. doi:10.1023/A:1008915208259

Shen, W., Xue, D., & Norrie, D. (1998). An agent-based manufacturing enterprise infrastructure for distributed integrated intelligent manufacturing system. In *Proceedings the 3rd International Conference on Practical Application of Intelligent Agents and Multi-Agent Systems,* London, UK (pp. 533-548).

Sheridan, T. B. (1993). Space teleoperation through time delay: Review and prognosis. *IEEE Transactions on Robotics and Automation, 9,* 592–606. doi:10.1109/70.258052

Sheskin, D. J. (2003). *Handbook of parametric and nonparametric statistical procedures.* Boca Raton, FL: CRC Press.

Siegelmann, H., & Sontag, E. (1991). Turing computability with neural nets. *Applied Mathematics Letters, 4*(6), 77–80. doi:10.1016/0893-9659(91)90080-F

Simon, D. (2002). Training radial basis neural networks with the extended kalman filter. *Neurocomputing, 48,* 455–475. doi:10.1016/S0925-2312(01)00611 7

Sinclair, M. C. (1995). Minimum cost topology optimisation of the COST 239 European optical network. In *Proceedings of the International Conference on Artificial Neural Networks and Genetic Algorithms* (pp. 26-29). Berlin, Germany: Springer-Verlag.

Sinclair, M. C. (1999). Evolutionary telecommunications: A summary. In *Proceedings of the GECCO'99 Workshop on Evolutionary Telecommunications: Past, Present and Future,* Orlando, FL (pp. 209-212).

Sinclair, M. C. (1999). Optical mesh network topology design using node-pair encoding genetic programming. In *Proceedings of the Genetic and Evolutionary Computation Conference,* Orlando, FL (pp. 1192–1197).

Sinclair, M. C. (2000). Node-pair encoding genetic programming for optical mesh network topology design. In D. W. Corne et al. (Eds.), *Telecommunications optimization: Heuristic and adaptive techniques* (pp. 99-114). New York: John Wiley & Sons.

Sing, J. K., Basu, D. K., Nasipuri, M., & Kundu, M. (2005). Face recognition using point symmetry distance-based RBF network. *Applied Soft Computing, 7*, 58–70. doi:10.1016/j.asoc.2005.02.004

Singh, S. (2002). Anomaly detection using negative selection based on the r-contiguous matching rule. In J. Timmis & P. J. Bentley (Eds.), *Proceedings of the 1st International Conference on Artificial Immune Systems (ICARIS)*, University of Kent at Canterbury (pp. 99-106).

Singh, S., & Markou, M. (2005). A black hole novelty detector for video analysis. *Pattern Analysis & Applications, 8*(1), 102–114. doi:10.1007/s10044-005-0248-3

Sipper, M. (1996). Co-evolving non-uniform cellular automata to perform computations. *Physica D. Nonlinear Phenomena, 92*(3-4), 193–208. doi:10.1016/0167-2789(95)00286-3

Sirovich, L., & Kirby, M. (1987). Low-dimensional procedure for the characterization of human face. *Journal of the Optical Society of America, 4*, 519–524. doi:10.1364/JOSAA.4.000519

Siwamogsatham, V., & Saygin, C. (2004). Auction-based distributed scheduling and control scheme for flexible manufacturing systems. *International Journal of Production Research, 42*, 547–572. doi:10.1080/0020 7540310001613683

Slorach, C., & Sharman, K. (2000). The design and implementation of custom architectures for evolvable hardware using off-the-shelf programmable devices. In *Evolvable Systems: From Biology to Hardware* (LNCS 1801, pp. 197-207). Berlin, Germany: Springer-Verlag.

Smedt, B., & Gielen, G. E. (2003). WATSON: Design space boundary exploration and model generation for analog and RF IC design. *IEEE Transactions on Computer-Aided Design of Integrated Circuits and Systems, 22*(2), 213–224. doi:10.1109/TCAD.2002.806598

Smith, K., & Sedra, A. (1968). The current-conveyor - a new circuit building block. *Proceedings of the IEEE, 56*(8), 1368–1369. doi:10.1109/PROC.1968.6591

Smith, P. (2000). Controlling code growth in genetic programming. In R. John & R. Birkenhead (Eds.), *Advances in soft computing* (pp. 166-171). Heidelberg, Germany: Physica-Verlag.

Smith, R. G. (1980). The contract net protocol: High level communication and control in a distributed problem solver. *IEEE Transactions on Computers, 29*(12), 1104–1113. doi:10.1109/TC.1980.1675516

Smith, S. F. (1980). *A learning system based on genetic adaptive algorithms*. Unpublished doctoral dissertation, University of Pittsburgh, Pittsburgh, PA, USA.

Smith, T., & Boning, D. (1997). A self-tuning EWMA controller utilizing artificial neural network function approximation techniques. *IEEE Transactions on Components, Packaging, and Manufacturing Technology Part C, 20*(2), 121–132. doi:10.1109/3476.622882

Sole, R., Ferrrer-Cancho, P., & Montota, R. (2003). Selection, Tinkering, and Emergence in Complex Networks. *Complexity, 8*(1), 20–33. doi:10.1002/cplx.10055

Solheim, I., Payne, T., & Castain, R. (1992). The potential in using backpropagation neural networks for facial verification systems. *Simulations, 58*(5), 306–310.

Solomon, E., Berg, L., Martin, D., & Villee, C. (1996). *Biologia*. Warszawa, Poland: Oficyna Wydawnicza.

Song, D. (2003). *A Linear genetic programming approach to intrusion detection*. Unpublished master's thesis, Dalhousie University, Halifax, Nova Scotia, Canada.

Song, D. X. (1999). Athena: A new efficient automatic checker for security protocol analysis. In *Proceedings of 12th IEEE Computer Security Foundations Workshop* (pp. 192-202). Piscataway, NJ: IEEE Press.

Song, D. X., Perrig, A., & Phan, D. (2001). AGVI – automatic generation, verification, and implementation of security protocols. In *Proceedings of the 13th International Conference on Computer Aided Verification* (LNCS 2102, pp. 241-245). Berlin, Germany: Springer-Verlag.

Song, D., Heywood, M. I., & Zincir-Heywood, A. N. (2003). A linear genetic programming approach to intrusion detection. In *Proceedings of the Genetic and Evolutionary Computation Conference* (LNCS 2724, pp. 2325-2336). Berlin, Germany: Springer-Verlag.

Sousa, P., & Ramos, C. (1999). A distributed architecture and negotiation protocol for scheduling in manufacturing systems. *Computers in Industry, 38*(2), 103–113. doi:10.1016/S0166-3615(98)00112-2

Spielman, D. J. (2005). Systems of Innovation: Models, methods, and future directions. *Innovation Strategy Today, 2*(1), 55–66.

Spinosa, E. J., & de Carvalho, A. C. (2005). Combining one-class classifiers for robust novelty detection in gene expression data. In *Advances in bioinformatics and computational biology* (LNCS 3594, pp. 54-64). Berlin, Germany: Springer.

Spinosa, E. J., de Leon, F., de Carvalho, A. P., & Jo, G. (2007). Olindda: A cluster-based approach for detecting novelty and concept drift in data streams. In *Proceedings of the ACM Symposium on Applied computing (SAC '07)* (pp. 448-452). New York: ACM.

Stan, Z. L., & Anil, K. J. (2004). *Handbook of face recognition*. New York: Springer-Verlag.

Stehr, G., Graeb, H. E., & Antreich, K. J. (2007). Analog performance space exploration by normal-boundary intersection and by Fourier-Motzkin elimination. *IEEE Transactions on Computer-Aided Design of Integrated Circuits and Systems, 26*(10), 1733–1748. doi:10.1109/TCAD.2007.895756

Suchak, R. P., & Lacovou, N. (1994). GroupLens: An open architecture for collaborative filtering for netnews. In *Proceedings of Conference on Computer Supported Cooperative Work,* Chapel Hill, NC (pp. 175-186).

Swaminathan, J. M., Smith, S. F., & Sadeh, N. M. (1996). A multi-agent framework for modeling supply chain dynamics. In *Proceedings of the NSF Research Planning Workshop on Artificial Intelligence and Manufacturing,* Albequerque, NM.

Swets, D. L., & Weng, J. (1996, August). Using discriminant eigenfeatures for image retrieval. *IEEE Transactions on Pattern Analysis and Machine Intelligence, 18*(8), 831–836. doi:10.1109/34.531802

Synopsys. (2007). *HSPICE RF user guide Z-2007.3* (pp. 95-104).

Szelke, E., & Monostori, L. (1999). Real scheduling in real time production control. In P. Brandimarte & A. Villa (Eds.), *Modelling manufacturing systems: From aggregate planning to real-time control* (pp. 65-114). Berlin, Germany: Springer-Verlag.

Takagi, H. (2001). Interactive evolutionary computation: Fusion of the capabilities of EC optimization of EC optimization and human evolution. *Proceedings of the IEEE, 89,* 1275–1296. doi:10.1109/5.949485

Tan, L. G., & Sinclair, M. C. (1995). Wavelength assignment between the central nodes of the COST 239 European optical network. In *Proceedings of the 11th UK Performance Engineering Workshop,* Liverpool, UK (pp. 235-247).

Tanenbaum, A. S., & van Steen, M. (2002). *Distributed systems: Principles and paradigms.* Upper Saddle River, NJ: Prentice Hall.

Tarassenko, L. (1995). Novelty detection for the identification of masses in mammograms. In *Proceedings of the 4th IEEE International Conference on Artificial Neural Networks,* Cambridge, UK (Vol. 4, pp. 442-447).

Tax, D., & Duin, R. (1998). Outlier detection using classifier instability. In A. Amin, D. Dori, P. Pudil, & H. Freeman (Eds.), *Advances in pattern recognition* (LNCS 1451, pp. 593-601.) Berlin, Germany: Springer-Verlag.

Teixeira, F., & Romariz, A. R. S. (2007). Optimum finite impulse response digital filter design using computational intelligence based optimization algorithms. In *Proceedings of the Seventh International Conference on Intelligent Systems Design and Applications* (pp. 635-640). Washington, DC: IEEE Computer Society.

Teixeira, F., & Romariz, A. R. S. (2008). Digital filter arbitrary magnitude and phase approximations: Statistical analysis applied to a stochastic-based optimization approach. In *Proceedings of the IEEE World Congress on Computational Intelligence* (pp. 4088-4095). Piscataway, NJ: IEEE Press.

Terrell, G. R. (1999). *Mathematical statistics: A unified introduction*. New York: Springer.

Thathachar, M. A., & Sastry, P. S. (2002). Varieties of learning automata: An overview. *IEEE Transactions on Systems, Man, and Cybernetics, 32*, 711–721. doi:10.1109/TSMCB.2002.1049606

The ORL database. (n.d.). *Cambridge University computer laboratory*. Retrieved from http//www.cam-orl.co.uk/facedatabase.html

Théraulaz, G., & Bonabeau, E. (2000). Swarm smarts. *Scientific American, 282*(3), 72–79.

Thoma, Y., & Sanchez, E. (2004). A reconfigurable chip for evolvable hardware. In *Proceedings of the Genetic and Evolutionary Computation Conference* (pp. 816-827).

Thoma, Y., Tempesti, G., Sanchez, E., & Arostegui, J. M. M. (2004). POEtic: An electronic tissue for bio-inspired cellular applications. *Bio Systems, 76*(1-3), 191–200. doi:10.1016/j.biosystems.2004.05.023

Thomaz, C. E., Feitosa, R. Q., & Veiga, A. (1998). Design of radial basis function network as classifier in face recognition using eigenfaces. In *Proceedings of the Vth Brazilian Symposium on Neural Networks*, Belo Horizonte, Brazil (pp. 118-123).

Thompson, A. (1997). An evolved circuit, intrinsic in silicon, entwined with physics. In *Evolvable Systems: From Biology to Hardware* (LNCS 1259, pp. 390-405). Berlin, Germany: Springer-Verlag.

Thompson, A., Harvey, I., & Husbands, P. (1996). Unconstrained evolution and hard consequences. *Towards Evolvable Hardware, The Evolutionary Engineering Approach* (. LNCS, 1062, 136–165.

Tlelo-Cuautle, E., & Duarte-Villaseñor, M. A. (2008a). Evolutionary electronics: Automatic synthesis of analog circuits by GAs. In A. Yang, Y. Shan, & L.T. Bui (Eds.),

Success in evolutionary computation (pp. 165-188). Berlin, Germany: Springer-Verlag.

Tlelo-Cuautle, E., Duarte-Villaseñor, M. A., & Guerra-Gómez, I. (2008b). Automatic synthesis of VFs and VMs by applying genetic algorithms. *Circuits . Systems and Signal Processing, 27*(3), 391–403. doi:10.1007/s00034-008-9030-2

Tlelo-Cuautle, E., Duarte-Villaseñor, M. A., Reyes-García, C. A., & Reyes-Salgado, G. (2007). Automatic synthesis of electronic circuits using genetic algorithms. *Computación y Sistemas, 10*(3), 217–229.

Tlelo-Cuautle, E., Moro-Frías, D., Sánchez-López, C., & Duarte-Villaseñor, M. A. (2008c). Synthesis of CCII-s by superimposing VFs and CFs through genetic operations. *IEICE Electronics Express, 5*(11), 411–417. doi:10.1587/elex.5.411

Toffoli, T., & Margolus, N. (1987). *Cellular automata machines: A new environment for modeling*. Cambridge, MA: MIT Press.

Trejo-Guerra, R., Tlelo-Cuautle, E., Cruz-Hernández, C., Sánchez-López, C., & Fakhfakh, M. (2008). Current conveyor realization of synchronized Chua's circuits for binary communications. In *Proceedings of the IEEE DTIS*, Tozeur, Tunisia (pp. 1-4).

Tribus, M. (1961). *Thermostatistics and thermodynamics* D. van Nostrand Company, Inc.

Trimberger, S. (1994). *Field-programmable gate array technology*. Boston: Kluwer Academic Publishers.

Tschudin, C. F. (2003). Fraglets – a metabolistic execution model for communication protocols. In *Proceedings of 2nd Annual Symposium on Autonomous Intelligent Networks and Systems (AINS 2003)*, Menlo Park, CA.

Tschudin, C.F., & Yamamoto, L. A. R. (2005). A metabolic approach to protocol resilience. In M. Smirnov (Ed.), *Autonomic communication* (LNCS 3457, pp. 191-206). Berlin, Germany: Springer-Verlag.

Turk, M. A., & Pentland, A. P. (1991). Eigenfaces for recognition. *Journal of Cognitive Neuroscience, 3*, 71–86. doi:10.1162/jocn.1991.3.1.71

Unno, N., & Fujii, N. (2007). Automated design of analog circuits accelerated by use of simplified MOS model and reuse of genetic operations. *IEICE Transactions on Electronics . E (Norwalk, Conn.)*, *90-C*(6), 1291–1298.

Upegui, A., & Sanchez, E. (2005). Evolving hardware by dynamically reconfiguring Xilinx FPGAs. In *Evolvable Systems: From Biology to Hardware* (LNCS 3637, pp. 56-65).

Upegui, A., & Sanchez, E. (2006). Evolving hardware with self-reconfigurable connectivity in Xilinx FPGAs. In *Proceedings of the 1st NASA/ESA Conference on Adaptive Hardware and Systems (AHS-2006)* (pp. 153-160). Los Alamitos, CA: IEEE Computer Society.

Upegui, A., & Sanchez, E. (2006). On-chip and on-line self-reconfigurable adaptable platform: The non-uniform cellular automata case. In *Proceedings of the 20th IEEE International Parallel and Distributed Processing Symposium (IPDPS06)* (p. 206).

Upegui, A., Peña Reyes, C. A., & Sanchez, E. (2005). An FPGA platform for on-line topology exploration of spiking neural networks. *Microprocessors and Microsystems*, *29*(5), 211–223. doi:10.1016/j.micpro.2004.08.012

Valentin, D., Abdi, H., O'Toole, A. J., & Cottrell, G. W. (1994). Connectionist models of face processing: A survey. *Pattern Recognition*, *27*, 1209–1230. doi:10.1016/0031-3203(94)90006-X

Van Belle, W. (2001). *Automatic generation of concurrency adaptors by means of learning algorithms*. Unpublished doctoral dissertation, Vrije Universiteit Brussel, Brussel, Belgium.

Van Belle, W., Mens, T., & D'Hondt, T. (2003). Using genetic programming to generate protocol adaptors for interprocess communication. In A. M. Tyrrell, P. C. Haddow, & J. Torresen (Eds.), In *Proceedings of the 5th International Conference on Evolvable Systems: From Biology to Hardware* (LNCS 2606, pp. 67-73). Berlin, Germany: Springer-Verlag.

Van der Plas, G., Debyser, G., Leyn, F., Lampaert, K., Vandenbussche, J., & Gielen, G. G. E. (2001). AMGIE-a synthesis environment for CMOS analog integrated circuits. *IEEE Transactions on Computer-Aided Design of Integrated Circuits and Systems*, *20*(9), 1037–1058. doi:10.1109/43.945301

Vancza, J., & Markus, A. (2000). An agent model for incentive-based production scheduling. *Computers in Industry*, *43*, 173–187. doi:10.1016/S0166-3615(00)00066-X

Vapnik, V. N. (1995). *The nature of statistical learning theory*. Berlin, Germany: Springer-Verlag.

Vasilakos, A. V., Anagnostakis, K. G., & Pedrycz, W. (2001). Application of computational intelligence techniques in active networks. *Soft Computing – A Fusion of Foundations . Methodologies and Applications*, *5*(4), 264–271.

Viano, G., Parodi, A., Alty, J., & Khalil, C. (2000). Adaptive user interface for process control based on multi-agent approach. In *Proceedings of the Working Conference on Advanced Visual Interfaces*, Palermo, Italy (pp. 201-204).

Vicsek, T. (1995). Novel Type of Phase Transition in a System of Self-Driven Particles. *Physical Review Letters*, *75*(6), 1226–1229. doi:10.1103/PhysRevLett.75.1226

Vidyasagar, M. (1993). *Nonlinear systems analysis* (2nd ed.). Englewood Cliffs, NJ: Prentice Hall.

Vinger, K., & Torresen, J. (2003). Implementing evolution of FIR-filters efficiently in an FPGA. In *Proceedings of the NASA/DOD Conference on Evolvable Hardware*, Chicago, Illinois (pp. 26-29).

Virginia, E. D. (2000). Biometric identification system using a radial basis network. In *Proceedings of the 34th Annual IEEE International Carnahan Conference on Security Technology*, Ottawa, Ontario, Canada (pp. 47-51).

Wang, L. X. (1994). *Adaptive fuzzy systems and control: Design and stability analysis*. Upper Saddle River, NJ: Prentice-Hall.

Wang, L. X., & Mendel, J. M. (1992). Back-propagation fuzzy system as nonlinear dynamic system identifiers.

In *Proceedings of the IEEE International Conference on Fuzzy Systems,* San Diego, CA (pp. 1409-1418).

Wang, L. X., & Mendel, J. M. (1992). Fuzzy basis functions, universal approximation and orthogonal least squares learning. *IEEE Transactions on Neural Networks, 3,* 807–814. doi:10.1109/72.159070

Wang, X., & Tang, X. (2004). A unified framework for subspace face recognition. *IEEE Transactions on Pattern Analysis and Machine Intelligence, 26*(9), 1222–1228. doi:10.1109/TPAMI.2004.57

Wang, Y. H., Yin, C. W., & Zhang, Y. (2003). A multi-agent and distributed ruler based approach to production scheduling of agile manufacturing systems. *International Journal of Computer Integrated Manufacturing, 16*(2), 81–92. doi:10.1080/713804987

Wang, Y., & Chakrabarti, D. (2003). Epidemic Spreading in real Networks: An Eigenvalue Viewpoint. *Proceedings of the 22nd Symposium on Reliable Distributed Computing,* pp. 242–262.

Watts, D. (1999) *Small World.* The Princeton University Press.

Watts, D. (2007). Influentials, Networks, and Public Opinion Formation. *The Journal of Consumer Research, 34*(4), 441–458. doi:10.1086/518527

Weise, T., Skubch, H., Zapf, M., & Geihs, K. (2008). *Global optimization algorithms and their application to distributed systems* (Kasseler Informatikschriften (KIS) No. 2008, 3). Distributed Systems Group, University of Kassel, Germany.

Werner, G. M., & Dyer, M. G. (1992). Evolution of communication in artificial organisms. In C. Langton et al. (Eds.), *Artificial life II* (pp. 659-687). Redwood City, CA: Addison-Wesley.

Whitley, L. D. (1994). A genetic algorithm tutorial. *Statistics and Computing, 4*(2), 65–85. doi:10.1007/BF00175354

Wickens, C. D. (1985). Engineering psychology and human performance. *Engineering Psychology, 36,* 307–348.

Wilcoxon, F. (1945). Individual comparisons by ranking methods. *Biometrics Bulletin, 1*(6), 80–83. doi:10.2307/3001968

Willsky, A. (1976). A survey of design methods for failure detection in dynamic systems. *Automatica, 12,* 601–611. doi:10.1016/0005-1098(76)90041-8

Wilson, G. F., & Lambert, J. D. (2000). Performance enhancement with real-time physiologically controlled adaptive aiding. In *Proceedings of the Human Factors and Ergonomics Society Annual Meeting,* Dayton, OH (pp. 61-64).

Wolfram, S. (2002). *A new kind of science.* Champaign, IL: Wolfram Media.

Wolpert, D. H., & Macready, W. G. (1997). No free lunch theorems for optimization. *IEEE Transactions on Evolutionary Computation, 1*(1), 67–82. doi:10.1109/4235.585893

Wonga, T. N., Leunga, C. W., Maka, K. L., & Fungb, R. Y. K. (2006). Dynamic shop floor scheduling in multi-agent manufacturing systems. *Expert Systems with Applications, 31*(3), 486–494. doi:10.1016/j.eswa.2005.09.073

Wu, K., Aggarwal, C. C., & Yu, P. S. (2001). Personalization with dynamic profiler. In *Proceedings of the International Workshop on Advanced Issues of E-Commerce and Web-Based Information Systems,* San Jose, CA (pp. 12-21).

Xi, B., Liu, Z., Raghavachari, M., Xia, C. H., & Zhang, L. (2004). A smart hill-climbing algorithm for application server configuration. In *Proceedings of the 13th International Conference on World Wide Web* (pp. 287-296). New York: ACM Press.

Xiang, W., & Lee, H. P. (2008). Ant colony intelligence in multi-agent dynamic manufacturing scheduling. *Engineering Applications of Artificial Intelligence, 21,* 73–85. doi:10.1016/j.engappai.2007.03.008

Xiaosong, D., Popovic, D., & Schulz-Ekloff, G. (1995). Oscillation-resisting in the learning of backpropagation neural networks. In *Proceedings of the 3rd IFAC/IFIP Workshop on Algorithms and Architectures for Real-time Control,* Ostend, Belgium (pp. 21-25).

Xilinx Corp. (2004). *XAPP151: Virtex series configuration architecture user guide.* Retrieved from http://www.xilinx.com

Xilinx Corp. (2004). *XAPP290: Two flows for partial reconfiguration: Module based or difference based.* Retrieved from http://www.xilinx.com

Xilinx Corp. (2005). *Virtex-II platform FPGA user guide.* Retrieved from http://www.xilinx.com

Yagmahana, B., & Yeniseyb, M. M. (2008). Ant colony optimization for multi-objective flow shop scheduling problem. *Computers & Industrial Engineering, 54*(3), 411–420. doi:10.1016/j.cie.2007.08.003

Yale Database (n.d.). *Department of computer science, Yale University.* Retrieved from http://cvc.yale.edu/projects/yalefaces/yalefaces.html

Yamaguchi, H., Okano, K., Higashino, T., & Taniguchi, K. (1995). Synthesis of protocol entities' specifications from service specifications in a petri net model with registers. In *Proceedings of the 15th International Conference on Distributed Computing Systems* (pp. 510-517). Washington, DC: IEEE Computer Society.

Yamamoto, L. A. R., & Tschudin, C. F. (2005). Genetic evolution of protocol implementations and configurations. In *Proceedings of the IFIP/IEEE International Workshop on Self-Managed Systems and Services (SELFMAN 2005),* Nice, France.

Yamamoto, L. A. R., & Tschudin, C. F. (2006). Experiments on the automatic evolution of protocols using genetic programming. In I. Stavrakakis & M. Smirnov (Eds.), *Autonomic communication* (LNCS 3854, pp. 13-28). Berlin, Germany: Springer-Verlag.

Yan, S. C., Wang, H., Tang, X. O., & Huang, T. (2007). Exploring features descriptors for face recognition. In *Proceedings of the 32nd IEEE International Conference on Acoustics, Speech, and Signal Processing,* Honolulu, HI (pp. 629-632).

Yang, F., & Paindavoine, M. (2003). Implementation of an RBF neural network on embedded systems: Real-time face tracking and identity verification. *IEEE Transac-*

tions on Neural Networks, 14(5), 1162–1175. doi:10.1109/TNN.2003.816035

Yao, X. (1999). Evolving artificial neural networks. *Proceedings of the IEEE, 87*(9), 1423–1447. doi:10.1109/5.784219

Yao, X., Wang, F., Padmanabhan, K., & Salcedo-Sanz, S. (2005). Hybrid evolutionary approaches to terminal assignment in communications networks. In W. E. Hart, N. Krasnogor, & J. E. Smith (Eds.), *Recent advances in memetic algorithms* (pp. 129-159). Berlin, Germany: Springer-Verlag.

Yen, G. G., & Lu, H. (2003). Dynamic multiobjective evolutionary algorithm: Adaptive cell-based rank and density estimation. *IEEE Transactions on Evolutionary Computation, 7,* 253–274. doi:10.1109/TEVC.2003.810068

Ying, H., & Chen, G. (1997). Necessary conditions for some typical fuzzy systems as universal approximators. *Automatica, 33*(7), 1333–1338. doi:10.1016/S0005-1098(97)00026-5

Ying, K.-C., & Liao, C.-J. (2004). An ant colony system for permutation flow-shop sequencing. *Computers & Operations Research, 31,* 791–801. doi:10.1016/S0305-0548(03)00038-8

Young, P. (2007) *Innovation Diffusion in Heterogeneous Populations: Contagion, Social Influence, and Social Learning,* CSED Working Paper No. 51, Center on Social and Economic Dynamics, Brookings.

Ypma, A., & Duin, R. P. W. (1997). Novelty detection using self-organizing maps. In *Progress in connectionist-based information systems* (Vol. 2, pp. 1322-1325). Berlin, Germany: Springer-Verlag.

Yu, X., & Ram, B. (2006). Bio-inspired scheduling for dynamic job shops with flexible routing and sequence-dependent setups. *International Journal of Production Research, 44*(22), 4793–4813. doi:10.1080/00207540600621094

Zhang, D., & Dong, Y. (2000). An efficient algorithm to rank Web resources. In *Proceedings of the 9th International World Wide Web Conference on Computer*

Networks: the International Journal of Computer and Telecommunications Networking (pp. 449-455). Amsterdam: North-Holland Publishing Co.

Zhao, W., Chellappa, R., Phillips, P. J., & Rosenfeld, A. (2003). Face recognition: A literature survey. *ACM Computing Surveys*, *35*(4), 399–459. doi:10.1145/954339.954342

Zhou, B., Wang, S., & Xi, L. (2008). Agent-based decision support system for dynamic scheduling of a flexible manufacturing system. *International Journal of Computer Applications in Technology*, *32*(1), 47–62. doi:10.1504/IJCAT.2008.019489

Zhou, J., Liu, Y., & Chen, Y. H. (2007). Face recognition using kernel PCA and hierarchical RBF network. In *Proceedings of the 6th IEEE International Conference on Computer Information Systems and Industrial Management Applications,* Minneapolis, MN (pp. 239-244).

Zitzler, E., Deb, K., & Thiele, L. (2000). Comparison of multi-objective evolutionary algorithms: Empirical results. *IEEE Transactions on Evolutionary Computation*, *8*(2), 173–195.

Zitzler, E., Thiele, L., Laumanns, M., Fonseca, C. M., & da Fonseca, V. G. (2003). Performance assessment of multiobjective optimizers: an analysis and review. *IEEE Transactions on Evolutionary Computation*, *7*(2), 117–132. doi:10.1109/TEVC.2003.810758

Zweig, K. A. (2007). *On local behavior and global structures in the evolution of complex networks*. Unpublished doctoral dissertation, University of Tübingen, Tübingen, Germany.

About the Contributors

Raymond Chiong is a tenured academic at the School of Computing & Design, Swinburne University of Technology (Sarawak Campus), Malaysia. He is leading the Intelligent Informatics Research Group under the Information & Security Research Lab (iSECURES Lab). He serves as an Associate Editor for the Interdisciplinary Journal of Information, Knowledge, and Management (IJIKM), and reviews for IEEE Transactions on Evolutionary Computation, Springer's Memetic Computing Journal as well as Springer's Soft Computing Journal. He also serves in the IEEE Computer Society Technical Committee on Intelligent Informatics (TCII), IASTED Technical Committee on Artificial Intelligence, as well as IASTED Technical Committee on Modelling and Simulation. His main research interests include nature-inspired computing and its application to complex systems. He has numerous publications in books, international journals and conference proceedings, and is currently involved with four edited books.

* * *

Marcelo Keese Albertini is currently a PhD candidate under the Program of Computer Science and Applied Mathematics of the University of São Paulo, Brazil. His research interests include machine learning, statistics and grid computing.

Li-Minn Ang received his PhD and Bachelor degrees from Edith Cowan University, Australia in 2001 and 1996 respectively. He has taught at Monash University Malaysia before joining the University of Nottingham Malaysia Campus in 2004, where he is currently an Associate Professor at the School of Electrical and Electronic Engineering. He is a member of the Visual Information Engineering Research Group. His research interests are in the fields of signal, image, vision processing, intelligent processing techniques, hardware architectures, and reconfigurable computing.

Walter Anheier received the Diploma and the Doctorate from Rheinisch Westfaelische Technische Hochschule (RWTH), Aachen, Germany, both in Electrical Engineering, in 1973 and 1980 respectively. From 1977 to 1981, he was an Assistant Professor in the Electrical Engineering Department at RWTH Aachen. His research interests emphasised on mathematical and physical aspects of numerical modelling of semiconductor devices. In 1981 he joined Philips Semiconductors in Hamburg, Germany, where he was involved in the characterization of MOS-devices and monolithic integrated circuits. Later on he was a project manager of several CAD-research and development projects in the field of MOS-modelling, circuit and hybrid simulation and in 1990 he was appointed as CAD-Manager of the Industrial IC Department at Philips. From 1985 to 1992 he was also a lecturer at FH and TU Hamburg. Since 1992, he has been working as a Full Professor with the Department of Electrical Engineering at the University of Bremen, Germany. His research interests include various aspects of microelectronics with emphasis on fast functional simulation, computer-aided testing (CAT), synthesis of digital systems, signal integrity analysis and ATPG for delay and crosstalk faults in digital circuits. He is an associate member of IEEE and a member of ACM and ITG.

Mariusz Boryczka was born in 1958. In 1982, he acquired his MSc in Computer Science at the Faculty of Automatic Control and Computer Science, Silesian University of Technology. He then obtained his PhD degree from the Faculty of Electrical Engineering at Poznań University of Technology in 1992. In 2008, he received the Doctor of Science (habilitation) degree in Computer Science from the Polish Academy of Science. Since 1982 he has been working in the Institute of Computer Science at University of Silesia. Starting from 2009 he acts as the deputy director (teaching affairs) of the Institute of Computer Science. His research interests include programming and programming languages, evolutionary algorithms, optimization, artificial life, and artificial intelligence.

José Ramón Cano received his MSc and PhD degrees in Computer Science from the University of Granada, Spain in 1999 and 2004 respectively. He is currently an Associate Professor in the Department of Computer Science, University of Jaén, Spain. His research interests include data mining, data reduction, data complexity, interpretability-accuracy trade-off, and evolutionary algorithms.

Siew Wen Chin received her Master of Science and Bachelor degrees from the University of Nottingham Malaysia Campus in 2008 and 2006 respectively. She is currently doing her PhD at the same university. She is a member of the Visual Information Engineering Research Group. Her research interests are in the fields of signal, image, vision processing, and audio visual speech recognition.

Miguel Aurelio Duarte-Villaseñor was born in Puebla, México, in 1981. He received the Bachelor degree in Electronics from the Faculty of Electronics Sciences (FCE-BUAP) in 2005, and the Master Sciences degree in Electronics from the National Institute of Astrophysics, Optics and Electronics (INAOE), México, in 2007. His research interests include electronic design automation, evolutionary electronics, modeling and simulation and circuit synthesis. He is now pursuing a PhD at INAOE.

Salvador García received his MSc and PhD degrees in Computer Science from the University of Granada, Spain in 2004 and 2008 respectively. He is currently an Assistant Professor in the Department of Computer Science, University of Granada, Spain. His research interests include data mining, data reduction, imbalanced problems, statistical inference, data complexity and evolutionary algorithms.

Ivick Guerra-Gómez received the BSc degree in Electronic Engineering (with Cum Laude distinction) from the Benemérita Universidad Autónoma de Puebla (BUAP), México, in 2006, and the MSc in Electronics from the Insituto Nacional de Astrofísica Óptica y Electrónica (INAOE), México, in 2008. He is working towards the PhD degree at INAOE and his research interests include evolutionary computation applied to circuit optimization and computer aided circuit design.

Francisco Herrera received his MSc degree in Mathematics in 1988 and PhD degree in Mathematics in 1991, both from the University of Granada, Spain. He is currently a Professor in the Department of Computer Science and Artificial Intelligence at the University of Granada. He has published more than 140 papers in international journals. He is the co-author of a book "Genetic Fuzzy Systems: Evolutionary Tuning and Learning of Fuzzy Knowledge Bases" (World Scientific, 2001). Besides that, he has co-edited 4 international books and 17 special issues in international journals on different soft computing topics. He also acts as associate editor of the following journals: IEEE Transactions on Fuzzy Systems, Mathware and Soft Computing, Advances in Fuzzy Systems, Advances in Computational Sciences and Technology, and International Journal of Applied Metaheuristic Computing. He currently serves as area editor of the Soft Computing Journal (on genetic algorithms and genetic fuzzy systems). He is also member of the editorial board of the journals: Fuzzy Sets and Systems, Applied Intelligence, Knowledge and Information Systems, Information Fusion, Evolutionary Intelligence, International Journal of Hybrid Intelligent Systems, Memetic Computation, International Journal of Computational Intelligence Research, The Open Cybernetics and Systemics Journal, Recent Patents on Computer Science, Journal of Advanced Research in Fuzzy and Uncertain Systems, and International Journal of Information Technology and Intelligent and Computing. His research interests include computing with words and decision making, data mining, data preparation, instance selection, fuzzy rule based systems, genetic fuzzy systems, knowledge extraction based on evolutionary algorithms, memetic algorithms and genetic algorithms.

King Hann Lim received his Master of Engineering from the University of Nottingham Malaysia Campus in 2007. He is currently doing his PhD at the same university. He is a member of the Visual Information Engineering Research Group. His research interests are in the fields of signal, image, vision processing, intelligent processing techniques, and computer vision for intelligent vehicles.

Rodrigo Fernandes de Mello is currently a Faculty at the Institute of Mathematics and Computer Sciences, Department of Computer Science, University of São Paulo, São Carlos, Brazil. He completed his PhD degree from University of São Paulo in 2003. His research interests include machine learning, autonomic computing and grid computing.

Akira Namatame is a Professor in the Department of Computer Science, National Defense Academy, Japan. He is well-known as an international research leader in the application of agent and evolutionary modelling technologies to problems in economics and social research, and in the past 10 years he has given over 20 invited talks in these areas. His research interests include multi-agent systems, complex networks, evolutionary computation, and game theory. He is the editor-in-chief of Springer's Journal of Economic Interaction and Coordination. He has published more than 200 refereed scientific papers, together with 8 books on multi-agent systems, collective systems and game theory.

Ajoy K. Palit, formerly a senior scientist of the Department of Electronics (DOE), Government of India, received his M.Tech. degree in Radiophysics and Electronics from the University of Calcutta in 1990 and the summa cum laude Ph.D. (Dr.-Ing.) degree in Electrical Engineering from the University of Bremen, Germany, in 1999. Thereafter, Ajoy worked in the Electrical Engineering Department of Delft University of Technology (TU Delft) in The Netherlands, as an Assistant Professor. He also worked in repas-AEG Information Technology GmbH, Germany, as a research and development engineer.

Since October 2002 he has been working in the Electrical Engineering Department of the University of Bremen, Germany, as a C1-scientist/faculty member. Ajoy teaches Masters degree courses on neural-fuzzy systems in modeling, prediction and signal processing, computational intelligence in time series forecasting, and fault modeling and test generation for VLSI circuits. He has over 40 publications in refereed international conferences and journals. He is also the principal author of the book "Computational Intelligence in Time Series Forecasting, Theory of Engineering Applications," published by Springer-Verlag, London, in 2005. He is the recipient of a Best Paper Award at the 2004 World Congress on Lateral Computing, in Fuzzy Logic Session. His research interests include signal integrity (crosstalk) fault modeling, GA-based-testing, test pattern generation and compaction, etc. He also pursues research on fuzzy logic, neural networks, neuro-fuzzy systems, genetic algorithms, etc. in system modeling and time series prediction. Ajoy has been the recipient of a National Scholarship of the Government of India, GATE scholarship, Institutes fellowship from Indian Institute of Technology, Bombay, UNDP/UNIDO fellowship, and DAAD fellowship of Germany.

Paolo Renna is an Assistant Professor at the Department of Environmental Engineering and Physics in the Engineering Faculty of Basilicata University, Italy. He received his PhD degree at Polytechnic of Bari in advanced production systems. His academic research principally deals with the development of innovative negotiation and production planning in distributed environments and manufacturing scheduling in dynamic environment. Several contributions have been presented on the design of Multi-Agent Architecture and tested by discrete event simulation in Business to Business environment. Among the contributions, he has been the co-author of two research books about e-marketplaces and production planning in production networks. Besides that, he has developed coordination approaches in multi-plant production planning environment and innovative scheduling approaches in flexible and reconfigurable manufacturing systems.

Carlos Alberto Reyes-García earned his PhD degree in Computer Science from the Florida State University. He has been a postdoctoral at the IIASS in Salerno, Italy. He is now a researcher in the Computer Science Department at INAOE, Mexico. He is also a National Researcher Level I at the Mexican SNI. He is the President of the Mexican Society for Artificial Intelligence (SMIA). His research interests are mainly in the fields of soft computing, speech, speaker and infant cry classification, and pattern recognition.

Alexandre Romariz received his B.S. degree in Electrical Engineering from the University of Brasília, Brazil, in 1992 and his MSc in Electrical Engineering from University of Campinas, Brazil, in 1995. He received his PhD degree in Electrical Engineering from the University of Colorado at Boulder, USA, in 2003. He is currently a Professor at the Electrical Engineering Department of the University of Brasília, teaching undergraduate and graduate courses in the areas of electronics, digital systems, random systems and computational intelligence. His research interests include applications of computational intelligence, optoelectronics, IC design and engineering education. He is currently the chair of the Brasília Section of the IEEE.

Kah Phooi Seng received her PhD and Bachelor degrees from the University of Tasmania, Australia in 2001 and 1997 respectively. She has taught at the University of Tasmania, Griffith University and Monash University Malaysia before joining the University of Nottingham Malaysia Campus in 2005, where she is currently an Associate Professor at the School of Electrical and Electronic Engineering. She is a member of the Visual Information Engineering Research Group. Her research interests are in the fields of intelligent visual processing, biometrics and multi-biometrics, artificial intelligence, and signal processing.

Flávio Teixeira was born in Brasília, Brazil on March 14, 1982. He received his B.S. degree in Computer Engineering from the UniCEUB in 2005 and the MSc degree in Electrical Engineering from the University of Brasília (UnB) in 2008, both in Brasília, Brazil. Currently, he is pursuing the PhD degree in Electrical Engineering at the University of Victoria, British Columbia, Canada. From 2004 to 2006, he was a telecommunication software designer at Autotrac, a company in the line of mobile data messaging and fleet monitoring in Brazil, focusing in satellite telecommunications. From 2006 to 2008, he was a software engineer in CEFTRU, a Multidisciplinary Research Center in Science & Technology for Transportation linked to the University of Brasília, concentrating on software design for transportation, including combinatorial optimization methods and geographic processing systems. His research interests include DSP algorithms, digital filter design, and multi-objective optimization for use in telecommunication applications.

Esteban Tlelo-Cuautle received the BSc degree from the Technologic Institute of Puebla (ITP), Mexico, in 1993, the MSc and PhD degrees from the Instituto Nacional de Astrofísica, Optica y Electrónica (INAOE), Mexico, in 1995 and 2000 respectively. Since January 2001 he is a full researcher at INAOE. He has authored and co-authored more than 100 papers on scientific journals, book chapters and conference proceedings. He is a senior member of the IEEE and an IEICE member. His research interests include modeling and simulation of circuits and analog and mixed-signal CAD tools. He regularly serves as reviewer of international conferences and international journals.

Andres Upegui is a senior researcher at the Reconfigurable and Embedded Digital Systems (REDS) Institute, HEIG-VD, Yverdon, Switzerland since 2006. He obtained a diploma on Electronic Engineering in 2000 from the Universidad Pontificia Bolivariana (UPB), Medellín, Colombia. He joined the UPB Microelectronics Research Group between 2000 and 2001. From 2001 to 2002, he did the Graduate School on Computer Science at the Ecole Polytechnique Fédérale de Lausanne (EPFL), and then in 2003 he joined the Logic Systems Laboratory (LSL) as a PhD student. In 2006, he received his PhD from the EPFL with a thesis entitled "Dynamically Reconfigurable Bio-inspired Hardware". He has co-authored more than 30 scientific publications, including book chapters, journal articles, and conference proceedings.

Thomas Weise has studied Applied Computer Science at the Chemnitz University of Technology in Germany with specialization in Information and Communication Systems, and obtained his Master's degree in 2005. From Chemnitz, he then went to the Distributed Systems Group of the University of Kassel where he works as a researcher and a PhD candidate. His research focuses on the applications of evolutionary computation, especially to various aspects of distributed systems. In his PhD thesis, he formalizes a new genetic programming approach known as Rule-based Genetic Programming (or in short RBGP), and shows how it can be applied to evolve distributed algorithms.

Gary G. Yen received the PhD degree in Electrical and Computer Engineering from the University of Notre Dame, Indiana, in 1992. He is currently a Professor in the School of Electrical and Computer Engineering, Oklahoma State University, USA. Before joining Oklahoma State University, he was with the Structure Control Division, U.S. Air Force Research Laboratory in Albuquerque, New Mexico. His research interests include intelligent control, computational intelligence, conditional health monitoring, signal processing and their industrial/defense applications. He is an IEEE Fellow. He was an associate editor of the IEEE Control Systems Magazine, IEEE Transactions on Control Systems Technology, Automatica, Mechantronics, IEEE Transactions on Systems, Man and Cybernetics, Part A and Part B, and IEEE Transactions on Neural Networks. He is currently serving as an associate editor for the IEEE Transactions on Evolutionary Computation and International Journal on Swarm Intelligence Research. He served as the General Chair for the 2003 IEEE International Symposium on Intelligent Control held in Houston, TX and the 2006 IEEE World Congress on Computational Intelligence held in Vancouver, Canada. He also served as Vice President for the Technical Activities of the IEEE Computational intelligence Society in 2005 and 2006, and is the founding editor-in-chief of the IEEE Computational Intelligence Magazine since 2006.

Index